Jewish Aspects in Avant-Garde

Perspectives on Jewish Texts and Contexts

Edited by
Vivian Liska

Editorial Board
Robert Alter, Steven E. Aschheim, Richard I. Cohen, Mark H. Gelber,
Moshe Halbertal, Christine Hayes, Moshe Idel, Samuel Moyn,
Ada Rapoport-Albert, Alvin Rosenfeld, David Ruderman, Bernd Witte

Volume 5

Jewish Aspects in Avant-Garde

Between Rebellion and Revelation

Edited by
Mark H. Gelber and Sami Sjöberg

DE GRUYTER

ISBN 978-3-11-065177-5
e-ISBN (PDF) 978-3-11-045495-6
e-ISBN (EPUB) 978-3-11-045290-7
ISSN 2199-6962

Library of Congress Cataloging-in-Publication Data
A CIP catalog record for this book has been applied for at the Library of Congress.

Bibliographic information published by the Deutsche Nationalbibliothek
The Deutsche Nationalbibliothek lists this publication in the Deutsche Nationalbibliografie;
detailed bibliographic data are available on the Internet at http://dnb.dnb.de.

© 2019 Walter de Gruyter GmbH, Berlin/Boston
This volume is text- and page-identical with the hardback published in 2017.
Typesetting: PTP-Berlin, Protago-TEX-Production GmbH, Berlin
Printing and binding: CPI books GmbH, Leck
♾ Printed on acid-free paper
Printed in Germany

www.degruyter.com

Contents

Acknowledgements —— vii

Sami Sjöberg and Mark H. Gelber
Introduction —— 1

The Avant-Garde and Jewish Traditions

Alfred Bodenheimer
Dada Judaism: The Avant-Garde in First World War Zurich —— 23

Radu Stern
Jews and the Avant-Garde: The Case of Romania —— 35

Sami Sjöberg
Towards an Ahistorical Jewishness: The Idea of Jewish Essence
in the German-Jewish Avant-Garde —— 53

Community Building and Cultural Conflicts

Andreas Kramer
Carl Einstein, Jewishness, and the Communities
of the European Avant-Garde —— 71

Laëtitia Tordjman
Challenging the Literary Community: The Warsaw Yiddish Avant-Garde
and *Khalyastre* —— 85

Maria Silina
Modern Jewish Sculptors and the Cultural Policy of the USSR
in the 1920s–1930s —— 101

Self-Representation and Anti-Semitism

Zoë Roth
Frontière humaine: Race, Nation, and the Shape of Representation
in Claude Cahun —— 119

Alana Sobelman
Arnold Schoenberg's Jewish Veil: The Workings of Anti-Semitic Rhetoric
in *Die glückliche Hand*, Op. 18 (1913) —— 141

Messianism, Syncretism, and Vanguard Philosophy

Małgorzata Stolarska-Fronia
Saints and Tsadikim – The Religious Syncretism
of Jewish Expressionism —— 161

Tom Paulus
Between Ecstasy and Lament: Revelationism and Messianism
in Epstein and Godard —— 193

Raphael Koenig
The Mad Book: Der Nister as Unreliable Author in *From my Estate* (1929) —— 207

Olivier Salazar-Ferrer
The Role of Judaism in Benjamin Fondane's Existential Philosophy —— 227

Jews in the Avant-Garde: A Historical Perspective

Steven E. Aschheim
The Avant-Garde and the Jews —— 253

Notes on Contributors —— 275

Acknowledgements

The editors would like to express sincere gratitude to those whose assistance made this book project possible. The volume began in early 2015 in the form of lectures delivered at the international conference on "The Avant-Garde and the Jews" that was held at the Institute of Jewish Studies at the University of Antwerp. We are greatly indebted to Vivian Liska, its director, and Jan Morrens its administrative assistant, for their support and practical expertise. They guaranteed that the conference would be both a professionally engaging and thoroughly enjoyable event. The dedicated help of numerous peer reviewers has been essential for our work in preparing the manuscript. These include: Haim Finkelstein, Peter Demetz, Howard Needler, Hanni Mittelmann, Scott Spector, Ilana Rosen, Konstantin Dudakov-Kashuro, Jakob Hessing, Lisa Silverman, Cosana Eram, Lisa Marie Anderson, Karolina Szymaniak, Ruth Klüger, Mikhail Krutikov, Vince Brook and Monique Jutrin. And last, Jeremy Schreiber has been especially helpful in putting the finishing touches on the book.

Sami Sjöberg and Mark H. Gelber

Sami Sjöberg and Mark H. Gelber
Introduction

Die Bücher der Juden vor allem das alte [sic] *Testament geben mir recht glaube an einen lebendigen Gott.*[1]
(Jakob van Hoddis)

The year 2016 marked the centenary of dada. German expressionism, Italian futurism and Russian cubo-futurism are even older than dada, and yet we are still far from a full understanding of these movements or of the avant-garde in general. This certainly has to do with the intrinsic complexity or versatility of the phenomenon, which incorporates many facets, including political and artistic revolt, international networks and temporal dynamics. Also, the avant-garde is open to various reinterpretations, such as feminist or post-colonial readings. As of yet, no serious attempt has been made to understand the Jewish dimension of the avant-garde. Hence, this volume charts and investigates the various ways in which the avant-garde, Jewishness and Judaism relate to each other.

Within the last ten years, a number of studies in various disciplines have addressed the relationship between Jewish topics and motifs and avant-garde movements. The topic of Jewish artists belonging to the avant-garde has also been of certain scholarly interest.[2] However, the phenomenon as such still remains largely uncharted, despite the fact that the degree of participation by Jewish avant-garde artists in literature, the visual arts, theater and film has been strikingly high. So far, studies have usually addressed the idea of "Jewish art,"[3] or surveyed Jewish characteristics in modernism[4] or focused on individual avant-garde artists of

---

[1] Jakob van Hoddis (1987, 233). "The books of the Jews, especially the Old Testament, give me the right faith in a living God." All translations are by the authors unless otherwise stated.
[2] Anderson 2011, Sandqvist 2006, and an early example is Apter-Gabriel 1987. Yet, such studies were not a new phenomenon, because important titles surveying avant-garde literature with a particular emphasis on Jewishness were published already in the 1920s, including Menachem Birnbaum's *Lyrische Dichtung deutscher Juden* (Lyric Poetry of German Jews, 1920), Gustav Krojanker's *Juden in der deutschen Literatur* (Jews in German Literature, 1922), along with studies such as Alfred Wolfenstein's *Jüdisches Wesen und neue Dichtung* (Jewish Essence and New Poetry, 1922) and Arthur Sakheim's *Das jüdische Element in der Weltliteratur* (The Jewish Element in World Literature, 1924).
[3] Classic studies on this topic are Sed-Rajna et al. 1997 and Van Voolen 2006.
[4] The Jewish characteristics in modernism are surveyed in studies such as Shaked 1987, Kampf 1990, Garb and Nochlin 1995, Bilski 1999, Wisse 2000, Baigell and Heyd 2001, Kirschenblatt-Gimblett and Karp 2008, and Washton Long, Baigell and Heyd 2010.

Jewish origin,[5] without developing or utilizing an overarching approach to this specific dimension of the avant-garde. This indicates that much of the important information is to be located at the fringes of academia, for instance in exhibition catalogues, or neglected material in archives and in various *Nachläße*.

In literature, the Jewish involvement in the avant-garde covers not only experimental texts produced in Jewish languages (Yiddish, Hebrew, Ladino) but also works in other languages by artists of Jewish descent. Overall, the significance of the avant-garde for modern Jewish culture and the impact of the Jewish tradition on the artistic production of the avant-garde are visible through the various and multiple reinterpretations of literary, artistic, philosophical or theological texts and traditions, which appropriate elements from Judaism or Jewish culture.

The focus of the present volume is European, owing to the fact that Europe was the birthplace of the artistic avant-garde. Moreover, with the advent of the Second World War, the majority of Jews resided in Europe.[6] During the interwar period, numerous Jews pursued careers in the arts, and they were especially visible in the "marginal" movements of the avant-garde. The aesthetic approaches of these movements were so varied that it has become commonplace to define the avant-garde in the plural.[7] That is certainly necessary regarding Jews in order to reflect the internal heterogenic reality of the avant-gardes they took part in.

Jewish Traces in the Avant-Garde

The avant-garde is undoubtedly a product of the modern period and it has been noted that this era brought about profound social, political, scientific and aesthetic upheavals and renewals.[8] The period exhibited contradictory impulses and

---

[5] For instance, Raileanu 2004, Hentea 2014. However, instead of a truly comparative approach, avant-garde studies have tended to focus on national languages and literatures, hence providing only fragmentary views of the avant-garde as a phenomenon. Granted, the various avant-gardes differ, but the lack of a realization of progressive art with a continent-wide social and political agenda underestimates the avant-garde as a transnational phenomenon.

[6] Approximately 9,5 million Jews lived in Europe in 1933 and comprised 1,7 % of the total population. These Jews represented more than 60 percent of the world's Jewish population at that time, which is estimated at 15,3 million. The Holocaust Encyclopedia, quoted March 2, 2016. www.ushmm.org/wlc/en/article.php?ModuleId=10005161.

[7] In this introduction avant-gardes refer to the various movements, whereas the singular form denotes the general phenomenon.

[8] Some date the starting point of the modern era to 1492, but it is usually considered to have begun in the late eighteenth century with the industrial revolution (economic) and rationalism (as a scientific paradigm).

dynamics: there was a general interest in the new (such as advances in technology) and due to religious skepticism also a heightened sense of the present moment, which is occasionally dubbed as "the shock of new."[9] However, to counter the progressive trends of social emancipation, internationalism and urbanization of the age, xenophobia and nationalism proliferated, which in turn fueled anti-Semitism and the rise of totalitarianism. Thus, the works of the avant-garde were produced in a social environment where liberal and conservative forces negotiated with each other, occasionally generating societal unrest. One might mention the Paris Commune, the Bavarian Council Republic or the May 1968 riots, and their subsequent suppression in this context.

From a historical perspective, the Jewish participation in the avant-gardes is noteworthy, because it can be seen as an alternative path to modernization. The avant-garde provided an alternative *Weltanschauung* to those uninterested in religious orthodoxy or bourgeois assimilation. Overall, the avant-gardists were often young and well-educated people.[10] For Jewish artists, the anti-nationalism of the avant-garde was particularly inviting, since the European Jewish population lived in a state of diaspora across the continent.[11] The religious tradition with its ties to Halakha, the Jewish law, provided extra-territorial features in the social reality of European Jewry. Indeed, for avant-garde artists of Jewish background, a primary dilemma was how to strike a balance between the historical continuity provided by religion and ethnicity and the novel aesthetic innovations that militated in favor of an explicit break with tradition. The avant-gardes often promoted anti-religious stances, as organized religion was seen by many to be outmoded, even though in reality multiple forms of religious thought and spirituality were cultivated in these groups.[12]

Latent religious influences are apparent in the manifesto "Gramatică" (Grammar, 1925) written by the Romanian Jewish avant-garde author Ilarie Voronca

---

[9] Major thinkers who promoted this conception are Nietzsche and Benjamin. For a further discussion, cf. Hughes 2013.
[10] This characteristic is evident, for instance, in Cheskel Zwi's manifesto-like text, "Wir jungen Juden" (We Young Jews, 1911), which indicates that many newcomers in the avant-garde circles considered themselves fundamentally as Jews. However, it should be noted that Zwi's outright affirmation was not shared by all his peers.
[11] For the sake of readability, the present volume utilizes a general notion of a "Jewish artist," which denotes those active in the arts and literature who are of Jewish origin, while acknowledging the complicated nature of such a formulation. For instance, the dada painter Marcel Janco identified himself as "an artist who is a Jew," rather than "a Jewish artist" (Sandqvist 2006, 377). The topic has been discussed at length elsewhere. See footnote 3.
[12] Illuminating examples of this are the "dissident Judaism" of Paul Adler and the neo-Kabbalah of the *Neue Club* member Oskar Goldberg.

(Eduard Marcus, 1903–1946). In fact, it includes all the main aspects of early twentieth-century avant-garde aesthetics. With the suggestive and subversive rhetoric characteristic of the manifesto genre, he denounced traditional art and conventional means of representation while promoting an alternative canon consisting of prominent figures in European experimental art, such as Stéphane Mallarmé, Arthur Rimbaud, Tristan Tzara and Marcel Janco – the latter two being Voronca's Jewish compatriots. Voronca echoes the works of these predecessors when stipulating the necessity for a *new* approach to words, which would establish a *new* logic. Already here looms a paradox: how can the "radically new" draw from literature written more than thirty years earlier? Similar specious neofilia proved to be an overarching theme in the various avant-gardes, together with various utopian and political aims.

In the light of such extensive neofilia, the omission of religion would seem to be necessary. Yet, amidst Voronca's rampant anti-traditionalist discourse a peculiar statement can be found, which mirrors his ethnic and religious background: "*Orice artist trebuie sa fie aducatorul unor alte principii, scoborand in concertul de fulgere de pe muntele Sinai cu tablele logicei noi in maini*" [Each artist must be the originator of novel principles, descending through the concert of fulgurations atop Mount Sinai with the tablets of a new logic in his hands] (Voronca 1925, 1).[13] This ambiguous statement describes and envisions the revealing of the Torah by God to Moses on Mount Sinai and attributes to the tablets of Law a novel sense: that is, a ground for a new logic. This goal was arguably one of the avant-garde's ultimate aims – to promote "*Andersdenken*," that is, thinking otherwise.[14]

While Voronca promoted his new avant-gardist logic, he concurrently suggested that Judaism had created a new logic as well, which perhaps refers to monotheism amidst polytheistic or pagan religions.[15] Voronca contextualized his tradition-recalling statement by claiming that a novel experience – which is free from conventional modes of thought – would result in a seemingly "neological," alternative logic, and that this logic would in time be subsumed into "old time logic" (Voronca 2002, 548). The inner dynamics of the avant-garde are apparent in the dialectic movement between the new and the old, in which the current "new"

---

13 Translated by Julian Semilian and Sanda Agalidi.
14 An early instance of such an approach is Carl Einstein's experimental novel *Bebuquin* (1908, full version 1912). It exemplifies that such modes of thought were not a question of mere dissidents opposing given aims within a determined system of thought; rather, the aim of these modes was to introduce alternative, non-systematic modes of thought. In this context, Einstein differentiated between the terms "thinking" (*Denken*) and "knowing" (*Erkennen*).
15 An instance of such emphasis can be found in Ladino where the Spanish singular word "*Dios*" (God) is replaced with "*El Dio*" to highlight Jewish monotheism.

becomes commonplace and is eventually replaced. More importantly, despite Voronca's somewhat enigmatic formulation, he obviously referred to a historical continuity between his avant-gardist experiments and the Jewish tradition.

The inevitable question arising from Voronca's statement above is how or in what ways his Jewishness should be taken into account. The text suggests a reading that acknowledges his background. Still, it may be asked whether the author's persuasion and intentionality may be understood in this same context. According to Carol Iancu, Voronca was influenced by his Jewish identity and never converted (Iancu 2016). Yet, this general information does not seem to add anything to our understanding of the text itself. On another level one may ask what the Jewish dimension reveals about the artistic production of Voronca and its potential relation to his and other avant-garde expression:

The aim of this volume is to respond to inquiries of this nature which probe the extent to which avant-garde artists of Jewish descent maintained productive relationships with their Jewishness. In order to reach this goal, of course, one must pose difficult questions concerning Jewishness. According to which criteria should Jewishness be defined? Is it ethnic, cultural, national, religion-based or social? So far, research attempts to deal with this problem, while declaring all-embracing aims, have proved to be lacking, because there is no single universal solution to the relation between the avant-garde and the Jews. However, one possible approach, adapted from social studies, is to acknowledge the avant-gardists' common intersectional positions. In short, intersectionality maps the possible sources and types of discrimination an individual might experience, such as race, class, gender, religious beliefs or language. This is to say that amongst the avant-gardists, the anomalous situation of an artist as a Jew and as an experimentalist may have produced similar experiences of in-betweenness or alienation.

Most of the artists discussed in this volume derived from the middle-class, and they rebelled against this background (Hirte 2009, 10). In their individual societies many encountered anti-Semitism including the outright threat of physical violence. Yet, the artists' backgrounds are very heterogeneous: German, Habsburg, French and East European Jews, whose cultural backgrounds and existential situations, including the extent of acculturation and ability to assimilate, were very different. However, assimilation usually occurred according to the educational, occupational and cultural conditions established by the middle-class, which is why assimilation may not have been very attractive to many of the young avant-garde artists. Moreover, it also proved to be difficult in many cases, such as Tzara's, whose dada production was considered to be a "foreign import" both in his native Romania, from where he emigrated, and in Switzerland, to where he relocated (Goga 1927, 36; Hentea 2014, 150).

Given the large number of individual cases, the concept of intra-European otherness outlined by Piotr Piotrowski is potentially useful in this context, since it is concerned with the history of the avant-garde. He distinguished the non-European other from a "close other," whose place is "on the margins of European culture, outside the center but still within the same cultural frame of reference" (Piotrowski 2009, 53). Instead of remaining outside the centers and in the *shtetlekh*, Jewish artists often formed alternative undercurrents in the metropolitan centers of the avant-garde. One might even say that they represented otherness in these centers. This tendency is perhaps nowhere as poignant as in the case of the German-Jewish author Carl Einstein (1885–1940), whose *Negerplastik* (1915) introduced African art into the European sphere. In this work the African imagery and cultural heritage are projected as the exotic non-European other, while Einstein himself remained in the position of the "close other," because Jewishness was one of his European "lived traditions." This otherness would eventually become evident during Einstein's forced exile beginning in 1933, which he accounts for in his so-called BEB II project:[16]

> ich sehe, immer mehr werde ich allein sein. jude, deutschsprechend, in frankreich. jude ohne gott und ohne kenntnis unserer vergangenheit, deutschsprechend [...]. in frankreich d i ohne leser. [...] nie werde ich in französischer dichtung zuhause sein; denn ich träume und sinniere deutsch. Also nun bin ich durch Hitler zu völliger Heimatlosigkeit und fremdheit verurteilt.[17]

> [I see that I will be more and more alone. jew, german-speaking, in france. jew without god and without the knowledge of our past, german-speaking. in france i.e. without readers. I shall never feel at home in french poetry; because I dream and muse in german. So now I am condemned by Hitler to complete homelessness and alienation.]

Einstein lamented the extent of his secular upbringing, since Judaism or the discourses of Jewishness could have served him as a *lingua franca* in France; in fact, it was required of him in order to become acquainted with French Jews. Einstein seems to represent a sort of a triple outsider: he was unwelcome in Germany and not being an observant Jew, he could not be easily accepted by the Parisian Jewish community. Additionally, even though he was an esteemed avant-gardist, the general appeal of the avant-garde has always been limited.

Beyond the illustrative case of Einstein, Piotrowski's argument is provocative in that he claims there are several histories and canons of the avant-garde. For example, Jews were especially prominent in expressionism. This fact can be explained by the need of many of the German-Jewish artists to resolve their German-

---

16 For a further discussion on this topic, see Kramer's essay in this volume.
17 Einstein, a fragment from BEB II. Quoted in Klaus Kiefer: *Avantgarde – Weltkrieg – Exil*, 26.

Jewish and Eastern-Western dichotomous dispositions. Expressionism tended to highlight otherness with the aim of demonstrating the need for Germans to create an inclusive society. It sought to force Germans to see and think in new ways, to expand their imaginations and dispense with many of their preconceptions. Expressionism's artistic program thus resonated with the historical experiences and modern desires of many German Jews.

Regarding Jewish artists who were often seminal in the avant-garde movements, it seems that their story has been told only partially. Often the place of these artists within a given movement is celebrated; sometimes their ethnic heritage is noted. But it is seldom analyzed according to any sort of group dynamics, despite the fact that Jewish participation in certain movements was prominent (such as in expressionism), while some major figures of the avant-garde, such as Hugo Ball or André Breton, were at least to some degree anti-Semitic.[18]

Another aim of the present volume is to consider the broader cultural environments in which the Jewish artists active in the avant-garde produced their works. This aspect addresses the inner dynamics of the various movements of the avant-garde and the attempt to achieve a balance between tradition and what is called "modern." This volume addresses the problematics of ethnic and religious Judaism in relation to authorship or artistic activity and production– here understood in the expanded sense that covers other arts as well. Evidently, some authors embraced Jewish concerns while avoiding a limited or unified concept of Jewish identity and encouraging an awareness of the non-Jewish environment (Liska 2008). The importance of Jewish motifs differs for individual artists: some authors fundamentally and consistently utilize them (Else Lasker-Schüler, Der Nister); some authors articulate them in religious border zones (Cahun), whereas some offer only few explicitly themed reference points (Einstein). This volume includes essays about a broad spectrum of ethnic Jewish artists, ranging from denominational (Meidner) to the seemingly indifferent (Tzara), who applied Jewish themes only intermittently.

Jewish Roots and Identity in the Avant-Garde

The term avant-garde derives from a medieval usage; it denoted a military advance guard. The term was appropriated to aesthetic use in the early 1800s in France (Wiesberger 1984, 18–19). In its current aesthetic sense, the term was first introduced in an essay entitled "l'Artiste, le savant et l'industriel" (A Dialogue be-

---

18 For a further discussion, see the essays of Stern and Aschheim in this volume.

tween the Artist, the Scientist and the Industrialist) in 1825 (ibid.). The text has been attributed to Benjamin Olinde Rodrigues (1795–1851), who was a Parisian banker and a Saint-Simonian socialist. Saint-Simonianism was a political and social movement, which envisioned a society that would discard both God and the idea of an afterlife and reorganize itself under the rubric of "useful work" in which all would participate (Saint-Simon 1975, 42). Thus, work would ultimately provide universal equality and emancipation.

Far from being a mere coincidence, the Jewish dimension of the avant-garde was present already at this early stage. Rodrigues was of Sephardi Jewish descent.[19] He had attended the French lycées and reportedly abandoned most forms of Jewish ritual by the 1820s, but his ethnic background nevertheless affected his life to a degree. Evidently, he was not able to secure a permanent teaching position at a French university because of his Jewish background (Altmann and Ortiz 2005, 60), Institutionalized anti-Semitism was a fact of life in post-revolutionary France. The Rodrigues family resided in a building on rue Montholon where Léon Halévy and other prominent Saint-Simonians lived. The house has been described by many as a center of the elite Parisian Jewish social world in the first decades of the nineteenth century. As it happens, Jews were more prominent in Saint-Simonianism than in any other contemporary organization. Pamela Pilbeam (2013, 13) has noted that the "Saint-Simonian movement provided a haven, a counterculture in which Jews could develop ideas on social reform and establish a collegial identity distinct from their faith. An eighth of the movement was Jewish." Saint-Simonian socialism almost certainly exerted an impact on the social aspect of the avant-garde, which emphasized the eventual merger of art, politics and everyday life and, hence, a better future. Yet, the relation between the avant-garde and Judaism is far more complicated.

There are numerous ways in which Jewishness and Judaism can be present in avant-gardist works of art. For instance, a work may include characteristics of the Jewish tradition, but also undermine these in terms of parody or deconstruction. In such cases the avant-garde should be seen in relation to tradition, because rereadings tend to mark a sovereign tradition, which is also established enough to withstand various forms of criticism. Exemplifying such criticism is the German-Jewish expressionist Alfred Lichtenstein (1889–1914) in his poem "Der Traurige" (The Sad Man, 1911):

---

[19] The spelling of his name suggests Portuguese instead of Spanish origins.

Heute hab ich größre Dinge vor –
Ach, ich will den Sinn des Daseins suchen.

Und am Abend werd ich etwas Rollschuh laufen
Oder mal in einen Judentempel gehn.
(Lichtenstein 1962, 22)

[Today I have bigger things in mind –
Ah, I shall seek the meaning of life.

And in the evening I shall do some roller-skating
Or maybe go to a Jewish Temple.]

In Lichtenstein's poem, the temple is a *locus* for the contemplation of life's meaning. However, the leisurely activity of roller-skating provides an equal chance for serious pondering. Indeed, Lichtenstein's poem exhibits a contemplative but ironic undercurrent paralleling the humorous details. Its blunt reference to roller-skating and attending a religious service in the same breath, however, is defiant. In a provocatory manner, Lichtenstein combines something particularly Jewish (the temple and activities therein) with a literary mode not foreign to avant-garde (irony or sarcasm).

Similar cases speak for a feeling of otherness. One may ask how did these tendencies relate to the identities of Jews in the avant-gardes? It should be emphasized that this question is not limited to a certain period but rather pertains even today. For example, Charles Bernstein, a leading American poet, claimed that "[the avant-gardist] Jewish identity is constituted by way of distance from a secure sense of what it means to be Jewish" (Morris 2010, 3). The "secure sense" can be read in a variety ways, but in essence it calls forth individual definitions of Jewishness. Indeed, it seems that regarding Jews and the avant-garde, one senses a variety of self-identifications on the one hand and, on the other, a resistance to accept imposed definitions about what "Jewishness" means.

Considering some explicit testimonies by Jews involved in the avant-garde, one notes a basic need to balance between different cultures, languages and religions. For instance, the early expressionist poet Jakob van Hoddis (Hans Davidsohn, 1887–1942) stated – after briefly leaning towards the Catholic faith – that "my Jewishness breaks through again. Catholicism was just an adventure" (van Hoddis 1987, 235). Yvan Goll (Isaac Lang, 1891–1950), the Alsatian poet, based his identity on in-betweenness: he defined himself as "by fate a Jew, by accident born in France, on paper a German" (Pinthus 1959, 341). Defining himself as an "apatrid" and taking this "close otherness" one step further, the Romanian-born Gherasim Luca (Salman Locker, 1913–1994) called himself an "*étranjuif*," a sort of "stranger Jew" – a stranger amongst other people who is also a stranger to himself (Luca 1962). After the Holocaust, Isidore Isou (Isidore Goldstein, 1925–2007), the Romanian founder of the lettrist movement, firmly stated: "I am fully, in each defect, in each light, in each impulse, in each curve, in each reluctance a Jew. I am so Jewish that it is perhaps the only word in my life that I write with a capital, without feeling that I add a dimension to make up for a deficiency" (Isou 1947, 209).

But not all artists of Jewish origin wanted to identify as Jews. For instance, Karl Kraus (1874–1936) and Walter Serner (Walter Seligmann, 1889–1942) rejected Judaism outright.[20] However, writers and artists of Jewish origin who distance themselves from Judaism have already addressed the relationship to Judaism on a personal level. Even though they might reject religion, they cannot discard their Jewishness so easily. Hence the process of refusal is a trace of self-definition. It normally means that people in this category have given sufficient thought to their background, which in turn allows for micro-historical mapping. Moreover, all of the stances above include an implicit understanding of respective Jewish communities, albeit these are necessarily imaginary ones. Still, they illuminate a given artist's relation to the community. It is of certain interest to probe the individual reasons for embracing or discarding the community, or remaining uninterested in it.

Taking some of the cases mentioned above into account, the notion of a rather polysemous nature of identity, which seeks to avoid reductive forms of Jewish identity, emerges. In the early twentieth century, Jewishness was often linked to either traditional religious orthodoxy or to acculturation that reduced or toned down the Jewish element. Of course, a variety of stances could be identified in between these extremes. Seen from the perspectives of both the avant-garde and Judaism, the Jewish artist provided a marginal voice. On the one hand, against an orthodox or even secular bourgeois assimilated Jewish backdrop, Jews active in the avant-garde are an anomaly.[21] They may have flirted with anti-bourgeois and unorthodox ideologies, such as revolutionary anarchism. On the other hand, Jewish artists were not to be found as a rule in the margins of the avant-gardes,

---

20 However, an unpublished manuscript entitled "Gott und 'Die Fackel'" (God and "Die Fackel") on Karl Kraus's Jewish influences by his peer Paul Hatvani suggests that Kraus' rejection of Judaism was far from a comprehensive one.

21 In their introduction to a theme issue on Jewish modernism, Amir Eshel and Todd Presner call this stance "double de-territorialization," which suggests that Jews active in the avant-garde were anti-traditionalists, thus unfitting for the established historical narratives of both modernism and Judaism. See Eshel and Presner 2006, 611.

such as dada, surrealism or lettrism. Rather they were key players who were able to register a seminal impact in the major manifestations of the individual groups.²²

Thus, as already stated, the Jews in the avant-garde formed distinct undercurrents in the artistic metropolitan centers of the time, like Paris and Berlin, where such undercurrents could manifest themselves and flourish in various ways.²³ They did not really constitute a kind of cultural periphery. For instance, the core of the Berlin-based "Der Neue Club" was Jewish; it included the neo-kabbalist Oskar Goldberg. This fact suggests that the group was both informed about neo-mysticism and that it probably differed from other expressionist groups. Furthermore, it seems that "Jewishness" in some avant-garde circles was radically different from what was conventionally considered to be Jewish at the time. It was open to elements that were derived from beyond the Jewish sphere, while also drawing on Jewish elements. For example, El Lissitzky's (Lazar Markovich Lissitzky, 1890–1941) excursion to the Pale of Settlement in the mid-1910s, where he copied old synagogue wall paintings, had a profound impact on his distinctly avant-gardist illustrations (see Apter-Gabriel 1987).

The role of Jews as mediators and art collectors was equally important for the avant-garde. The "little magazines" that were the primary distribution channel of avant-gardist literary works, would have been unimaginable without Jewish networking. Christian Weikop (2013, 696) notes that during the 1910s and 1920s a network emerged that was "closely linked to patterns of artistic and literary production, dissemination, and patronage, in complex processes of Jewish assimilation that in many respects determined the paths of German modernism." Indeed, key figures like Herwarth Walden (Georg Levin, 1878–1941) introduced European avant-gardes to German readers while publishing articles related to Jewish topics. However, his and other little magazines were not unilaterally a sign of assimilation; rather, they reflected a wide spectrum of the everyday life of the Jews involved in the avant-garde.

All in all, for several Jews the avant-garde seemed to be a way of balancing between aspects of the Jewish past and present. Equally, it sought an equilibrium between the Jewish and non-Jewish worlds. An instance of this characteristic was provided by Alfred Wolfenstein (1883–1945), who regarded the avant-garde through a messianic spectrum with the eventual aim of erasing distinctions and thus the position of the Jew as the "close other." Even though we now

---

22 Here, especially, Jews from Romania are significant. For instance, Tzara and the brothers Janco were prominent dadaists. Claude Sernet, Gellu Naum and Voronca were renowned surrealists, and Isou was the founder of the lettrist movement. See Ion Pop (ed.) *La réhabilitation du rêve. Une anthologie de l'avant-garde roumaine*. Paris: Maurice Nadeau, 2006.
23 For a further discussion, see Bilski 1999.

know his quest was unsuccessful, it speaks volumes for the contemporary self-understanding of the Jews in the avant-garde who were subject to intra-European otherness during the early decades of the 20th century.

From Micro-History Towards a Non-Reductive Comparative Approach

From the aspect of research, the main question this volume attempts to answer is how Jewish studies and avant-garde studies may benefit reciprocally from each other as interdisciplinary fields that complement each other's methodological repertoire. The investigations contained in this volume take into account new historical and theoretical perspectives, which facilitate new views of Jewish artistic, literary and cultural production on the one hand, and a better understanding of the avant-garde on the other.

The micro-historical level, where we can map how individual artists or delimited groups reconciled or accommodated Judaism and the avant-garde, is potentially informative because it does not reduce Jewishness into a monolithic community or expression. However, beyond micro-history a method to clarify how one can approach both the avant-garde and Jewishness together on a more general level is still lacking. In other words, in order to arrive at a more comprehensive picture of the "close other," one needs to venture beyond micro-history.

Thus, it is a challenge to compare and to "cross expose" two elusive and contentious fields of study. Firstly, the term "Jewish," in the manner it is used in Jewish studies, accounts for, but is not limited to, the Jewish tradition with its rituals, texts, customs, ethics, and geographical displacements. These should be regarded from both the religious and the secular spheres. For instance, what meaning did rituals and religious texts convey in a secular context? Secondly, the avant-garde is no less elusive with its geopolitical networks, overlapping temporal aspects, heterogenic texts and various local appropriations. In fact, the fragmentary and varied character of the manifestations of the avant-gardes often lack a common theme and a method of execution. The label "avant-garde" could be characterized as a manifold repertoire of works of art that do not fit for the readily established categories of their time.

There is a deliberate *aporia* looming in the pairing of the avant-garde and the Jews. Jewishness is defined historically via culture and ethnicity (in addition to religion or nation), which means that each definition and depiction of Jewishness must negotiate with or at least acknowledge this complexity. The avant-garde averts imposed definitions and categorizations and cannot be self-defining, because if it were it would relinquish its vanguard position. This position necessitates that avant-gardist art remain indefinable, at least to the extent that art is an institution in its own right. In this sense, once particular art is defined and designated "avant-garde," as is usually done by critics and scholars, it is avant-garde no more. In other words, the avant-garde may be understood as a temporal phenomenon and various attempts that acknowledge the problematics of definition will fall victim to the same trap. One such instance is Isou's (1946, 37) characterization of his own movement as the "avant-garde of the avant-garde," which entails two distinct senses of the term. The first is the "bygone avant-garde" (futurism, dada, surrealism) that preceded his movement in time, and the second is a more loosely defined "avant-garde" that succeeds the first one. Yet, every time art is characterized as avant-garde, it loses its avant-gardist quality, because its novelties have become conventional – in the vein Voronca outlined in his manifesto.

The aporetic combination of the terms "avant-garde" and "Jews" seems to require a so-called "emptying out" of the other so that the two distinct elements cannot be reconciled. Yet, an either/or option is a highly problematical point of departure for analysis, because it is contrafactual. Moreover, it will not clarify or explicate the situation of the Jews active in the avant-garde through the lens of intra-European otherness. By nature, there seems to be a suspended co-existence of aporetic terms. In fact, any attempt to overcome the aporetic suspension of these terms requires reductionism. Yet, one might still ask: what can we learn about the Jews and the avant-garde without reductions? Is a non-reductive comparative approach possible?

In an attempt to circumvent the aporia, some so-called third terms should be considered. Third terms indicate features that are common to the avant-garde and Judaism, but which are merely regarded from within two distinct disciplines with incompatible presumptions and hypotheses. Avant-garde studies and Jewish studies approach their subjects and conceptualize them quite differently. However, the undeniable fact is that Jewish people were disproportionately active in the avant-gardes. It is logical to assume that when encountering new ideas they interpreted them to an extent by means or categories which were already familiar to them, namely those deriving from the Jewish tradition. This possibility would explain the existence of numerous overlaps, of which some are accounted for in the essays contained in this volume. Furthermore, it may point to a continuum in the Jewish history of ideas.

Firstly, there seems to be a common socio-political pursuit among the Jews and the avant-garde, namely the *idea of an ideal community*, which has been seminal in the avant-garde from Saint-Simonianism onwards. It does not denote a delimited congregation of any sort but a more broadly defined community that shares the same values and beliefs. This characteristic was prominent in expressionism and in some variants of dada. In Judaism, it denotes the Jewish community in general. Secondly, and closely connected with the first example, are the *utopian tendencies* of Judaism and the avant-garde. These have a long tradition in Judaism in the form of messianism, which promotes the idea of a messianic age or an eternal divine kingdom. There are more secular messianic ideas advanced by Jewish thinkers, such as those of Walter Benjamin or Ernst Bloch, the latter of whom was associated with expressionism. The avant-garde contains a utopian impulse, which is the amalgamation of art and life. In this context, Jews in the avant-garde often adopted messianic rhetoric from the Jewish tradition. Thirdly, in the same way that the Messiah may transgress Jewish law, the avant-garde artist was no less *antinomian* with respect to bourgeois culture and its so-called "good taste." For instance, the German-Jewish expressionist Albert Ehrenstein (1886–1950) wrote to Karl Kraus in 1911: "*Es ist vielleicht nicht ganz geschmackvoll, davon zu reden, immerhin beging ich impertinent genug das Verbrechen, Jesus Christus nicht den Vortritt zu lassen und am 23. Dezember zur Welt zu kommen*" [It is perhaps of slightly bad taste to mention this, but anyway, I was impertinent enough to commit the crime of not allowing Jesus Christ to go first by entering the world on the twenty-third of December] (Ehrenstein 1989, 88). Fourthly, both Judaism and the avant-garde are *cosmopolitan*, which is, of course, apparent owing to the abundant pejorative uses of the term. This characteristic does not only pertain to the various appropriations of certain aesthetic currents but also to the individual artists themselves. The avant-garde fostered linguistic displacement, intercultural encounter and cross-fertilization.

Essential for literary analysis in particular are *thematic and technical continuities*. Ehrenstein explained that the significant Jewish participation in the avant-garde resulted from "the religious tradition of the Word" (Beller 2005, 231). This tradition originated from the Torah and its commentary literature, especially the myth of or belief in God's oral creation of the world, which was a main focus of medieval Kabbalah (e.g. Abraham Abulafia, Joseph R. Gikatilla and Moshe Cordovero), especially in the form of the investigation of the significance and polysemy of the Hebrew letters. Writers like Lasker-Schüler, Goll, Isou and others utilized Jewish themes in their avant-garde poetry, most often kabbalistic ones, envisioning transcendent realms or mythical events.

The Kabbalah was a source of avant-gardist textual techniques, a fact which signals that these "new" techniques were not at all novel. For instance, Georges Perec's (1936–1982) *oulipian* essay, "Histoire du lipogramme" (History of the Lipogram, 1970), launched the history of the lipogrammatic technique with references to the Zohar, the name of God and key kabbalistic techniques (gematria, notarikon, temurah). Another case is Tzara's *La rose et le chien. Poème perpetuel* (The Rose and the Dog. Perpetual Poem, 1958), which he completed with the help of Picasso. The poem was written on overlapping circular discs, which enabled multiple readings reminiscent of the visual permutation wheels in Abulafia's *Hayyei ha-Olam ha-Ba* (Life of the World to Come, 1280). An even earlier instance of such techniques in Tzara's œuvre is his visual poem "Calligramme" (1916), which mimics or lampoons Hebrew micrography, that is, Jewish calligrammes with their origins in the ninth century.

The thematic continuity of avant-garde includes references to the vast Jewish textual corpus (both religious and secular texts). Van Hoddis provides an example in his early poem "Sprichwörtliches" (Proverbial, 1905–1906), which quotes the Talmud in its last two lines:

Wer wird groß? Der nur er selber ist
Wer gut? Der freudig das Leben betrachtet.
Wer ist weise? Der von jedem lernt.
Wer ist achtbar? Der die Menschen achtet.
(van Hoddis 1987, 215)

[Who is great? He who is only himself
Who is good? He who views life happily.
Who is wise? He who learns from everyone.
Who is respectable? He who respects people.]

Van Hoddis recontextualizes the Biblical lines, while departing from the Talmud *in spiritu*. Hence, the new connotations the poem produces with its somewhat comic self-confidence and optimism reflect obliquely the Talmudic verses (*Pirkei Avot* [Chapters of the Fathers], 4, verse 1.). Van Hoddis's poem is an illuminating example of the reappropriation of a classical Jewish text in the context of the avant-garde. It emulates the formal elements of the Talmudic text while placing it into a contemporary German-Jewish milieu, thereby recontextualizing also the connotations the text conveys. The poem is directed or addressed to readers who are not only familiar with the Talmud, but also liberal regarding the possibilities of reforming the sacred text.

Similar points of contact and mutual themes reoccur throughout the chapters of the present volume. The essays in the first part discuss the early avant-gardes' stances on the various manifestations of tradition in the Jewish context. With a clear-cut focus on avant-garde literature produced by some of the most renowned avant-gardists of Jewish origin, Alfred Bodenheimer points out how the radical textual experimentation in dada by Tzara and others offered resistance to the current stereotypical views on the degenerate quality of Jewish language which crystallized in the debates concerning "Judeo-German," that is, Yiddish as a variant of German. By focusing on Tzara's and Marcel Janco's Romanian Jewish background, Radu Stern analyzes how the historical constraints established by nationalism facilitated the absorption of cosmopolitan and transnational values among Jews. The European Jewish population in the diaspora was characteristically transnational and this characteristic required negotiations on various levels with country-specific nationalisms. In addition to its cosmopolitanism, the avant-garde provided novel textual means that were regarded as potential solutions to the dichotomy between the national and the transnational. Sami Sjöberg looks into Alfred Wolfenstein's groundbreaking interpretation of the avant-garde in the framework of German expressionism. Wolfenstein promoted avant-gardist "new literature" as a means of overcoming the linguistic differences between the varieties of German spoken by Jews and Germans respectively. His utopian approach called for a comprehensive cultural reboot and mutual integration.

The Jewish endeavors to integrate or at least to coexist with the society at large gave birth to various communities, which – in the context of the avant-garde – could also be imaginary. Andreas Kramer's essay opens the second part and highlights how the contradictory striving for national belonging and maintenance of emigrant otherness are visible in the *œuvre* of Carl Einstein. Today Einstein, is considered one of the most esteemed avant-garde authors; he sought to de-emphasize his Jewishness owing to his sense of being a secular person with preciously little background in religious Jewish life. Parallel to his half-forced exclusion from the Jewish community, Einstein attempted to convey a notion of a new kind of collective Jewish identity, which was analogous to the communities of the European avant-garde. A more concrete manifestation of a particularly Jewish community in the avant-garde circles is provided by Laëtitia Torjman, who focuses on the Polish Khalyastre group. Her investigation shows how the works of the core group transgressed various geographical and symbolic borders of the more conservative Jewish community. Such experimentation was met with backlashes from both the Jewish and non-Jewish domains. Fittingly, Maria Silina accounts for the eventual repression of the so-called Russian Jewish renaissance by Stalin from the mid-1920s onwards. The idea of a minority-particular, or communal, form of avant-garde came to an abrupt end in the USSR in the 1930s, after modern artists of Jewish origins were forced to reject Jewish motifs altogether.

The two essays constituting the third part of this volume address Jewish avant-gardists in relation to the non-Jewish cultural environment and especially anti-Semitism. The French-Jewish artist Claude Cahun challenged representations of race and ethnic minorities in her self-portraits by adopting avant-garde aesthetics. Zoë Roth indicates that Cahun's images and writings overturn representations derived from the outside while forming a coherent personal identity in a multi-minoritarian frame – addressing issues related to race, sexuality and gender. Alana Sobelman discusses anti-Semitic debates and stereotypes in Viennese cultural circles at the turn of the century while unearthing Arnold Schoenberg's manner of challenging anti-Semitic discourse. Several of Schoenberg's works at the time sought to revise the dominant views of the Jewish body and mind as fundamentally effeminate. Schoenberg's engagement illustrates how such issues were not merely theoretical debates; rather, they were also addressed in the arts.

The fourth part sheds light on some particular aspects of the relationship between the avant-garde and the Jewish tradition. The example of messianism both as a doctrine and a structure of thought, together with religious syncretism and its connection to various avant-garde topoi pertain to this section. Małgorzata Strolarska-Fronia examines the intersection of avant-garde aesthetics and imagery, traditional Judaism, and interwar Jewish philosophical thought. Through an iconographical analysis she reveals how some Jewish artists formed their religious identity by amalgamating elements from various overlapping and, occasionally, contradictory modes of thought. A parallel trend occurred in European avant-garde cinema of the 1920s. Tom Paulus, by investigating a revelationist tradition, argues for acknowledging a relation between early film theory, dialectical materialism and various modes of Jewish mysticism. He cites the films of Epstein and Godard in this regard. A personalized version of messianism occurs in the works of the experimental Yiddish writer Der Nister, whose contribution to the Soviet avant-garde is examined by Raphael Koenig. Overcome by repressive cultural policies, Der Nister utilized the avant-gardist literary topos of the "mad author," while redefining his relationship with the Jewish tradition. Olivier Salazar-Ferrer detects a similar method of redefinition in the existential poetics of Benjamin Fondane. Salazar-Ferrer argues that Fondane's understanding of Judaism derived from the philosophy of Lev Shestov, while Fondane eschewed inclusive modes of Judaism and contemporary avant-garde.

The final section of the volume diverges from the main foci, which are the manifestations of avant-garde aesthetics and various modes of Jewish thought, customs, and themes in literature and other arts. Steven E. Aschheim's essay provides a historical and biographical overview of the various Jewish figures active in the avant-gardes of the twentieth century. His detailed analysis emphasizes the inevitable difficulties in defining a phenomenon that might be labeled "Jewish avant-garde." Aschheim's contribution highlights the need for new methodological tools and approaches, some of which are introduced in this volume. However, approaches such as the use of third terms are preliminary or tentative and they call for further analysis in this field of study.

Admittedly, the current volume has some limitations that have constricted its scope, such as the focus on the earlier part of the twentieth century. Even though the geographical focus of the volume is Continental, one should not neglect the importance of North American Jewish literature, the full extent of the Russian Jewish renaissance, the few proponents of Jewish futurism (such as Bruno Jasieński) or vanguard poets of Jewish origin predating the historical avant-garde, such as Gustave Kahn, the free verse poet of the late nineteenth century. In addition, the later cases of avant-garde production in relation to Jewish issues require further investigation, especially regarding the Adornian post-Auschwitz paradigm shift and current cultural trends. For instance, the aesthetics and thematic frameworks of Gustav Metzger, the creator of auto-destructive art with his background in Orthodox Judaism, and of the Austrian-Jewish experimentalist Hermann Nitsch should be taken into account. Especially Nitsch's books *Die Eroberung von Jerusalem* (The Conquest of Jerusalem, 1976) and the Hebrew-German *Levitikus* (2010) would benefit from a detailed analysis based on some of the perspectives introduced in this volume.

This volume attempts to answer, at least tentatively, questions concerning the renegotiation of the relation between religion and secularity in the avant-garde, and the varied manifestations of the contact between tradition and the ideas of novelty and "modern" in the avant-gardist works by Jewish artists. Furthermore, it illuminates how texts produced by Jews involved in the avant-garde document and comment on the state of Judaism and Jewishness at the time they were produced. The insights which the individual essays record provide the necessary intellectual background for understanding how these issues are recurring in current cultural debates concerning minorities and avant-garde output.

Bibliography

(anon.): The Holocaust Encyclopedia. www.ushmm.org/wlc/en/article.php?ModuleId= 10005161 (7 March 2016).
Altmann, Simon, and Eduardo L. Ortiz (eds.). *Mathematics and Social Utopias in France: Olinde Rodrigues and His Times*. Providence: American Mathematical Society, 2006.
Anderson, Lisa Marie. *German Expressionism and the Messianism of a Generation*. Amsterdam: Rodopi, 2010.
Apter-Gabriel, Ruth (ed.). *Tradition and Revolution: The Jewish Renaissance in Russian Avant-Garde Art 1912–1928*. Jerusalem: The Israel Museum, 1987.
Baigell, Matthew, and Milly Heyd. *Complex Identities: Jewish Consciousness and Modern Art*. New Brunswick, New Jersey, and London: Rutgers University Press, 2001.
Beller, Steven. "Albert Ehrenstein." *Encyclopedia of Modern Jewish Culture*. Ed. Glenda Abramson. London: Routledge, 2005. 230–231.
Bilski, Emily D. (ed.). *Berlin Metropolis: Jews and the New Culture*. Berkeley: University of California Press, 1999.
Birnbaum, Menachem. *Lyrische Dichtung deutscher Juden*. Berlin: Welt-Verlag, 1920.
Ehrenstein, Albert. *Briefe*. Göttingen: Wallstein Verlag, 1989.
Einstein, Carl. *Bebuquin oder die Dilettanten des Wunders*. Berlin: Aktion-Verlag, 1912.

Eshel, Amir, and Todd Presner. "Introduction." *Modernism/modernity* 13.4 (2006): 607–614.
Garb, Tamar, and Linda Nochlin (eds.). *The Jew in the Text: Modernity and the Construction of Identity*. London: Thames and Hudson, 1995.
Goga, Octavian. *Mustul care fierbe*. București: Imprimeria statului, 1927.
Hentea, Maurice. *TaTa Dada: The Real Life and Celestial Adventures of Tristan Tzara*. Cambridge and London: MIT Press, 2014.
Hirte, Chris. *Erich Mühsam: Eine Biographie*. Freiburg: Ahriman Verlag, 2009.
Hughes, Robert. *The Shock of the New*. New York: Alfred A. Knopf, 2013.
Iancu, Carol. *Voronca, Ilarie*. The YIVO Encyclopedia of Jews in Eastern Europe. www.yivoencyclopedia.org/article.aspx/Voronca_Ilarie (7 March 2016).
Isou, Isidore. *La dictature lettriste: Cahiers d'un nouveau régime artistique*. Paris: [s.n.], 1946.
Isou, Isidore. *L'agrégation d'un nom et d'un Messie*. Paris: Gallimard, 1947.
Kampf, Avram. *Chagall to Kitaj – Jewish Experience in 20th Century Art*. New York: Praeger, 1990.
Kiefer, Klaus. *Avantgarde – Weltkrieg – Exil*. Frankfurt am Main: Peter Lang, 1986.
Kirschenblatt-Gimblett, Barbara, and Jonathan Karp (eds.). *The Art of Being Jewish in Modern Times*. Philadelphia: University of Pennsylvania Press, 2008.
Krojanker, Gustav. *Juden in der deutschen Literatur*. Berlin: Welt-Verlag, 1922.
Lichtenstein, Alfred. *Gesammelte Gedichte*. Zürich: Arche, 1962.
Liska, Vivian. "Secret Affinities: Contemporary Jewish Writing in Austria." *Contemporary Jewish Writing in Europe: A Guide*. Ed. Vivian Liska and Thomas Nolden. Bloomington: Indiana University Press, 2008. 1–22.
Luca, Gherasim. Cahier de 1962. Bibliothèque littéraire Jacques Doucet. Fonds Ghérasim Luca, Bibliothèque littéraire Jacques Doucet, Paris, 1962.
Morris, Daniel. "Introduction." *Radical Poetics and Secular Jewish Culture*. Ed. Stephen Paul Miller and Daniel Morris. Tuscaloosa: The University of Alabama Press, 2009. 1–11.
Perec, Georges. "Histoire du lipogramme." *Oulipo: La littérature potentielle*. Paris: Gallimard, 1973. 73–89.
Pilbeam, Pamela. *Saint-Simonians in Nineteenth-Century France. From Free Love to Algeria*. Basingstoke and New York: Palgrave Macmillan, 2013.
Pinthus, Kurt (ed.). *Menscheitsdämmerung. Ein Dokument des Expressionismus*. Reinbek: Rowohlt, 1959.
Piotrowski, Piotr. "Toward a Horizontal History of the European Avant-Garde." *Europa! Europa? The Avant-Garde, Modernism and the Fate of a Continent*. Ed. Sascha Bru, Jan Baetens, Benedikt Hjartarson, Peter Nicholls, Tania Ørum and Hubert van den Berg. Berlin and New York: De Gruyter, 2009. 49–58.
Raileanu, Petre. *Gherasim Luca*. Paris: Oxus, 2004.
Rodrigues, Olinde. "L'artiste, le savant et l'industriel." *Œuvres de Saint-Simon et d'Enfantin*. Aalen: Otto Zeller, 1964. 201–258.
Saint-Simon, Henri. *Henri Saint-Simon (1760–1825): Selected Writings on Science, Industry, and Social Organization*. London: Holmes and Meier, 1975.
Sakheim, Arthur. *Das jüdische Element in der Weltliteratur*. Hamburg: Hazoref, 1924.
Sandqvist, Tom. *Dada East: The Romanians of Cabaret Voltaire*. Cambridge and London: The MIT Press, 2006.
Sed-Rajna, Gabrielle. *Jewish Art*. New York: Harry N. Abrams, 1997.
Shaked, Gershon. *The Shadows Within: Essays on Modern Jewish Writers*. Philadelphia: Jewish Publication Society, 1987.

van Hoddis, Jakob. *Dichtungen und Briefe*. Ed. Regina Nörtemann. Zürich: Arche, 1987.
Van Voolen, Edward. *My Grandparents, My Parents and I: Jewish Art and Culture*. München: Prestel, 2006.
Voronca, Ilarie. "Gramatică." *Punct* 2.6–7 (1925): 1.
Voronca, Ilarie. "Grammar." *Between Worlds: A Sourcebook of Central European Avant-Gardes, 1910–1930*. Ed. Timothy O. Benson and Éva Forgács. Trans. Julian Semilian and Sanda Agalidi. Cambridge and London: The MIT Press, 2002. 547–549.
Washton Long, Rose-Carol, Matthew Baigell and Milly Heyd (eds.). *Jewish Dimensions in Modern Visual Culture: Antisemitism, Assimilation, Affirmation*. Waltham: Brandeis University Press, 2010.
Weikop, Christian. "Introduction." *The Oxford Critical and Cultural History of Modernist Magazines. Vol. III: Europe 1880–1940*: Part 2. Ed. Peter Brooker, Sascha Bru, Andrew Thacker and Christian Weikop. Oxford: Oxford University Press, 2013. 693–708.
Weisgerber, Jean. "Le mot et le concept d'avant-garde: Français." *Les avant-gardes littéraires au XXe siècle. Vol. I. Histoire*. Ed. Jean Weisgerber. Amsterdam and Philadelphia: John Benjamins, 1984. 17–20.
Wisse, Ruth. *The Modern Jewish Canon: A Journey through Language and Culture*. New York: The Free Press, 2000.
Wolfenstein, Alfred. *Jüdisches Wesen und neue Dichtung*. Berlin: Erich Reiss, 1922.
Zwi, Cheskel. "Wir jungen Juden!" *Die Aktion* 1.42 (1911): 1315–1316.

The Avant-Garde and Jewish Traditions

Alfred Bodenheimer
Dada Judaism: The Avant-Garde in First World War Zurich

> *Wir armen Juden clagend hungersnot*
> *vnd müßend gar verzagen, hand kein brot.*
> *oime las compassio*
> *cullis mullis lassio*
> *Egypten was guot land,*
> *wau wau wau wiriwau,*
> *Egypten was guot land.*

This is not a dada text, yet it is similar to dada texts in several ways: like many dada poems, it consists of a mix of semantically recognizable words (in German), especially in the first two verses, as well as in the fifth and the last; it also has a syntactic order and suggests a meaning in the sense of practical, conventional language. Likewise, there are lines with unrecognizable words, either with a tonality recalling Latin, or evoking the barking of a dog, additionally parodying the threefold *"wau"* (German for "woof") with the line ending *"wiriwau."* The main difference from dada texts is that the latter never spoke so explicitly about Jews (*"Wir armen Juden"*).

The quoted text was printed in 1583, in a revised version of the Lucerne Passionsspiel. I have quoted it from the German translation of Sander L. Gilman's *Jewish Self-Hatred. Anti-Semitism and the Hidden Language of the Jews*.[1] Gilman presents this quotation, spoken by the figures representing the Jews in the Passionsspiel, in order to demonstrate "the subhuman nature of the Jews' language, a language of marginality" (1986, 76). Gilman also stresses that here, unlike in many other cases, the comic effect of Jewish speech prevails over fear of Jews and is more about making the audiences laugh rather than making them angry.

A long line of discrimination and ridiculing of "Jewish language" can be drawn from the sixteenth century to 1912, shortly before the outburst of the First World War, when Moritz Goldstein's famous article "Deutsch-jüdischer Parnass" led to the so-called *"Kunstwart-Debatte"* in Germany. Goldstein's central statement, that *"wir Juden verwalten den geistigen Besitz eines Volkes, das uns die*

---

[1] Wyss, Heinz (ed.). *Das Luzerner Osterspiel*. Bern: Francke, 1967, 196. Here quoted from: Gilman, Sander L. *Jüdischer Selbsthaß. Antisemitismus und die verborgene Sprache der Juden*. Trans. Isabella König. Frankfurt a. M.: Jüdischer Verlag, 1993, 72. The quote has been taken from the German translation of Gilman's book, because unlike Gilman's English original version, it quotes the original medieval German version of the Osterspiel.

Berechtigung und die Fähigkeit dazu abspricht" [We Jews uphold the intellectual property of a people that denies our right to do so], caused a wave of reactions about whether and to what degree Jews were (or were not) legitimate speakers and writers of the German language.[2]

Since the nineteenth century the use not just of German but of European languages in general had undergone a process of ethnification and nationalization. Intellectuals of the non-Jewish majority contested the legitimacy, or at least authenticity, of the literary production of Jews in these languages. At the same time, Yiddish, the Jewish *lingua franca* before the Holocaust, was disparagingly termed "Jargon," not least by Jews themselves, as we know for example from Kafka, himself an admirer of Yiddish theatre. In an increasingly nationalized Europe, the mastering of many languages characterized eastern Jewish intellectuals, some of whom were able to author books in multiple languages (such as Simon Dubnow, who wrote in Russian, Yiddish, Hebrew, and German); nevertheless, such multilingualism was perceived as a sign of homelessness and lack of roots, not as a positive, multicultural quality.

There are several reasons to consider dada as having been among the more radical forms of the avant-garde. Dada, from its outset, was an international issue, not least in the various origins of its founders, in the multilingualism it practiced as part of its program, and in the development of several European centers where it was realized. It was a combination – indeed, an amalgamation – of art, poetry, and performance. And, it was a radical way of challenging language, not only as a manifestation of personal or collective belonging, but also as an instrument of semantics, of sending a message and of making sense.

The dada movement had a clear point and place of departure. It had its beginnings in 1916, in Zurich, where it was centered around the group of poets and artists active at the Cabaret Voltaire in the Spiegelgasse, a few houses from where Lenin resided in the months before being transported back to Russia in a sealed wagon. The main protagonists of early dada are well known: German poets Richard Huelsenbeck and Hugo Ball, as well as the latter's companion and later wife, Emmy Hennings; Alsatian artist Hans Arp and, to a certain extent, his companion Sophie Täuber-Arp; later, Hans Richter, an artist of wealthy German-Jewish descent (although this became known to the public only in 1989); and Walter Serner, a writer born in Bohemia as a Jew with the family name Seligmann who converted to Catholicism in 1913 (he was killed by the Nazis in 1942). Finally,

---

[2] For an overview of the article, its historical context and reception see: Julius H. Schoeps et al. (eds.). *Deutsch-jüdischer Parnaß. Menorah Jahrbuch für deutsch-jüdische Geschichte.* Berlin and Wien: Philo Verlagsgesellschaft, 2002.

there were two young Jews from Romania: Marcel Janco and Tristan Tzara. Janco, born Marcel Hermann Iancu, was an artist at the beginning of a remarkable career. He later turned to Zionism and returned to Romania, from where he escaped to Palestine, at the last minute in 1941. He went on to become one of Israel's leading artists and turned the village of Ein Hod into an artists' colony, where a museum bearing his name was founded in 1983, the year before his death. Tzara was an author, poet and performer; he was born Samuel Rosenstock in Moinesti (in the province of Moldavia), in 1896. By the age of eleven, he had been sent to boarding school in Bucharest (where he became a schoolmate and friend of Janco) and had begun his publishing activity in Romania. Towards the end of 1915 he came to Zurich to study, but almost certainly also to avoid being drafted, in case Romania (then neutral) entered the war. In Zurich he made the acquaintance of Hugo Ball and soon joined the Cabaret Voltaire, adopting French as his literary language. As this was a foreign language to him and he had, as a schoolboy, mastered German with consistently better grades than in French (Hentea 2014, 27)[3], this feat is quite remarkable, especially in the German-speaking environment of Zurich.

One may speculate why Tzara chose French as the language for his poetry and performances. One reason may be that he feared that performing in German with a Romanian accent could, in Swiss-German-speaking Zurich, expose him to the public as a stranger in manifold ways, or even more clearly as an Eastern European Jew. It may also be that his speaking French was a political statement. Coming from a country whose traditional adoration of French culture had been suppressed in the years before and during the First World War by a blunt (and anti-Semitic) nationalism, he was perhaps making a statement by using French as a kind of "counter language" to the nationalistic chauvinism of his home country. Concerning the importance of French to him, it is striking and surely not accidental that Tzara later organized his dada soirée on 14 July 1916, Bastille Day.

For many years, the Jewish origin of various dadaists was not a central issue for research, though it was not concealed, either. The reason it was downplayed may have been the impression that neither the dadaists themselves nor their environment seemed to emphasize the issue. Nor did it become visible in their texts and performances of the time. There may also have been a certain self-restraint involved, stemming from concern that stressing the participation of Jews could inadvertently be seen to be in line with the disqualification of "Entartete Kunst" by the National Socialists, who mixed criteria of origin and modernism in denouncing major artists of the early twentieth century.

---

[3] Hentea (2014, 83) also mentions the "halting and at times ungrammatical French" of Tzara's dada texts.

Yet in recent years, researchers such as Tom Sandqvist, Milly Heyd, Haim Finkelstein, and Marius Hentea have given new emphasis to the Jewishness of the Romanian contributors to dada Zurich, centrally among them Tzara. Albert Boime's article "Dada's Dark Secret" (2010) highlights how Hugo Ball, especially, expressed anti-Semitic feelings that were largely blurred in some later editions of his works but which influenced his approach to Tzara and Janco during and after the dada years. All this sheds new light on dada in Zurich.

Milly Heyd considers Tristan Tzara, along with another groundbreaking Jewish avant-garde artist, Man Ray, in terms of "The Hidden Jew and the Avant-Garde" (2010, 194). She assumes a rather conventional view of the Jew, trying but finally failing to flee or conceal his Jewish identity in a turn to universalistic forms of art.

In showing that the Hasidic and Kabbalistic influences of his youth are evident in Tzara's language practice, Tom Sandqvist (2006) raises a well taken point, as this fact renders language a performative medium of change and creation, rather than viewing it as an instrument of communicating preformed and seemingly unambiguous meaning. But for dada, Judaism has more to it than the transformation of some more traditional or "authentic" forms of Judaism into secular art and literary production. For dada, Judaism is more an attempt to cope with the task of creating new forms of art, in which the general Jewish experience of exile, dispersal, contempt, and non-acceptance is simultaneously transformed, elevated, and abrogated in universalist expression.

For Tzara, dada was not a refuge from Judaism or a means to introduce elements of Judaism (like the Kabbalah) into art. Rather, it was a form of expressing Judaism, clearly not as an explicit form of identity, but in a way that visualized the paradoxical form and essence of being, an experience which could be described as fundamental for contemporary European Jews. This refers to more than just the fundamental paradox recognized clearly by many Europeans of his generation, namely, the irrational consequences of a seemingly rationalized bourgeois way of thinking that had led Europe into a disastrous war. The specific paradoxical experience of European Jews of the age had, even long before, been that of an existence that was "out of order." The simultaneity of affirming the circumstances of one's existence (by assimilation to the ruling classes), yet at the same time negating them (as discriminatory), of creating (national) identity by destroying (Jewish) identity, while defining it as the lack of full participation in the national project, of performing (the national) language by suppressing (the Yiddish) language, while making being Jewish as such into the denial of the ability to write and speak national languages fluently – this was the paradoxical mode of existence of Jews in the early twentieth century.

In Tzara's case, this paradoxical mode of existence is evident even in his name, which he first used as a *nom de plume* in a Romanian publication in October 1915, shortly before leaving for Switzerland. Heyd has collected various explanations for this choice of name:

> Beyond the obvious allusions to Tristan and Isolde, it has been suggested that it may mean "sad in the country" (trist en tsara). Tzara is also based on "tara," Rumanian for country, more specifically, insinuating land. Another view holds that the pseudonym echoes the name of the poet Tristan Corbière. A further reading of the name was offered by the French poet Max Jacob, namely, that "Tzara" is short for Zarathustra implying a Nietzschean influence. Finally, "Tzara" also suggests the word "problem" in Yiddish, implying "problem" in a Jewish context.
> (Heyd 2010, 198)

Another point can be added: Tzara's parents' first language was reportedly Yiddish, and even if (as was likely) it was not spoken at home by a family striving for assimilation, he may have had knowledge of it (Dickerman 2006, 22). If so, the word "Tzara" in its Yiddish (or Hebrew) sense as "problem" would be a kind of complement to the first name Tristan, insofar as it would combine the Romanian word for sadness with the Yiddish word for "problem." Finally, in a permutational reading, "Tzara" could also be understood as a reversal of "*eretz*" or "*aretz*," the Hebrew word for "land," thus reversing the Romanian term ("*tara*"). It would probably be a mistake to try to identify the "correct" reading of this pseudonym – its quality might instead be found in the very multivalence of its associations and connotations, including a variety of multilingual and multicultural combinations. Moreover, it seems that it is precisely the monistic way by which a language seemingly "makes sense" that Tzara tries to attack in his dada activity. Considering Talmudic and Aggadic textual interpretation, one might call this practice of multifaceted readings itself "Jewish" – I refrain from doing so, because it would again be an attempt to clearly and essentially define a "Jewish" way of acting. I focus instead on Tzara's act of de-essentializing and in fact de-constructing readings and methods of thinking and acting.

Tzara himself never discussed his *nom de plume*. But, it is revealing that in his "Manifeste Dada 1918," he offers several interpretations for the word "dada," similar to the manifold interpretations that have been proffered for the name "Tristan Tzara":

> Dada does not mean anything
> If you find it futile and don't want to waste your time on a word that means nothing ... The first thought that comes to these people is bacteriological in character: to find its etymological, or at least its historical or psychological origin. We see by the papers that the Kru Negroes call the tail of a holy cow Dada. The cube and the mother in a certain district of Italy are called: Dada. A hobby horse, a nurse both in Russian and Rumanian: Dada. Some learned

journalists regard it as an art for babies, other holy Jesuscallingthelittlechildrenuntohims of our day, as a relapse into a dry and noisy, noisy and monotonous primitivism. Sensibility is not constructed on the basis of a word; all constructions converge on perfection which is boring, the stagnant idea of a gilded swamp, a relative human product.
(Tzara, 1916)[4]

Stephen Forcer urges us "to read Tzara's poetry in its own terms as polyvalent text" (2012, 264), and Bernard Noël notes of Tzara "that his name is synonymous with the invention of dada and that in any case that's what history has decided" (2011, 241).[5] Since Tzara was the first to use the word dada in print (although the word may have been introduced by Hugo Ball), one may add that, in its intrinsic lack of significance, and concomitant programmatic polyvalence, the name Tristan Tzara can itself be understood as an expression of dada – even though his pseudonym preceded the artistic movement. Tzara had previously used other pseudonyms, and in time he may have discarded this one, too, had it not become entangled with the dada movement.

Like Tzara, Ball associated the term dada with its meanings or allusions in various languages. He described the coining of the term in the context of naming a new journal in April 1916, although it would be over ten years until this note was published in his work *The Flight out of Time*: "Dada is 'yes' in Romanian, 'rocking horse' and 'hobbyhorse' in French. For Germans it is a sign of foolish naiveté, joy in procreation, and preoccupation with the baby carriage" (Dickerman 2006, 33). Although it is interesting to notice that Ball's reflection on the notion begins with its Romanian and French meanings, it is even more important to mention that in his own public explanation of the word "dada" in July 1916, Ball was looking for a positive meaning of the word. Andreas Kramer quotes Ball's remark from his opening of the dada soirée on 14 July 1916: Dada was "*Ein internationales Wort. Nur ein Wort, und das Wort als Bewegung*" [An international word. Only one word, and the word as a movement]. Kramer adds that, "[w]here other avant-garde movements announce their intentions in their names, Ball's remark seems to suggest that the signifier "dada" refuses to be tied to any specific signified – that it was portable as well as moveable, transient and vagrant, and emphatically not at home anywhere" (2011, 203).

It is striking, then, that Tzara's and Ball's respective definitions of dada, seemingly identical in their references to nothing specific but the movement itself, differ greatly in how they circumscribe the non-significance of the word. Whereas

---

4 For the French original see: Tzara, Tristan. *Oeuvres completes. Vol. 1*. Ed. Henri Béhar. Paris: Flammarion, 1975 [1912–1924]. 360.
5 "*que son nom est synonyme de l'invention de Dada – et qu'en tout cas ainsi en a décidé l'histoire*".

Ball does not offer any meaning, dissolving the word "dada" in the term "international" and as a bare "movement" (which may mean a kinetic act as well as a group of artists), thereby trying to describe dada as a kind of Hegelian synthesis of the national clashes in the Great War, Tzara does not use the word "international." Instead, he offers numerous, quite real yet entirely unconnected meanings of the word in various languages. Tzara's definition dissolves any meaning that Ball's "internationality" might eventually develop. According to Tzara, the multilingual potential of the word does not multiply or constitute its sense, but rather eliminates it. Tzara, in other words, does not aim to develop his own dada language; he seeks to unmask language itself as a construction that draws its value, and sometimes its claim to superiority, from an equally constructed concept of identities and values. In themselves, all languages are equal, but equal in their differences. This claim to the right of equality while upholding difference is the basic Jewish claim to a secular society. But the European peoples, be it first for religious or later for nationalist reasons, have never managed to actually understand this right, let alone grant it to minority societies.

If we compare, then, the performative poetry of Ball and Tzara, we realize that their respective concepts of dada poetry differed greatly. Famous poems by Ball, for example, like his "Karawane" or the poem "Gadji beri bimba," gather words that, for the most part, make no sense in any conventional language, although they contain words or morphemes of specific languages. T.J. Demos has summarized Ball's practice of poetry and performance as follows:

> It is undeniable that there is something intensely private and opaque about Ball's speech that resists communication, just as his strange costume projects an image of alterity. [...] this solipsistic element highlights the singularity of identity, which refuses to collapse into any unified and essentialized (but nevertheless "imaginary") community of nationalism. (Demos 2003, 154)

Tzara, in contrast, never used this form of opaque poetry. Creating a language of fantasized wording may have run counter to the specific universalism of art that he was striving for, a universalism based on the pluralism of myriad different elements. He came from a background in which jingoistic and anti-Semitic arguments had long reproached Jews for using impure, falsified language, from early examples in the sixteenth century (as quoted at the beginning of this chapter) all the way to the arguments of Romanian intellectuals in Tzara's time, who attacked Jews as "foreigners" importing "diseased ideas" into Romanian literature and culture (Hentea 2014, 44). Therefore, Tzara had a different way of expressing himself than Ball. As Henri Béhar (2005, 56f.) makes clear, Tzara's style is characterized by a formally correct grammar and syntax. The provocative and irritating character of Tzara's poetry, Béhar claims, stems from the use of a seemingly disturbing semanticism, combining notions that seem completely out of place, not in their singularity but in their combination.

This underlines the argument that Tzara's concept of dada poetics was different from Ball's, and that this difference can be depicted as "Jewish." Ball, who was traumatized by a visit to the Belgian front (he himself had been rejected for service in the German army, due to health reasons) was obviously searching for a new and newly composed language by which to challenge the language of war. In a way, he looked for poetic ways out of the frenzy of war. It is unsurprising, then, that Ball, at a certain point, stepped out of dada and turned strongly to Catholicism, striving for resolution through religion. Tzara was less driven by pacifist or religious feelings; instead, he was fascinated by the issue of sense and nonsense, using language as a means to serve and simultaneously destroy the needs of meaning in a conventional sense.

Another mode of resistance to Western culture appears in Tzara's "Poèmes nègres" ("Negro poems"), based on poetry from various African languages, as well as from the Fijian and Maori languages. These poems must of course be considered in the context of the general boom, at the beginning of the twentieth century, in what was called "primitive art"; in fact, the poems transform the primitivism of plastic and visual arts into poetry. As quoted earlier, Tzara, in his manifesto of 1918, used the word "primitivism" as one of the characteristics of dada. By mixing translation and original language, a new form of what is termed "*Verfremdung*" (translated, insufficiently, into English as "alienation") is created. It fits Tzara's tendency to use language in order to question the supremacy of language. Sense giving and sense killing might be understood as emerging from the same source – it is not the words that express seemingly irresistible truths, but only their subjugation under the dictates of convention. It may be the case, then, that it was less the oft-quoted "primitivism" of the original that challenged western thinking, but rather the admission of non-understanding. As a Jew, Tzara had many reasons to call into question the so-called disastrous truths and rationalizations of European thinking, one result of which was the First World War – with the discrimination of Jews for centuries being another.

It is in line with this concept of his alienating of languages that, aside from his plays and manifestos, Tzara's most well-known literary work is his creation of and participation in simultaneous poetry. As avant-garde researchers know, the concept of simultaneous poetry was developed not by dada but by the founder of futurism, Filippo Tommaso Marinetti. Yet dada, and at its forefront Tristan Tzara, gave simultaneous poetry a new function, quite the opposite of Marinetti's nationalist – indeed, pre-fascist – ideology. Béhar has identified fourteen examples of simultaneous poetry by dada, with Tzara as the only dada group member involved in each. All these poems, each composed by more than one person, contain simultaneously recited texts in at least two languages, usually French and German. Tzara's partners in this simultaneous poetry were Richard Huelsenbeck, Walter Serner, Hans Arp, and, once, even Marcel Janco – but never Hugo Ball, although it must be noted that he did write a simultaneous Christmas play (Béhar 2005, 64 f.).

The most famous of Tzara's simultaneous poems comprises lines to be performed in three languages: German (by Richard Huelsenbeck), French (by Tristan Tzara), and English (by Marcel Janco). Its title, which is only in French, is "L'amiral cherche une maison à louer" [The admiral is looking for a house to rent]. The poem was performed on 30 March 1916 at the Cabaret Voltaire in Zurich (Tzara 1975 [1912–1924], 492–493).

The analogous performance of entirely different texts in three languages is a well-composed cacophony, actually a composition of voices and languages subdued to an exact rhythm. Within this composition, it becomes clear that the French part, composed and performed by Tzara, is the one most clearly connected to the conventional meaning of the French title, especially here:

> *Le télégraphiste assassine la concierge qui m'a trompé elle a vendu l'appartement que j'avais loué*
> [The telegraphist kills the concierge who has cheated on me she has sold the apartment that I had rented]

The title also echoes in this line:

> *La rue s'enfuit avec mon bagage à travers la ville*
> [The street escapes with my luggage through the city]

And of course, the theme is picked up in the final line, when the voices speak in unison, in French: "*L'Amiral n'a rien trouvé*" [The admiral found nothing].

Researchers have understood the admiral's homelessness to be a symbol of the exile that was also felt by the performers of the poem, each of whom was, in some way, an emigré. Of course, the comic aspect of the symbol is that here the person to whom this homelessness is ascribed is a member of the governing classes and the highest military ranks. Without over-interpreting the text, it is remarkable, then, that the quoted French lines spoken by Tzara are those in the poem that most explicitly focus on the concrete reality of being homeless, of being robbed of and denied a home, which, from the outset, would be a home that one did not own but only rented.

In his biography of Tzara, Marius Hentea explains that the style of the texts in the three languages was adapted to each of the speakers:

> A gifted musician, Janco sang his Engish lines. This created another layer of opposition beyond language and provided an underlying melody to the piece [...] Huelsenbeck's aggres-

> sive performance style was brought out by the greater number of pure sounds in his lines: "Ahoi ahoi ... prrzza chrrza prrrza." Tzara, whose small frame and young bespectacled face set him apart, had the narrative center, so the helpless, gentle little boy who has a simple story to tell struggles against a bombastic Huelsenbeck and a melodic Janco.
> (Hentea 2014, 70)

Later, Hentea adds that "Tzara, who was juggling three languages (Romanian, French, and German), found a natural home in this multilingual ambiance" (2014, 71).

At the same time, however, the languages also neutralize one another, losing their claims to superiority and exclusivity, as well as to such a fictitious quality as "purity." Language becomes subordinate to rhythm and sound. There is more research to be done regarding how this simultaneous poetry was composed, whether it was written or only performed by a team of dadaist artists and writers. It seems that researchers disagree on this matter. But maybe, in the end, such differentiation between authorship and performance would, in dada, be an unpromising point of departure, considering the necessity of close cooperation.

I have provided a preliminary sketch of what I believe can be recognized as a sort of "dada Judaism" in Zurich. Tracing Jewish origins in a context where extensive measures were taken to conceal explicit Jewishness (which, in this case, did not in the least prevent Ball and Huelsenbeck from eventually referring to Tzara's or Janco's Judaism in rather polemical ways) is a tricky process, and I have tried to avoid over-interpretations. My main argument is that the Jewish character of Tristan Tzara's dadaism is evident in his stressing the multivalence of words and the pluralism of distinct but equally important languages.

Dada without its Jewish protagonists would certainly have had a much different face – probably with more of Ball's Nietzschean melancholy and introversion, less Latin easiness and playing with conventional language, and fewer of the marketing strategies for the performances that Tzara and Janco doubtlessly brought with them. This issue has not been touched on in this article. Were it ascribed to "Judaism," it might awaken unwanted connotations, even if it was decisive for the future of dada. For after Ball left dada Zurich, in 1917, it was Tzara who assumed the movement's leading position. By attracting famous artists to Zurich who presented their works in the context of dada, and with effective promotion of the movement's name, Tzara may have been crucially responsible for the tremendous career of dada, which was later transferred to other, larger European cities and became one of the most prominent and sustainable notions of European avant-garde.

Bibliography

Béhar, Henri. *Tristan Tzara*. Paris: Oxus, 2005.
Boime, Albert. "Dada's Dark Secret." *Jewish Dimensions in Modern Visual Culture. Antisemitism, Assimilation, Affirmation*. Ed. Rose-Carol Washton Long, Matthew Baigell and Milly Heyd. Hanover and London: Brandeis University Press, 2010. 90–115.
Demos, T.J. "Circulations: In and Around Zurich Dada." *October* 105 (2003): 147–158.
Dickerman, Leah. *Dada*. Washington: National Gallery of Art, 2006.
Forcer, Stephen. "The Importance of Talking Nonsense: Tzara, Ideology, and Dada in the Twenty-First Century." *Dada and Beyond. Vol. 2: Dada and its Legacies*. Ed. Elza Adamowicz and Eric Robertson. Amsterdam and New York: Brill, 2012. 263–273.
Gilman, Sander L. *Jewish Self-Hatred. Anti-Semitism and the Hidden Language of the Jews*. Baltimore and London: The Johns Hopkins University Press, 1986.
Gilman, Sander L. *Jüdischer Selbsthaß. Antisemitismus und die verborgene Sprache der Juden*. Trans. Isabella König. Frankfurt a. M.: Jüdischer Verlag, 1993.
Hentea, Marius. *Dada Tata. The Real Life and Celestial Adventures of Tristan Tzara*. Cambridge, MA and London: MIT Press, 2014.
Heyd, Milly. "Tristan Tzara/Shmuel Rosenstock. The Hidden/Overt Jewish Agenda." *Jewish Dimensions in Modern Visual Culture. Antisemitism, Assimilation, Affirmation*. Ed. Rose-Carol Washton Long, Matthew Baigell and Milly Heyd. Hanover and London: Brandeis University Press, 2010. 193–219.
Kramer, Andreas. "Speaking Dada: The Politics of Language." *Dada and Beyond. Vol. 1: Dada Discourses*. Ed. Elza Adamowicz and Eric Robertson. Amsterdam and New York: Brill, 2011. 201–213.
Noël, Bernhard. "Dada PaDada Dada." *Dada and Beyond. Vol. 1: Dada Discourses*. Ed. Elza Adamowicz and Eric Robertson. Amsterdam and New York: Brill, 2011. 239–246.
Sandqvist, Tom. *Dada East. The Romanians of Cabaret Voltaire*. Cambridge, MA: MIT Press, 2006.
Schoeps, Julius H. et al. (eds.). *Deutsch-jüdischer Parnaß. Menorah Jahrbuch für deutsch-jüdische Geschichte*. Berlin and Wien: Philo Verlagsgesellschaft, 2002.
Tzara, Tristan. *Dada Manifesto*. www.391.org/manifestos/1918-dada-manifesto-tristan-tzara.html#.VKFdUECAw. Quoted June 8, 2016. Zürich: 1916.
Tzara, Tristan. *Oeuvres completes. Vol. 1*. Ed. Henri Béhar. Paris: Flammarion, 1975 [1912–1924].
Wyss, Heinz (ed.). *Das Luzerner Osterspiel. Vol. 1*. Bern: Francke, 1967.

Radu Stern
Jews and the Avant-Garde: The Case of Romania

Linking the avant-garde to Jews was a common way to make an argument against radical modernism, often described as a Jewish endeavor. In an extreme way, the association between avant-garde and the Jews was used by the Nazis, who combined their aversion for formal experiments with their hatred of the Jews and called both "degenerate." The so-called "degeneration" of the avant-garde was easily explained as a consequence of the racial "degeneration" of those who created it, namely the Jews. Like their Nazi counterparts, the Romanian Legionaries linked avant-garde to Jews and leftist politics. The Legionary critic Nicolae Roșu believed that Jews were responsible for dadaism, surrealism, German socialism, the Weimar constitution, and Russian bolshevism. For him, Picasso, the founder of cubism, was necessarily Jewish: "*Evrei sunt Tristan Tzara și Pablo Picasso, promotorii dadaismului si cubismului,*" [Tristan Tzara and Pablo Picasso, promoters of dadaism and cubism, are Jews.] (Roșu, 1937, 156.) A year later, in 1938, Marcel Janco sarcastically commented: *Picasso, despre care toată lumea știie ca e evreu, afara de el.* [Everyone knows Picasso is Jewish, except Picasso himself.] (Janco 1938, 18.) Strangely, this phrase, present in the original text, disappeared from a modern edition of Marcel Janco's writings recently published in Romania. (Șerban 2011, 197.) According to Neil Levi, the anti-Semitic interpretation of modernist form as a symptom of the Jewish spirit gave birth to the myth of the Judaization of modern art. Nonetheless, it should not be interpreted only as an anti-Semitic attack against the new experimental culture but also as an integral part of modernism itself. (Levi 2014, 3.) However, in Romania this connection between Jews and radical modernism was no myth but reality. Even if Picasso was not Jewish, it is a fact that in Romania the majority and the most important avant-garde artists were indeed Jews. How could this fact be explained?

In a seminal article, Steven A. Mansbach noticed the unusually high proportion of "foreigners," especially Jews, among the avant-garde in Romania and emphasized their essential input for the advent of the dada movement. (Mansbach 1998, 53.) Following Mansbach, the Swedish art historian Tom Sandqvist claimed in his *Dada East: The Romanians of Cabaret Voltaire* that "*Ex Oriente*, Dada" (that is, dada) had been born in the East, and its true origin is to be found in Romania. (Sandqvist 2006, 13.) Sandqvist connected dada's early roots in Romania to the hasidic culture that was still very much present around 1900 in the *shtetls* of Moldavia, from where the Jews Arthur Segal, Tristan Tzara, and the Janco brothers originated. Therefore, Sandqvist linked explicitly the avant-garde from Romania to Jewish religious roots. According to him, hasidism should be considered one of the main sources for modern art.

This idea is not a new one. Already in 1996, the Swedish Yiddishist Salomon Schulman, whom Sandqvist quotes, related Tzara's poetry to hasidism and interpreted dada as a neo-mystical movement (Schulman 1996, 1). Schulman's attempt is not even the first one; in 1987 Amelia Pavel, an art historian from Romania, tried to establish a link between hasidism and Arthur Segal and she stated that his theory of light in painting was influenced by kabbalism. (Pavel 1987, 79–81.)

However intriguing these hypotheses may be, the direct links betweeen Tristan Tzara, Marcel Janco, Arthur Segal and hasidism cannot be proven. Even if Sandqvist mentioned the Baal Shem Tov several times, he could not produce any concrete evidence of the *Besht*'s first-hand influence on any of these artists. All three were very far from *hasidut*, the kind of special piety a Hasid is expected to display. Moreover, although in different ways, all three rejected Orthodox Judaism in favor of modern civilization. Although he spoke Yiddish at home – also it seems that Tzara spoke in Yiddish with Isaak Babel at the Writers' Congress in Paris in 1937 – and went to the Israelite-Romanian primary school, Tzara was raised in a bourgeois family that, while maintaining the Jewish tradition, was not observant. According to the most recent Tzara biographer, Marius Hentea, the poet's father, Filip Rosenstock, marked "atheist" as his religion when he filed for a passport. (Hentea 2014, 7.) The Rosenstocks were more interested in the social and political situation of European Jewry than in religious subjects. Tzara's cousin Irina Atanasiu remembered that, during a vacation in the family house at Gârceni in the Vaslui county, the young Samy was running all over the place shouting: "Dreyfus innocent! Esterhazy guilty!" (Atanasiu 1998,16.) Defiantly anti-religious, Tzara maintained for his entire life an ambiguous stance towards his Jewishness. (Heyd 2010, 193–219.) In a letter from 1992, his son Christophe specifically rejected any influence of the Jewish religion on Tzara and stated that: "My father never showed the slightest religious concern in front of myself or in front of his friends." (Tzara 1998, 171.)

Marcel Janco's family was also resolutely modern. Kashruth dietary rules were not observed and, after a very short attempt, secular teaching was preferred to the traditional *heder* to educate the children. (Janco, Jules, 3.) Later, Janco would even marry the Swiss Amélie Micheline (Lily) Ackermann, a Gentile, which would have been unheard of in a truly hasidic or religious environment. Several years later, in 1925, Tzara would do the same; he married the Swedish Greta Knutson, also a Gentile. Their son born in 1927 was called Christophe, which would have been impossible in an observant Jewish environment. While Arthur Segal's family was religious, an excerpt from his unpublished autobiography states clearly that he himself was not attracted by religion:

> I hated to go to the synagogue, and I did not like the orthodox Jews with their long black coats, sidelocks and their language. Here I would like to admit that customs of other religions are strange to me as well. I do not like Nations, I do not want to belong to them. I hate Nationalism wherever I encounter it, but I am sure that I would find everywhere people with whom I would feel united. I hated the synagogue because the prayers made no sense to me and I said one day to my father: 'I cannot understand events 2000 years ago or the contents of today prayers.' I got my ear boxed and from then on I kept my mouth shut.
> (Segal, 46)

The families of the two other major Jewish avant-garde artists from Romania, Victor Brauner and M.H. Maxy, were not religious either. Brauner's father was even seriously interested in spiritism, a terrible sin for an observant Jew. The artists from the second wave of the avant-garde from Romania, Paul Păun and Jules Perahim, were also secular Jews.

Sandqvist's error is easy to elucidate. In his Western perspective, Marcel Janco, Tristan Tzara, and Arthur Segal were necessarily Romanian nationals whose religion was Jewish. For that reason, their Jewish identity was "obviously" identified mainly with the religious dimension, with Judaism. Hasidism, with its fascinating mystical element, was just a tempting overbid.

However, the situation was different in Romania, where Jews were perceived not only as a specific religious group, but also as a different ethnic community. Even today, Jews are considered one of the officially recognized nineteen national minorities. If for Westerners all Romanian citizens are Romanian nationals, in Romania there is a distinction between "citizenship," in the sense of the German *Staatsangehörigkeit* or *Staatsbürgerschaft* and "nationality," which is understood as ethnic affiliation. Taking into account these realities is essential. Therefore, in order to analyze the identity and the perception of these artists, all of whom were secular Jews, it is imperative to make a methodological distinction between Judaism as a religion and Jewishness as an ethnic designation and community. Any serious analysis of the artists' status must have this distinction as a starting point.

If "Jewish" means Judaism, one could ask if there was anything specifically Jewish in their art? If the answer to this question is "yes," then it was not at the level of content. Except for a group portrait by Victor Brauner that might be representing Jews and one late work by M.H. Maxy, *Jews cleaning snow,* an evocation of the forced labor imposed on Jews in Romania during World War Two, a time when Maxy was no longer an avant-garde artist, there were no Jewish subjects in their creation. Marcel Janco would paint Jewish subjects only after his emigration to Palestine in 1941. In a late interview published in an Israeli magazine, Janco declared that until then, he was not attracted by religion. (Janco 1980.)

Though Judaism seems to have no discernible influence, at least in the content of their art, what is then the role played by their Jewishness in their artistic choices? To begin with, the artists themselves never claimed that their art was Jewish. This would have been contrary to avant-garde aesthetics, which were internationalist. With the noteworthy exception of futurism, the other avant-gardes discarded every kind of nationalism and favored a transnational approach to artistic creation. Nationalism was seen mostly as a chauvinistic abomination that produced the horrors of the First World War. For Roman Jakobson, dada's *Fronde* was directed precisely against the "zoological nationalism" of the European countries. (Jakobson 1990, 40). A dada manifesto from January 21, 1921 signed, among others, by Tzara begins as follows: "The signatories of this manifesto live in France, America, Spain, Germany, Italy, Switzerland, etc. but have no nationality." In an article from the surrealist magazine *Unu* (One), the poet Ilarie Voronca, born Eduard Marcus, took the same internationalist stand: "... *dintre toate NAȚIUNILE, eu aleg imagi-NAȚIUNEA !*" [... from all NATIONS, I choose the imagi-NATION.] (Voronca 1928, 1.)

Could all of the above mean that the very high percentage of artists of Jewish descent in the avant-garde from Romania, both in literature or in the visual arts, was just a coincidence? As will be shown, it was not just by chance.

Several outstanding Romanian cultural personalities believed that there was a special affinity between Jews and modernism. In his most important work, published in 1941, *Istoria literaturii române de la origini până în prezent* (The History of Romanian Literature from its Origins to the Present), a famous book in Romanian culture, the literary critic and historian George Călinescu dedicated a special chapter to the Jewish writers. Thus, they were separated from the other authors. He asserted that: "*In literatură, ei sunt totdeauna informați, colportorii de lucrurile cele mai noi, anticlasiciști, mderniști, agitațti de probleme. Ei compenseză inerția tradiției și o fac sa se revizuiască.*" [In literature, they [the Jews] are always informed, mongers of the newest things, anti-classicists, modernists, agitated by problems. They compensate the inertia of tradition and make it to revise itself.] (Călinescu 1941, 2nd ed. 1992, 976.) Călinescu's older rival, Eugen Lovinescu, had already written about the same phenomenon at the end of 1920s. However, he maintained that the Jewish propensity for novelty was not only literary but also cultural and political: "In all the avant-garde movements, be they social, such as old times socialism or today's communism, or literary, such as French symbolism or German expressionism, the role of the Jew as a promoter of novelty is everywhere identical." (Lovinescu 1981, II, 396.) Even if this special affinity between Jews and modernism really existed, which is debatable, (Slezkine 2001, 52–60;

Levi 2014) could this explain entirely the overwhelming majority of Jewish artists among the ranks of the Romanian avant-garde?

To understand the relation between the artists' Jewishness and their avant-garde art, one should analyze it against the background of the complex and complicated situation of Jews in Romania. The emancipation of Jews in Romania was a very sluggish and painful process. The achievement of national unity and the attainment of independence of the newly-founded Romania (1866) were accompanied by a certain economic development, which brought about an increase in urban population and a modification of its structure. The number of non-ethnic Romanians in the population increased in a significant way. These transformations challenged the rural population of Romania, traditionally mistrustful of foreigners. Two celebrated verses from one of the most famous poems of the "national poet" Mihai Eminescu, *Doina* (1884), underline a typical response to these developments:

Cine-au indrăgi străinii
Mânca-i-ar inima câinii

[He who gets to love foreigners,
Let the dogs eat out his heart]

The Jews had a peculiar position among these foreigners and they faced a specific hostile reaction, which combined general xenophobia with extremely virulent anti-Semitism. Worshippers of another religion and reluctant to intermarry, the Jews were considered non-assimilable. For many, they represented "foreigners from the inside," perceived as more dangerous for the Romanian population than foreigners from abroad. The "Jewish problem" became one of the most debated subjects of the Romanian political scene. Although anti-Judaism, that encouraged the Christians to hate those, as they said, "who killed Jesus," was very present, many Romanians resented also what they felt as a Jewish over-representation in the new economy and believed that Jews were the main obstacle blocking the emergence of a Romanian-owned trade.

Nevertheless, economic considerations cannot explain everything. In the eyes of Romanian nationalists, who advocated one nation for one country, the very existence of Jews among the population challenged the project of a pure, ethnically Romanian homogenous society. After the First World War, Greater Romania, an obviously multiethnic country, was proclaimed a "national state" but "nation" was biologically defined as a community of blood, not as a community of citizens. This perception had been summarized long before the war by the philosopher and politician Vasile Conta in a speech about the *Jewish Problem* he gave in the Romanian parliament on September 4, 1879:

> *Dacă ținem seama că același sânge curge în vinele tuturor membrilor unui popor, înțelegem că toți acești membri vor avea, prin efectul eredității, cam aceleași sentimente, cam aceleași tendințe și chiar cam aceleași idei; așa încât, la vreme de nevoie, la ocaziuni mari, inima tuturor va bate în același fel, mintea tuturor va adopta aceeași opinie, acțiunea tuturor va urmări același scop; cu alte cuvinte, națiunea care va fi de o singură rasă, va avea un singur centru de gravitate; și statul care va fi format dintr-o astfel de națiune, acela și numai acela va fi în cele mai bune condiții de tărie, de trăinicie și de progres. Prin urmare, după cerințele chiar ale ființei, cea dintâi condițiune pentru existența unui stat este ca poporul să fie de aceeași rasă.*
>
> [If we keep in mind that in the veins of all members of a given people there is the same blood, we will understand that all these members will have, because of heredity, more or less the same feelings, the same tendencies and even the same ideas; so, in times of need, at great opportunities, all people's hearts will beat in the same way, all minds will adopt the same opinion, all actions *will have the same aim. In other words, the nation of a single race will have one center of gravity: the state formed by this kind* of nation, this state, and only this one, will have the best conditions of strength, of durability and progress. As a consequence, the first condition for a state is that the people should be of the same race.]
> (Conta 1879, 5755)

For this reason, the nationalists saw the Jews, more than any other "foreigners," as the enemy from within, a threat to the unity of the nation, which they understood as a community of blood. In this respect, Jews were seen not only as culturally different, but as racially different. They were not simply called *"străini"* (foreigners), but *"venetici,"* a pejorative word that could be translated as "allogenic intruders that do not belong."

Unfortunately, popular anti-Semitism was accompanied by an intellectual anti-Semitism that contaminated the Romanian elites, who blamed Jews for "the lack of a profound knowledge of the language, lack of adherence to the ethnocultural and historical Romanian realities, alteration of the Romanian literary specificity ("Judaization" of Romanian literature), genetic inclination towards immorality (pornography) etc." (Voicu 2003, 138.) Astonished, the French ambassador in Bucharest, A. Henry, wrote in 1900: "Anti-Semitism is more than an opinion in Romania, it's a passion shared by politicians from all parties, the representatives of Orthodoxy and, one can add, by all Wallachian and Moldavian peasants." (Morar 2006,10.) In his *Autobiography*, Arthur Segal recalled: "All the time I felt persecuted, contempt, I felt a pariah as I was a Jew, to whom one was allowed to say and do anything." He wrote that in school he was punished more than other boys "only because [he] was a Jew." (Segal, 14 and 29.) Tristan Tzara's penname is a pun, *"trist in țară,"* which means "sad in my own country"; it may be related to the virulent anti-Semitism which he experienced in Romania.

Although anti-Semitism was present in almost any area of everyday life, the animosity towards Jews crystallized around Romania's refusal to naturalize them.

(For the history of the Jews' emancipation in Romania, see Iancu, 1979, 1986, 1992; Volovici.) Article 46 of the Paris Convention from 1858, which followed the Crimean War, granted civil rights in Wallachia and Moldavia only for Christians. Article 7 of the Romanian constitution from 1866 stipulated that only foreigners who were Christians could be naturalized. It is obvious that the real objective of this article was to prevent the naturalization of Jews. Article 44 of the Berlin Treaty of 1878, which recognized the independence of the Romanian kingdom, asked for the suppression of Article 7. This demand met with a fierce refusal on the part of Romanian politicians, but also poets, writers, philosophers, historians, and other cultural personalities, who maintained that granting citizenship to Jews meant the suicide of the Romanian people. These ideas persisted well after citizenship was finally granted to Jews. In the same year that the new constitution was promulgated, 1923, the anti-Semitic university professor A.C. Cuza published a *numerus clausus*, in which he advocated the severe limitation of the number of Jews active in Romanian cultural and economic life. In his eyes, the *numerus clausus* was meant to be just a preliminary phase to attain the final goal, a *numerus nullus*. (Cuza 1923.) Unfortunately, A.C. Cuza *was* not just an author but a successful politician who attempted to put his ideas into practice. In 1923 he founded *Liga apărării național creștine* (The League of National Christian Defence), the first fascist organization in Romania. In 1937, he was named vice-prime minister in the Goga-Cuza government, which issued drastic racial laws directed against the Jewish population. (Bozdoghină 2012.)

For the anti-Semites, there was no incompatibility between their Christian faith and their hatred for Jews. In 1927, Nicolae Roșu asserted that *"antisemitismul înseamnă cristianism. Cu cât suntem mai buni creștini, cu atât suntem antisemiți."* [Anti-Semitism means Christianism. The more we are better Christians, the more we are anti-Semitic.] (Roșu, 1927.) The old idea that only a Christian could be a "true Romanian" still aplied for many. For Nae Ionescu, undoubtedly the most influential Romanian philosopher of the 1930s, even fellow Christians who were not orthodox, were not eligible to be called true Romanians: *"Sa fii român, nu un bun român, ci român pur si simplu inseamnă să fii ortodox."* [To be Romanian, not a good Romanian but just Romanian, it means to be orthodox.] (Ionescu 1937, 201.) The same opinion was shared by Olga Greceanu, who wrote in 1939 in her book *Specificul național în pictură* (The National Specificity in Painting) that: *"Noi, românii, am fost născuți ortodocși [...] noi am fost mai întâi ortodocși și numai dupa aceea români."* [We, Romanians, we were born orthodox ... we were first of all orthodox and then Romanians.] (Greceanu 2012, 33–34).

In Romania in 1896, the Jew Tristan Tzara was not a Romanian citizen at birth. His birth certificate read: "Samuel Rosenstock, of parents of Mosaic religion, Israelite nationality [sic], not subjected to any protection." (see Fig. 1)

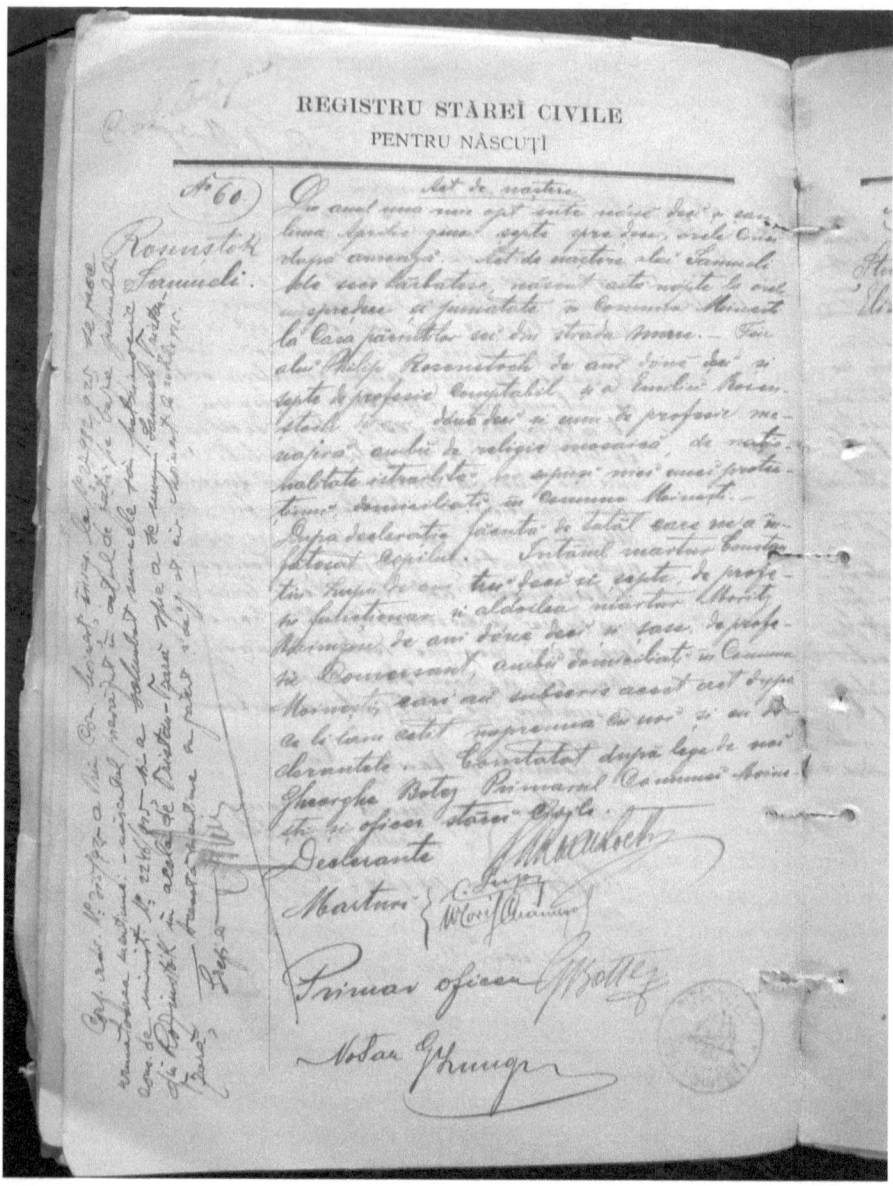

Fig. 1: The birth certificate of Samuel Rosenstock.

The situation was the same for M.H. Maxy, son of a "foreign carpenter of Israelite nationality." (M.H. Maxy's birth certificate, MNAR archives, Bucharest.) He applied for citizenship on June 5, 1923, even though he was born in Romania and had fought as a volunteer in the Romanian army during the First World War (Pelin 2005, 376). Although Marius Hentea (2014, 32) claims in his Tzara monograph that Marcel Janco was a Romanian citizen at birth, this was not the case. In 2010, Dr. Vlad Solomon discovered in the Janco archives in Tel-Aviv a copy of Janco's request from 1923 for Romanian naturalization for his wife and himself, which clearly proves that, as the others, he could become a Romanian citizen only after the new Constitution came into effect (see Fig. 2). Thus, the subtitle of Sandqvist's book, "the Romanians of Cabaret Voltaire" is historically wrong: none of figures refered to by the title was a Romanian citizen at the time of their activity in the Cabaret Voltaire.

In a paper from 2007, Irina Cărăbaş curiously mentions the Constitution of 1923 as "proof" of the low level of anti-Semitism in Romania in the 1920s (Cărăbaş 2007). While the new 1923 Constitution confirmed the Jews' right to citizenship, less than fifteen years later, royal decree No. 169 from January 21, 1938 compelled Jews to reclaim their citizenship. In order to do this, it was necessary to supply a considerable number of documents – a very difficult task to perform within a time frame that was purposely too short. As a consequence, 36.3 % of the Jews lost their civic rights (Voicu 2003, 158). Both M.H. Maxy and Marcel Janco had to submit to this humiliating procedure (Pelin 2005, 377). Marcel Janco's documents for reclaiming his citizenship may be found in the Janco archives in Tel-Aviv.

Vasile Conta's nationalistic and anti-Semitic conceptions were shared by many Romanian intellectuals and they strongly influenced A.C. Cuza. Quite early in his career, Cuza applied these ideas to the realm of artistic creation. In 1908, he published *Naţionalitatea în artă* (Nationality in Art). Even if in 1935 the "ethnocratic" ideologist Nechifor Crainic, who described A.C. Cuza's text as "a fundamental truth of our life," regretted that it did not become "a classic guide for Romanian creativity," (Crainic 1935) still, the book had a considerable impact and was republished several times. It became, undoubtedly, the reference text of Romanian extreme cultural nationalism and artistic anti-Semitism. The motto of the book is: *"Naţionalitatea este puterea creatoare a culture umane-cultura, puterea creatoare a maţionalităţei."* [Nationality is the creative power of human culture – culture is the creative power of nationality.] Thus, following Conta, A.C. Cuza considered the nation as an ethnically homogenous group that must have the same body and the same soul. This unity based on blood must also be territorial because *"pe acelaşi teritoriu [...] nu se poate devolta decât o singură naţionalitate."* [any given territory [...] can serve the development of only one nationality.] (Cuza 1908, 124.) National identity is established for A.C. Cuza by "the ethnic individu-

Fig. 2: Marcel Janco's naturalization request.

ality of any people." *"De indata ce imiteaza cultura altor neamuri, ele (poparele) se confunda cu dansele si nu mai exista."* [From the moment that peoples imitate the culture of other peoples, they will merge with the other peoples and no longer exist.] (ibid., 12.) Art, as the highest expression of culture, and the artist are deeply linked to their nationality. The artist must necessarily represent his nationality. Thus, art can exist *"decât ca artă națională"* [only as a national art.] (ibid., 9.) A national art implies a national style as *"este evident că opera de artă care nu va purta semnele vădite ale naționalității, nu va putea fi decât operă **neadevărată**."* [It is obvious that a work of art that does not bear the manifest signs of nationality could be only *untrue.*] (ibid., 51.) Consequently, the representatives of Romanian culture must be ethnically Romanians (ibid., 144.) Foreigners could only fake the true character of Romanian culture. The "foreigners" that A.C. Cuza had in mind were the Jews, the actual target of the book. The *jidani* (kikes), to use A.C. Cuza's terms, "*o combinațiune etnică absolut inferioară*" [an absolutely inferior ethnical combination] (ibid., 154) are of a different race, of a different faith, with other principles of culture, and they are not assimilable. In spite of this, "*cu obraznicia caracteristică neamului*" [with the characteristic impudence of their people] they dare to aspire to play a role in Romanian culture, wanting to spread unhealthy ideas and dissolve the national soul. Therefore, "*jidanii nu pot să creeze cultură română.*" [kikes cannot create Romanian culture] (ibid., 216) and they must be barred from entering the Romanian cultural scene.

A.C. Cuza's warning against the menace of "judaization" of Romanian culture became a standard theme in the Romanian cultural debate. In the 1930s, authors such as Nicolae Roşu or Nicolae Davidescu continued to state that "judaization" is the main danger that threatens Romanian culture (Roşu 1937; Davidescu 1939). Although he took risks by including Jewish writers in *The History of Romanian Literature*, for which he was heavily attacked by the extreme right, George Călinescu affirmed that "*Evreii [...] rămân un factor dinafara cercului rasial, făcând puntea de legatură între national și universal.*" [The Jews [...] remain outside the racial circle, being the bridge between the national and universal.] (Călinescu 1992, 976.) Favorable perhaps at the first glance, this statement shows, nevertheless, that the distinguished literary historian considered Jews a different race. After the description of Jewish writers' qualities quoted above, Călinescu concluded that

> *aceste însu șiri sunt legate de tipicele iriitante cusururi: dezinteres total pentru creație ca scop, trăirismul exagerat, negarea criticii (de care noi, rasă constructivă, avem trebuință) umanitarismul, împins până la negarea drepturilor și notelor noastre naționale. Prin această lipsă de tactla noi ca și oriunde, evreii atrag asupră-le periodic, toate fulgerele*

[these characteristics are linked to their typical irritating shortcomings: total lack of interest for creation as such, exaggerated "*trăirism*" [a trend in philosophical thinking from Romania that proclaimed the primacy of instinct and the unconscious over reason] negation of critique (which is needed by us, as a constructive race), humanitarianism extended until the negation of our national notes and rights. Because of this tactless behavior, the Jews attract periodically, with us and everywhere, all lightnings against them.]

The publication of Eugen Lovinescu's *Memoirs* and *Diaries* showed that the critic, who asked for accommodation with Western culture and accepted Jewish writers in his literary club, was also not completely immune to anti-Semitism For instance, he swiftly dismissed *75 H.P.*, the most radical avant-garde magazine from Romania, as "purely Jewish" (Gulea 2007, 204). He frequently used the pejorative *jidani* (kikes) and did not refrain from speaking about "the impudence of the sidelock-bearers." (Bogdan 2004.)

Cuza's affirmations that true Romanian art must be a national art, as well as the idea that only Romanians by blood could be genuine Romanian artists, were widely accepted at the time. The attacks were not usually directed against the Jewish avant-garde artists' formal creations; rather they targeted their ethnic origin for the most part. For instance, Brauner's first exhibition of 1924 was described as a product of the "dark foreignness," which should be reported as subversive action to the State Secret Police (Anonymous 1924, 6). Surprisingly, the attempt to describe (Jewish) avant-garde art as essentially anti-national and serving the interests of Romania's enemies has survived. Stelian Tănase, a contemporary Romanian literary historian, has explored the files of the *Siguranța*, the bourgeois secret police, and found, supposedly, evidence of the avant-garde's involvement in destabilizing the Romanian state. He described Victor Brauner, who was for a very short period a member of the then clandestine Communist party before he left in 1937 after the Moscow trials, as a Komintern agent who worked for the Stalinist Soviet Union and who used his artistic practice mainly as a cover for his secret activities (Tănase 2008, 44).

The traditionalist artist Horia Igiroșanu, who was also the art critic of *Clipa* (The Instant), the conservative journal of the Society of Fine Arts, called Marcel Janco and M.H. Maxy "*nebuni*" [crazy] but also "*străini de țară*" [aliens to our land.] (Igiroșanu 1924.) In another article, Igiroșanu declared:

> *E o nemaipomenită îndrazneală ca in țara noastră de plugari si de ciobani, cu câmpii intinse si mănoase, sa apară asemenea specimene are nu au țară si care nu înțeleg sa o aibă, nu au ce căuta in mijlocul nostru [...] Sunt încă destui în țara asta care sa lupte pentru arta noastră, sa o ridice, nu sa o coboare, si sa trimeata la balamuc pe nebuni si peste graniță pe acei care nu înțeleg și nu pot sa iubească această țărișoară.*

> [It is an unprecedented impudence that in our ploughmen's and shepherds' country, with vast and fertile plains, [we] have these intruders in our fine arts [...] Artists who do not have a country and do not understand [how] to have one, do not have anything to do amidst ourselves [...] There are enough people in this country to fight for our art, to develop it, not to diminish it, and to send to the madhouse and abroad those who do not understand and cannot love this small country.]

He added in a threatening tone: "*Cu nebunii aceştia nu voi sta preamult de vorbă, voi termina în alfel, dacă nu vor înțelege să plece în altă parte.*" [I will not talk a lot to these fools. I will deal with them in another way, if they do not understand to get out of here.] (Igiroșanu 1923.) Alexandru Hodoș, the managing editor of *Țara noastră* (Our Country), the magazine of Octavian Goga, who, later on, in 1937, became undersecretary of state in the anti-Semitic Goga-Cuza government, not only called Marcel Janco "crazy" but also asked if he and Tristan Tzara, then Romanian citizens: *"dar, cel puțin, sunt ei compatrioții noștri?"* [were truly our fellow countrymen?] He claimed that Marcel Janco's grandfather came to Moldavia fifty years ago and that Tristan Tzara must have some cousins and uncles in Krakow." (Hodoș 1924, 142.)

These attacks aimed at the ethnic origin of the avant-garde permeated all cultural fields. For example, the architect I.D. Enescu, the president of the Society of Romanian Architects, established a link between modern architecture, "more international than national" and *"cei care n-au luat parte la război, cei care n-au o patrie precisă"* [those who did not take part in the war and do not have a definite homeland] – the later being an obvious hint to Jews and, possibly, a direct allusion to Marcel Janco, who had spent the war years in Zurich (Enescu 1934, 18). Even in 1937, when M.H. Maxy was no longer an avant-garde artist, he was still attacked for his ethnic origin, as in an anti-Semitic cartoon from *Porunca Vremii*, (Marți 23 Noiembrie 1937) in which he was caricatured as Maxy "Goldenmayer-Stern," with a "Jewish" hooked-nose, using "kosher painting," and his brush being replaced by a venomous serpent with which the "kike" poisoned art (see Fig. 3).

The demand for a "national art" became the central element of Romanian debate concerning artistic creation. The discussion concentrated obsessively around the definition of "national specificity." In practice, the "national specificity" was thought to be connected to the values of autochthonism, which idealized the Romanian national values as embodied by the peasant and contrasted them to the urban and decadent "foreign" population. For A.C. Cuza, the idea that "beauty has no homeland" was heresy. Romanian national art had to have a Romanian inspiration only:

> **Arhitectii** *nostri, să caute dar a cultiva stilul național al clădirilor-si să nu creadă ca sunt arhitecți români – sau artiști – întrucât se vor mărgini a copia monumentele străine.*
> **Pictorii,** *să răsfrângă frumusețile naturei noastre, splendorile cerului românesc, din propria lor inspirație, nu sa vadă lumea deafară cu ochi de imprumut – si sa fie orbi pentru noi.*
>
> [Our *architects* should cultivate the *national style* of buildings – and they should not believe they are Romanian architects – or artists – if they limit themselves to copy foreign monuments. *Painters* should reflect the beauties of our nature, the splendors of the Romanian sky, not to see the world with borrowed eyes, being blind to us.]
> (Cuza, 1908, 138–139.)

Consequently, "national art" should be traditional, dealing with Romanian subjects, and "truly" Romanian artists should not be lured by imported modernist formal experiments.

Fig. 3: M.H. Maxy depicted in an anti-Semitic cartoon in 1937.

In light of the above, the rather general unwillingness to accept Jews as fellow Romanians was even more restrictive in the sensitive artistic domain. If only ethnic Romanians could create a "national art," it followed that there was no hope in this field for the Jewish artists, condemned forever to be excluded from a cultural domain they were told that they did not belong to. Assimilation, including religious conversion, for those who were willing to do so, was not a valid path in order to be accepted as a Romanian artist. Even the abandonment of their faith could not modify the Jews' status, as baptism could not modify their blood. "Câteva picături de agheasmă" [Several drops of holy water] – wrote A.C. Cuza – cannot change anything. For many, they would have remained just "christened" Jews, pejoratively called "Pseudo-Romanians." As such, they were still inevitably rejected as essentially not-native, as missing the organic link with the soil and with the genuine Romanian ethos. "*Evreii sut incapabili de o viziune totalitară a vieții românești* [...] *Evreii nu pot avea* [...] *perspectiva peisagiului larg, a pitorescului artistic ce se revarsă din plin in arta românească, deoarece, trăind departe, viața le e sfărîmată in chinurile revoltei si neputinței*" [The Jews are unable to have a global vision of

Romanian life [...] The Jews could not have [...] the perspective of the wide landscape, of the artistic, picturesque flooding Romanian art because, living faraway, their life is crushed by revolt and helplessness.] (Roșu, 1937, 190.)

These ideas were the theoretical foundation on which the gradual exclusion of Jews from Romanian cultural life had been built. Indignant, Marcel Janco tried to fight the criteria of *"faith, sex, nationality,* and *ethnicity,"* which produced an unacceptable racialization of art. He pleaded for the autonomy of the aesthetic: "the work of art is, in its essence, without sex, nationality or religion." He also pointed out the obvious anti-Semitic intent, central to A.C. Cuza and his followers' understanding of the "national specificity": *"Nu e nevoe să adaugăm că aceste subtile tălmăciri de artă se aplică numai 'poporului ales.'"* [It is unnecessary to add that these subtle art interpretations are applied only to the "chosen people".] (Janco 1938b, 2.)

For the promoters of "national specificity," art had absolutely to be "national art," and it could not be neutral. Moreover, as national specificity included a compulsory orthodox component, no Jewish artists were considered to be able to express it, no matter how talented they were. "Truly" Romanian artists were expected to express their "Romanianism" and to refuse the transnational approach of modernism. It is obvious that given these conditions it was difficult for Jewish artists to identify themselves with this cultural trend, since it rebuffed them. The barrier erected between them and "national art" constrained them to search for another kind of art, for which their "otherness" was not insuperable. *"Noi respingem falsa tradiție a solului și ne înclinăm in fața nesfârșitei tradiții a omului. Prima este conservatism, a doua este civilizație."* [We reject the false tradition of the soil, and we bow to the endless tradition of man. The first is conservatism, the second is civilization.] This formulation was printed in an editorial of the avant-garde magazine *Integral* (Voronca 1925). The universalism and cosmopolitanism of avant-garde art were an obvious target. In this sense, the Jewishness of the artists, perceived as an insurmountable obstacle to create a "national art," offered a somehow easier access to modernity than that afforded to some of their Romanian colleagues, busy searching for "national specificity." After all, the Jewish artists constituted the majority of the avant-garde in Romania, also because there were so few Romanian avant-garde artists. In other words, one could view the fact that the majority of the avant-garde artists from Romania were Jewish as a problem of Romanian culture rather than only a problem of Jewish culture.

Bibliography

Anonymous. "Expozitia Victor Brauner. Sala sindicatului artelor." *Contimporanul* 9 (1924).
Atanasiu, Irina. "Vacances à Gârceni." *Les Cahiers/Caietele Tristan Tzara* 1 (1998).
Bogdan, George Radu. "Problema antisemitismului lui E. Lovinescu." *România literară*, 33 (2004): www.romlit.ro/problema_antisemitismului_lui_e._lovinescu, retrieved January 4 2015.
Bozdoghină, Horia. *Antisemitismul lui A.C. Cuza în politica românească*. București: Editura Curtea Veche, 2012.
Călinescu, George, *Istoria literaturi romăne ; de la origini pâna în prezent*, (1941) 2nd ed., București: Editura Minerva, 1981.
Cărăbaș, Irina. "'Down with the avant-garde for it has prostituted itself': Avant-Garde, Jewishness and Totalitarianism in Romania. Paper presented at *Avant-Garde and Violence*, 4th Annual Conference of the Nordic Network for Avant-Garde Studies, Reykjavik University, September 2007.
Conta, Vasile. "Cestiunea evreiască." *Monitorul Oficial* 201 (September 5, 17 1879).
Crainic, Nechifor. "Naționalitatea in artă." *Gândirea* XIV, March 3 1935. www.oocities.org/imjhsourcebook2/Crainic1.htm, retrieved January 4 2015.
Cuza, A.C. *Naționalitatea in artă: principii, fapte, concluzii. Introducere la doctrina naționalistă creștină*. București: Editura Minerva, 1908.
Cuza, A.C. *Numerus clausus*. București: Editura Ligi apărării național creștine, 1923.
Davidescu, Nicolae. *Primejdia judaică: pagini de îndrumare românească*. București: Editura Vremea, 1939.
Enescu, I.D. "Arhitectura și economia națională." *Arhitectura* (1934).
Greceanu, Olga. *Specificul național în pictură*. Editia a II-a. Otopeni: Editura Idaco, 2012.
Gulea, Dan. *Domni, tovaraşi, camarazi: o evoluție a avangardei romăne*. Pitești: Editura Paralela 45, 2007.
Hentea, Marius. *Dada Tata. The Real Life and the Celestial Adventures of Tristan Tzara*. Cambridge, MA: The MIT Press, 2014.
Heyd, Milly. "Tristan Tzara/Shmuel Rosenstock: The Hidden/Overt Jewish Agenda." *Jewish Dimensions in Modern Visual Culture: Antisemitism, Assimilation, Affirmation*. Ed. Rose-Carol Washton Long, Matthew Baigell and Milly Heyd. Waltham, MA: Brandeis University Press, 2010. 193–219.
Hodoș, Alexandru. "Dadaism, cubism – et caetera." *Țara noastră* 6 (1924).
Iancu, Carol. *Les Juifs en Roumanie: 1866 - 1919: de l'exclusion à l'émancipation*. Aix-en-Provence: Editions de l'Université de Provence, 1979.
Iancu, Carol. *Les juifs en Roumanie: de l'émancipation à la marginalisation*. Paris and Louvain: E. Peeters, 1986.
Iancu, Carol. *L'émancipation des Juifs de Roumanie (1913–1919): de l'inégalité civique aux droits de minorité: l'originalité d'un combat à partir des guerres balkaniques et jusqu'à la conférence de paix de Paris*. Montpellier: Centre de recherches et d'études juives et hébraiques, 1992.
Igiroanu, Horia. "Nebunia secolului. Arta ultra modernă. Cazul Maxy." *Clipa* (18 November 1923).
Igiroșanu, Horia. "Un alt nebun: Marcel Iancu." *Clipa* (January 6 1924).

Ionescu, Naen. "Noi și catolicismul." in *Roza vânturilor*. București: Editura Cultura Nationala, 1937.
Jakobson, Roman. "Dada." *Language in Literature*. Ed. Krystyna Pomorska and Stephan Rudy. Harvard: The Belknap Press, 1990. 34–40.
Janco, Jules. *Memories*. Unpublished typescipt by Amit Janco. Jules Janco's archives, Montreal.
Janco, Marcel, "Mărturii iudaice despre artă", *Cultura*, June 1938a
Janco, Marcel. "O olimpiada a artei evreești." *Adam X.123–124* (June-July-August 1938b).
Janco, Marcel. "Arta mea și sionismul." *Shevet Romania* 8–9 (September 1980).
Lovinescu, Eugen, *Istoria literaturii române contemporane*, (1937) 2nd ed., București: Editura Minerva, 1981.
Mansbach, Stephen A. "The 'Foreignness' of Classical Modern Art in Romania." *Art Bulletin* 80 (September 1998): 534–554.
Morar, Ovidiu. "Intelectualii români și problema evreiască." in *Problema evreiască: Perspective românești*, in Ed. Aura Christi. București: Editura Ideea europeană, 2006, 10–33.
Pavel, Amelia. "Arthur Segal – Lebensperiode und Schaffen in Rumänien." *Arthur Segal 1875–1944*. Ed. Wulf Herzogenrath and Paul Liška. Berlin: Argon, 1987, 77–86.
Pelin, Mihai. *Deceniul prăbușirilor (1940–1950)*. București: Editura Compania, 2005.
Roșu, Nicolae. "Antagonismul ireductibil." *Cuvântul studențesc* IV.5 (25 December 1927).
Roșu, Nicolae. *Orientari în veac*. București: Editura Cugetarea, 1937.
Sandqvist, Tom. *Dada East: the Romanians of Cabaret Voltaire*. Cambridge, MA: The MIT Press, 2006.
Schulman, Salomon. *Jiddishland. Bland rabbiner och revolutionärer*. Nora: Nia Doxa, 1996.
Segal, Arthur. *Autobiography. Part I. My Boyhood in Romania*. Unpublished typescript. Leo Baeck Institute, New York.
Slezkine, Yuri. *The Jewish Century*. Princeton: Princeton University Press, 2001.
Solomon, Vlad. "Marcel Iancu – evreu și sionist." *Acum*, January 9 2011. http://acum.tv/articol/23972, retrieved January 12 2011.
Șerban, Geo. *Întâlniri cu Marcel Iancu*. București: Editura Hasefer, 2011.
Tănase, Stelian. *Avangarda românească in arhivele Siguranței*. Iași: Editura Polirom, 2008.
Tzara, Christophe. "Letter to Vasile Robciuc from April 15 1992." *Les Cahiers/Caietele Tristan Tzara* 1 (1998): 171.
Voicu, George. "Romanian Literary Anti-Semitism: Historical-Ideological Facets." *Studia Hebraica* 3 (2003): 138–162.
Volovici, Leon. *Ideologia naționalistă și problema evreiască : eseu despre formele antisemitismului intelectual in România anilor '30*. București: Editura Humanitas, 1995.
Voronca, Ilarie. "Precizări. Pentru Cezar Petrescu și alții." *Integral* 5 (1925).
Voronca, Ilarie. "Ora zece dimineața." *Unu* 6 (October 1928): 1.

Sami Sjöberg
Towards an Ahistorical Jewishness: The Idea of Jewish Essence in the German-Jewish Avant-Garde

Es ist Frühling im Abendlande. Die Dichtung mit zwei Gesichtern singt Untergang und Aufgang. Vielleicht verkündet sich hier eine Vereinung von Orient und Occident.[1]

The idea of a "Jewish essence" (*Jüdisches Wesen*), denoting a particular and recognizable Jewish quality or mode of being, was a controversial issue in early-twentieth-century cultural debates in Germany. The concept was originally devised in order to write the first accounts of "Jewish history," providing the necessary continuity for such narratives. In the sense applied in this essay, the notion surfaced during the fin-de-siècle era and survived well into the 1930s, with similar notional inquiries being topical even today.

The expressionist author Alfred Wolfenstein (1883–1945) wrote several pieces about the relation between Jews and the so-called "new poetry," which in the German-speaking world refers to the avant-garde. The image "*Die Zeit der Übergänge verstärkt ihr Gewimmel auf allen Brücken*" [The time of transitions causes a rush on all bridges] begins many an essay that Wolfenstein (1922b, 428) devoted to the topic.[2] He envisioned a Jew, whose status is all but certain, standing in the middle of some congestion. In Wolfenstein's metaphor the old shore belongs not to the Jew, and neither yet does the bridge; instead, the "*Bewegung darüberhin ist sein Schicksal und das Kommende winkt ihm so gut wie den andern*" [movement from there is his fate and the Coming already beckons him just like the others] (Wolfenstein 1922, 428). The future thus holds a promise of equality with these others, here denoting the mainstream German population, which is inscribed in the portentous fate of the Jew. For Wolfenstein, being Jewish signifies striving towards the future, with the subtextual promise that this future is preferable to the current moment, and it was this striving he grasped as the very "essence" of Jewishness.

---

[1] "Spring has arrived in the West. Poetry with two aspects [i.e., Jewish and German] sings of decline and emergence. Perhaps a union between the Orient and Occident is being heralded." Wolfenstein 1922a, 357. All translations are by the author unless otherwise indicated.

[2] Wolfenstein's works on the topic include *Jüdisches Wesen und neue Dichtung* (1922), "Das neue Dichtertum des Juden" (1922), "Jüdisches Wesen und Dichtertum" (1922), "Von der Dichtung des Juden" (1934) and "Vom deutschjüdischen Dichter der Gegenwart" (1935–1936).

Wolfenstein's emphasis on the future echoes the avant-garde, which is by definition forward-looking. He recognized this similarity, and the avant-garde had an instrumental role in the future he had predicted. Arguably, for him, the avant-garde was an essential method in the eventual overcoming of the distinction between the German and German-Jewish populations – as is evident in the epigraph of this essay. However, his aim was not to identify the avant-garde with Judaism in any traditional sense of the latter term, but rather to fashion it into a common groundwork for modern Jews and Germans.

Hence, Wolfenstein's understanding of "Jewish essence" was disconnected from such orthodox-theological definitions of Jewishness that derived from Judaism, that is, religion. Indeed, Wolfenstein (1993a [1936], 402) regarded the avant-garde as an emancipation from Jewish history, or what he called "our false selves." Therefore, the key question his stance raises is how did German-Jewish artists who were active in the avant-garde understand the idea and contexts of a Jewish essence? What kinds of traditional and modern connotations did it have, and how did they link it with contemporary attitudes towards religion and secularism? Moreover, how did it affect these artists' work? Given the emphasis of the epigraph above, the framework for this inquiry is decidedly esthetic. In Wolfenstein's case, unlike most characterizations contemporary to his, there is no direct causality between the ethnic origin of the artist and any possible "Jewishness" of his or her work. Yet, in the context of the avant-garde, it seems that in addition to explicit characteristics there is also an implicit "Jewish" quality to the works of the artists whom Wolfenstein addresses: this quality derives not only from the theme of the works but from the way things are seen and how their intrinsic values are displayed.

Wolfenstein (1993b [1935–1936], 215) regarded poetry as the most immediate form of art, due to its medium: words required no recoding into other media. The present essay will thus delve into Wolfenstein's poetics and politics of "amalgamation" by examining the German-Jewish background from which his ideas emerged. The mapping of the modern usage of "Jewish essence" illuminates the latter part of the inquiry, which focuses on the relation between Judaism and the avant-garde, and especially on the futurospective emphasis of Wolfenstein's interpretation of "Jewish essence" and how its religious content is appropriated to esthetics.

Debates Regarding Jewish Essence

Wolfenstein explains that the "Jewish essence" is found exclusively in the German language. According to him, there remains no trace of it in the Romance languages, whereas the Jew appears as a Doppelgänger of the German (Wolfenstein 1922b, 437). Evidently, Wolfenstein postulates a difference between Germans and Jews. It should be noted that "Jewish essence" is necessarily a set of construed reifications and essentialisms, which are in turn perceived to somehow define the Jews' unique mode of being. Moreover, its creation was essential, because it enabled the construction of a narrative around fragmentary instances that would be labelled "Jewish history" (Hughes 2014, 15, 52). Indeed, the core of this "essence" was seldom defined unambiguously or universally: for instance, obeying Jewish law, Halakha, could hardly be regarded as a decisive factor in any modern and secular environment. Moreover, the term "Jewish essence" could equally well prove constraining when people with highly varied religious beliefs, political pursuits or esthetic preferences were set under its normative umbrella. Wolfenstein sought, at least in part, to unravel the rather strict frame erected from, for instance, Max Brod's views on "Jewish essence."[3]

A radical change in the German intellectual climate occurred following the disaster of the First World War, and led to the emergence of debates concerning a "Jewish essence." Germany experienced a temporary spiritual revulsion against war and materialism; this atmosphere prompted expressionism to engage in a struggle for peace, world brotherhood and the dignity of humanity. For the numerous Jewish members of the movement, it was also, simultaneously, a striving to find one's place in the world. This identity-focused political quest concerned Jews beyond the sphere of the avant-garde, which helps to explain why universalism became one of the key characteristics of expressionism's ideas about "Jewish essence."

In the context of the avant-garde, Wolfenstein (1922b, 433) clearly states that a "Jewish essence" was notable in expressionism but not equally in dada.[4] The expressionist "Jewish essence" should be seen in relation to the overall situation

---

[3] Brod ascribed to each artist of Jewish origin a "Jewish essence," regardless of whether there was anything particularly "Jewish" in the artist's work. For further discussion, see Móricz 2008, 7–9.

[4] In contrast to the expressionists, the dadaists tended to eschew subjects relating to religion, especially those that did so in an affirmative way. A unique exception to this was John Höxter's 1919 special issue of *Der blutige Ernst* (Bloody Earnest), themed "Der Jude" (The Jew). It was a reaction to the post-revolutionary anti-Semitism in Germany and did not seek to assert any mode of "Jewish essence."

in Germany. Coinciding with expressionism a second movement arose, one which aimed at the intellectual, moral and political rebirth of the Jewish people. This movement introduced its own idea of "Jewish essence," against which artists such as Wolfenstein reflected their understanding of the term. The main figures behind this intellectualist aspiration were Martin Buber and Franz Rosenzweig. Buber turned to East European Jews (*Ostjuden*) for a "genuine" kind of "Jewish essence," though he himself was an assimilated German Jew, a *Westjude* (e.g., Aschheim 1982, 129–133). He appropriated pseudo-nationalistic strategies, suggesting that the character of a people would derive from its past, and that this narrated past is always held in higher esteem than the corrupted present. Rosenzweig fell for a similar nostalgia. He imagined a past in which the "Jewish essence" he sought to revive in the modern period existed in a full and authentic form. In fact, his incorruptible "Jewish essence" meant that anything he deemed detrimental derived from the Jews' attempts to look to the outside world for political solutions to their problems. Rosenzweig concluded that these attempts could not solve anything for the Jews, because non-Jewish solutions overlooked the fact that Jews were unlike others (Hughes 2014, 90–92). Not only did Rosenzweig establish "Jewish essence" as a constricting frame; he also advocated Jewish particularity.

Hence, the signification of "Jewish essence" was problematic for the assimilated *Westjuden* who were native speakers of German and who had never embraced the Jewish tradition in the same manner as the Yiddish-speaking *Ostjuden*. The case of expressionism and the traditional *Ostjuden* was also complicated: expressionism's stance vis-à-vis tradition was influenced by avant-garde ideals, which were secessionist in character. However, in the avant-garde such separations were seldom transparent and final. From the avant-garde's point of view, the debate over "Jewish essence" meant that German Jews needed to determine both how to modernize Judaism and how a "Jewish essence" would fit into this undertaking. Appropriately, the German-Jewish theatre critic Julius Bab (1880–1955) associated himself with the *Westjuden* when engaging in the debate. According to him, German Jews were rooted exclusively in German culture and expressed their Jewishness only insofar as they tended to become mediators rather than creators of "Germanness" (*Deutschtum*). Echoing Rosenzweig, Bab rationalized that "Jewish creative instincts" were repressed when under the dictates of a "foreign culture" (Bab 1912, 4–5). It becomes apparent that Bab is arguing for a Jewish particularity that does not intermingle with the special indigenous character of German culture.[5]

---

[5] Another aspect to this stance is Ludwig Strauss's (1998, 448) interpretation of Bab's writings, which highlight assimilation. Strauss avers that Bab in fact believed in the existence of a Jewish race within the German people.

Regardless of his isolationism, Bab did not regard the *Ostjuden* as a solution in the manner of Buber. He argued that German Jews could not solve their problems by simply attaching themselves to Eastern Jewry because their relationship to German culture was too deep and natural (Bab 1912, 3; Aschheim 1982, 118). Bab was against every kind of cultural retrogression, especially the kind he recognized in Buber's vision. As Steven Aschheim (1982, 118) noted, according to Bab the *Ostjuden* could be integrated into the European community, but to propose the opposite for German Jews was absurd and would sever their roots from that community. This is to say that Bab regarded the *Westjuden* as an integral part of a modernizing Europe and did not see how relinquishing modernization would be feasible or even possible.

Following Bab's arguments, the literary critic Gustav Krojanker reflected on the place of Jews in German culture and among the literati.[6] Focusing on Bab's statement concerning the Jew's position as a cultural outsider, Krojanker contended that the problem arose from Jewish authors not developing an "authentic" voice:

> *Von je ist [...] jüdisches Wesen als ein Komplex von nicht nur andersartigen, sondern vor allem minderwertigen und verderblichen Eigenschaften so laut und verletzend dargestellt worden, dass der Jude, der sich die Werte nicht setzt, sondern von aussen bezieht, es ängstlich vermeidet, Dingen nachzugehen, als deren Resultat er von vornherein den Beweis seiner Drittrangigkeit und die Rechtfertigung seines Ausgeschlossenseins erwartet.*
> (Krojanker 1922, 7)

> [As a complex of not only dissimilar, but rather particularly inferior and perishable properties, the Jewish essence has been illustrated loudly and hurtfully, [which has suggested] that the Jew, who does not set the values himself but rather applies them from outside, avoids the anxious pursuit of things, as a result of which he awaits *a priori* proof of his third-ratedness and a vindication of his debarment.]

In Krojanker's view, the Jewish author is a passive mediator unless he or she takes cultural background into account. Only in such cases can the full Jewish particularity be manifested, which would eventually shatter the preconception of the Jew's fundamental "foreignness." Krojanker's text is therefore a step towards a self-assertion of the Jewish author and, hence, the recognition of a "Jewish essence."

---

6 Krojanker edited an anthology entitled *Juden in der deutschen Literatur* (Jews in German literature, 1922), which collected essays about German-Jewish authors penned by Jewish writers. Avant-gardists such as Meir Wiener, Albert Ehrenstein and Wolfenstein were represented in the volume – even Buber contributed an essay.

Although Krojanker describes the Jews' relation to society at large, he does not pinpoint the characteristics that render the avant-garde "Jewish." Concerning the concrete characteristics of a "Jewish essence," Bab argued that these were first and foremost thematological. He stated that the use of traditional biblical themes would give rise to a work of art with Jewish particularity which would manifest this essence (Bab 1918, 397–398). Indeed, biblical themes had been widely used even by expressionists (e.g., Paul Adler and Ernst Toller), but not exclusively by Jewish ones. In fact, the most common religious variant in German drama amalgamated Jewish and Christian elements (cf. Anderson 2011, 81–92).

Regardless of the intermingling of these elements, or perhaps because of it, Bab decided to attack the avant-garde and its pursuits of cultural renewal. He stated that one should look for "*das wahre jüdische Wesen mehr in seinen zeitlos großen Manifesten als in zufälligen Erscheinungen einer oft sehr unmassgeblichen Gegenwart*" [the true Jewish essence rather in its great timeless manifestations than in the random phenomena of an often very non-substantial presence] (Bab 1918, 401). For Bab, the avant-garde was only one of the many contemporary manifestations of a "Jewish essence." Neglecting the avant-garde's paralleling with modernization, and the artists still wishing to identify themselves as Jews, Bab defined the avant-garde and Jewishness as antithetical. Any potential "Jewish avant-garde" would thus be defined via tradition – ultimately an oxymoron. Backtracking to Wolfenstein's image of the bridge, in Bab's vision the Jew seems to stand on it somewhat reluctantly, his nostalgic gaze fixed on the old shore, in the very vein of Buber and Rosenzweig.

Jewish Essence in German-Jewish Expressionism

In Bab's view, contemporary phenomena were unsubstantial in relation to Jewish history and the necessary narrative that dovetails with it. Wolfenstein, for one, represented a perspective that was opposite to that of Bab. In relation to the debate on "Jewish essence," expressionism's stance vis-à-vis tradition was made clear through, among other things, the participation of Jewish artists in expressionism. Wolfenstein characterized the idea of "Jewish essence" as a manifestation of the Jewish mode of being in a heterogeneous social world. He saw the Jew as the penultimate contemporary bearer of the signs of transition (*Zeichen des Übergangs*), and noted quasi-theologically that, as "old Judaism" had no female deity, Jewishness was necessarily male in spirit, which becomes apparent through varied symptoms of "restlessness" (Wolfenstein 1922b, 428). Such ambiguous characterizations were unfamiliar to the more tradition-inclined Jews.

The expressionists' rather eccentric interpretations of Judaism and Jewishness evoked criticism in conservative circles. For instance, Rabbi Leopold Fuchs expressed concern over the lack of theological essentialism – that is, a complete lack of Jewish essence – in the expressionists' understanding of Judaism:

> Schon streitet man weniger um das, was nicht zum Judentum gehört, um die Negation, als darum, was positiv Judentum sei. Schon hört man seltener das Wort: mein Judentum besteht darin, das ich ein guter Mensch bin. [...] ich bin doch ein guter Jude! [...] Man sagt nicht mehr: Ich bin kein rechter Jude, denn ich glaube nicht an Bibel und Talmud, Wunder, Schöpfung, Verbalinspiration, persönlichen Messias, [oder] Verpflichtung zum Religionsgebet.
> (Fuchs 1924, 1)

> [Already we argue less about what does not belong to Judaism, about the negation, than what positive Judaism is. Even more rarely does one hear the word: my Judaism is that I am a good person. Therefore, I am a good Jew! One no longer says: I am not a real Jew, because I do not believe in the Bible and Talmud, miracles, creation, verbal inspiration, a personal Messiah, or commitment to religious prayer.]

Fuchs regards the avant-garde as a middlebrow exercise when considered from a religious point of view. The rabbi's lamentation illustrates how the avant-garde had transmuted elements of Judaism into forms that were unrecognizable to conservative Jews. He highlights the neglect of traditional Judaism in the avant-garde, without noting the fundamentally antithetical character of each.

The renewal of religion was indeed related to modernization in Wolfenstein's case. His conception of "Jewish essence" is unique in that he implies that the avant-garde is a Jewish phenomenon: the Jew on the bridge faces modernization, and the so-called new shore *could* be his – hence, a sort of conditional promise looms over Wolfenstein's reckoning. The condition is related to urbanization: Wolfenstein (1922c, 29) acknowledges that the avant-garde arises from urban culture, which ultimately precludes the *Ostjuden*. As the avant-garde was closely linked with modernization, it was also concerned with how accustomed the Jews were to modern metropolitan life. Such consideration is undoubtedly worthwhile on a microhistorical level, yet what does it reveal about the role of the artist and the works of art in relation to a "Jewish essence"?

On this topic, Brod's formulations of Jewish art are noteworthy. He mapped the delicate interrelations between self-consciousness, intentionality and artistic work, but ended up declaring that Jewish art necessitates "a miracle" in which consciously and unconsciously Jewish factors amalgamate (Brod 1922, 207–208). Wolfenstein, for one, circumvented Brod's esoteric tones by noting that artists were allowed to reflect in a special way on the question of identity. According to him, the author recognizes a difference between the reality of his life and the reality of his work, which is to say that being Jewish does not automatically render one's *œuvre* Jewish (Wolfenstein 1922c, 11). As the identities of the Jew as a person and as a poet are distinct, Wolfenstein's view on "Jewish essence" avoids the all-embracing yet constrictive elements characteristic of Brod's definition.

For Wolfenstein (1922c, 36), the avant-garde contains something essentially Jewish, because *"Der Jude ist der unklassische Dichter"* [the Jew is the non-classical poet]. Even though some now-canonized German writers such as Heinrich Heine and Theodor Lessing were Jewish, Wolfenstein's definition situated the Jewish author as parallel to the avant-garde, and thus outside German classical tradition. Obviously, in Wolfenstein's view the identity prompted by the avant-garde could not derive from the *Ostjuden* (Jewish tradition) or from classicism (German tradition). Hence, the critical question is where the avant-gardist element in Wolfenstein's "Jewish essence" derived from.

The early history of expressionism provides an answer. In its formative stages, expressionism witnessed the involvement of several artists of Jewish origin who were essential in developing and transforming the new aesthetics. For instance, Jakob van Hoddis, Georg Heym and Kurt Hiller launched the Neopathetic Cabaret in 1910, one of the most influential soirées of early expressionism in Berlin. In addition, in the 1910s the expressionist magazines *Der Sturm* and *Die Aktion* were headed by Jewish editors – Herwarth Walden and Franz Pfemfert, respectively. These magazines (especially Walden's) introduced avant-garde aesthetics and movements to the German public, while also addressing (as did Pfemfert's magazine, in particular) a broad spectrum of issues of Jewish interest.[7] The sort of modernized Jewishness envisioned in these magazines presented the cultural avant-garde as an organic part of the pursuit.

In short, the avant-garde provided an esthetic platform where the Jew would not be considered an imitator or outsider. Whereas Bab had reduced the Jews to mere mediators of German culture, Wolfenstein (1922b, 439) states that the Jews would bring about *"eine frische Vermählung mit den Dingen nicht naturalistisch sondern mythisch"* [a fresh marriage of things, which is not naturalistic but rather mythical]. In other words, the "Jewish essence" thus lies in one's relation to things, things which are not grasped in any straightforwardly realistic or rational manner. Therefore, Wolfenstein's idea of "Jewish essence" does not involve the use of biblical themes, which could be (and were) applied by non-Jews as well; rather, it concerns the particular ways of ordering one's perceptions and ideas. In the midst of modernization, such an emphasis is understandable: urban culture, technology and new means of communication provided a renewed sense of reality, a sense that art could not disregard. Accordingly, Wolfenstein needed

---

7 For a more detailed analysis, see Sjöberg 2016.

to consolidate "Jewish essence" and modernization with what "Jewish" meant to him.

Appropriately, Brod (1918, 2) marvelled that Wolfenstein had created a Jewish mode of linguistic expression "within the German language, as paradoxical as that sounds." Wolfenstein was keen on bridging the demarcated halves of the term "German-Jewish" through the avant-garde. He sought to construct an aesthetic symbiosis between "German clarity" (rationalism) and Jewish intellectual spirituality (*Geistigkeit*) by means of a new art (Wolfenstein 1922c, 439). The introduction of the avant-garde as a unifying factor would require both Jews and Germans to disavow their vernacular, which they assumed to represent the world "realistically," and to adopt a new perspective, a new way of relating to phenomena. Wolfenstein's stance suggests that, for him, the experiential world of the individual had undergone a radical change through modernization and that poetic language should follow suit.

Indeed, the "*neue Dichtung kennt diese Unzufriedenheit mit dem Worte, als eine schwere Wahrheit*" [new poetry is familiar with this dissatisfaction with the word, as a severe truth] (Wolfenstein 1922c, 23). Conventional language is here regarded as a hindrance to modernization, and thus a new form of language is required. The avant-garde is suitable for this, as it includes both an analysis of the situation and the means to recover from it. Hence, through the successful renewal of language a linguistic comradeship can be envisioned. Accordingly, Wolfenstein (1993b [1934], 398) concludes that "*Die Dichtung löst durch Bewahrung und Verneinung deutschen und jüdischen Wesens den Hass auf – in ihrer Sprache ist die Freundschaft vollbracht*" [Poetry dissolves [mutual hatred] through preservation and unification of the German and Jewish character – in their language friendship is accomplished]. Hereby the Jew would relinquish the role of Doppelgänger.

To succeed, the new poetry should modulate any religious element regardless of whether it was acting under the rubric of a "Jewish essence." This is to say that Wolfenstein sought to reinvent Jewishness as independent of religious tradition. Therefore, the remaining characteristically "Jewish" element in avant-garde art is the numerous unexpected interrelation between things, phenomena and the observers. Such a mode of Jewishness is related to tradition only by virtue of an interpretative "method" – an avant-gardist hermeneutics of sorts – and not through historical narrative, religion or ethnicity. Wolfenstein's "Jewish essence" is not a categorizable essence as such, but rather a mode of being that is manifested through its relation to the world.

Wolfenstein's Poetics of Jewish Essence

Even though Fuchs's comment may have been applicable to certain expressionists, it was not especially valid for Wolfenstein. He aimed at shifting away from history and tradition and towards the modern era, without fully relinquishing the element of faith in favor of straightforward secularism. Wolfenstein regarded the situation through a certain revolutionary ethos, whereby the "new man" of the avant-garde was also the "new Jew." Approaching the issue by acknowledging the conservative perspective of Fuchs, he noted that *"wir in einer auch für das Judentum revolutionären Epoche leben"* [we live in an epoch that is revolutionary also for Judaism], meaning that Judaism itself would need to be modernized (Wolfenstein 1993a [1936], 402).

Wolfenstein's most precise formulation of the mismatch between religion and the avant-garde identifies the former with a certain inertia: *"Religionen sind da, um zu trösten, zu beruhigen, das zackige Hiersein abzurunden, und für solche überirdische Ergänzung benötigen andere Menschen andere Gottheiten. Die Kunst aber will ein irdisches Gegenüber des Lebens [sein], sie will nicht versüssen, nicht beschönigen, nicht [...] einschläfern. Sie will aufregen, will fort bewegen"* [Religions are there to comfort, to soothe, to round off the jagged being-here, and for those unearthly supplements other people need other deities. But art wants to be an earthly opposite to life, it does not want to sweeten, to gloss over, to sleep. It wants to incite, wants to move forward] (Wolfenstein 1922b, 433). Instead of postulating a transcendent realm, the avant-garde focuses on the immediate.

This obvious dissimilarity between religion and the avant-garde led to the rabbis' regressive point of view losing influence, especially with young artists who were feeling estranged from traditional Judaism. *"Eine neue Religion kann uns nicht einfallen"* [A new religion cannot overrun us], as Wolfenstein (1993a [1936], 403) phrased it. His idea of modernization was not the one prompted by Haskalah; rather, it was a new path, one enabled by the still largely unexplored potential of the "new poetry." However, Wolfenstein was discussing religion, not *faith* as such. In this sense, his formulations seem to derive from a more basic form of belief. He states: *"Ich spreche hier vom spirituell schwebenden Wesen des Juden und seinem neuen Dichtertum"* [I speak here of the spiritually suspended essence of the Jews and their new "poetness"] (Wolfenstein 1922b, 429). This spiritual suspension refers to a partially transcendent quality of the "Jewish essence," which is not fully here in this world at the present moment. This further connotes messianic aims and an eventual full realization of the very essence in the future.

Consequently, Wolfenstein balances between the avant-garde and the more conservative stances in revising the "Jewish essence" according to contemporary requirements. Hence, he characterizes the significance of the avant-garde to contemporary Judaism as follows:

> *In den Knieen der Epoche wartet, nach dem ersten irren Falle, vielleicht ein großer Sprung. Auch der Jude wird eine neue Gestalt gewinnen. Sein Auftreten im Aufrruhr der Gegenwart, Leben, Tod und Dichtung, kündigt sie schon an. Sie wird nur noch entschiedener seine spirituelle Sendung zu erkennen geben. So aber wird sie nicht nur deshalb wirken, weil dies Wesen sich in ihr wie für die Ewigkeit verstärkt, sondern auch weil die Gestalt, die es trägt, an Eigenschaften, es zu tragen und es auszudrücken, wachsen wird. Viele wünschen sich neuen Boden. Herrlicher ist die Unabhängigkeit einer neuen jüdischen Gestalt. Der Boden kann verloren gehen, das Geschick kann sich wütend immer wiederholen, weil man es nicht erkennt, ewige Zerstreuung, – Jerusalem kann wieder zerstört werden: die schwebende Sendung nicht. Sie fühlt grenzenlos durch Länder hindurch die unverwehrte Welt, die Gott gehört und ihre Bewohner von ihm erlangt.*
> (Wolfenstein 1922b, 440)

[The knees of our era, after a first mistaken fall, may be flexed for a great leap forward. And the Jew will acquire a new form as well: he will emerge as a distant figure amidst the uproar of the present – life, death, and literature have already proclaimed as much, making his spiritual mission that much more decisive and clear. Literature will play a decisive role not because the essence of Judaism will become spiritually stronger, but because the new forms it assumes will increase its expressive capabilities. Many now seek a new land. But the independence of new forms of Jewish literary expression is more splendid still. A land can be lost, and fate can furiously be repeated because it has not been understood, producing an eternal diaspora – Jerusalem can be destroyed once more: but Judaism's transcendent mission, never. This mission transcends every state, envisioning an open world that belongs to God, and that citizens of its various states receive from him.][8]

Wolfenstein depicts a "Jewish world of writing" where literature and Jewishness are inseparable. Literature will assume new forms from avant-garde aesthetics, which will transform the preceding literary language and supplement its expressive capabilities. Moreover, literature is seen as the home of the "landless," nomadic Jew. By virtue of this formulation, Wolfenstein produces a vision that is among the most poignant versions of the avant-garde's utopian aim of unifying art and life. The Jews who would previously have identified themselves as belonging to a certain creed and tradition – via Judaism's seminal texts, such as the Torah and Talmud – should now identify with the avant-garde. In other words, Wolfenstein saw the avant-garde as a textual homeland by virtue of which Jews could affirm their identity.

---

8 Translated by Hermann Levin Goldschmidt.

Appropriately, one of the new forms derived from the avant-garde was anti-realism. Wolfenstein (1922b, 439) notes that Jews did not take part in realist movements, and that the *"jüngere Generation [der Juden] schlug geistige Richtungen ein, mit denen sein Wesen zusammentraf, um spirituelle Dichtung zu werden"* [younger generation of Jews struck out in spiritual directions, by which they met their essence, to become spiritual poetry]. The preference for an abstract "space" over nations is summarized in Wolfenstein's rather ambiguous idea of Judaism's transcendent mission. Due to its abstract character, this mission is unbound and mobile, potentially manifesting itself wherever the Jew is.

The equation's inclusion of Germans in this particularly Jewish textual "homeland" seems incongruent. This is due to the limited temporal perspective, however, and the situation should be seen in terms of the idea of suspension. The arrival of the avant-garde meant that Jews were not limited to imitating German literature, and that the new literary means at their disposal enabled them to master the qualities of the language of their expression. In other words, they renewed the poetic repertoire of the German language. Evoking Benjamin's idea of the Angel of History, the language of poetry itself epitomizes the messianic anticipation: *"Die Lyrik, an sich schon eine Kunstart des klingenden Untergangs der Gegenstände in der Form, – begegnet sich mit dem hereinbrechen Gefühl eines Weltuntergangs. [...] Aber im Gedicht gibt sich die Gefahr zugleich wie überwunden"* [The poetry is in itself an art form of the sounding doom of items in the form – met with the feeling of a doomsday closing in. But in the poem, the risk is as good as overcome] (Wolfenstein 1922a, 347). Wolfenstein envisions a modernization where the conventional relations between things are ruptured, severed and lost. Poetry mediates the chaotic state where language is ruptured and, simultaneously, overcomes this development by appropriating it as a poetic device. Reality changes and so will poetry, which embodies the future in its vanguard character.

In its Wolfensteinian sense, avant-garde poetry negotiates between two temporalities. Logically, the new literature is a manifestation of the "Jewish essence" in which Wolfenstein recognized both a present and a future. The present is characterized by this "Jewish essence," in other words, particularity. Yet he wrote illuminatingly that poetry bears a foretaste of the future: *"In der Dichtung wie in einem Paradiese des Menschen wandelt Gott"* [God strolls in poetry like in a human paradise] (Wolfenstein 1922c, 46).[9] In this messianic phrase, poetry is the artificial paradise where God roams – suggesting that the future envisaged by Wolfenstein

---

9 Here Wolfenstein echoes the Kabbalistic thought that identifies the original text (Torah) with divinity. Hence, his avant-garde poetry would include the Jewish God, whose preferred residence, according to the lore, was a "house of words."

would become available through literature. As noted, literature would be the Jews' home, which posits them in the vanguard of the messianic future.

Wolfenstein's postulation of the new shore underlines his focus on the aspect of becoming. Hence, his aim is a messianic one where literature holds the promise of eventual paradise. According to Wolfenstein, "*die Kunst besteht in ihrer Gegenwart. Sie bedeutet bereits die Erfüllung, das Paradies (dem man nicht wortwörtlich zumarschieren kann)*" [Art is made of its contemporariness. It already signifies fulfilment, the paradise (through which one literally cannot march)] (Wolfenstein 1922b, 433). Here the contemporariness of art denotes the avant-garde that, for its part, embodies a paradise that is presently abstract. Paradoxically, the promised paradise that one aspires to is thus already in the avant-garde, in which the "now" becomes highlighted.

Art is indeed the indicator of the future in the present. The two temporalities of Jewish essence are suspended in poetry, which Wolfenstein recognized as the earthly opposite to life. Life can be lived only in the present, so anything opposite to life denotes what exceeds the temporality that life occupies. Regarding the aspect of becoming, there is already a hint of the potential future in the present: "*Der Jude ist [...] ein Mensch [...] der Zeitkunst: Ein Mensch des Werdens, des Ganges, der Zeit – raumlos*" [The Jew is a person of contemporary art: A man of becoming, of passage, of time – spaceless] (Wolfenstein 1922c, 48). Characterized in such a manner, the Jew embodies the desire to move forward, futurospection, and thus becomes parallel with messianism and the avant-garde. In short, being a Jew means living in a state of constant messianic tension that involves anticipation of a better future.

Wolfenstein's latent adoption of Jewish messianism seems to be practical in terms of socio-historical ends. The apocalyptic tones of expressionist poetry are not in his focus as much as art is, in its functioning as a platform that produces a sense of solidarity between Germans and Jews. To this end, Wolfenstein revises the Jewish tradition, by incorporating modern elements, and puts it at the service of modernization amongst his Jewish peers.

Coda

The task Wolfenstein imagined for the avant-garde – the unification of two cultures – was enabled by new means of literary expression. His rationale was that the new grammatical and linguistic anomalies, being neither German nor Jewish in character, would provide untrodden ground for a unified German-Jewish culture, where such a term would be regarded as a symbiosis instead of an oxymoron.

The avant-garde seemed to offer the possibility of building a new future together. Poetry, being composed of concepts and words, was indeed in a special position to unite the fractions, for it applied the medium of people's thoughts. Wolfenstein's statements suggest the utopian aspiration of changing perspectives and creating objectivity via poetry.

Bab and Wolfenstein grasped the meaning of the contemporary to Jewishness in opposite ways. Bab looks to what he postulates as the resplendent history of the Jews, the Tanakh, the Talmudic tradition, from antiquity to exile and diaspora, and actualizes all of this in the current state of things, arguing for acknowledgement of these features in art. Wolfenstein, on the other hand, seeks to renew Jewishness in such a way that it is reborn and thereby united with German culture in a transnational modern era.

Wolfenstein was aware that solving the German-Jewish dilemma required stepping outside the Jewish cultural canon yet simultaneously striving towards a messianic future. Even though Wolfenstein excludes religion, it is present via textuality and the status of the (divine) word as the basis of the Jewish tradition. Appropriately, he ties together, in a single sentence, the religious textual tradition and the avant-garde: "*Das Wort insbesondere, die Sprache,* [ist] *das Ausdrucksmittel der Kunst und zugleich des Lebens*" [The word in particular, language, is the means of expression of art and – at the same time – life] (Wolfenstein 1934, 213). The avant-garde is seen as an anticipator of the future in the present.

Yet, there looms a dilemma in Wolfenstein's conception of "Jewish essence." The new interrelatedness of things is noted as a trait that derives from Jewish tradition, but when appropriated into the sphere of the avant-garde, it did not relinquish this particularity. Regardless of Wolfenstein's outspoken efforts, in his usage the avant-garde becomes another denominator for Jewish particularity instead of the utopia of universalism. In a rather conventional fashion, Wolfenstein falls victim to providing a set of reifications and essentialisms: the Jew who resides in avant-garde textuality can hardly be regarded as an overarching goal with the aim of inviting Germans in.

Bibliography

Anderson, Lisa Marie. *German Expressionism and the Messianism of a Generation*. Amsterdam: Rodopi, 2011.

Aschheim, Steven E. *Brothers and Strangers: The East European Jew in German and German Jewish Consciousness, 1800–1923*. Madison: University of Wisconsin Press, 1982.

Bab, Julius. "Der Anteil der Juden an der deutschen Dichtung der Gegenwart." *Mitteilungen des Verbandes der jüdischen Jugendvereine Deutschlands* 3.12 (1912): 3–9.

Bab, Julius. "Die Wiederkunft des biblischen Motivs im jüngsten deutschen Drama." *Neue jüdische Monatshefte* 3.17 (1918): 396–401.
Brod, Max. "'Die Freundschaft' von Alfred Wolfenstein." *Selbstwehr* 11.6 (1918): 2.
Brod, Max. *Heidentum, Christentum, Judentum. Ein Bekenntnisbuch*. Teil 1. Berlin: Kurt Wolff, 1922.
Fuchs, Leon. "Expressionistisches Judentum." *Jüdisch-liberale Zeitung* 4.4 (1924): 1–2.
Hughes, Aaron W. *Rethinking Jewish Philosophy: Beyond Particularism and Universalism*. New York: Oxford University Press, 2014.
Krojanker, Gustav (ed.). *Juden in der deutschen Literatur: Essays über zeitgenössische Schriftsteller*. Berlin: Welt-Verlag, 1922.
Móricz, Klára. *Jewish Identities: Nationalism, Racism, and Utopianism in Twentieth-Century Music*. Berkeley: University of California Press, 2008.
Sjöberg, Sami. "Jewish Communality in German Avant-Garde Magazines of the 1910s and 1920s." *Orbis litterarum*, forthcoming.
Strauss, Ludwig. "Ein Dokument der Assimilation." *Gesammelte Werke 4: Dramen, Epen, vermischte Schriften*. Göttingen: Wallstein Verlag, 1998. 448–452.
Wolfenstein, Alfred. "Das neue Dichtertum des Juden." *Juden in der deutschen Literatur: Essays über zeitgenössische Schriftsteller*. Berlin: Welt-Verlag, 1922a. 333–359.
Wolfenstein, Alfred. "Jüdisches Wesen und Dichtertum (aus einer größeren Arbeit)." *Der Jude* 6.7 (1922b): 428–440.
Wolfenstein, Alfred. *Jüdisches Wesen und neue Dichtung*. Berlin: Erich Weiss Verlag, 1922c.
Wolfenstein, Alfred: "Von der Dichtung des Juden." *Der Morgen: Monatsschrift der Juden in Deutschland* 9.5 (1934): 208–215.
Wolfenstein, Alfred. "Jüdische Haltung." *Werke. Vermischte Schriften: Ästhetik, Literatur, Politik*. Eds. Hermann Haarmann and Günter Holtz. Mainz: Hase and Koehler, 1993a. 400–404.
Wolfenstein, Alfred. "Vom deutschjüdischen Dichter der Gegenwart." *Werke. Vermischte Schriften: Ästhetik, Literatur, Politik*. Eds. Hermann Haarmann and Günter Holtz. Mainz: Hase and Koehler, 1993b. 394–398.

Community Building and Cultural Conflicts

Andreas Kramer
Carl Einstein, Jewishness, and the Communities of the European Avant-Garde

The work of the German-Jewish writer, art critic, and theorist Carl Einstein (1885–1940) provides an intriguing perspective on the relationship between Jews and the European avant-garde of the early twentieth century. In this context, the fact that Einstein has been hailed as a "prophet of the avant-garde" (Siebenhaar 1991) becomes particularly resonant. In the Jewish tradition, prophets are both predictors of the future and guardians of a collective past or memory, simultaneously looking both forward and backward. In the age of secular modernity, Einstein believed, art should fill the gap left by religious tradition, and accordingly, avant-garde art should not merely dismantle cultural tradition, but bring about a new one that would bind society together again. As an art theorist, Einstein took the term "vision" seriously. A lifelong champion of cubism's visual revolution, he regarded avant-garde activity as a commitment to a comprehensive "*Umbildung des Sehens*" [transformation of vision], which would resonate beyond the confines of art and transform the way we see and inhabit the world (Einstein 1992, 153). This essay will argue that Einstein's thinking about the nature and the purpose of avant-garde art and literature in the twentieth century bears resemblance to the Jewish model, particularly in avant-garde art's emphasizing the importance of individual and collective agency, the role of a community sustained by religious and cultural tradition, and a view of history and temporality that sidesteps the protocols of modernity.[1]

Regardless of whether they actually possess prophetic quality, Einstein's life and work offer a number of entry points into exploring Jewishness in relation to the avant-garde. However, the most straightforward approach – the analysis of Jewish themes and ideas in his writings, and through them, consideration of the author's biography and cultural context – is fraught with difficulties. It seems appropriate enough that Ludwig Rubiner and Karl Otten anthologized some of Einstein's literary writings in collections that foreground the Jewish experience of modernity (Einstein 1919, 1920 and 1962), even if the volumes disregard his critical and theoretical writings. Yet, Einstein tended to view his Jewish background as being largely irrelevant to his avant-garde commitment. He adopted the role of the radical intellectual outsider whose very marginality enabled him to attack

---
[1] See the essay "Das Gesetz" (1914), in Einstein 1980, 218–219.

bourgeois culture and society. This stance distinguished him from many other German-Jewish writers and intellectuals of his generation who promoted Jewish avant-gardism as a political or poetic force with the power to redeem modernity (cf. Rubiner 1920; Wolfenstein 1922). At the same time, Einstein's consideration of how he and the wider avant-garde came to adopt that marginal position sheds light also on the Jewish experience, even where it is not explicitly mentioned. In other words, the multiple negativity evident in Einstein's presentation of his own avant-garde commitment betrays a cultural logic, one that I will address. Finally, the notion of Einstein as a "German-Jewish" writer and critic is too narrow to account for the many contradictions that mark both his life and work (cf. Kiefer 2000). Born in Wilhelmine Germany, he belonged to the expressionist generation, but his lifelong avant-gardism extended far beyond Germany. His work overlaps with, and responds to, several avant-garde movements in art and literature, chiefly expressionism, cubism, and surrealism.[2] Einstein knew, worked with, and wrote about Picasso, Braque, Gris, the Blue Riders Kandinsky and Marc, the artists of the Bauhaus (at one point, Einstein was approached about taking a professorship at the institution), Russian avant-gardists such as Ehrenburg, Eisenstein, El Lissitzky, and Mayakovsky (many of whom he met in Berlin), and the surrealist writers and painters in Paris. Among the German artists and writers close to Einstein and his concerns were Arp, Benn, Dix, Grosz, Rubiner, Rudolf Schlichter, and Carl Sternheim.

A brief look at Einstein's biography is necessary, to establish both his complex relationship with the country and culture of his birth and his commitment to the cosmopolitan ideals of the avant-garde. Einstein was born in Neuwied, in the Rhineland, where his father served as a rabbi, educator, and Jewish community leader. His father continued in these roles in Karlsruhe, in Baden, where the family moved in 1888. Each town had a long tradition of religious tolerance and Einstein would have learned Hebrew and attended one of the local synagogues. Profoundly affected by his father's premature death in 1899, Einstein showed little interest in maintaining or reforming Jewish religious tradition or in participating in the emerging Jewish cultural renaissance. He went to Berlin and quickly established himself as a writer and critic at the forefront of expressionism, publishing mainly in Franz Pfemfert's journal *Die Aktion*. His 1915 pamphlet on African sculpture, *Negerplastik,* was more than just an example of European avant-garde fascination with the primitive; it broke new ground in recognizing African masks and carvings as vital and self-present works resistant to historicizing Western discourse. The

---

2 For detailed accounts see Kiefer 1994, Meffre 2002, Creighton / Kramer 2012.

pamphlet further crystallizes Einstein's early belief that art, if it claimed to have any power beyond itself, needed to have a basis in religion or some other form of allegiance.

Einstein's disillusionment with the German war effort stemmed partly from his experience of anti-Semitism in the German army. Perhaps as a result of this, he turned to political commitment. At the end of 1918 he was actively involved in the short-lived soldiers' council in Brussels (where he had served in the German military government), and he continued his radical-left commitment upon return to Berlin. He spoke at the funeral of Rosa Luxemburg and involved himself with Grosz, Herzfelde, and others in the political wing of Berlin dada. His essay "Zur primitiven Kunst" (On Primitive Art), first published in Rubiner's anthology *Die Gemeinschaft* (Einstein 1920), is an avant-garde manifesto of sorts, as it welcomes the end of art and the beginning of an egalitarian politics which would render art obsolete. In 1926 Einstein published an influential volume on modern art, *Die Kunst des 20. Jahrhunderts*, which went through three editions in just five years, the last containing a substantial chapter on the "romantic generation," the surrealists. In 1928 he permanently settled in Paris, where he joined the dissident surrealist circles around Bataille and Leiris, with whom he would edit the magazine, *Documents*. He was advisory editor to *transition*, the famous small magazine which brought European avant-garde art and literature to an Anglophone audience. In his final years, Einstein drafted *Die Fabrikation der Fiktionen*, his theory of the avant-garde, wherein he criticizes the European avant-garde (and, implicitly, his own contributions to it) for its ultimate failure to have any social impact. Einstein's account, at once scathing and mournful, repeatedly turns on the notion that the avant-garde failed to translate artistic subjectivity into a broader, more objective "*Gemeinschaftsgefühl*" [sense of community] (Einstein 1973, 42–43, 74). Running through *Die Fabrikation* is a broadly Marxist perspective which parallels elements of Frankfurt School theory, most notably Peter Bürger's account of the failure of the historical avant-garde to reach beyond its own institutionalized status and achieve lasting social change.

According to Marianne Kröger, it was Einstein's experiences of war, anti-Semitism, and, above all, exile which compelled him to confront Jewishness as an important part of his social and cultural identity (Kröger 2009, 158). Confronting Jewishness did not, however, mean emphasizing his own Jewish background; he did not, for example, produce an autobiography in which this background was elaborated (as did Ernst Toller and Alfred Döblin, among others). This was partly because he regarded the genre as inherently "heroizing," a flimsy means to prop up what he labelled "the wavering self-confidence of a minority under threat," i.e., of avant-garde artists and intellectuals (Einstein 1973, 93). Important and detailed studies by Portmann / Wolf (2006) and Kröger (2009) offer much in revealing and assessing the Jewish aspects of Einstein's life and work, even if they effectively affirm the "heroic" notion of biographical identity that he dismissed.³

Despite Einstein's own scepticism towards the biographical model, he did write a "Kleine Autobiographie" (Little Autobiography, 1930). First published in a Festschrift celebrating publisher Gustav Kiepenheuer's fiftieth birthday, the short text subverts the autobiographical genre and becomes an essay in non-identity. Comprising just a few (generous) pages in the Festschrift, the pithy text recalls Einstein's upbringing in the Rhineland and in Baden. It eschews overt references to Judaism or Jewishness; yet the silence speaks volumes about the "small" or minority status of Jewish culture within a larger field of hegemonic cultures. The text is about discovering the "Other," be it in the form of working-class families and their children, or other religious communities. (The text mentions Calvinists, Lutherans, Catholics, and the Herrnhuter Gemeinde.) In the one instance where Einstein addresses Jewishness directly, he presents a short scene involving a kind but "different" uncle who was originally from the East. The scene invokes a typical Shtetl narrative, enabling Einstein to present Eastern European childhood and diaspora as part of the all-encompassing otherness encountered in Karlsruhe (Einstein 1985, 109–111).

During his Parisian years of exile, Einstein embarked on a project entitled "BEB II." Unfinished, fragmentary, and existing only in note form, it includes scenes and episodes from Einstein's childhood and adolescence, and reactivates the early Bebuquin figure to explore "*die jüdische existenz*" (Jewish existence) through the lenses of avant-garde activity and exile. Unsurprisingly, the examination of an autobiographical self through the Bebuquin figure yields multiple negativity, with Einstein invoking standard tropes such as diaspora, persecution, and geopolitical displacement. When Einstein explores the cultural origins of his avant-gardism, he dismisses it as a product of circumstances: "*all diese artistik ist I. die jüdische heimatlosigkeit, II. die sueddeutsche ueberkultiviertheit*" [all this artistry is 1. Jewish lack of Heimat, 2. the hypertrophied culture of Southern Germany] (cited in Kröger 2009, 146). Writing in exile, Einstein here turns to history and geography in order to explain his stances as radical antibourgeois, social outsider, and member of a minority.

---

3 Cf. Portmann and Wolf's assertion that "*Einsteins ganzes Leben und Werk* [!] *ist dadurch eine einzige Auseinandersetzung, zuerst mit dem jüdischen Gott und später mit dem spinozistischen Gott oder dem Judentum ohne Gott. Einstein entwickelte sich dabei vom gläubigen jüdischen Mystiker* [!] *über den Juden ohne Gott zum dunklen Aufklärer*" [Einstein's whole life and work thus becomes a singular confrontation, first with the Jewish God, then with the Spinozist God, or Judaism without God. In the process, Einstein developed from being a believing Jewish mystic to a Jew without God to a dark rationalist.] (Portmann / Wolf 2006, 172).

In "BEB II," Einstein further revisits the avant-garde concern with questions of religion and God. In a note dated 18 February 1933, he writes: *"ich sehe immer mehr werde ich allein sein. jude, deutschsprechend, in frankreich. jude ohne gott und ohne kenntnis unserer vergangenen zeit"* [I see I am going to be alone more and more. Jew, German-speaking, in France. Jew without God and without knowledge of our past] (cited in Kröger 2009, 148). The community Einstein is referring to may be the Jewish diaspora; yet it is one that has discarded tradition. The quote continues: *"deutschsprechend, doch gewillt die deutsche sprache nicht wie meine landsleute und gleichzüngige faul und müde versacken zu lassen"* [German-speaking but determined not to let the German language decay, lazy and tired like my countrymen]. Expelled from the political community sustained by ideas of national and ethnic identity, Einstein affirms the German language as a space of cultural belonging. But another note from "BEB II" talks about language in these terms: *"EIN TRAINING GOTT ZU VERGESSEN? Überall wischt er den Namen Gottes aus – DAS WORT selber nicht mehr selber zu kennen, damit alle alte Literatur aus"* [A TRAINING IN ORDER TO FORGET GOD? He wipes out the name of God everywhere – not to know THE WORD itself, and thus wipes out all old literature] (cited in Kröger 2009, 154). The doubling of "selber" complicates the reflexive relation between self and language. Such acts of erasure evoke the avant-garde gesture of destroying tradition orientated towards the "name," but in doing so they reveal what may be the fundamental contradiction of the avant-garde: that even the most radical negativity towards tradition and language cannot escape their combined power.

Einstein's early prose fiction, *Bebuquin oder die Dilettanten des Wunders* (1912), besides largely sustaining his reputation as an innovative writer, allegorizes the search for identity, community, and temporality that differ radically from the normative regime of bourgeois modernity. The fragmented narrative, ironic and absurdist in turn, presents young Bebuquin's search for existential meaning as he passes through a bohemian world of late-night bars and theatres; intent on leaving behind an unproductive life of reflection and ennui, he discusses (albeit incongruously) philosophical ideas about logic, religion, and art. Bebuquin's composite foreign name renders him an assemblage of contradictory elements, the childlike and the bookish. Moreover, he functions as the author's puppet or mannequin, as the exhilaratingly meta-fictional text makes clear at several points. "Bookish" references abound, including some to Jewish ideas. At one point, the possibility of the titular "miracle" is figured as an ecstatic transgression of the boundaries of self, speech, and literary form in the vein of

Martin Buber's model of ecstatic language, before being cynically dismissed.[4] For Erich Kleinschmidt, the hapless protagonist's name is a Frenchified corruption of "*be-buqin*" [in bottles], which, on a literal level, would resonate with the story's bohemian settings and general sense of absurdity. Kleinschmidt further suggests that Einstein re-writes the Hebrew phrase in order to conceal the "name" (Einstein 1985, 73). Reviewing *Bebuquin* in 1913, Kurt Hiller read the text as Jewish avant-garde prose, asking rhetorically whether Einstein might have written the "Semitic Faust" (Hiller 1913, 173). By this question the critic means that Einstein's prose and Bebuquin's search remain rigorously abstract and intellectual, averse to any compromise with the earthly world. Einstein's narrative features a paternal (or Mephistophelian) *bohémien*, called Nebukadnezar Böhm, who is heard quoting from both Spinoza and Jacob Böhme, i.e., the reflective-critical and the mystical poles of early modern Jewish thought, which, it might be said, were continued in the early twentieth century by Hermann Cohen and Martin Buber. If Böhm allegorizes paternal tradition, then the symbolic son, Bebuquin, is compelled to pursue both reflection and mysticism in the form of prayers and dialogues. Bebuquin is often seen as a character who reflects some of Einstein's own concerns – religious and epistemological doubt; the rebellion against the literal and symbolic father; antipathy towards the bourgeois world (Schmidt-Bergmann 1992, 10) – and a licence to experiment with literary form and language. Portmann and Wolf go so far as to read *Bebuquin* as a *"religiöser Entwicklungsroman"* [novel of religious development] that closely mirrors Einstein's confrontation with Jewish thought in particular (Portmann / Wolf 2006, 144); however, their biographical reading necessarily downplays the text's formal, avant-gardist features. For Heidemarie Oehm, Einstein conducts in *Bebuquin* a kind of "messianic experiment," specifically in relation to the idea that one's most profound self-recognition is also the point at which one's self might coincide with God, or the divine self (Oehm 1976, 177). Messianism, however, is but one of multiple layers of allusion, and it is one which the text takes to its absurd conclusion: *"Zwei Methoden gibt's, entweder man glaubt und ist bei Gott, ist Mystiker und verblödet an einer nagelnden Idee fixe, oder man platzt und wird gesprengt. Immer ist der Wahnsinn das einzig vermutbare Resultat"* [There are two methods: either you believe and are with God, a mystic imbecile with a stupid idée fixe, or else you explode and blow up. Either way, the only possible result is madness] (Einstein 1980, 112).

---

4 In *Ekstatische Konfessionen* (1909), Buber defined ecstatic language as the language of images and dreams that transcends the world of everyday communication; this language contains the desire, and also the inability, to say the unsayable. Buber's ideas were important for expressionist debates about language. Cf. Anz / Stark 1982, 578–581.

Whereas *Bebuquin* is clustered around the religious idea of the miracle that disrupts a world dominated by logic and reason, Einstein's critical essays use political and philosophical terms to postulate an avant-garde which both disrupts the bourgeois world of history and tradition while simultaneously constructing a new world which is based upon a shared creative vision. In "Anmerkungen" (1912), Einstein distinguishes between absolute, avant-gardist "revolt" and mere "dialectical opposition," which operates within the framework of reason and logic (Einstein 1980, 122–123), while his more complex piece, "Totalität," (1914) outlines an aesthetics of the avant-garde (Einstein 1980, 223–229).

The representation of Jewish characters in Einstein's work presents another angle from which to consider identity and communities. This representation is generally in the context of social and political critique rather than religious affinity. A satire published during the First World War about a fictitious "*Gesellschaft für religiöse Gründungen*," or "*G.F.R.G.*" (Society for the Founding of Religions), features a wily Swabian businessman who cons a Jewish banker into providing money to recruit "*falsche Messiasse*" [false Messiahs] from the local lunatic asylum (Einstein 1980, 135–165). Other stories feature Jewish merchants named "Kohn," "Levi," or "Poschatzer," who invariably function as a critique of how art, culture, and religion become tradable commodities (e.g., Einstein 1981, 34). Einstein's dada satires feature the post-war profiteer, often Jewish and of lower-class background, whose newfound wealth compels him to mimic the odious behaviours of the ruling class. Activating anti-Semitic stereotypes, the figure of the "Schieber" is found in the discourse and imagination of the political Left, as exemplified in the dada magazine *Der blutige Ernst* (Bloody Seriousness) of 1919, which was first edited by John Höxter and then by Einstein and George Grosz. Despite this, Einstein's view of why the German revolution failed was largely based on awareness of the continued hold of capitalism in post-1918 Germany. However, a special issue of *Der blutige Ernst*, entitled *Der Jude*, challenged the political expediency of conspiracy theories that blamed the Jews for both the defeat in the war and the revolution.[5] Dada's critique notes that both the reactionary right and the communist or socialist left resorted to stereotypes which presented the Jews as agents of both capitalism and communism. Far from being an instance of Jewish self-hatred, Einstein's critique of Jewish profiteers and a Jewish upper middle-class embodied in the refined "Kurfuerstendammjuden" seeks to expose

---

5 A case in point is Mehring's satire: "Die Schuld der Juden am Weltkrieg, der Revolution und den nivellierenden Witterungsverhältnissen" (The Guilt of the Jews for the World War, the Revolution, and the Levelling Weather Conditions).

a mindset in modern capitalism which turns culture and religion into valuable commodities.⁶

Einstein's play *Die schlimme Botschaft* (1921, its title a direct negation of the Christian "*frohe Botschaft*") is set in contemporary, post-revolutionary Germany (Einstein 1981, 146–199). It presents Jesus as a dangerous anarchist who challenges the authority of church and state, but whose potentially messianic power is grotesquely curtailed by social and political conditions. These include rampant anti-Semitic stereotyping by odious "*Odinsmänner*" and by a sinister pseudo-academic "*Magister*," who holds forth about racial characteristics (Einstein 1981, 176 and 180–181). The play turns the crucifixion into a media spectacle which provides new business opportunities. Both Jews and Germans profiteer from the public denigration and the killing of the foreign other, which at one point is staged as an anti-Semitic pogrom (Einstein 1981, 176), while images of the crucifixion are said to be worth more if they were marketed as expressionist art (Einstein 1981, 185–186). Underneath the trenchant satire, Einstein presents Jesus as someone who possesses political and religious integrity which is kept distinct from forms of Christian, nationalist, and anti-Semitic ideology. This integrity seems to rest upon his desire to build a community of others, even if the project fails spectacularly given the economic interests of Jewish capitalists and financiers. Beyond the play, in the real world, a powerful lobby agitated successfully for blasphemy charges to be brought against the play's author (the first such trial in the new Weimar Republic), resulting in Einstein being sentenced to pay a substantial fine.⁷

When he writes critically about Jewish artists, Einstein tends to use the first-person plural pronoun "*wir*," rather than the impersonal pronoun "*man*," which he uses elsewhere to describe individual artists' actions or choices. His use of "*wir*" in relation to Jewish artists suggests that he feels an affinity with these artists in terms of belonging to a minority. However, the community of "*wir*" equally suggests the minority of avant-garde artists within mainstream culture, and the community of artists in a marketplace that turns culture into monetary value. "*Nous sommes des juifs et c'est bien comme ça*," Einstein writes laconically to the Polish-born painter Moise Kisling, in November 1921 (Meffre 1997, 117).⁸ Einstein's comments about Jewish avant-garde artists are not extensive; they are nevertheless important, for he views the European avant-garde movements as a whole, and,

---

6 Portmann / Wolf read this particular critique as a form of allegiance, as Einstein's desire to fight for Judaism and the Jews (Portmann / Wolf 2006, 172).
7 For a brief account of the trial and the various charges (including one of anti-Semitism against Einstein), see Kröger 2009, 98.
8 This letter forms part of an extensive correspondence in which Einstein can be seen to explore Jewishness, in the context of increasing anti-Semitism and nationalism in Germany.

although he operates with concepts of identity, community and tradition, his discussion of Jewishness and avant-gardism has the potential to destabilize those very concepts.

The fragility of the avant-gardist community derives not merely from the fact that it includes Jewish artists and writers, but also from the realities of geographic and cultural displacement. In this vein, Amadeo Modigliani is cast as "*der immer fremde Jude*" [the Jew who will always be foreign], who lacks creative inventiveness but is a skilfully eclectic painter borrowing from both European and non-European models ranging from Botticelli to Cézanne and African sculpture. It is in this sense that Einstein can claim for the uprooted Jewish artist a sense of cultural belonging: "*der italienische Jude gehört ganz in die französische Malerei*" [the Italian Jew belongs fully to French painting] (Einstein 1996, 89). Einstein, the cosmopolitan avant-gardist, draws here on national discourse in order to emphasize these Jewish artists' debt and contribution to French painting; his discourse thus responds to a debate in post-war France that branded large swathes of the artistic avant-garde as non-French, Jewish and "*boche*" (Golan 2010).

Elsewhere in his art criticism, Einstein deploys the standard trope of Jewish displacement and international mobility to other effects. Writing in the 1920s, Einstein casts Kisling, Marc Chagall, and Leon Bakst, the Russian stage designer of the Ballets Russes, as "Orientals," artists originally from the East who are marked by an "*ethnographisch fremden Leben der Juden*" [ethnographically foreign life of the Jews] (Einstein 1996, 234). This phrase reprises the standard Western trope which constructs Eastern Jews as an isolated, culturally distinct minority. But, Einstein implies, as avant-garde artists who rejected or subverted regional or national styles, they were also artistic outsiders. In an article on Kisling, Einstein, sometimes repeating material verbatim, narrates the Polish-born artist's attempt at finding acceptance in the West in three stages; the specific form of the essay points to the idea of time as being non-linear, and the interrelatedness of Eastern and Western cultures and times (Einstein 1981, 205–213). Jewishness functions here as something that disrupts historical continuity through geographical mobility, offering some degree of escape from the constraints of being a religious, artistic, and social outsider – even if such escape entails a return to figuration. Einstein writes similarly about Bakst and Chagall, tracking these artists' trajectories to Paris, the geographical and cultural center of the Western avant-garde. Einstein comes close to associating Jewish otherness in the arts with a transnational or cosmopolitan practice (cf. Kröger 2009, 111). Bakst even becomes an artistic type, the Jewish "*Emigrant, dessen Geschick die Schicksallosigkeit ist*" [emigré whose fate is that of not having a fate]. This punning phrase ("*Geschick*" can mean "fate" as well as "skill") also alludes to the fact that the history of Jewish persecution ensured a perception of the Jews as a people who cannot escape their destiny. For

Einstein, Bakst's eclecticism is a series of cultural appropriations and transformations which oscillate between East and West, Russian and French, Jewish and non-Jewish influences and traditions, both resisting and confirming these categories. Bakst's muted avant-gardism is due to "*dem intellektuellen Geschick, der kritischen Begabtheit des Juden, der oft eher vermittelt oder umschreibt als ursprünglich schafft*" [the intellectual skill, the critical talent of the Jew who is frequently a mediator and someone who paraphrases, [more] than he is an original creator] (Einstein 1981, 352).[9] Writing in the late 1920s, Einstein suggests that it is not so much an innate lack of originality but rather the facts of geographical migration and cultural mediation that characterize Jewish avant-gardism, and that the space created by such encounters may temporarily suspend any mechanisms of exclusion and generate the hope for a new, binding vision of society.

A different outcome of an encounter between East and West, Jewishness and cubist avant-garde, is registered when Einstein considers Marc Chagall's artistic and geographical trajectories. Using the impersonal pronoun to indicate distance and disapproval, Einstein describes how Chagall responded to the innovations of Matisse, the cubists, and Delaunay: "*Man griff die neuen Formen und füllte sie mit russischer oder jüdischer Ethnologie; das 'Simultané' des Delaunay wurde episch*" [One seized the new forms and filled them with Russian or Jewish ethnology; Delaunay's simultané became epic] (Einstein 1996, 235). Chagall's ability to adopt a new formal language was always competing with Jewish content, with the result that the dynamism of cubist pictorial space becomes fixed so as to accommodate quite specific content: "*Haggadah und Epos werden zum 'Simultané' geschichtet*" [haggadah and the epic become layered into the simultané] (Einstein 1996, 236). Chagall's combination of new form and old content starkly indicates issues of identity, community, and temporality which are often at stake in this version of a Jewish avant-garde; yet Einstein finds Chagall's solution too obvious and facile. He singles out Chagall's painting *Feiertag* (Feast Day, 1914), which shows a rabbi on whose head stands a miniature version of himself, facing backwards. For Einstein, this doubling and reversal, along with the difference in scale, may allude to the fragility of the religious community and its place in time. However, according to Einstein, rather than encountering a visual revolution, the viewer is instead caught in an impasse between old content and new form; or as Einstein puts it in reference to one of Chagall's favorite pictorial tropes, "*man fliegt zwischen Mythe und Witz*" [one flies between myth and joke] (Einstein 1996, 236).

---

9 Einstein first used the notion of "*Umschreiben*," or paraphrase, in an early essay, "Paraphrase" of 1911, to critique derivative, unambitious and unoriginal culture, without giving it specifically Jewish connotations (Einstein 1980, 167–169).

It is politics, rather than Jewish ethnography, that becomes significant in Einstein's view of Suprematism and Constructivism.[10] Einstein identifies a clear parallel between the sociopolitical revolution which nationalized private property, and the artistic revolution of non-representationalism: "*Man zerschlug mit Recht die Dinge, diese rückständig versteinerten Übereinkünfte* [...] *enteignete die Malerei vom Motiv*" [One rightly smashed the objects, these retrograde and petrified conventions [...] expropriated the motif from painting] (Einstein 1996, 239–240). But this parallel would become subject to a historical dialectic, as Einstein suggests when he remarks (in reference to El Lissitzky) on the striking contrast between Suprematist abstraction from reality and the "*gesteigerte Wirklichkeitssinn*" [heightened sense of reality] in post-revolutionary Russia (Einstein 1996, 239). He notes another version of the contrast: "*Man hatte den alten Fetisch Objekt ausgetrieben, doch die seelische Gestimmtheit, nämlich die alte Rechtsgläubigkeit war geblieben*" [One had expelled the object, that old fetish, but the inner mood, that is the old belief in the Law, remained] (ibid.). This leads Einstein to suggest that what appears radically non-representational and utopian is merely the flipside of a very old metaphysics (ibid.). His reference to the law, and religious law, resonates here, not merely because it is made in relation to Jewish Suprematists and Constructivists, but because it is shorthand for the avant-garde's failure to create a binding vision for a new culture and society that would fully replace religious tradition.

In conclusion, Einstein's writings offer a range of ideas about the relationship between Jews, Jewishness, and the avant-garde. For Einstein, there is no essential or elective relationship between Jews and the avant-garde, but only various structural similarities or analogies between Jewishness and the constitution of the European avant-garde of the early twentieth century. The analogical relationship derives more from Einstein's view of the avant-garde, his commitment to it, and the role he thinks avant-gardism should play in the modern world, than Jews do from his own biographical and social experience as a German Jew. In short, Einstein, the self-declared "*jude ohne gott*," commits the avant-garde – operating as it does in the age when God has died – to playing the same role that Jewish religious tradition played: providing a strong bond for a community of "others." It is in this sense that Einstein regards avant-garde activity not primarily as a radical destruction of tradition, but as a form of renegotiation to create, ultimately, a new tradition. Einstein differs, however, from proponents of the Jewish cultural renaissance or of messianic expressionism in that his idea of avant-gardist rene-

---

10 For a fuller account, see Michel 2012.

gotiation is predicated on both the spirit of discontinuity and a radical critique of contemporary culture and society.

On a more structural level (though this also derives from Einstein's and the avant-garde's historical situation), references to Jewishness in Einstein's writings – whether biographical, fictional, or critical – draw attention to the continuity of the Other in modern culture, the discursive and imaginative construction of the Other, and the resulting social and cultural marginalization. As such, the structural analogy of Jews and the avant-garde would be able to highlight questions of social, cultural, and artistic identity and community, and approach such questions in a way that is neither conceptually nor historically fixed, but open-ended. This might suggest that Jewishness in the avant-garde constitutes a heightened form of an "uncommon community," a modus operandi that, as Vivian Liska has argued in relation to German-Jewish modernist writers before and after the Shoah (Liska 2011, 7–21), both sustains and subverts established ideas of community in the face of unprecedented upheaval and rupture.

On this structural level, Einstein's writings can be seen to map the "uncommon communities" of the European avant-garde by invoking, sporadically or implicitly, the analogy with Jewish tradition and experience. Both are orientated towards a transnational, cosmopolitan community of "others"; both are liable to a complex interplay of identification and difference, of complicity and resistance, of belonging and exclusion, to constant negotiation of the parameters by which identities are discursively and imaginatively constructed. If the avant-garde artist operates in a cultural space that might be structurally analogous to that of the Jews in modern society – the status of outsider, or minority, and identifiable as such – then the avant-garde might capitalize on its own marginal or exilic position and destabilize the rigid fixity and putative universality of national and other identity concepts it finds itself subjected to. Moreover, if modelled on the Jewish analogy, the "uncommon communities" of the European avant-garde would be shifting and mobile, not merely as regards national, ethnic, or linguistic borders, but also in terms of history and temporality. In the early twentieth century, both European Judaism and the avant-garde were entwined in Western modernity, to the extent that they shared a negative or sceptical approach to tradition, even though each remained – or should remain, as Einstein believed of the avant-garde – committed to creating a new, binding tradition in the absence of the old one. For Einstein, the avant-garde artist's individualism must be bound into a larger sense of community, within which the "*Einsamkeit*," the loneliness and alone-ness of the modern Jewish artist participating in the cultural avant-garde, might be contained within a form of "*Gemeinsamkeit*," a fragile, shifting community sustained by shared commitment to the establishment of a new, utopian world rather than to exclusive maintenance of tradition. However, for Einstein and many other Jewish avant-garde artists and writers of the first half of the twentieth century, this would remain a vision whose time was yet to come.

Bibliography

Anz, Thomas, and Michael Stark (eds.). *Expressionismus: Manifeste und Dokumente zur deutschen Literatur 1910–1920*. Stuttgart: Metzler, 1982.
Creighton, Nicola, and Andreas Kramer (eds.). *Carl Einstein und die europäische Avantgarde. Carl Einstein and the European Avant-Garde*. Berlin: De Gruyter, 2012.
Einstein, Carl. "Der Leib des Armen." *Kameraden der Menschheit*. Ed. Ludwig Rubiner. Potsdam: Kiepenheuer, 1919. 85–87.
Einstein, Carl. "Zur primitiven Kunst." *Die Gemeinschaft: Dokumente der geistigen Weltwende*. Ed. Ludwig Rubiner. Potsdam: Kiepenheuer, 1920. 175–176.
Einstein, Carl. "Gedichte I – V" and "Der Leib des Armen." *Schofar: Lieder und Legenden jüdischer Dichter*. Ed. Karl Otten. Neuwied: Luchterhand, 1962. 186–192.
Einstein, Carl. *Die Fabrikation der Fiktionen*. Ed. Sibylle Penkert. Reinbek: Rowohlt, 1973.
Einstein, Carl. *Werke*. 4 vols. 1980–1992. Vol. 1: *1908–1918*. Ed. Jens-Peter Kwasny. Berlin: Medusa, 1980. Vol. 2: *1919–1928*. Ed. Marion Schmidt. Berlin: Medusa, 1981. Vol. 3: *1929–1940*. Ed. Marion Schmid and Liliane Meffre. Berlin: Medusa, 1985. Vol. 4: *Texte aus dem Nachlass*. Ed. Hermann Haarmann and Klaus Siebenhaar. Berlin: Fannei & Walz, 1992.
Einstein, Carl. *Bebuquin*. Ed. Erich Kleinschmidt. Stuttgart: Reclam, 1985.
Einstein, Carl. *Die Kunst des 20. Jahrhunderts*. Ed. Uwe Fleckner and Thomas Gaethgens. Berlin: Fannei & Walz, 1996.
Golan, Romy. "The École Français versus the École de Paris: The Debate about the Status of Jewish Artists in Paris between the Wars." *Jewish Dimensions in Modern Visual Culture: Antisemitism, Assimilation, Affirmation*. Ed. Rose-Carol Washton Long, Matthew Baigell and Milly Heyd. Waltham, MA: Brandeis University Press, 2010. 77–89.
Hiller, Kurt. "Bemerkungen zu *Bebuquin*." *Die Weisheit der Langenweile. Eine Zeit- und Streitschrift*. Leipzig: K. Wolff, 1913. 171–177.
Kiefer, Klaus H. *Diskurswandel im Werk Carl Einsteins: Ein Beitrag zur Theorie und Geschichte der europäischen Avantgarde*. Tübingen: Niemeyer, 1994.
Kiefer, Klaus H. "Carl Einstein." *Metzler Lexikon der deutsch-jüdischen Literatur: Jüdische Autorinnen und Autoren deutscher Sprache von der Aufklärung bis zur Gegenwart*. Ed. Andreas B. Kilcher. Stuttgart and Weimar: Metzler, 2000, 131–134.
Kröger, Marianne. "Carl Einstein als jüdischer Autor? Überlegungen zu einem neuen Forschungsparadigma." *"Jüdische Ethik" und Anarchismus im spanischen Bürgerkrieg: Simone Weil – Carl Einstein – Etta Federn*. Frankfurt/M.: Peter Lang, 2009, 63–159.
Liska, Vivian. *Fremde Gemeinschaft: Deutsch-jüdische Literatur der Moderne*. Göttingen: Wallstein, 2011.
Meffre, Liliane. "Lettres de Carl Einstein à Moise Kisling (1920–1924)." *Les Cahiers du Musée National d'Art Moderne* 62 (Winter 1997) : 74–123.
Meffre, Liliane. *Carl Einstein: Itinéraires d'une pensée moderne*. Paris: Presses de l'Université de Paris-Sorbonne, 2002.

Michel, Andreas. "The False Collective: Carl Einstein and the Russian Avant-Garde." *Carl Einstein und die europäische Avantgarde. Carl Einstein and the European Avant-Garde.* Eds. Nicola Creighton and Andreas Kramer. Berlin: De Gruyter, 2012. 242–254.

Oehm, Heidemarie. *Die Kunsttheorie Carl Einsteins.* Munich: Wilhelm Fink, 1976.

Portmann, Werner, and Siegbert Wolf. "Carl Einstein (1885–1940), dunkler Aufklärer zwischen Gott und Nichts – eine Spurensuche." *"Ja, ich kämpfte": Von 'Luftmenschen', Kindern des Schtetls und der Revolution: Biographien radikaler Jüdinnen und Juden.* Münster: Unrast, 2006. 130–194.

Schmidt-Bergmann, Hansgeorg. *"Die Stadt der Langeweile": Carl Einstein und Karlsruhe.* Spuren, vol. 19. Marbach: Deutsche Schillergesellschaft, 1992.

Siebenhaar, Klaus (ed.). *Carl Einstein: Prophet der Avantgarde.* Berlin: Fannei & Walz, 1991.

Washton Long, Rose-Carol, Matthew Baigell and Milly Heyd (eds.). *Jewish Dimensions in Modern Visual Culture: Antisemitism, Assimilation, Affirmation.* Waltham, MA: Brandeis University Press, 2010.

Wolfenstein, Alfred. *Jüdisches Wesen und neue Dichtung.* Berlin: Reiss, 1922.

Laëtitia Tordjman
Challenging the Literary Community: The Warsaw Yiddish Avant-Garde and *Khalyastre*

Warsaw in the early 1920s was a boisterous "Jewish metropolis" (Dynner and Guesnet 2015), "the center of all the centers of Yiddish literature" (Shmeruk 1993, 129), and, according to some contemporaries, "the heart of a Jewish national 'kingdom'"[1] (Moss 2015, 390). During the Second Polish Republic, with nearly one-third of its population being Jewish, Warsaw reflected almost all the Jewish cultural and political opinions of the time, from deep ideals of assimilation to radical anarchism, from Hasidism to Zionism and cultural nationalism.[2] This heterogeneous milieu became the playground of one of the most turbulent Yiddish avant-garde groups: di Khalyastre – "the gang."

In interwar Warsaw, "Jewish nationalism" was one of the main political and cultural movements and took every possible form, from political territorialism to cultural diasporism. Despite the fact that Polish nationalist feelings were increasing at the time – and concomitantly anti-Semitism was intensifying amongst a large segment of the Polish population – Jewish nationalism could still express itself without much fear of censorship.[3] In its cultural form, nationalism had a profound impact on literary production in Yiddish and Hebrew. As concerns Yiddish literature, this "national" tendency dates to the beginnings of what is generally acknowledged as "modern Yiddish literature." It was at least partly influenced by a kind of essentialist "Herderian" belief in the power of the vernacular language, a "family tongue"[4] that can reveal the "richness of the folk" and the "treasures of popular culture" (Sauder 2003[5]). By the turn of the twentieth century, at a moment when national emancipation was becoming a general concern for minorities throughout Central and Eastern Europe, the three Yiddish "masters" – Mendele Moykher Sforim, Sholem Aleichem, and Y.L. Peretz – had laid the foundation stone for Yiddish culturalism. The Yiddishists' purpose was to promote a

---
1 Moss quotes Moyshe Zonshayn, *Yidish-varshe* (Buenos Aires: Tsentral-farband fun poylishe yidn in Argentine, 1954, 23–24).
2 For extensive information about interwar Warsaw Jewish political culture, see Moss 2015.
3 On 28 June 1919, Polish leaders signed the "Little Treaty of Versailles" (also known as the "Minorities Treaty"), which promised equal treatment and legal protection for national minorities.
4 Abramovitsh speaks of "the language of my people" when referring to Yiddish. See multiple occurrences in his correspondence gathered in *Dos Mendele bukh* (Mayzel 1959).
5 Sauder refers to Johann Gottfried Herder's *Werke*, I: *Frühe Schriften 1764–1772*. Frankfurt a. M.: Ulrich Gaier, 1985.

secular Yiddish culture as the basis of Jewish collective identity. Their works display their attempts to negotiate between heterogeneous literary influences and different conceptions of literature's impact on the "people" or the "nation" and of the figure of the author (as a spokesperson or as a singular poetic voice). These tensions echo throughout Yiddish literary production and seem to have multiplied in myriad ways in interwar Warsaw, not least as they paralleled the political and intellectual turmoils of the time.

For the young aspiring Yiddish poets and writers who had just moved to Warsaw, the cultural scene offered many opportunities: on one hand, Jewish cultural institutions like the *Fareyn fun Yidishe Literatn un Zhurnalistn in Varshe*[6] (Association of Jewish Writers and Journalists in Warsaw) and its literary journals *Varshever almanakh* (Warsaw almanac, 1923) and *Varshever shriftn* (Warsaw writings, 1926)[7] functioned as social meeting places and raised funds for young authors; on the other hand, their revolutionary aspirations resonated with a cosmopolitan and bohemian lifestyle that promoted an autonomous modernist literature, emancipated from any political or national goal.

This essay focuses more specifically on one particular journal, *Khalyastre*, named after the Khalyastre group and published in 1922.[8] This journal provides new insights into the Yiddish avant-garde's project. It may be understood as a polyphonic literary ensemble[9] and interpreted as an attempt to challenge and reshape the Yiddish literary community. By recalling Jacques Rancière's analysis of avant-garde aesthetic practices as a "redistribution of the sensible" (Rancière 2004), I argue that *Khalyastre* shapes a kind of non-elitist cosmopolitanism, which challenges both the figures of the Yiddish author and of the Yiddish public. My essay begins by contextualizing the publication of *Khalyastre* in the Warsaw Yiddish literary milieu and with a more global perspective regarding some typical avant-garde trends of the early twentieth century. It then turns to literary analysis of specific poems and short stories in order to illustrate how the Yiddish literary imaginary is challenged and renegotiated in *Khalyastre*, thus unveiling fluid and

---

[6] I use the guidelines of the YIVO Institute to transliterate Yiddish.

[7] First an apolitical institution, the "Warsaw Association of Jewish Writers and Journalists" "gradually became identified with radical leftist Yiddishist parties (the Bund and the Communists)" (Cohen, 2010).

[8] The Khalyastre movement participated in the publication of numerous journals: *Yung-yidish* in 1919, with the Łódź group; *Ringen* (1921), under the editorship of Michal Weichert and Alter-Sholem Kacyzne; and in the period of 1922–1924 *Khalyastre* (first published in Warsaw in 1921, and then in Paris in 1924), *Vog* (The Scale, edited by Melech Ravitch), and *Albatros*, Uri Tsevi Grinberg's expressionist journal.

[9] As an avant-garde text, *Khalyastre* is fragmented, unfinished. And yet, a kind of cohesion emerges when all the singular authorial voices resonate together.

complex identities. Finally, it questions the kind of renewed literary community that implicitly emerges throughout the journal.

The Publication of *Khalyastre*: Yiddish Warsaw in the 1920s and Beyond

Long before the 1920s, Warsaw was already a dominant center of Yiddish literature. According to Chone Shmeruk (1993), Yiddish literary life developed rapidly between 1890 and 1905, thanks to the massive increase in publishing houses and to the presence of leading literary figures in the city – including Y.L. Peretz. Moreover, even before 1914, the proliferation of Yiddish newspapers such as *Der Veg* (The Way, first edited by Zvi-Hirsch Prilutski in 1905), *Haynt* (Today) and *Der Moment* (The Moment) offered a large arena to young journalists and writers; publications in these newspapers shaped the literary tastes of the Yiddish public, by providing a familiarity with modern literature. Finally, massive Jewish urban migrations brought newcomers from various backgrounds to the Yiddish literary scene: "The colorful and many-faceted Warsaw Yiddish center was the creation of generations of non-native writers and cultural activists, not only at its beginnings, but also in the eighteen-eighties [...]. One can [...] assert, with some certainty, that it continued to apply to Warsaw until the Holocaust" (Shmeruk 1993, 129).

These factors may explain the myriad opinions in Warsaw Jewish political and cultural spheres in the early 1920s, including the non-elitist cosmopolitanism of the youngest Yiddish avant-garde writers.[10] The latter were of course also deeply sensitive to modernist literary movements such as Russian cubo-futurism and German expressionism, whose proponents congregated in interwar Warsaw despite the political and social uncertainties that followed the end of the First World War, the Polish-Soviet War (February 1919 – March 1921), and the birth of the Second Polish Republic.

Khalyastre, as a group, appeared in 1919 with publication of the journal *Yungyidish* (Young Yiddish, published by Moyshe Broderzon), and lasted until 1924. It was a time of intense creativity for the poets, artists, and novelists who published multiple articles and essays in various journals, and organized controversial

---

10 Interestingly enough, none of the major figures in the *Khalyastre* group are originally from Warsaw: Perets Markish (1895–1952), born in Polonnoye (Volhynia) left Kiev for Warsaw in 1921, Uri Tsevi Grinberg (1896–1981), born in Galicia, arrived the same year from Lwôw. Melech Ravitch (1893–1976) was born in Radymno, eastern Galicia, while Oyzer Varshavski (1898–1944), born in Sochaczew, settled with his family in Warsaw at the age of fourteen.

public events such as exhibitions and poetry readings. According to Seth Wolitz (2010), the Khalyastre movement can be divided into three periods: the year 1919, the "transitional period 1921–1922," and "the golden period of 1922–1924." This "golden period" is the most vivid example of the Khalyastre's aesthetic revolution. The event that triggered the beginning of the period is in itself revolutionary, as it exemplifies the artists' desire to rebel against the Yiddish literary establishment and to break free from all traditions. On Saturday, January 22, 1922 – during Shabbat – Perets Markish, Uri Tsevi Grinberg, Melech Ravitch, and Moyshe Broderzon organized a public poetry recital. According to the organizers, seven hundred persons attended, plus a hundred more who could not enter and stayed outside (Ertel 2001). In front of the crowd, the poets declaimed in agitprop style that artists must destroy the old and welcome the new. Stormy debates over the future of Yiddish literature and even harsh criticisms against what was then described as a "depraved" literature and an "outrage" to artistic practices and "good taste" ensued.[11]

Such a critical shock reveals the revolutionary character of the *Khalyastre* group. Yet the event – both in form and content – was not a mere poetry recital. It can easily be interpreted as an artistic performance, both because it occurred on a Shabbat morning, and because it deprived poetry of its highest rank in the *belletristic* hierarchy by using it as a means to profess revolutionary slogans. In 1922, however, such performances were a completely new artistic form. Their first occasion was the *"Mise en accusation et jugement de Maurice Barrès par Dada"* (Maurice Barrès's indictment and trial by dada), held in Paris on May 13, 1921. Because it so deeply renewed the ways of practicing art –which exerted an impact on the meaning of art itself – the event organized by the Khalyastre group in January 1922 was as "decisive" (Clerc 2013) as the dadaist's fake trial.

Following this crucial event, the members of the Khalyastre group decided to publish a new literary journal which could sustain their revolutionary aesthetic claims. In his autobiography, Melech Ravitch (1962, 87) recounts that the idea of *Khalyastre* emerged after he shouted: "Guys! Let's publish a journal – a journal of the present-day – no, of tomorrow – no, of the day after tomorrow!"[12] Whether this was actually pronounced or not, the sentence tells much about the spirit of the young artists, who were willing to create a radically new form of art and to share it with their Yiddish readers.[13]

---

[11] Between February and March 1922, Hillel Zeitlin (at the time an enthusiast and promoter of modern Yiddish literature) wrote in *Der Moment* four ferocious articles against *"di khaliastre."* Ravitch answered these critics with a brochure entitled *Pro Perets Markish* (Warsaw, 1922).
[12] My translation.
[13] Despite the large number of publishing houses in Warsaw, *Khalyastre* was published by the Khalyastre group.

This call for absolute novelty cannot obscure the fact that such a literary avant-garde journal or "little magazine" was part of a much broader phenomenon that appeared not only in the Yiddish avant-garde in Europe, Russia, and New York,[14] but also throughout the entire international modernist scene of the time. As one of the starting points of modernism in the arts, little magazines are "non-commercial enterprises founded by individuals or small groups [...]. Defying mainstream tastes and conventions, some little magazines aim to uphold higher artistic and intellectual standards than their commercial counterparts, while others seek to challenge conventional political wisdom and practice" (McKible and Churchill 2005, 3). From this perspective, *Khalyastre*'s politically radical and aesthetically anti-conformist writers are a link in the modernist global network – an "internationally variegated and often internationally counter-cultural sphere" (Brooker and Thacker 2009, 2). They nonetheless never gave up on negotiating modern Jewish identities by renewing Yiddish literature. Like many "paranational avant-garde formations," the Khalyastre group "[expressed a] consciousness and practice [...] developing in the directions of metropolitan and international significance" (Williams 1981, 85), yet never abandoned the Yiddish language or its cultural identity. In *Khalyastre*, the avant-garde poets and writers reshaped Yiddish literature – not as a legacy of the past, but as a bridge to the future.

Several Ways to "Deparochialize"[15] the Yiddish Literary Imaginary

Yiddish avant-garde literature is less an attempt to find a hypothetical synthesis between tradition and modernity than an effort to explore the literary imaginary in light of modernist aesthetics. Since the beginning of the twentieth century,[16] the modern Yiddish "literary canon" rests on a literary pantheon or "triumvirate of classic masters": Mendele Moykher Sforim, Sholem Aleichem, and Y.L. Peretz. In just a few decades, these three figures, plus other writers, literary critics, and

---

14 The Yiddish avant-garde in the 1920s was an international phenomenon, with many groups that developed their own aesthetic specificities. In New York: *Di Yunge* (with Mani Leib, H. Leivick Y. Opatoshu) and *In Zikh* (Glanz Leyeles, Y. Glatshteyn, N.B. Minkoff). In Russia: the Kiev group (with D. Bergelson and Der Nister), which published *Eigns* and *Shtrom* (1922–1924, Moscow). In Vilnius: *Yung Vilne* (Chaim Grade, Leyzer Wolf, and Avrom Sutzkever).
15 I borrow this term from Moss (2009).
16 And more specifically after the Czernowitz Conference (30 August 3 – September 1908), which declared Yiddish "a national language of the Jewish people."

journalists, established an entire Yiddish literary field, with its own literary codes, themes, motives, typical characters, places, and public. Despite certain disagreements, they formed a literary community, with shared social imaginaries and beliefs. In order to be part of the field, each new Yiddish author had to refer to the literary canon, either to imitate it or to try to overtake or transcend it. For the young authors in interwar Warsaw who were attracted by bohemian life and the figure of the *"poète maudit,"* such canonical literature may have seemed obsolete.[17] Yet they never turned their backs on the literary past. However rebellious they may have been, the modernist literary forms that took shape in *Khalyastre* are mostly about fluidity, complexity, and negotiation, and not about simple rejection – even in Grinberg's most blasphemous poem. It seems that their general idea was that the Yiddish language, despite the traditional or national imaginary attached to it, could nonetheless express the widest array of modern ideas, including internationalism and anarchism, and even more importantly of modern sensibilities.[18] Each writer's task was to find a way to overcome the national, canonical, or ancestral aspects of Yiddish – to "deparochialize" or even "denationalize" the Yiddish literary canon. Using specific examples from *Khalyastre*, three different means of "deparochializing" will be explained: syncretism and adaptation of folkloric motives with modernist aesthetics; transposition of Jewish canonical motifs into "non-Jewish" environments; and the use of a paroxysmal poetic voice that radically transforms the inherent meaning of the literary imaginary itself.

Concerning the adaptation of folkloric motives with modernist aesthetics, the most obvious example would be the beautiful Hebrew calligraphy on the front cover of *Khalyastre* (Fig. 1). It is a direct reference to Jewish folklore, as it clearly evokes the medieval tradition of "illustrated micrography" that decorated the manuscripts of the Bible. Here, however, the calligraphy illustrates the cover of a blasphemous literary journal whose manifesto, formulated by Markish, proclaims that *"Unzer mos iz nit sheynkayt – nor shoyderlikhkeyt"* [Our measure is not beauty – but horror]. The religious dimension of the calligraphy is being challenged and the Hebrew letters thus remain as material signs that evoke Jewish traditional culture. Moreover, the front cover of *Khalyastre*, with its angular letters whose shape resembles smoke rising from a fire, is typical of the expressionist

---

17 This feeling may have led the painter and graphic designer Henryk Berlewi – notably after he discovered futurism and dada during the First World War – to proclaim, in the first volume of *Ringen* in 1921: *"Mir hobn keyn bodem unter di fis, di amolike traditsie iz farshvunden"* [We have no ground under our feet, our time-honored tradition has disappeared] (Weichert 1921, 3).

18 An initial idea they shared with many Yiddishists. Whereas for the Yiddishists, literature had to take part in a wider national and cultural project, *Khalyastre* was an attempt to bring Yiddish literature to an autonomous form.

style of many modernist magazine cover pages, such as *Blast, Little Review*, and *Others*. Thanks to this cover, *Khalyastre* thus claims at first sight to belong both to the international network of avant-garde little magazines and to the Yiddish (and in this case Jewish) culture.

Fig. 1: Challenging the literary community.

As regards content, many folkloric motives are rewritten here in a modernist style. The figure of the dybbuk is but one example. In Jewish mythology, a dybbuk is an evil spirit that takes possession of living persons and speaks through them. Its existence can be traced to sixteenth-century manuscripts, when examples of possessed Jews were not especially different from hundreds of accounts that reported possession of Catholic individuals in Southern Europe (Chajes 2003). Until the nineteenth century, the dybbuk played an important part in Kabbalistic and folkloric mythology, in Jewish tradition, especially in rural areas, but it was mostly forgotten by the metropolitan Jewish intelligentsia. In 1912–1914, during his ethnographical expeditions to Volhynia and Podolia, S. An-ski collected a huge amount of folkloric material[19] – some of it concerning the dybbuk, which he later used to write his most famous play, *Tsvishn tsvey veltn: Der dibek* (Between Two Worlds:

---

19 Contrary to his Russian contemporaries such as Hayim Nahman Bialik and Yehoshu'a Rana Ravnitski, who were more intrigued by the Hebrew folklore of the Talmud, An-ski was seeking to collect ethnographic material from living sources. According to Gabriella Safran (2010), Russian

The Dybbuk).[20] The play premiered in Warsaw on December 9, 1920. Performed by the Vilna Troupe, it introduced into Yiddish theater a "New Jewish Style" that broke with the carnivalesque traditions of the *Purimshpiel* (Purim play) by using expressionist means as a way "to embody on the stage a visionary artistic linkage between theater and ritual" (Steinlauf 2006, 237). The play was an immediate and stunning success. This public triumph may have had an impact on the *Khalyastre*'s writers, who adapted the dybbuk folkloric motif in an even more expressionist style. Melech Ravitch's "Gezang tsum mentshlekhn kerper" (Song to the human body) echoes with the uncanny idea of a moving dead body in a visual and vibrant depiction:

Un az men hoybt oyf aza pniak fun a hant
git zikh a treysl makhtloz dos kleyd
mit dem leybikn kholel
vos iz a geshtorbene hant

[And if we raise the stump of such a hand
the clothes start to shiver, helpless,
with the empty orbit
that is a dead hand] (13)[21]

In the same spirit, Perets Markish, in "Tsum oremen meltsayt" (To the poor's dinner), curses:

Vey iz aykh, sharbns farneyte, o, beynerne moyekh-katafalkes
fun shoymikn blut-toy, fun zudikn vanzin
oyf shtendike khupes un lents fun levayes.

[Woe upon you resewn skulls o catafalque of brain bones
of the foaming dew of blood and of the steaming insanity
to the eternal wedding and the funeral dance.] (66)

Here, the vivid descriptions of living-dead bodies as well as the morbid fascination with death, the association of opposite motifs (blood and wedding) and bright colors (red and white), and Markish's apocalyptic tone are clearly expressionistic. By intertwining Jewish and non-Jewish motifs and forms, the poet manages to

---

populists such as Gleb Uspensky, whom An-ski met in Saint Petersburg in the late nineteenth century, inspired him significantly.

20 In the play, Khonen, as a dybbuk, takes possession of his beloved Leah's body on her wedding day.

21 All page numbers from *Khalyastre* (Markish 1922) are now directly given after the English translation. All translations from Yiddish are mine.

overcome the conflict between folkloric imaginary and modernist aesthetic, thus developing an aesthetic syncretism.

Such syncretism embraces the idea that Yiddish modernist expression still needed to be rooted in Jewish traditions. But for other writers, Yiddish literature would have to break free from any particular "Jewish" content. In Oyzer Varshavski's and Yoysef Opatoshu's short stories for example, Yiddish literature reaches hitherto unexplored places, thus escaping the literary imagination of the *shtetl* and its typical characters. In *In di berg* (In the mountains), Varshavski brings his Yiddish readers to the Tatras Mountains and tells of the everyday life of Christian *gazdy* (peasants) who grapple with natural and supernatural forces. While the language and superstitions of the Tatras peasants had been a common motif in Polish literature since the end of the nineteenth century and an indication of the intelligentsia's growing interest in folk culture, they are here introduced in Yiddish literature for the first time. Varshavski ironically challenges the Polish nationalist belief in the purity of the folk by writing about one of its favorite motifs in an allegedly "corrupted" (sic) language (Yiddish) and for a supposedly "alien" (sic) audience (Yiddish readers).

Yoysef Opatoshu – who moved to New York in 1907 – sets his story *Fir nigers* (Four negroes) in the prejudiced South of the United States. In a small, unnamed town, the white inhabitants walk toward the local prison, their faces disfigured by hatred, to lynch John, a black man whose crime the reader is not aware of. With a small vestige of human compassion in the surrounding chaos, the three other black men in the prison first wonder whether they should give John up or protect him. But their last vestiges of humanity soon disappear as they undergo a metamorphosis into the same kind of human beasts as the white perpetrators; finally, they condemn John to his inevitable death:

> Di negers zaynen geblibn shteyn on loshn, derzen dem toyt far di oygn, mit amol hobn zey zikh a varf geton oyf Djonen, geefnt di tir, im aroysgeshteydert, vi me varft a kalb, tsi a ferd a stade volf, az tsu konen antloyfn, zikh rateven dos lebn.

> [The negroes froze, voiceless, facing death, then suddenly they rushed towards John, opened the door, dragged him outside as one throws a calf or a horse to a pack of wolves in order to flee and save his own life.] (26)

A similar eruption of monstrous feelings and behaviors in facing racial violence is evoked in Lamed Shapiro's short stories which thematize pogroms, for example "The Kiss" (1907) and "The Cross" (1909). But whereas Shapiro recalls his own experience after the pogroms he witnessed in late-nineteenth-century Ukraine, Opatoshu sets his story in the American South, an environment unknown to Yiddish literature in Poland. Opatoshu's and Varshavski's Yiddish readers may have experienced a kind of otherness and strangeness while reading the two short stories in their own day-to-day language. At the same time, common Jewish motifs, such as rural superstitions, anti-Semitism, and racial violence, were being transposed into foreign contexts. In a way, both Opatoshu and Varshavski try to find their own literary voices by negotiating an unexpected path between familiarization and defamiliarization. In their short stories, literature is shaped as a kind of third space in which to experiment with new collective and individual identities.

Uri Tsevi Grinberg's attempt to "deparochialize" the Yiddish literary canon by dismantling all religious beliefs and replacing them with an apocalyptic and blasphemous chaos testifies to his perfect mastery of Yiddish and its literature. In *Velt barg-arop* (The World Down the Slope) the poet, as the prophet of the Apocalypse, describes a world where all human values – and above all every religion – are turned upside down. Contrary to the new prophetic poet, whose voice seems to equal the voice of the divine Creator in its ability to build or destroy, the "ancient" prophets – Moses and Jesus – are nothing but lost men. While Moses has simply disappeared ("*Un Moyshe rabeynu gefint men in gas nisht*" [and we cannot find Moses in the streets], 32), Jesus is doomed to suffer Promethean torment:

> *Un s'entfert der mentsh oyfn tseylem: ikh hob nisht*
> *a trit oyf der erd ton… ikh veys nisht* […]
> *tselakht zikh di lester-khaliastre un khoyzekt:*
> *heng, heyliker, heng un hot yikhed mit vrones,*
> *kol-zman s'hobn vrones dayn guf nisht tsefresn …*
> *mir lozn dir.*
>
> [And the man on his cross answers: I cannot walk
> on the ground. I don't know […]
> And the gang of blasphemers bursts out laughing and mocks:
> Stay hung, o Saint, stay hung and make love
> to the crows
> until the crows devour your body …
> We leave you.] (31)

While several Yiddish artists were wont to judaize the Christ theme – Jesus' martyrdom becoming the prime example of the sufferings of the Jewish nation – Grinberg goes even further and blasphemously desacralizes all religious motives by violently prophesizing their replacement by a kind of bloody and zoophilic orgy. Therefore, religions – and God – are doomed to disappear. However, if the prophets are now deprived of their transcendental powers and left helpless, their sufferings reconnect them with their human nature. Thus, the blasphemous poet finally reasserts the equality of all religions, and thus the equality of all human beings – at least before death. Similarly, the poet depicts the Virgin Mary as the naked queen of prostitutes, desperately seeking her son:

[...] *in veg kumt akegn*
a makhne fun zoynes, berosh – a madone:
a kroyn oyfn kop un s'iz naket di erve
vos iz funem ruakh-hakodesh bafrukhpert.
O, vu iz mayn eyniker Yeshu? Vu iz er?

[[...] and here comes towards them
a group of whores lead by a Madonna
with a crown on her head and a bared sex
who was fecundated by the Holy Spirit ...
Oh, where is he my own Jesus? Where is he?] (31–32)

Beyond their obviously blasphemous aspect, these lines are interesting in their use of multiple linguistic layers: the Virgin Mary laments in colloquial Yiddish (which is already subversive enough), while the poet skillfully intertwines biblical Hebrew words, Christian vocabulary, and Yiddish. In doing so, Grinberg pushes the syncretic dimension of Yiddish to its extreme limits, and thus manages to "deparochialize" the language by using its potentialities to generate paroxysm. Eventually, blasphemy is not about total rejection, but in its negative climax it evidences the possibility of new forms of human associations, and therefore buoys hope for a different kind of human community. Furthermore, Yiddish poetry here demonstrates its ability to utilize or draw upon complex expressionist aesthetics and to profess a revolutionary modernity.

The literary pieces analyzed above are but a few examples of the multiplicity of literary positions and aesthetic revolutions displayed in *Khalyastre*. In any case, even if the writers may have later endorsed clear political positions in their public or private lives,[22] their literary achievements in *Khalyastre* are variegated and nuanced. They demonstrate a desire not only to "denationalize" Yiddish literature, but also to explore what a range of modern identities could be.

---

[22] Perets Markish settled in the Soviet Union in 1926, and was considered in the 1930s as one of the most important Soviet Yiddish writers. He joined the Communist Party in 1946. Uri Tsevi Grinberg joined Vladimir Jabotinsky's Revisionist Zionists in the 1930s, and endorsed the role of a "national Hebrew poet." He immigrated to Palestine when the First World War broke out in Europe. Melech Ravitch's cosmopolitanism took him to Australia, Argentina, Mexico, and finally Montreal in the 1930s. In *Kontinenten un okeanen* (Continents and oceans, 1937), he draws the figure of the Yiddish poet as a citizen of the world. Oyzer Varshavski settled in Paris, where he frequented the bohemian artistic scene of the Parisian cafes of Montparnasse. Although his literary production diminished in the 1930s, he is probably the one who remained the most faithful to Yiddish avant-garde aesthetics.

The "Distribution of the Sensible" and the Shaping of a New Literary Community

The individual writers' various singular sensibilities and their multiple ways of negotiating their own identities as Yiddish authors explain the great diversity of literary forms found in *Khalyastre*. Taken as a whole, however, the magazine sheds new light on the Khalyastre group's project. In fact, even if specific authorial voices are displayed here, each depends on the existence of the others. Each poem or short story assumes its full meaning only in relationship with every other literary piece in the journal, which is above all a polyphonic and discursive literary object. In this way, the individual voice is no less decisive than the collective one. Such a collective dimension is further evidenced in the texts themselves, where one easily notices the omnipresence of the personal pronoun "*mir*" [we].

The final section of this essay will focus on the multiple aspects of the pronoun "*mir*" in the journal. I argue that the way *Khalyastre* radically challenges the Yiddish literary canon, as well as how it profoundly negotiates the limits of a Jewish "we," has ethical and even political consequences. According to Jacques Rancière in *The Distribution of the Sensible*: "aesthetic acts [are] configurations of experience that create new modes of sense perception and include novel forms of political subjectivity" (Rancière 2004, 19). In fact, literature may have accurate effects on reality when it transforms so profoundly both the writers' and the readers' perceptions or sensibilities. Rancière argues that avant-garde aesthetic movements convey a "meta-political idea of global political subjectivity, [...] that anticipates a community to come" (Rancière 2004, 30). Thus, it is important to understand the "community to come" that implicitly appears in *Khalyastre*.

In order to comprehend the unusual scope of the pronoun "*mir*" in *Khalyastre*, a brief enumeration of several of its occurrences may be useful. Uri Tsevi Grinberg's *Velt barg* ends with the birth of an overwhelmingly poetic "we" with God-like demiurgic powers:

Mir zenen tseklingen fun toyznter glokn.
Mir zenen tseshpilte fun ale kley-niguns.
Mir zenen tseoygte fun eybikn zeen,
mir zenen tseoyert fun eybikn hern.

[We are the ringing of a thousand bells.
We are the melodies of all the instruments.
We are the eyes of eternal vision,
We are the ears of eternal listening.] (34)

Or, in the few lines that serve as a preliminary statement to the entire journal, Moyshe Broderzon writes:

> *Mir yungen, mir a freylekhe tsezungene khalyastre*
> *Mir geyen in an umbavustn veg,*
> *In tife moreshkhoyredike teg*
> *In nekht fun shrek*
> *Per aspera ad astra!*
>
> [We, the young, a happy, boisterous gang
> We're trodding an unknown path
> through deeply melancholy days
> through nights of fright
> *Per aspera ad astra!*] (10)

The word *"Mir"* notably opens the entire journal. Thus, Perets Markish's literary manifesto can be read in a sense as an attempt to define that "We":

> *Un azoy geyen mir: tsevarfn, ayntsikvayz un ineynem – in anarkhistishe khaliastres bandes un federatsies.*
>
> [And here we go, dispersed, one by one and together, in gangs, in anarchical groups and in federations.] (12)

But his definition radically differs from many others in *Khalyastre*, such as that provided by Melech Ravitch:

> *ikh,*
> *du!*
> *Its kenen mir ersht geyn un zukhn iber der velt*
> *Got.*
>
> [I
> You!
> Now we can really go and look around the world
> for God.] (21)

Obvious variations in the simple meaning of "we," such as Markish's "gangs" and "anarchical groups," and Ravitch's "I" plus "You," reveal a major difference between *Khalyastre* and many modernist magazines. Indeed, if the "we" is typical of avant-garde discourse, and above all of manifestos, it often marks the precise limits of the group. A series of principles defines the "we" as an artistic movement, in contrast to other movements or even to the rest of society. More generally, the aspect of the "we" is often ambivalent: socially, it might include the whole of the "community," the "people," or the "nation," and at the same time exclude "them" or the "other."

However, the "we" in *Khalyastre* is, on the contrary, highly metamorphic and fluid, thus displaying a wide range of individuation processes and multiple possibilities for collective associations. Therefore, the writers challenge the ambition to delimit precisely the "we" – whether as the artistic "we" of an avant-garde movement or as the national "we" of the "Jewish nation" – without professing any absolute or utopian universalism. Simultaneously, they challenge two opposite mythical figures of the poet: the guide or prophet of the nation and the lonely and misunderstood *poète maudit*. By negotiating between these multiple identities, they finally give shape to a new figure: the cosmopolitan writer.

In refiguring the Yiddish literary imagination and the contours of a collective identity through the emergence of a variegated *"mir,"* the Khalyastre group created "new modes of sense perception" (Rancière 2004, 19) and broadened the range of possible individual and collective experiences. Reunited in one artistic collective, the writers of *Khalyastre* formed a cosmopolitan and transnational literary group. Moreover, they were not so much addressing a "public" with whom they potentially shared common social imaginaries and definitions of the national community. Rather, they were addressing a transnational audience of readers with their own private tastes and sensibilities. The *Khalyastre*'s readers and writers, taken together, thus form an unconstrained and cosmopolitan literary community. In this way, *Khalyastre* marked an important stage in the development of an autonomous Yiddish literature, emancipated from political or cultural nationalisms – yet nonetheless still Yiddish.

Bibliography

Brooker, Peter, and Andrew Thacker. *The Oxford Critical and Cultural History of Modernist Magazines. Volume I, Britain and Ireland 1880–1955*. Oxford and New York: Oxford University Press, 2009.

Casanova, Pascale and Fredric Jameson. *Des littératures combatives: L'internationale des nationalismes littéraires*. Paris: Raisons d'agir, 2011.

Chajes, Jeffrey Howard. *Between Worlds: Dybbuks, Exorcists, and Early Modern Judaism*. Philadelphia: University of Pennsylvania Press, 2003.

Clerc, Thomas. 2013. "Le procès de Maurice Barrès par les Dadaïstes." www.inculte.fr/dans-les-archives-de-la-revue-inculte-4-le-proces-de-maurice-barres-par-les-dadaistes-par-thomas-clerc/. *Inculte* 4, September 2013 (July 10 2015).

Cohen, Nathan. 2010. "Association of Jewish Writers and Journalists in Warsaw." www.yivoencyclopedia.org/article.aspx/Association_of_Jewish_Writers_and_Journalists_in_Warsaw. YIVO Encyclopedia of Jews in Eastern Europe, 2010 (January 6 2016).

Cohen, Richard, Jonathan Frankel and Stefani Hoffman (eds.). *Insiders and Outsiders: Dilemmas of East European Jewry*. Oxford and Portland: The Littman Library of Jewish Civilization, 2010.
Dynner, Glenn and François Guesnet. *Warsaw. The Jewish Metropolis*. Boston: Brill, 2015.
Ertel, Rachel. "Khaliastra et la modernité européenne." *Khaliastra, revue littéraire Varsovie 1922–Paris 1924*. Paris: Lachenal et Ritter, 2001. 263–304.
Gottesman, Itzik Nakhmen. *Defining the Yiddish Nation: the Jewish Folklorists of Poland*. Detroit: Wayne State University Press, 2003.
Krutikov, Mikhail. *From Kabbalah to Class Struggle: Expressionism, Marxism, and Yiddish Literature in the Life and Work of Meir Wiener*. Stanford: Stanford University Press, 2011.
Markish, Perets, and Israel Joshua Singer. *Khaliastre: erster almanac*. Warsaw: Khaliastre, 1922.
Mayzel, Nakhman. *Dos Mendele-bukh: Briv un oytobiografishe notitsn*. New York: Ikuf, 1959.
McKible, Adam and Suzanne W. Churchill. "Little Magazines and Modernism: An Introduction." *American Periodicals: A Journal of History, Criticism and Bibliography* 15.1, 2005. 1–5.
Miron, Dan. *A Traveler Disguised. The Rise of Modern Yiddish Fiction in the Nineteenth Century*. New York: Schocken Books, 1973.
Moss, Kenneth. *Jewish Renaissance in the Russian Revolution*. Cambridge: Harvard University Press, 2009.
Moss, Kenneth. "Negotiating Jewish Nationalism in Interwar Warsaw." *Warsaw. The Jewish Metropolis*. Ed. Glenn Dynner and François Guesnet. Boston: Brill, 2015. 390–434.
Polonsky, Antony. *The Jews in Poland and Russia*. Oxford: Littman Library of Jewish Civilization, 2010.
Rancière, Jacques. *The Politics of Aesthetics: The Distribution of the Sensible*. London: Continuum, 2004.
Ravitch, Melech. *Dos mayse-bukh fun mayn lebn*. Buenos Aires: Tsentral-Farband fun Poylishe Yidn in Argentine, 1962.
Safran, Gabriella. *Wandering Soul: The Dybbuk's Creator, S. An-Sky*. Cambridge: Belknap Press of Harvard University Press, 2010.
Sauder, Gerhard. "La conception herdérienne de peuple/langue, des peuples et de leurs langues." *Revue germanique internationale* 20 (2003): 123–132.
Sherman, Joseph. *A Captive of the Dawn: the Life and Work of Perets Markish (1895–1952)*. London: Legenda, 2011.
Shmeruk, Chone. "Aspects of the History of Warsaw as a Yiddish Literary Center." *Studies from Polin. From Shtetl to Socialism*. Ed. Antony Polonski. London and Washington: Littman Library of Jewish Civilization, 1993. 120–133.
Steinlauf, Michael. "'Fardibekt!': An-sky's Polish Legacy." *The Worlds of S. An-sky. A Russian Jewish Intellectual at the Turn of the Century*. Ed. Gabriella Safran and Steven J. Zipperstein. Stanford: Stanford University Press, 2006. 232–251.
Trachtenberg, Barry. *The Revolutionary Roots of Modern Yiddish, 1903–1917*. New York: Syracuse University Press, 2008.
Veidlinger, Jeffrey. "Culture and the Public: A Yiddish Perspective." *Canadian-American Slavic Studies* 47 (2013): 123–136.
Weichert, Michal, and Alter Kacyzne. *Ringen*. Warsaw: 1921.
Weiser, Kalman. *Jewish People, Yiddish Nation: Noah Prylucki and the Folkists in Poland*. Toronto: University of Toronto Press, 2011.
Williams, Raymond. *Culture*. London: Fontana Press, 1981.

Wolitz, Seth. "Between Folk and Freedom: The Failure of the Yiddish Modernist Movement in Poland." *Yiddish* 8.1 (1991): 26–51.
Wolitz, Seth. "Khalyastre." www.yivoencyclopedia.org/article.aspx/Khalyastre. YIVO Encyclopedia of Jews in Eastern Europe, 2010 (January 7 2016).

Maria Silina
Modern Jewish Sculptors and the Cultural Policy of the USSR in the 1920s–1930s

The artist Nathan Altman (1889–1970) actively participated in Jewish cultural life in Russia in the 1910s. In his self-portrait, *Portret molodogo evreia* (Portrait of a Young Jew, bronze, wood), from 1915, the future promoter of futurism for the Russian proletariat revealed the contradictory traits of his nature. The left side of the face belongs to a Jew with a traditional Hassidic hat and side-lock, the right side to a young man without religious attributes. The bronze surface of this self-portrait, slightly touched by a cubistic deformation, remains stuck to the strict frontality of ancient Egyptian portraiture. The piece was of great importance to secular Jewish culture worldwide, as it was the first self-portrait by a Jewish sculptor (Orlov 2004). The message of the piece can be read as follows: a Jewish artist had to choose between either traditional religious culture or assimilation into a pan-European lifestyle. In another sculptural portrait, this one the work of Beatrisa Sandomirskaya (1894–1974), an assimilated Jewish artist, entitled *Portret* (Portrait, wood, iron). Its subject is an unidentified person around 1921. In it, she revealed a dilemma about depicting modern people. Half of the face has robotized features, the other bearded, folklorized Slavonic traits. This represents the dialectics of two civilizations, one modern and technical, the other archaic. In the 1920s Sandomirskaya started working in wood, adopting a neo-archaic manner in depicting peasant types and heroes of Russian folklore. These two works of art outline the range of the artistic quest of modernist Jewish sculptors in the 1910s–1930s in Soviet Russia, from the creation of secular Yiddishist culture by means of cubism, constructivism, or neo-archaism in the early 1920s, to the complete assimilation of religious attributes along with persistence of the same stylistic manner by the mid-1930s. This article will argue that thinking of national identity in terms of international avant-garde and modernism allowed Jewish sculptors to integrate into the overall Soviet Socialist culture of the 1930s.

Modern Yiddish Sculpture and the First Sculpture Studios in the 1910s

In Tsarist times Jewish sculptors such as Mark Antokolsky (1843–1902) and Ilia Ginzburg (1859–1939), both of whom were successful promoters of Russian imperial ideology, were faced with anti-Semitism and conditions unfavorable for developing Jewish culture. By the 1910s, however, the situation in Europe had changed considerably with the beginning of contemporary national Jewish art. Martin Buber (1878–1965) raised the problem of Jewish art at the first Zionist Congress in Basel in 1901, though official acknowledgement of a specifically Yiddish cultural tradition dates to the Czernowitz conference in 1908. These activities led to questions about Jewish national art, whether its creation was possible at all, and how Jewish ethnos could contribute to European art (Bland 2000; Olin 2001). Yoysef Chaikov (1888–1979), a key representative of modern Jewish art, left Kiev in 1910 for Paris, the artistic capital of modernist pan-European art, where he met other Jewish émigrés. In 1912 he had become one of the founders of the first Hebrew-language art magazine, *Mahmadim* (Precious), which presented graphical images made in the dominant style of the period. These artists expressed Jewish themes in terms of European Art Nouveau style, a style that was also popular in the Jewish *Bezalel art school* in Palestine at the time (Olin 2001, 45–56). This was contrary to the conceptions held by Paris-based artists like Ossip Zadkine and Leon Indenbaum concerning what Jewish art should be. Since the 1910s they had been searching for the basis of national Jewish sculpture in neo-archaism, a style which drew on ancient Egyptian and Assyrian art (Shatskikh 2007, 58). They linked this interest in orientalism to their ethnic and religious heritage, whereas artists of other nationalities were keen on rethinking the plastic arts in general. Archaic style was implemented in *taille directe* technique and indebted to non-academic directions in European art history (Mendes-Flohr 1991, 77–88; Curtis 1999, 77–91). In short, working in Paris on new themes that could reflect national culture, Jewish artists were at the epicenter of the specifically professional tasks of European art.

In Russia, during the period following the 1917 Revolution, there emerged political and cultural organizations, new schools, and newspapers for the creation and dissemination of secular Yiddish culture (Kampf 1984; Apter-Gabriel 1988; Moss 2009). This process was boosted by the Provisional Government's abolishment of the Pale of Settlement in March 1917 and by the right of Self-Determination of Nations supported by the Soviets after the Bolshevik revolution in autumn 1917 (Kostyrchenko 2009, 35). Soon, artists who had left for Europe after the First World War began to return to Vitebsk, Petrograd, Kiev, and Moscow. Around this time, two art schools became especially important for modern Jewish art: the Kiev *Kultur-Lige* art section and the Vitebsk Art School.

In January 1918 in Kiev, under the Ukrainian People's Republic (UNR) government and closely connected with the Jewish Labour Bund, the autonomy of Ukrainian Jews was proclaimed in order to develop Yiddish language and culture. At this time the *Kultur-lige* was established; it was the first institute for secular Yiddish culture in Europe (Kazovsky 2003). By the end of 1919, the *Khudozh-*

estvennaya Sektsia (Artistic Section) of the *Kultur-lige* was formed. It included a sculpture studio, led by Yoysef Chaikov, where non-decorative national Jewish sculpture, including life-size statues, was produced. Chaikov's works, combining kinetic balance and figures expressing laconism and dynamic force, were exemplary in educational programs of contemporary Jewish sculpture, and were very influential in the studio from 1918 until 1922. After Chaikov left for Moscow in 1922, the central role in promoting new artistic methods in the sculpture studio was played by Mark Epstein (1899–1949), an active member of the Kiev *Kultur Lige* (Kazovsky 2003, 87; Hamm 2010, 80). In his art practice Epstein endorsed modernist art and experiments on construction and new sculptural structures, and the use of modern and non-conventional materials (Kazovsky 2003, 87). The Artistic Section of the Kultur-Lige became known as *Evreiskaia khudozhestvenno-promyshlennaia shkola* (Jewish Arts and Trades School) in 1924, and Epstein was its main supporter. The students worked on everyday scenes of *shtetl* life and modern classics of Jewish literature. As his students recalled later, he taught them to work so "that it could be seen that it was the work of a Jew" (Mastbaum 2009).

Vitebsk was another center for Jewish art activists in the post-revolutionary years. A non-figural art system, elaborated by Kazimir Malevitch (1879–1935) in the 1910s, was successfully introduced to the educational system of the Vitebsk Art School. In his 1915 manifesto *Ot kubizma i futurizma k suprematizmu: novyi zhyvopisnyi realizm* (From Cubism to Suprematism: the New Realism in Painting), Malevich analyzed movements such as cubism and futurism, rejecting their exclusively pictorial and imitative nature. According to Malevitch, suprematism was the only new and non-narrative, non-imitative but completely independent system of art, freed from illusionistic conventions. Under Malevich's influence, one of the most active promoters of secular Jewish culture, El (Lazar) Lissitsky (1890–1941), proceeded from the Yiddishism of the *Kultur-lige* to non-Nationalist suprematism in Vitebsk (Apter-Gabriel 1988, 50). The findings of a non-figural art system expressed in spatial graphic compositions were also successfully adapted by the young artist David Yakerson (1896–1947), who taught sculpture in Vitebsk from autumn 1919 until 1922 (Shatskih 2007, 37–38). In less than a year, students of the Vitebsk sculpture studio managed to shift from the traditional program introduced by Latvian artist Yanis Tilberg, a former student of the Fine Arts Academy in St. Petersburg, to the new educational system that promoted formal experimentation and suprematism. Yakerson was a student of the famous Vitebsk painter Yehuda Pen (1854–1937), who fostered generations of Jewish artists including Marc Chagall, El Lissitsky, and Osip Zadkine. On entering the Vitebsk School, Yakerson quickly recognized the unique power and potential of the Malevich system and he incorporated it into his teaching. He introduced an analytical method that included such formal features of an object as space, *faktura*, volume, color, and avoidance of visual resemblance to nature. Abstract models in the Yakerson sculpture studio were made by building up geometric volumes in main figures such as pyramids and cubes that enhanced comprehension of the formal features of the space. The majority of professors and students were of Jewish origin, but the school positioned itself as a center of the new art without nationalist character.

Yoysef Chaikov and the First Treatise on Secular Sculpture in Yiddish

In 1921 Yoysef Chaikov, writing under the umbrella of the Kiev *Kultur-lige*, authored *Skulptur* (Sculpture), the first Yiddish treatise on secular sculpture. In this short text Chaikov scrutinized the major directions in sculpture from a Yiddishist perspective. These were initial steps towards the "New Sculpture" that was to come. Chaikov credited futurists with introducing dynamic and unconventional new materials into sculpture, although this had led to the loss of monumentality. Cubism gave a new form to contemporary artists, especially a monolithic and archaic one, but it did not take into account the inherent *fir zaytn* (four-sidedness) of sculpture. Suprematists and expressionists created new artistic forms based on the economy of expression while making their art pictorial. Constructivists combined material as pictorial *faktura* (visual texture of material surface) or as a utilitarian architectural object, such that sculpture approached engineering.

Affection for the plastic sculptural idea was crucial to Chaikov. His critique was not aimed at figuration in general; rather, he saw sculpture in every conscious formation of an object, knowledge of the true "essence" of things, in contrast to the illusionism of academics (Wood et al. 2012, xvi–xxi). Moreover, Chaikov regarded the connection between the expression of plastic form and the ethnicity of an artist as key in the creation of contemporary sculpture. As he explained it, "*Reyne plastishe form iz tif national un der direkter tsugang tsu kunst shaft ot di form*" [Pure plastic form is deeply national and the direct approach to art creates its own form] (Apter-Gabriel 1988, 231). If the rejection of illusionism and the search for a pure plastic idea refined traditions, then the new industrial culture of European cities provided up-to-date issues. According to Chaikov, "*Dos yidishe zelbstbavustzayn in der shilderungs-kunst hot zikh dervekt in der tsayt fun elekretsitet, industrieler tekhnik un ayzn-beton.*" [Jewish self-awareness in the arts emerged in the time of electricity, industrial technology and reinforced concrete] (Chaikov 1921, 2). Jewish art, in the form defined by Chaikov, was seen as the will to actively transform the Jewish world through adoption of new technologies and new methods in the arts. Moreover, this renewal, raised in the absence of plastic, that is, sculptural, tradition in Jewish art, made it easy to ignore established traditions and facilitated a clearer direction towards new sculpture. Likewise, art freed from the bonds of traditionalism provided a "direct" expression of the artist's ethnicity.

Chaikov's works of the late 1910s, images of which were published in the books *Brikboyer I, II* (Bridgebuilder I and II, iron, 1920), and *Fidler* (Violin Player, 1921), were of great importance not only for the maturation of new Jewish sculpture of the 1920s in the works of his students, but also for his personal artistic career. He used simple geometric figures as free elements and as relief projection, creating a balanced system. In his 1921 relief *A yid a geyer* (A Walking Jew) these geometric forms express both centrifugal forces and fragile equilibrium in their composition. Its main formal element is the use of pure volumes, which are particularly expressive due to their geometric exposition and pictorial role in the composition. Like most contemporary artists, Chaikov was interested in carrying out formal tasks on revealing surface/*faktura*, geometricization, and shifts in relief levels, consistence, and valorization. This is evident in plaster reliefs of 1921–1922 such as *Violin Player* and *Shveya* (A Sewing Woman), where the main effect is achieved through the intense dynamics of sharp, polished shapes and angles. Chaikov kept this special sensitivity to such dynamic forces in composition throughout his life, moving from figurative abstractions in the late 1910s to Socialist realism in the 1930s (Bowlt 2012).

The figure *Soyfer* (Sribe, plaster, 1923) is particularly exemplary for the emergence of Jewish contemporary sculpture. Visual tension between the abstract, almost architectural, parts of the figure create a composition full of inner energy and dynamism. Chaikov was raised in the family of his grandfather, who was a scribe by profession; thus the subject of the sculpture had biographical significance. However, his purely religious subject was meant to find its place in contemporary art due to its expressive formal language. Nothing except the theme should remind one of traditional Jewish culture. This exemplifies how this new, deeply national, and, paradoxically, thoroughly non-traditional art was born.

Jewish Public Sculpture in the Post-revolutionary Years (1918–1921)

The impact of the Bolshevik revolution extended to the theory and teaching of Jewish secular sculpture. National public sculpture emerged during these years, and its rapid spread even in the Jewish community was unexpected, especially given the long-standing tradition of aniconism codified in Judaism (Mann 2000,

34–36). Prominent Tsarist Russian sculptor Ilia Gintsburg recollected in his memoirs that neither his grandfather nor he had ever seen a work of art in their hometown (Orlov 2008, 390). Soon after the 1917 Revolution, the Kharkov-based author Kalman Zingman wrote a story in Yiddish called *Edeniya* (Edenland), in which he describes a city of the future where mass theatrical performances are common. His description is remarkable not only for its inclusion of a monument to the Ukrainian poet Taras Schevchenko (which is installed in the city's downtown), but also for the many city streets adorned by statues of Jewish writers (Moss 2009, 60–63). Kenneth B. Moss dates *Edeniya* to the end of 1917 or beginning of 1918; however, 1918–1920 seems more plausible, as from autumn 1918 impressive numbers of monuments to revolutionary heroes and forefathers of socialism had been erected in territories controlled by Bolsheviks. This was known as the "*plan monumental'noi propagandy*" [monumental propaganda plan] (Tolstoi 2010, 47–119). By 1919 the Bolshevik public art initiative had reached the provinces that included places in the former Pale of Settlement. As in *Edeniya*, in the Ukraine and Belarus images from the pantheons of writers, poets, and politicians were erected. Many of these figures were thought of as emancipatory symbols and were associated with anti-imperial ideology, including the Ukrainian Shevchenko. The monuments in his honor were made by Latvian artist Yanis Tilberg (in Vitebsk), Polish sculptor Bernard Kratko (in Kiev and Kharkov during 1921), Ukrainian-Georgian artist Ivan Kavaleridze (in the small town of Romny in 1918), and Jewish *Kultur-lige* activist Epstein (in Kiev in 1919). Marxist politicians enjoyed the most popularity, however. Chaikov installed two monuments of Marx in Kiev (one in 1919, another in 1922), as well as monuments in honor of Leo Trotsky and Karl Liebknecht, also in Kiev (Silina 2014, 257). These were made according to the same scheme: a larger than life-sized cubist-archaic portrait head was installed on the pediment, which served as a tribune with a sophisticated dynamic composition.

Especially noteworthy were the monuments made by Vitebsk-based David Yakerson, as he was the first to introduce suprematism into public sculpture. His 1919 monuments of Marx (in Polotsk), Nevel, and Liebknecht (in Vitebsk) were similarly constructed, being made of a massive portrait head, carved in *taille direct* technique, that was then installed on a suprematist base.[1] The idea of the

---

[1] The *taille direct* method, widely used since ancient times, was seen in the beginning of the 20th century as a revival of an ancient mastership ethos. It was reintroduced by Parisian sculptor Joseph Bernard in the 1900s. David Yakerson taught this method in Vitebsk sculpture studios using a hardened concrete. Though it was thought to be synergic to work in non-academic materials such as wood, rocks (especially hard ones like granite, basalt, etc.), it was impossible in practice due to the poor material equipment of early Soviet art schools. Yakerson could know about this technique of chiseling half-set cement or clay from sculptor Oskar Meshchaninov, one of the most

suprematist pedestal was in fact a predecessor of Malevich's *architectons*, universal modules of non-utilitarian functions, which he began creating in 1923. Unfortunately, Yakerson's monuments were destroyed by 1923, and his contributions to suprematist public sculpture were excluded from art history until recently.

Another important yet often forgotten chapter in the history of secular Jewish sculpture in the early Soviet Union is the promotion of local Jewish revolutionary heroes. Their images were considered by Bolshevik municipal authorities to be part of a new Socialist culture. In 1922 the Minsk *Evsektsiia* (Jewish section of the Communist Party of the Soviet Union) proposed to erect a monument in Minsk to Hirsh Lekkert (1879–1902). The son of a Jewish tailor, Lekkert had joined the *Bund* in the 1890s, where he was a passionate propagandist and fighter against Tsarism. Soon after the Revolution he was recognized as a martyr of the Jewish workers' movement, although any connections to his Bundist past were soon suppressed. The monument was to be installed in Minsk's central square, not in his hometown of Vilna, in order to emphasize his importance in the pantheon of local Bolshevik heroes (Bemporad 2013, 65–67). Construction began in 1922 in the square, which was previously occupied by an obelisk in honor of Tsar Alexander II. Local authorities borrowed the base of the Tsarist monument and engraved a new commemorative inscription, in Hebrew. In 1924, Chaikov created his version for a Lekkert monument of plaster and glass (Silina 2014, 257) (see Fig. 1). This was a non-specified image of a personality constructed of extremely geometrized and well-balanced volumes. In this work Chaikov further developed techniques of the Ukrainian sculptor Alexander Archipenko, who was active in France and America. These techniques can be seen in Archipenko's *Carrousel Pierrot* (Pierrot Carousel, painted plaster, 1913), and Chaikov here translated them into public sculpture.[2] He attempted to rethink the monumental imaging of a hero in a country that had torn apart the hierarchical organization of society. Due to a lack of funding, construction on the monument was halted until 1927 and was rescheduled to coincide with the tenth anniversary of the Bolshevik Revolution. The end result was installation of a realistic bust made by Abram Brazer (1892–1942) in 1927. This image broke completely with the historical and folklorist interpretations of a Jew: it contained no visible orientalist or accentuated Semitic traits, nor any traditional

---

successful practitioners in the Joseph Bernard studio, with whom he shared family ties (Shatskih 2007, 170). The *taille direct* technique was also taught in the Kiev *Kultur Lige* sculpture studio; Sergey Bulakovsky, who mastered hard-rock carving in Paris, briefly worked there in 1918 (Silina 2014, 210).

2 Chaikov had already singled out Alexander Archipenko's *Skulptur Malerei* (sculpto-painting) in his *Skulptur* treatise. It was the dynamic strain of geometric figures in Archipenko's works such as *Medrano I* (mixed media, 1912) that so appealed to Chaikov (Chaikov 1921, 6–9).

Fig. 1: Yoysef Chaikov. Project of Lekkert monument for Minsk. Plaster, glass. 1922–1924. Not preserved.

Jewish symbols or attributes. Instead, Lekkert was represented as a contemporary Soviet hero, with messianic resolve in his eyes and self-determination in his posture. By the 1930s, however, Jewish public heroes had disappeared from public spaces and local initiatives had sunk into oblivion. David Yakerson installed a monument to local revolutionary Lev Garfunkel in the Yanovichi *shtetl* in 1919, but little is known about the monument or the seventeen- or eighteen-year-old young man it honored, who died in 1919 during the Civil War (Silina 2014, 260). This monument shared a similar fate; in 1937 it was removed and forgotten (Bemporad 2013, 67–69). Of all the initiatives of Yiddish activists, only Chaikov's work as an active member of the state-controlled Union of Artists of the USSR was used to legitimize the "monumental propaganda plan." In the 1960s his works were incorporated into the state-approved narrative of early Soviet art (Chaikov 1968).

Yiddish Culture and the Soviet Art Institutions in the 1920s

The first signs of the dramatic changes awaiting Jewish culture in the USSR were visible by 1921, when the Fine Arts department of *Narkompros* (Commissariat of Enlightenment of the RSFSR) was liquidated and contemporary artists who had led its central and local branches in 1918 were removed. By the 1920s a wide range of restrictive measures had been implemented against religious practice and teaching in Hebrew. Instead of supporting traditional religious Jewish culture, it was claimed that a new proletarian Yiddish culture had been created. In 1920, the *Kultur Lige* Central bureau in Moscow and the Kiev branch came under Bolshevik control, which saw in them a convenient instrument for Sovietization of the Jewish cultural milieu. By 1924 all educational units of the *Kultur Lige* were under *Narkompros* jurisdiction (Kazovsky 2003, 25–27). The Jewish Arts and Trades School became dependent on state aid, as well as on support from the American Jewish Joint Distribution Committee. By the late 1920s, the school administration was under constant attack for its lack of a Soviet proletarian agenda; the school was ultimately closed in 1931 (Kazovsky 2003, 53–55).

During the 1920s a significant number of young Jews entered Soviet universities, which were forced to conform to the framework of an all-Soviet "universal" culture (Bemporad 2013, 3–4, 44). Likewise, artists such as Yoysef Chaikov had to undergo a transition to become Soviet artists. In 1924 he became a professor at *Vkhutemas* (known from 1920–1926 as the Higher Art and Technical Studios; from 1926–1930 as *Vkhutein*, the Higher Art and Technical Institute). Shortly thereafter he became the head of the Sculpture department, and in 1927 chairman of the *Obshchestvo russkikh skul'ptorov* (ORS, Society of Russian Sculptors) (Matsa et al. 1933, 327). At *Vkutemas*, Chaikov's students experimented with non-conventional materials and technical aesthetics of the new era; for example, a student work from the 1920s by A.V. Kikin, entitled *Oborona SSSR* (Defense of the USSR), is strikingly reminiscent of early works by Chaikov, such as *Bridgebuilder* (wood, cardboard, wire, 1921). Chaikov continued creating experimental constructions such as *A Young Jew* (plaster, 1923) and *A Walking Jew* (wood, 1925) until 1925. One of his last works on Jewish life in the prewar period was the 1929 relief panel

Evrei na zemle (Jews on the Land). The rendering still pointed to the *Kulture Lige*-era reliefs like the 1921 *Violin Player*, its surface treated as a space executed in sunk and bas relief. Yet it also marked the emergence of a new semi-folklore, almost *lubok* (Russian popular prints) style. His later polychrome art deco figurines representing sports and leisure time, such as *Futbolisty* (Football Players, plaster, 1928), *Mototsiklist* (Motocyclist, ceramics, 1931), and *Voleybol* (Volleyball, ceramics, 1934), had nothing to do with Yiddish sculpture of the late 1910s but had very much in common with the laconic images of the typical Jewish population in works by Marc Chagall or Issachar Ben Ryback from the 1910s.

Chaikov's new manner, which he also taught to his *Vkhutemas* students, can be seen as a sculptural analogue to the effect the *Obshchestvo khudozhnikov-stankovistov* (OST, Society of Easel Painters) had on the legacy and works of former *Kultur Lige* members like Alexander Tyshler. The *OST* aesthetic was expressed in a highly distinctive synthesis of neo-primitivism and topics from dynamic modern city life. The manner is exemplary in the early legacy of Ilia Slonim (1906–1973), a student of Chaikov's who, judging by the testimony of his relatives in private conversation with the author, did not associate or refer his art practice to Jewish culture. Stylistically, however, his works of the 1920s, created during his study at *Vkhutemas-Vkhutein*, are difficult to separate from contemporary Yiddish culture. His 1929 relief *The Strike of 1905* exhibits a neo-archaic style with strong orientalist overtones, and the national Jewish traits in depicting characters are still recognizable (see Fig. 2). Instead of depicting proletarian struggle and heroic typification, Slonim nearly created Old Testament martyrs. Later he would take interest in the legacy of Antoine Bourdelle and Gothic art, which allowed him to deepen his affection for the Archaic past.

Another of Chaikov's students, Meer Aisenshtadt (1895–1961), initially received a traditional Jewish education and was patronized by a local Jewish community. According to the memoirs of his wife, Ariadna Arendt, "two sources were constantly struggling in his mind: national and international" (Meer Aisenshtadt 1991) and he regretted that there was no tradition of Jewish art. Aisenshtadt's works, such as his final *Vkhutein* project, *Symphony of the Factory* (1930–1931), or his *Homage to Lucas Cranach* (1929–1933), display inherited complex constructivist spatial compositions and Malevich suprematist experiments of the 1920s, which combine with the lyric narrativism of the *OST* group. These works depicted Socialism through the means of neo-primitivism, however, and were not demanded by political leaders striving to set the standards of the unified Socialist realism culture.

Fig. 2: Ilia Slonim. *The Strike of 1905. Plaster. 1929.* Not preserved.

Reduction of Jewish Art to Stalinist Unified Culture and Ethnography in the 1930s

A 1932 decree by the Central Committee of the VKP(b) entitled *O perestoike literakurno-khudozhestvennykh organizatsiy* (On Restructuring Literary-Artistic Organizations) denounced the institutional freedom of artists (Matsa et al. 1933, 644–645). At the time, Yoysef Chaikov was head of the *Moskovskii oblastnoi soiuz sovetskikh khudozhnikov-skul'ptorov* (Moscow Soviet Sculptors' Union), an ill-fated organization that was merged with *Moskovskii oblastnoi soiuz sovetskikh khudozhnikov* (Moscow Union of Soviet Artists) in 1940. By 1933 the critical campaign against formalism had been launched, aiming against any innovative and stylistically independent direction in art; the activities of former Yiddish art activists were mentioned only as formal *oshibki* (mistakes) (Ternovets 1933, 153). In an article dedicated to Chaikov's legacy, Alexander Romm, an art historian formerly active in Jewish artistic life in Vitebsk, tendentiously linked the neo-archaic style that he practiced in Paris to the rise of Nationalism, a style he saw almost as a manifestation of territorial ambitions (Romm 1933, 111). In 1937, Chaikov's group for Meyerhold theatre, as well as works of Ilia Slonim, came under criticism for being formal and therefore opposed to Socialist realism (Protiv formalizma 1937, 72, 74).

A 1934 issue of *Iskusstvo* (Art), an official magazine of the *Moscow Union of Soviet Artists*, contained only one article on a Jewish sculptor. It was an obituary of Solomon Strazh (1870–1934), in which he was explicitly labelled a mediocre master. The main pathos of the piece was its emphasis on the emancipatory power of Soviet culture and class struggle issues, which enabled Jewish artists to free themselves from religious taboos and to find their own way. This popular biography for Soviet readers mentioned the cruel "*melamed* of the *heder*," the young sculptor's sacral fear of "*narushenie vekovechnogo zapreta, nalozhennogo Bibliei,*" [the break with the everlasting commandment of the Bible] (Rayhinstein 1934, 79–80). Before the 1917 Revolution, Strazh had made sculptures in neo-Archaic and Art Nouveau styles on Jewish themes. In the 1920s he pursued sculptures that touched Jewish contemporary history (such as *Pogrom* in plaster, 1929), but by the 1930s he had switched to common Socialist themes. The production of mass sculpture became the major source of income for the greater number of Soviet sculptors in the 1930s. Dissemination of such work was aimed at forging a unified and approved Socialist culture over the vast and multiethnic territory of the USSR. Former head of the Jewish Arts and Trades School Mark Epstein and Meer Aisenshtadt, Solomon Strazh, and others became involved in the production of partisan and Party-oriented art. The fate of Abram Brazer is also exemplary in this respect. In 1931 he was criticized for the Nationalistic motives of his oeuvre; he was said to use art directly against proletarian dictatorship, using Western formalism in his creative work (*Iskusstvo natsionaljnikh respublik* 1931, 23). In the 1930s Brazer began producing political portraits of local party leaders, including a monument to Felix Dzerzhinsky, a head of the Soviet secret political police (Cheka/GPU/OGPU). For this monument he was honored in 1940 with the title *Narodnyi Khudozhnik Belorussii* (People's Painter of Belorussia) and his work became the classic example of Belorussian Socialist sculpture (Voronovich 2010).

While national discourse was gradually being displaced by that of class, Soviet ethnography was being established. Both in themes and in artistic methods, neo-archaism became the road that led sculptors away from a national agenda that was emancipatory to one that was colonial. During the 1920s, David Yakerson turned to figurative wooden sculpture in neo-Archaic style, collaborating with the *Muzei Narodovedenia* (Museum of Ethnology) in Moscow. The existence of diverse ethnic and cultural groups in the USSR afforded impressive possibilities for portraying a variety of nations in sophisticated archaic and primitivist styles. At the 1926 exhibition of the *Assotsiatsia khudozhnikov revolutsionnoi Rossii* (AKhRR, Association of Artists of Revolutionary Russia), entitled *Zhizhn' i byt narodov SSSR* (Everyday Life of the Peoples of the USSR), Yakerson showed works representing national and social types of various indigenous ethnic groups, including his works *Tunguz* (Tungus) and *Belorusskii evrei* (Belorussian Jew) (Shatskikh 1984, 164). However, already in the early 1930s he was being attacked by critics who accused him of promoting "*simvolitcheski traktovannoe rassovoe i biologicheskoe, a ne klassovoe*" [symbolically interpreted racial and biological [traits], that dominate over class-specific [traits]] in his work *Iakut* (Yakut) (A.M. 1931, 26). The class concept allowed Soviet critics to advocate a progressivist vision of the nation, but also to ultimately denounce the cultural particularity of any nation suspected of separatism.

In 1934 the *Evreistkaia avtonomnaia oblast'* (Jewish Autonomous Republic, EAO), with its administrative center in Birobidzhan, was founded, and thus creation of a truly national Socialist Jewish culture was anticipated. However, the ambitious projects were confined to vague generalities (Ivanov 2010). The US-based *John Reed Club* made a gift of numerous Jewish art pieces to commemorate the creation of Jewish autonomy in Birobidzan. (The majority of the club's New York branch were Jewish immigrants from Eastern Europe and the former Russian Empire.) The exhibition of these donated pieces opened with great fanfare in New York and later in Moscow, yet never reached its destination of Birobidzhan (Weinstein 2001, 143, 158). The *EAO* participated in the 1939 *Vsesoiuznaia sel'skokhoziaistvennaia vystavka* (All-Union Agricultural Exhibition, VSKhV) in Moscow, but the theme of the Jewish section was purely agricultural. No Jewish art piece in style or theme was present, which was typical at the other pavilions, where traditional religious albeit heavily desacralized and decontextualized ornamentation was used (Zhirnova 2011). David Yakerson also took part in the *VSKhV* exhibition, but not as part of any Jewish community of artists, which no longer existed by then; instead, he presented as one of the designers of Bashkir pavilion. He created a statue of Salavat Yulaev, the official national hero of the Bashkir people. The statue was thought to resemble traditional national Bashkirian herms (Tolstoi 2005, 427). For his *VSKhV* wooden reliefs he used the "1930s sketches of the folklore motives that he earlier created in Rashkov and other Jewish places," (Foll 2007, 68) which had become repressed into the domain of historicized ethnography. Having lost the possibility to establish a truly transnational style in autonomous national institutions, the basis for Jewish cultural identity was not only lost but also merged with State cultural organizations.

Bibliography

"Iskusstvo natsionalnykh sovetskih sotsialisticheskih respublik." [Art of National Soviet Socialist Republics] *Za proletarskoye iskusstvo* 6 (1931): 22–27.
A.M. "Na perestroyku fronta sovetskoy skulpturi." [For Reconstruction of Soviet Sculptural Front] *Za proletarskoye iskusstvo* 9 (1931): 24–27.
Apter-Gabriel, Ruth (ed.). *Tradition and Revolution: The Jewish Renaissance in Russian Avant-Garde Art 1912–1928*. Jerusalem: The Israel Museum, 1988.
Bemporad, Elissa. *Becoming Soviet Jews: The Bolshevik Experiment in Minsk*. Bloomington: Indiana University Press, 2013.
Bland, Kalman. *The Artless Jew: Medieval and Modern Affirmations and Denials of the Visual*. Princeton, NJ: Princeton University Press, 2000.
Bowlt, John. "Icarian Games: Iosif Chaikov and the Jewish Legacy." *Experiment* 18. 1 (2012): 166–193.
Chaikov, Yoysef. *Skulptur*. Trans. from Yiddish into Russian by Velvl Chernin. Kiev: Gosudarstvennoe izdateljstvo, 1921.
Chaikov, Yoysef. "Kiev, god 1919." *Tvorchestvo* 4 (1968): 6.
Curtis, Penelope. *Sculpture 1900–1945: After Rodin*. New York: Oxford University Press, 1999.
Foll, LeClaire. *Vitebskaya khudozhestvennaya shkola (1897–1923)*. Minsk: Propilei, 2007.
Golan, Romy. "École Française vs École de Paris: The Debate about the Status of Jewish Artists in Paris between the Wars." *Jewish Dimensions in Modern Visual Culture. Antisemitism, Assimilation, Affirmation*. Eds. Rose-Carol Washton Long, Matthew Baigell and Milly Heyd. Waltham, MA: Brandeis University Press, 2010. 77–89.
Hamm, Michael F. "'Special and Bewildering': A Portrait of Late-Imperial and Early Soviet Kyiv." *Modernity in Kyiv. Jubilant Experimentation*. Ed. Irena R. Makaryk and Virlana Tkacz. Toronto: University of Toronto Press, 2010. 52–97.
Ivanov A. "'Evrei v tsarskoy Rossii' – vystavka dostyzheniy evreyskogo khoziaystvennogo y kulturnogo stroitelstva v Strane Sovetov." *Novoye Literaturnoye Obozrenie* 102 (2010). http://magazines.russ.ru/nlo/2010/102/iv14-pr.html (April 20 2015).
Kampf, Avram. *Jewish Experience in the Art of the Twentieth Century*. South Hadley: Bergin and Garvey, 1984.
Kazovsky, Hillel. *Khudozhniki Kul'tur-Ligi / The Artists of the Kultur-Lige*. Moscow and Jerusalem: Mosty kulturi, Gesharim, 2003.
Kostyrchenko, G.V. *Stalin protiv "kosmopolitov". Vlast y evreyskaya intelligentsiya v SSSR*. Moscow: ROSPEN, 2009.
Mann, Vivian B. (ed.). *Jewish Texts on the Visual Arts*. New York: Cambridge University Press, 2000.
Mastbaum, Itella. "Posmotri y vspomni. Skulptor Haim ben-Bezalel Mastbaum." *Zametki po evreiskoy istorii* 16 (2009). www.berkovich-zametki.com/2009/Zametki/Nomer16/Mastbaum1.php (March 18 2015).
Matsa, I., L. Reyngardt, and L. Rempel (eds.). *Sovetskoe iskusstvo za 15 let. Materialy I dokumentatsiya*. Moscow and Leningrad: Ogiz-Izogiz, 1933.
Meer Aisenshtadt, 1895–1961: skulptura, grafika: katalog vystavki. Moscow: Sovetskiy khudozhnik, 1991.
Mendes-Flohr, Paul. *Divided Passions: Jewish Intellectuals and the Experience of Modernity*. Detroit: Wayne State University Press, 1991.

Moss, Kenneth B. *Jewish Renaissance in the Russian Revolution*. Cambridge: Harvard University Press, 2009.
Olin, Margaret. *The Nation Without Art: Examining Modern Discourses on Jewish Art*. Lincoln: University of Nebraska Press, 2001.
Orlov, Alina. "Beyond Nationalism: Natan Altman's 'Self-Portrait; a Jewish Youth' (1915)." *Transversal* 5.1 (2004): 100–108.
Orlov, Alina. "First There Was the Word: Early Russian Texts on Modern Jewish Art." *Oxford Art Journal* 31. 3 (2008): 383–402.
Protiv formalizma y naturalisma v iskusstve. Moscow: Ogiz-Izogiz, 1937.
Rayhinstein, M. "Skulptor S. N. Strazh." *Iskusstvo* 6 (1934): 78–85.
Romm, A.G. "O tvorchestve Yoysefa Chaikova." *Iskusstvo* 3 (1933): 109–126.
Shatskikh, A.S. "Derevyannaya skulptura D. Yakersona (1897–1946)." *Sovetskaya skulptura*. Vol. 8. Moscow: Sovetskiy khudozhnik, 1984. 160–169.
Shatskikh, A.S. "Arkhitekturno-plasticheskie kompozitsii skulptora M.B. Aisenshtadta." *Skulptura v gorode*. Moscow: Sovetskiy khudozhnik, 1990. 165–174.
Shatskikh, Aleksandra. *Vitebsk: The Life of Art*. New Haven and London: Yale University Press, 2007.
Silina, Maria. *Istoriya y Ideologia: Monumentaljno-Dekorativniy Reljef SSSR 1920–1930-h godov*. Moscow: BuksMart, 2014.
Ternovets, B.N. "XV let sovetskoy skulpturi." *Iskusstvo* 5 (1933): 131–160.
Tolstoi, V.P. (ed.). *Vystavochnye ansambly SSSR. 1920–1930-e gody: materialy I dokumenty*. Moscow: Galart, 2006.
Tolstoi, V.P. (ed.). *Khudozhestvennaya zhizn Rossii. 1917–1932. Sobytia, fakty, kommentarii. Sbornik materialov y dokumentov*. Moscow: Galart, 2010.
Voronovich, Irina. "Sudba mastera." *Mishpocha* 25 (2010): 52–56.
Weinstein, Andrew. "From International Socialism to Jewish Nationalism: The John Reed Club Gift to Birobidzhan." *Complex Identities: Jewish Consciousness and Modern Art*. Ed. Matthew Baigell and Milly Heyd. New Brunswick, NJ: Rutgers University Press, 2001. 142–161.
Wood, Jon, David Hulks and Alex Potts (eds.). *Modern Sculpture Reader*. Los Angeles: J. Paul Getty Museum, 2012.
Zhirnova, I.A. Utchastie Evreiskoy avtonomnoy oblasti vo Vsesoyznoy selskohozyaystvennoy vystavke. I Mezhdunarodnaya konferentsiya "Evreyskaya kultura na idish: istoki, traditsii, transformatsiya I sovremennoye sostoyanie". Birobidjan, 7–8 September 2011. www.nasledie-eao.ru/news/detail.php?ID=1530 (20 March 2015).

Self-Representation and Anti-Semitism

Zoë Roth
Frontière humaine: Race, Nation, and the Shape of Representation in Claude Cahun

"*Sous ce masque, un autre masque; je n'en finirai pas d'enlever tous ces visages*" [Under this mask, another mask. I will never finish taking off all of these faces]. So wrote the French surrealist Claude Cahun (née Lucy Schwob, 1894–1954) in 1930 (2002 [1930], 406). In a 1928 self-portrait, these many faces adorn Cahun's dark robe, while her face, obscured by a japanesque mask (Shaw 2013, 49), refuses the notion of an essential self beneath the veneer of appearances (Fig. 1). Cahun's aesthetic play with identity positions has often been attributed to her desire to undermine normative conceptions of gender and sexuality (Rice 1999; Adamowicz 2004; Doy 2008; Shaw 2013). A lesbian, Cahun worked with her lifelong partner and stepsister Suzanne Malherbe (later Marcel Moore, 1892–1972) to produce works celebrating cross-dressing and masquerade. But Cahun also came from a prominent, assimilated Jewish family. Just as the Asian-like mask in the self-portrait points to a racial register, so too can we read her work and identity in terms of race. In this essay, I will argue that the intersection of Jewish, gendered, and sexual difference animates Cahun's avant-garde exploration of the limits of representation. However, she also demonstrates how these forms of difference have been marginalized in histories of the avant-garde. Cahun and Moore long collaborated with the French surrealists, including André Breton, Robert Desnos, and René Crevel, but they existed on the group's edges. She was largely omitted from surrealist histories, which often cast female participants as the "muses" of men, while ignoring Jewish participants' origins altogether.

Two images – a negative and the printed photograph – depicting Cahun at the International Surrealist Exhibition in London in 1936 inadvertently capture how Cahun embodies the double erasure of gender and racial difference from the avant-garde (Unknown 1936) (Fig. 2). In the negative, a coterie of surrealist "who's-who" that includes ELT Mesens, André Breton, Roland Penrose, David Gascoyne, Cahun, and an unknown woman are lined up from left to right in front of an empty shop. Cahun is on the far right, while the unknown woman is largely cut off. A rough rectangle has been drawn around the male participants, presumably to indicate how the photograph should be trimmed. She is completely absent from the printed photo of this event, which marked the emergence of British surrealism. In these images, Cahun is gradually pushed to the edge of the scene, until she is entirely effaced.

DOI 10.1515/9783110454956-009

Fig. 1: Claude Cahun. *Self Portrait*. c. 1928. Jersey Heritage Archive. JHT/1995/22/w.

Only in the 1990s did François Leperlier revive interest in Cahun with the publication of *Claude Cahun: L'Écart et la metamorphose* (Claude Cahun: Distance and Metamorphosis) (1992). Her use of mirrors, masks, and doubles produces multiple identity positions that unfold through a project of self-portraiture challenging the very nature of representation – both political and aesthetic. She conceived of cosmopolitan forms of belonging that provide a counterpoint to exclusionary nationalist and racial discourses that targeted Jews. The Jewish body stands at the center of her work, allowing her to embody simultaneously multiple forms of difference. She deploys visual stereotypes of the parasitic, deviant Jewish body in order to denaturalize mimetic forms of representation. But while her strategies unveil the aesthetic processes that construct race, her work also hints at racial tensions between France's "indigenous" Jews and the more recently arrived *Ostjuden* (Eastern

Fig. 2: Unknown. *Untitled. Negative of ELT Mesens, Roland Penrose, André Breton, and David Gascoyne.* 11 June 1936. Jersey Heritage Archive. JHT/1995/00022/x.

Jews). Her work provides an alternative genealogy of the French avant-garde, in which questions about the visibility of race gave rise to new representational urgencies. Using Cahun's work as a focal point, I argue that a series of social and political phenomena in the late nineteenth and early twentieth centuries, including immigration, the Dreyfus affair, and organized anti-Semitism, produced anxieties concerning Jewishness that propelled the interwar French avant-garde to question conventional modes of representation. While this article focuses on surrealism, these tensions are also apparent in other avant-garde movements, such as dada and Georges Bataille's *Documents* group. Reading the avant-garde crisis of representation via Jewish difference in Cahun's work demonstrates the way marginalized identities – figures cut out of the frame – helped shape the avant-garde's engagement with experiences of alterity.

The crisis of aesthetic representation has been widely understood as a reaction to the social and political upheavals of WWI, when movements such as surrealism and dada produced new forms of artistic practice to depict a radically altered world (Short 1978; Perloff 2010). By exploring how race and anti-Semitism helped shape the avant-garde's self-reflexive practice, however, this essay contributes to scholarship that challenges the commonplace narrative situating the origins of the crisis in representation in WWI (see for example Sheshagiri 2010; Sell 2011; Harding 2014). I will trace a longer genealogy of the crisis of representation in France back to the way Jews' political and racial belonging in the Republic was thrown into question in the *fin-de-siècle*. My essay connects the avant-garde's radical break with conventional forms of representation to anxieties around the visibility of race and the persistence of anti-Semitism.

If scholarship has often overlooked the avant-garde's multiple origins, it has also elided the way Jewish identity shaped the French interwar avant-garde. Until recently, the Jewish identity of some of the French avant-garde's most important participants, including Man Ray and Tristan Tzara, was overlooked (Heyd 2001, 2010). Although Man Ray and Tzara played down or outright rejected their Jewish origins, ignoring their ethnic and religious backgrounds elides the political and racial anxieties of the time. Such artists may not have put stock in their backgrounds, but, as I shall explore later, their Jewishness played a role in how both fellow artists and political institutions viewed them. Mirroring the way women were largely omitted from avant-garde histories until the 1980s (Adamowicz 2004, 50), important Jewish participants, such as Wolfgang Paalen, have been marginalized in accounts of the avant-garde (Winter 2001). In exploring Cahun's work, I will demonstrate how racial and nationalist anxieties pertaining to Jewishness are crucial aspects of the avant-garde's exploration of otherness.

Emancipation, Immigration, Representation

Claude Cahun was born Lucy Schwob to a prominent literary family in Nantes in 1894. Her uncle, Marcel Schwob, a symbolist writer who influenced Guillaume Apollinaire, was a contemporary of Proust. Due to her mother's mental illness she spent most of her childhood in the company of her grandmother, Mathilde Cahun. Her father, Maurice René Schwob, owned *Le Phare de la Loire* (The Loire Lighthouse), the openly Republican Nantes daily. Anti-Semitism played a pivotal role in Cahun's early family life. She was born in the same year Captain Alfred Dreyfus was tried for treason, and was equally affected by the anti-Semitic attacks following his 1906 exoneration. In Nantes, the *Ligue antisémite* (Anti-Semitic League) targeted Schwob, who they saw as embodying "the influences of the Jewish colony, so prominent in Nantes" (Birnbaum 2011, 241). Schwob strongly identified with the persecuted officer, as Cahun writes in *Confidences au miroir* (Secrets Told to the Mirror): "*il envisagea même l'affaire Dreyfus sous l'angle national* [...] *Je ne doute pas qu'à la place du capitaine il eût courbé la tête, péri 'déshonoré'* [...] *à l'île du Diable"* [he even envisaged the Dreyfus affair under a national angle [...] I don't doubt that he would have bowed his head, dead 'dishonored' [...] on Devil's Island in the captain's place] (2002, 600). If the personal was political for her father, Cahun also suffered from the resurgence of anti-Semitism. *"Un jour"* [one day] in 1907, as she states in a letter to Charles Henri Barbier (1951), *"liée avec des cordes à sauter à un arbre de la cour de récréation, je fus lapidée avec du gravier"* [tied to a tree in the playground with a jump rope, I was stoned with gravel] (cited in Leperlier 2006, 27). Following such attacks, Cahun was sent to England where she attended school for a year before reluctantly returning to live with her father.

In 1917, Cahun changed her name from Lucy Schwob to Claude Cahun (Leperlier 2006, 41). While playing on the surrealist use of pseudonyms to question stable authorship, her name change also points towards expressions of both Jewish and gendered identity: Claude is gender-neutral, while she reinforces Judaism's matrilineal lines by adopting her grandmother's name, Cahun. As Leo Spitzer argues in his discussion of the role names play in constructing diasporic identities, naming provides both an outward facing social identity and a personal identity (2010, 22). Cahun's name change signaled the way gender, sexuality, and Jewishness intertwined to construct both the social and private realms of her identity. Indeed, her renaming coincided with a series of physical changes – shaving her head, cross-dressing, and masquerade – that embodied the performative aspect of gender (Krauss 1999, 29). Yet little has been made of the racial aspect of her name change. What happens to Jewishness when she changes her name from Schwob, an illustrious patronymic associated with Proust, to the French version of "Cohen," a sign of the Jewish priestly class?

To answer this question, it is necessary to situate Cahun's choice within the nineteenth-century bureaucratic practice of requiring Jews across Western and Central Europe to adopt family names (Spitzer 2010, 24). The operation was linked to emancipation and integration, but it also enabled states to more easily identify Jews (Spitzer 2010, 24). In this way, Jewish naming represented a shift in the visibility of Jews. It brought them into the fold of civic life as well as methods of bureaucratic categorization. By choosing to leave behind an acculturated name for one that was clearly religious – and more of a target in the atmosphere of growing anti-Semitism – Cahun alludes to the breakdown of the assimilationist model that underpinned French Jews' participation in the life of the nation, gesturing back to the Dreyfus affair and earlier emancipation reforms. At a time when Jews across Europe were changing their names to more "Christian" variants (Spitzer 2010, 27), Cahun was *demasking* the limits of emancipation and assimilation. Her name not only mediated between the social and the private, but also between two images of Jews: one acculturated, the other foreign.[1]

France holds a privileged place in the modernization of European Jewry (Samuels 2009, 6). The French Revolution triggered the set of political reforms now known as Jewish emancipation, which gradually granted Jews the same political representation as other citizens. Indeed, as the French Revolution did away with self-governing groups – granting Jews citizenship as individuals rather than as a collective – their assimilation was a pivotal factor in the creation of the modern French state. Jewish emancipation thus proved a litmus test both for the Enlightenment's philosophical ideals and the founding of the Republic on an individual basis (Schechter 2003).

In the nineteenth century, many French Jews eagerly assimilated, while still retaining their ethnic and religious affiliations. The name *Israélite* signified a modern Jewish identity that molded communal affiliation with acculturation (Samuels 2009, 81). French Jewry's relatively untroubled acculturation and integration in the first half of the nineteenth century instilled in them a confidence in state institutions. Their identification with the state culminated in an increase in Jews, such as Dreyfus, joining the civil service and army during the Third Republic (1871–1940) (Birnbaum 1992; Samuels 2009, 14).

French Jews were bound up with the project of French universalism, but they also suffered from the exclusive particularism that accompanied this model. In contrast to conceptions of a nation-state predetermined by blood, such as the one found in Germany, the republic that emerged from the French Revolution was founded on a universal contract between the state and free individuals (Silverman, 1992, 19–20). However, the boundary between biological and cultural conceptions of the nation in France has not always been clear. French political and social values, such as individualism and universalism, helped racialize the "French" (Silverman 1992, 7–8) – and exclude those considered different – by constructing a seemingly immutable notion of *la race française* that naturally cohered to the nation's boundaries. In the context of immigration and the emergence of racial

---

[1] Emancipation, acculturation, integration, and assimilation are terms that, while connected, denote distinct changes in Jewish communities in nineteenth- and twentieth-century Europe. Emancipation refers to "the acquisiton of rights and privileges enjoyed by non-Jewish citizens/subjects of similar socioeconomic rank." Acculturation denotes the obtaining of "the cultural and social habits of the dominant non-Jewish group." Integration describes "the entry of Jews into non-Jewish circles and spheres of activity." The term assimilation has often been used to describe this nexus, but it was also a prescriptivist program of cultural and political transformation. For this reason, I also take assimilation to describe the way some Jews identified primarily with "a larger, non-Jewish nationality." These definitions derive from Edelman 2013.

theories at the end of the nineteenth and beginning of the twentieth centuries, political doctrines increasingly equated race with nation (Camiscioli 2009, 56). Pseudo-scientific racial discourses emerged from discoveries in evolutionary science and biology that sought to provide positivist categories for phenotypical phenomena (Benbassa 2001, 137). In addition, racial categorization, particularly as it was applied to Jews, combined physiognomic traits with nationality and religion. Increased immigration, emboldened nationalism, and racialism proved disastrous for Jews in France, who came to be seen as threatening French national identity based on racial purity (Silverman 1992, 19–20; Camiscioli 2009). The Dreyfus affair brought these tensions to a fever pitch, casting Jews as a foreign race that threatened French sovereignty.

The secular reforms that derived from Dreyfus' exoneration calmed widespread French anti-Semitism. Although reactionary nationalist groups, like *L'Action française*, and writers, like Édouard Drumont, kept political and cultural anti-Semitism alive, the French Jewish community quickly rebounded from the affair (Hyman 1998, 113). The challenge that now faced French Jews in the years up to the First World War was the influx of Eastern European Jewry. France's acculturated, integrated Jewish population feared immigrants would threaten their social and political gains, because they were seen as a visible sign of Jewish difference (Benbassa 2001, 134; Lindemann 1991, 62).

Beginning in the 1880s, successive waves of immigration from Eastern Europe had brought many *Ostjuden* to France. Although France was simply a stopping-off point on the way to the New World in the period up to WWI, the arrival of Jewish immigrants increasingly tested France's assimilationist model (Hyman 1998, 116; Benbassa 2001, 134). The influx coincided with the resurgence of nationalism following France's defeat in the Franco-Prussian War and the loss of Alsace-Lorraine, which compelled many Alsatian Jews to move to Paris (Lindemann 1991, 60). The nationalism that emerged during the early Third Republic (1870–1940) was more chauvinistic and anti-Semitic than previous revolutionary nationalisms, which had vaunted France's humanitarian ideals (Girardet 1983). This reactionary nationalism often singled out Jews as the enemy weakening France from within (Winock 2000, 99). Tensions began to emerge both within France's Jewish community and between French Jews and the state. Rising anti-Semitism threatened the inroads they had made into French civic, economic, and cultural life, while successive waves of Eastern European Jewish immigrants challenged their self-understanding as acculturated French citizens (Hyman 1998, 122, 115). The arrival of Jewish immigrants, in other words, also forced French Jews to interrogate the boundaries of Jewishness.

The outbreak of WWI provided an opportunity for immigrants to more fully integrate into native French Jewish communities, as both groups collaborated to support France's war effort. But the war only held in abeyance a dangerous, building confluence of forces that exploded in the interwar period, including immense numbers of immigrants and virulent, nationalist anti-Semitism (Hyman 1998, 133, 135). Many of these immigrants, who included Tristan Tzara and his dada cohort, as well as the "École de Paris," the largely Jewish circle of artists working in Montparnasse, produced some of the most important avant-garde works of the twentieth-century. The anxieties that crystallized around these immigrants and their cultural influence once again merged anti-Semitism, nationalism, and racialism. Mirroring the charges previously leveled at Jews during the Dreyfus affair, the avant-garde artists working in Paris at the time were attacked for being both "boche" (German) and Jewish (Golan 2010, 78).

These Jews had to contend with the disdain of both French nativists and *Israélites*. Reflecting French Jews' earlier anxieties about the visible difference of *Ostjuden*, the Jewish art critic Louis Vauxcelles wrote:

> A barbarian horde has rushed upon Montparnasse, descending on [the art galleries] of Rue La Boétie from the cafés of the 14th arrondissement [Montparnasse], uttering raucous Germano-Slavic screams of war [...]. These are people from "somewhere else" who ignore and in the bottom of their hearts look down on what Renoir has called the gentleness of the French School – that is, our race's virtue of tact.
> (Cited in Golan 2010, 81)

The French avant-garde often staged clashes of civilization in order to stake out new artistic territories – think, for example, of the surrealist map, "Le Monde au temps du surréaliste" (The Surrealist Map of the World). In this passage, however, two kinds of "races" confront each other in a battle for French artistic values. In other words, this is a battle about who will control the terrain of representation. Moreover, at the moment Vauxcelles aligns himself with the French race – "our race" – he comes up against the boundaries of his own Jewishness.

Reflecting the double onslaught of internal and external tensions affecting Jewish communities in France, avant-garde participants were also battling over modes of representation with their Jewish counterparts. André Breton's staging of *Le Procès Barrès* (The Trial and Sentencing of Maurice Barrès by Dada) (13 May, 1921) provides a telling example. While purportedly intended to prosecute the reactionary nationalist Maurice Barrès for having betrayed his early revolutionary impulses, Breton sought to associate him with dada – and by extension Tzara – in order to relegate dada to the dustbin of history and thus setting the stage for surrealism (Harding 2013, 35). The contradiction of aligning Tzara, a Romanian Jewish émigré, with Barrès, a vitriolic anti-Semite and anti-Dreyfusard, would later resurface in Breton's angry denunciation of Tzara as a *"un personnage connu pour le promoteur d'un mouvement venu de Zurich qu'il n'est pas utile de désigner autrement et qui ne répond plus aujourd'hui à aucune réalité"* [a person known as a promoter of a 'movement' that comes from Zurich, which demands no other designation, and which today no longer corresponds to any reality] (cited in Polizzotti 1997, 170–171). There was more than just a touch of xenophobia in Breton's contradictory denunciation of a foreigner at the International Congress of Paris (Josephson 1962, 148–149). He set off a series of accusations among dada and surrealist factions reminiscent of the public intellectual debates played out during the Dreyfus affair. By appropriating the judicial space of the courtroom to insist dada no longer had the means to interpret reality, Breton sought to take hold of – and expel Tzara from – "the means of representation" itself (Harding 2013, 29, 32). Beyond the latent anti-Semitism in Breton's actions, James Harding reads this event as evidence of the historical avant-garde's contradictory dynamics – dynamics that were non-linear as well as forward-looking. Breton's reactionary return to *fin-de-siècle* anti-Semitism, then, produced a typically avant-garde form of public performance. But it also demonstrated an alternative genealogy of the avant-garde's spectacular nature, tying the avant-garde's crisis of representation to anxieties around the visibility of race and Jewishness.

Visualizing Jewishness

The highly visual nature of Jewish racial "otherness" during the *fin-de-siècle* and interwar period meant that the question of what it was to be Jewish was partially negotiated through exploring the limits of representation. But Jewish difference was not an isolated category. Indeed, as a classification and an identity that has been continually contested, Jewishness provides a site for exploring the intersection of race, gender, and sexuality (Pellegrini 1997, 108). As Lisa Silverman (2012) has shown, this intersection has made it a fruitful site for artists' and writers' exploration of the self. In this way, Jewishness can provide an "analytic framework" for understanding the historical construction of identity, as well as to what extent cultural practices can be considered "Jewish" (Silverman 2009, 103). But precisely because Jewishness crosses such boundaries, it has also been a source of anxiety for those concerned with "policing" difference.

In his discussion of anti-Semitic interpretations of modernism as Jewish, Neil Levi (2014, 9) describes how "the figure of the Jew provides both a personification and an explanation for otherwise unrepresentable, disorienting experiences that, in modernity, are associated with a kind of crisis, whether subject formation, transformations in economic, political, and aesthetic value, or the experience of change itself." The confrontation with the boundaries of Jewishness – and the intersection of Jewishness with other forms of difference – shaped an interrogation of the way representations come into being. This sort of self-reflexive process is characteristic of the avant-garde, and Cahun's work is exemplary in this regard. She self-consciously stages an encounter between Jewishness, gender, and sexuality in order to visualize the crisis of modernity.

Both overt and inferred references to Jewish identity, race, and anti-Semitism exist in Cahun's work. For example, she reimagines the Biblical stories of Salome, Judith, and Delilah in *Vues et visions* (Views and Visions) (1914) and *Heroïnes* (Heroines) (1925). In her examination of Jewish allusions in Cahun's writing, Michelle Gewurtz (2012, 8) argues that the title of Cahun's artist book *Aveux non avenus* (Disavowals) is a play on the Kol Nidre prayer, which translates into French as "*tous les vœux*" [all vows] and finishes with the words "Our vows (to God) shall not be vows." Beyond Biblical and religious symbols, Cahun also scatters behind traces of modern Jewish identities. Urged by a friend, she dedicated her 1934 pamphlet *Les Paris sont ouverts* (Place Your Bets) to Trotsky, "*émue du sort d'un Juif errant au passeport sans visa*" [moved by the situation of a wandering Jew with a passport but no visa] (Cahun 2002, 584). Reprising the image of the wandering Jew to represent Trotsky's contemporary statelessness, *Les Paris sont ouverts* criticizes art used in the service of propaganda, whether by nationalism or communism. In the pamphlet, Cahun constructs an imagined space of revolutionary aesthetics – she cites Max Ernst's *frottage* works – that challenges systems of capitalist and nationalist exploitation (Thynne 2010, 7).

More overtly, Cahun was clearly sensitive to the onset of fascism and the resurgence of anti-Semitism between the two World Wars. Alongside Georges Bataille, she was active in the militant surrealist group *Contre-Attaque* (Counter-Attack), which aimed to wed artistic praxis and revolutionary politics (Thynne 2010, 1). This adherence to committed art culminated in her involvement in the resistance on the island of Jersey, where she and Malherbe were living when the Nazis invaded in 1940. Although it appears her artistic activity ceased during this period, her revolutionary aesthetic experiments paved the way for her radical political activities. In a 1946 letter to Breton she linked her political and surrealist activities, stating that "*la suite logique de mon activité d'écrivain à l'époque du Front Populaire*" [the next logical step of my activities as a writer during the time of the Popular Front] naturally derived from "*une activité surréaliste militante comme nous avons voulu en avoir lors de Contre-Attaque*" [a militant surrealist activity, similar to the one we had wanted in Counter-Attack] (cited in Leperlier 1992, 267). But her acute awareness of the dangers of fascism can be situated on a timeline reaching back to the debate around human rights set off by the Dreyfus affair, and even farther, to a long history of anti-Semitic persecution and discrimination against homosexuals. Writing to Paul Levy in 1950, she declared:

si j'ai lutté avec des camarades d'extrême gauche, c'est que cette cause, sans être la mienne, me paraît juste, qu'elle était la seule qui s'opposât efficacement au racisme hitlérien, et que le maintien de certaines valeurs, parmi lesquelles la liberté d'expression – et, par elle, non seulement le maintien mais la conquête de la liberté des mœurs, des droits de l'être humain opprimé par des siècles de superstitions féroces – m'importaient personnellement.

[if I fought alongside my extreme-left comrades, it's because this cause, without being my own, seemed just, that it was the only cause that was effectively opposing Hitlerian racism, and that maintaining certain values, including freedom of expression – and not simply maintaining freedom of expression, but also the liberty to behave as we please, the rights of human beings oppressed by centuries of brutal superstitions – directly concerned me.] (Cahun 2002, 715–716)

On Jersey, Cahun and Moore produced pamphlets that ridiculed the Germans under the propaganda figure of the "Soldier with No Name." In a reversal of Dreyfus, the French army captain accused of corrupting France from within by collaborating with the Germans, the "Soldier with No Name" was presented as a German officer speaking out against his own army. In the carnivalesque tone of a dada performance (Thynne 2010, 13), one pamphlet declares: "*HITLER fuehrt uns ... GOEBBELS spricht fuer uns ... GOERING frisst fuer uns ... LEY trinkt fuer uns ... Himmler? ... HIMMLER ERMORDET FUER ... aber niemand stirbt fuer uns!*" [HITLER guides us ... GOEBBELS speaks for us ... GOERING gorges himself for us ... LEY drinks for us ... Himmler? HIMMLER ASSASSINATES FOR ... but nobody dies for us!] (Cahun and Moore, 1940–1945). Another leaflet subverts the anti-Semitic trope of the parasitic Jews by painting Hitler as a "*nichtdeutschen Vampir das Blut unseren Jugend säuft!*" [non-German vampire who gets drunk on the blood of our youth] (Cahun and Moore, 1940–1945) (Thynne 2010, 15). The tone of the tracts even provoked the Gestapo agents who questioned Cahun and Moore, suspecting they were written by "an internationalist German intellectual" (Cahun 2002, 629).

Several of Cahun's images demonstrate her desire to produce forms of representation that critique political modes of belonging and subvert national boundaries. Taken together they construct a web of imagined spaces of belonging. In a 1925 self-portrait (Fig. 3), Cahun stares down at the camera. A figure that appears to be Moore peaks out behind her, teasing the viewer with the gaze of a hide-and-seek alter-ego. Although Cahun's shoulders are bare, suggesting nudity, she sports a luminescent six-pointed star. What looks like a reflection of glass suggests that the image has been double-exposed to make it appear as if her head is encased in a bell jar. A series of four images entitled *Studies for a Keepsake* (c. 1925) also depict Cahun's head exhibited under bell jars like a scientific specimen, recalling practices of museum display. Whereas her expression is somewhat playful in *Keepsake*, Cahun looks constrained in *Self Portrait*. The star, although flamboyant, is suspended on a tight chain around her neck that cuts into her skin. It becomes a grotesque stereotype of Jewish visibility that suffocates her under glass, like a specimen on show. But the superimposition of the bell jar self-consciously critiques the supposedly transparent ways of looking associated with the museum (Bal 2003, 14). By bringing attention to the way visual knowledge of a subject is constructed, Cahun denaturalizes the representative nature of the stereotype.

A 1936 image of Cahun reprises the star (Fig. 4). The image's plain lighting, shallow background, conventional front angle, and her neutral expression suggest that it may have been intended as a passport photo. A self-conscious form of identity construction is still at work here, however (Doy 1999, 19). In stark contrast

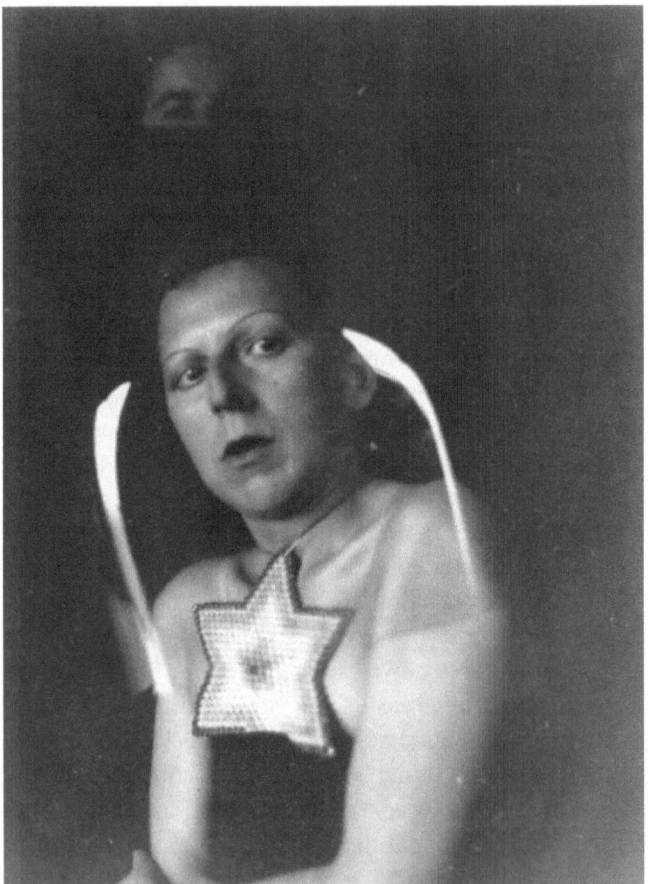

Fig. 3: Claude Cahun. *Self Portrait*. c. 1925. Black and white photograph. Collection Leslie Tonkonow and Klaus Ottmann.

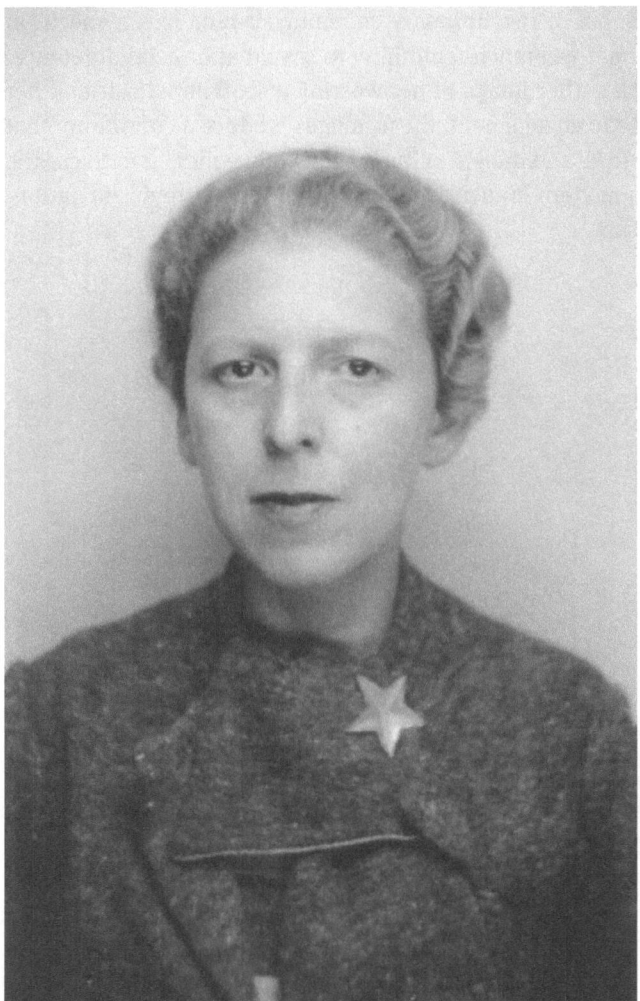

Fig. 4: Claude Cahun. *Passport Photograph*. c. 1936. Black and white photograph. Private collection, UK.

to her raucous gender-bending works, her demure attire, primly coiffed hair, and retiring gaze reproduce conventions of French femininity. This "identity card" offers a snapshot of citizenship that personifies France in female form – a visual convention beginning with the Revolution. The star in this image is a five-pointed brooch, a symbol of revolutionary communism that she also wears in the negative discussed earlier. However, here it adorns a heavy overcoat that resembles the sumptuary visual codes associated with Eastern European Jews in France's popular press. This symbol of revolutionary communism produces a spectrum that stretches from normative French femininity to sexual and racial difference. Placed in relation to the earlier image of her wearing a six-pointed star and her political forms of aesthetic engagement, these images produce a continuum that reveals the presence of Jews and queers in the French body politic, and traces the historical arc of Jews in modern France from the Revolution to Dreyfus to nationalism and nascent fascism.

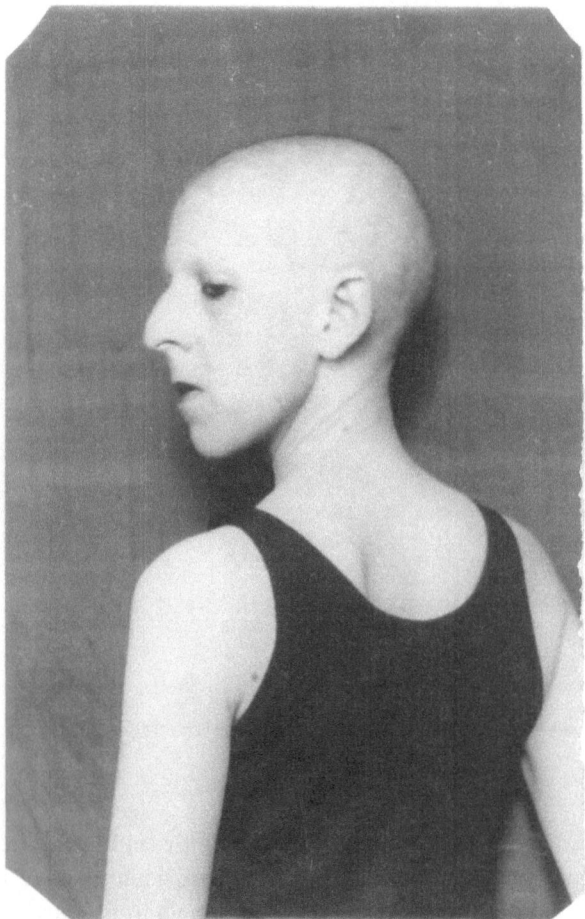

Fig. 5: Claude Cahun. *Self Portrait*. c. 1920. Black and white silver/gelatin photographic print. Jersey Heritage Archive. JHT/2003/00001/006.

If the portrait above traces out a more capacious French national imaginary, the following image seems to return to the polarized racial climate of the Dreyfus affair (Fig. 5). The photograph, entitled *Self-Portrait*, appeared as the cover of the surrealist magazine *Bifur* in April 1930, as well as the cover of the surrealist writer Georges Ribemont-Dessaignes' novel *Frontière humaine* (Human Frontier) (1929) (Shaw 2013, 125). But it was taken in 1920 as a part of a series of photographs, some of which appeared in *Aveux non avenus*. In it, Cahun's staging of a stereotypical Jewish profile draws on *fin-de-siècle* images of a hyper-racialized Jewish body, an invasive foreign organism within the body politic of the French nation. Cahun's "monstrous" profile evokes what Jennifer Shaw calls the post-WWI *rappel à l'ordre*, when reactionary political forces sought to bring into line seemingly dangerous forms of social and cultural difference (2013, 30, 125).

The "policing" of difference particularly affected Jews in *fin-de-siècle* and interwar France. Scientific and pseudo-scientific discourses including psychiatry, criminology, and sexology often targeted the Jewish body, which seemed to crystallize the intersection of race, sexuality, and gender. During the Dreyfus affair, for instance, the proliferation of anti-Semitic imagery associated the supposedly deformed body of Jewish men with criminality and degeneracy. The newspaper *La Lanterne* (The Lantern) physically mapped Dreyfus' criminal disposition in a phrenological diagram. And Alfonse Bertillon, the French policeman who inaugurated *l'anthropologie criminelle* with his forensic methods of photographing criminals' bodies, provided "expert witness" testimony that helped convict the army captain (Kleeblatt 200, 80). Drawing on these associations, the popular press often represented Jews with hooked noses, large ears, bumpy heads, and thick lips (Kleeblatt 2000, 76). Such images cast Jewish men as "matter out of place" (Douglas 1984, 36; Levi 2014, 6) that needed to be expelled from the chauvinist French body politic (Freedman 2003, 344). In the French imaginary of the *fin-de-siècle* and interwar periods, visualizations of Jewish difference helped define the imagined racial boundaries of the French nation.

Notions of the Jewish body as a dangerous criminal or political element converged with fears about Jewish sexual difference. In the German and French *fin-de-siècle* imaginary, the stereotypically hooked nose served as a prosthesis for the Jewish male's circumcised penis, while anti-Semites invoked circumcision as proof of the Jewish man's effeminacy or homosexuality (Gilman 2003, 116; Gilman 1991, 188–189). The figure of *la belle juive*, on the other hand, cast Jewish women as sexually voracious and exotic. By identifying Jewish racial difference, the social and political disorder that "abnormal" sexual and gender identities seemed to represent, could be regulated. But Jewishness was also a conductor of difference. Sander Gilman, for example, reads the Jewish nose as a pathological boundary in Proust – "an incurable disease" – that defines the boundaries of what it means to be French (Gilman 2003, 116–118). The nose of Proust's half-Jewish protagonist, Swann, finally reveals his deathbed fealty to *la race maudite* (Freedman 2003, 348–349; Samuels 2009, 256–257). The damned sign of Jewishness shadows homosexuality, the other "cursed race" that flickers across the countenances of the novel's characters.

The supposedly Jewish nose provided the most prominent index of political anxieties about Jews' racial difference. Although the association of Jews with large, hooked noses in visual imagery dates to at least the thirteenth century (Lipton 2014, 95), anti-Semitic discourses during the late nineteenth century often homed in on the Jewish nose in order to question the racial, and therefore civic, status of Jewish bodies (Gilman 2003, 111). In *Scènes et doctrines du nationalisme* (Scenes and Doctrines of Nationalism), for example, Barrès (later "tried" by Breton) associated Dreyfus' "ethnic nose" with "his face from a foreign race" (1902, 135). Barrès joined Édouard Drumont in a long French intellectual tradition that identified Jewishness as the source of French national decline. *La France juive* (Jewish France), with "*ce fameux nez recourbé*" [that famous hooked nose], presents a veritable dress-up box of racist stereotypes, which also includes "*les yeux clignotants, les dents serrées, les oreilles saillantes, les ongles carrés*" [flashing eyes, sharp teeth, prominent ears, [and] square nails] (Drumont 1886, 34).

These racial indexes of monstrosity seemed to promise identification. But, as with the association of Jews and homosexuality, anxieties surrounding the Jews' presence in France stemmed from the fear that Jews had become indistinguishable from the French. If acculturated French Jews could "pass" as white, it implied that the host country had become "Judaized" (Levi 2014). The fear of passing also informed representations of the Jew as a vector for everything from communicable diseases to parasites such as lice (Raffles 2007; Levi 2014, 150). Reflecting Drumont's vivid illustration, certain stereotypes conceived of the Jew as a monstrous parasite, embodied in the figure of Nosferatu, a mysterious *Ostjude*-like figure, who threatened social and gender order by feeding off the blood of the nation (Gardenour 2011, 52–53; Halberstam 1993, 333). The vampire crystallized anxieties about modernity – urbanization, capitalism, mobility, miscegenation – often associated with Jews in anti-Semitic discourses. In a similar manner to the way in which Jewishness intersects with other forms of difference, Judith Halberstam (1993, 337) has described the body of the vampire as one that "is not female, not Jewish, not homosexual, but [that] bears the marks of the constructions of femininity, race, and sexuality." The fact that grotesque racial stereotypes about Jews existed along with fears that they were indistinguishable, had more to do with *constructing* rather than *identifying* Jews' racial nature (Bach 1999, 73). Infamous physical characteristics signified, on the one hand, the "truth" about a supposedly Jewish racial nature, or, in the absence of such visible markers, Jews' devious ability to slip under the physical radar.

Cahun's portrait (in Fig. 5) condenses these political, historical, and cultural associations. Cahun appears in profile against a dark background. The high contrast and heavy front lighting flatten the photo's perspective and throw into relief her hooked nose and pointed chin and ears. Reminiscent of the 1922 German film *Nosferatu*, which Cahun saw in Paris (Leperlier 2006, 39), the drained, bleached photograph stages stereotypes of the parasitic Jew. The pointed, bat-like ears, too, reflect another anti-Semitic bodily trope linking the Jew's body to the animal that allows the vampire to travel "under the radar" and insinuate itself into society's dark corners, wreaking havoc from within (Gilman 2003, 121). The protruding nose and pointed ears writ large on the face of Jewish men were signs of their racial difference. Jewish women, on the other hand, could "pass" by covering their ears with long hair (Gilman 2003, 123). But in the photograph, Cahun's head is shorn, her ears prominent, her nose aquiline. She cannot hide her racial difference in the closet. This subversion of the gender clichés central to anti-Semitic discourses accomplishes a double revelation, however. By dragging the Jewish man out of the closet she lays bare the racial categories that construct the Jewish man as effeminate. Yet in her adoption of the parasitic visage of the vampiric Jew, she strips his racialized twin, *la belle juive*, of attraction; the beautiful woman who attaches herself to gentile men is revealed as a gruesome fantasy of racial difference.

These multiple layers of identity construct a self-reflexive aesthetic that implicates the viewer. In the image, the opaque aperture of her eye both fixes the viewer and summons us to position ourselves behind the mask, even as the play of surfaces reveals there is nothing underneath. By manipulating anti-Semitic racial typologies, she chips away at the natural characteristics – the *frontières humaines* – that give identity a physiological, racial appearance. The image questions how we construct representations of race, forcing us to acknowledge that seeing and reading are practices of masquerade, rather than revelation. By manipulating her body to show how representations form, Cahun exposes the processes whereby knowledge about racial and gendered subjects comes into being. And she reveals how the figure of the "Jew" operates as an allegory for racial difference in the French imaginary.

To a certain extent, Cahun discloses the operations whereby racial representations become naturalized. But it would be utopian to see her works as dissolving national or racial categories in favor of pluralistic modes of belonging. Despite the radical visual critique Cahun undertakes here, she draws on stereotypes associated with a certain kind of Jew – the unassimilated, foreign *Ostjude* – that contrast sharply with the model of an acculturated French Jew. The self-reflexive distance simultaneously denaturalizes Eastern Jewishness, naturalizing "French" Jewishness in the process. Thus Cahun relies on pre-existing racial concepts that are stabilized through her performance. In this sense, Cahun's image operates along the lines of what Gilman calls "the double-bind of the assimilated or assimilating Jew" (cited in Golan 1995, 165), a tension that was particularly acute in the divisions between *Israélites* and immigrant Jews in France. Do Cahun's aesthetics move beyond these internal and external divisions to open up Jewish identities to multiple expressions? Or do they reinscribe racial and national differences between Jewish communities? Instead of offering a utopian deconstruction of Jewish racial identity, Cahun's image performs the double-bind of French Jews: caught between assimilation and exclusion, they could not help but be defined by what they were or what they were not.

During the *fin-de-siècle*, attempts to pin down Jewish difference brought together the dislocating forces of modernity and new modes of visuality. The anxieties around race and nation embodied by Jews produced new representational urgencies, which the avant-garde took up through an exploration of otherness. The question of how to represent race and Jewishness, then, must be seen as a central aspect of the avant-garde's crisis of representation. The Jewish body, in particular, provided a natural staging ground for the avant-garde reconception of representation. Cahun's self-reflexive work reveals the aesthetic categories – beautiful and ugly, normative and degenerate – that govern the Jewish body's visibility. But it is also made possible *through* a confrontation with the limits of representation. In this way, Cahun points to the way attempts to represent Jewishness incarnate the reactionary forces at play in modernity itself.

Bibliography

Adamowicz, Elza. "'Sous ce masque, un autre masque': Claude Cahun's Photomontages." *Exposure: Revealing Bodies, Unveiling Representations*. Ed. Kathryn Banks and Joseph Harris. London: Peter Lang, 2004: 49–61.
Bach, Raymond. "Identifying Jews: The Legacy of the 1941 Exhibition, 'Le Juif et La France.'" *Studies in 20th & 21st Century Literature* 23.1 (1999): 65–92.
Bal, M. "Visual Essentialism and the Object of Visual Culture." *Journal of Visual Culture* 2.1 (2003): 5–32.
Barrès, Maurice. *Scènes et doctrines du nationalisme*. Paris: Félix Juven, 1902.
Bein, Alex. "The Jewish Parasite: Notes on the Semantics of the Jewish Problem, with Special Reference to Germany." *The Leo Baeck Institute Yearbook* 9.1 (1964): 3–40.
Benbassa, Esther. *The Jews of France: A History from Antiquity to the Present*. Princeton: Princeton University Press, 2001.
Birnbaum, Pierre. *Les Fous de la République. Histoire politique des Juifs d'État, de Gambetta à Vichy*. Paris: Fayard, 1992.

Birnbaum, Pierre. *The Anti-Semitic Moment: A Tour of France in 1898*. Trans. Jane Marie Todd. Chicago: University of Chicago Press, 2011.
Boime, Albert. "Dada's Dark Secret." *Jewish Dimensions in Modern Visual Culture: Antisemitism, Assimilation, Affirmation*. Ed. Rose-Carol Washton Long, Matthew Baigell, and Milly Heyd. Waltham, MA: Brandeis University Press, 2010. 90–115.
Cahun, Claude. *Écrits*. Ed. Francois Leperlier. Paris: Jean-Michel Place Editions, 2002.
Cahun, Claude, and Marcel Moore. "Variety of Original and Carbon Copied Propaganda Leaflets Produced by Lucie Schwob and Suzanne Malherbe during the German Occupation of Jersey including 'die Soldaten ohne Namen.'" 1940–1945. Jersey Heritage Archive. JHT/1995/00045/53.
Camiscioli, Elisa. "Race Making and Race Mixing in the Early Twentieth-Century Immigration Debate." *Transnational Spaces and Identities in the Francophone World*. Ed. Hafid Gafaïti, Patricia M.E. Lorcin and David G. Troyansky. Lincoln: University of Nebraska Press, 2009. 53–70.
Douglas, Mary. *Purity and Danger: An Analysis of Concepts of Pollution and Taboo*. London: Routledge, 1984.
Doy, Gen. *Claude Cahun: A Sensual Politics of Photography*. London: I.B. Tauris, 2008.
Drumont, Edouard. *La France juive: Essai d'histoire contemporaine*. Paris: C. Marpon & E. Flammarion, 1886.
Edelman, Todd M. "Assimilation." *YIVO Encyclopedia of Jews in Eastern Europe* 13 July 2010. http://yivoencyclopedia.org/article.aspx/Assimilation (20 November 2015).
Freedman, Jonathan. "Coming out of the Jewish Closet with Marcel Proust." *Queer Theory and the Jewish Question*. Ed. Daniel Boyarin, Daniel Itzkovitz and Ann Pellegrini. New York: Columbia University Press, 2003. 334–364.
Gardenour, Brenda. "The Biology of Blood-Lust: Medieval Medicine, Theology, and the Vampire Jew." *Film & History: An Interdisciplinary Journal of Film and Television Studies* 41.2 (2011): 51–63.
Gewurtz, Michelle. "Equivocally Jewish: Claude Cahun and the Narratives of Modern Art." *Hadassah-Brandeis Institute* (2012). Working Papers: The Donna Sudarsky Memorial Series.
Gilman, Sander L. *The Jew's Body*. New York: Routledge, 1991.
Gilman, Sander L. *Jewish Frontiers: Essays on Bodies, Histories, and Identities*. New York: Palgrave Macmillan, 2003.
Girardet, Raoul. *Le Nationalisme français: 1871–1914*. Paris: Seuil, 1983.
Golan, Romy. "From Fin de Siècle to Vichy: The Cultural Hygienics of Camille (Faust) Mauclair." *The Jew in Text: Modernity and the Construction of Identity*. Ed. Linda Nochlin and Tamar Garb. London: Thames and Hudson, 1996. 156–173.
Golan, Romy. "The École Française versus the École de Paris: The Debate about the Status of Jewish Artists in Paris between the Wars." *Jewish Dimensions in Modern Visual Culture: Antisemitism, Assimilation, Affirmation*. Ed. Rose-Carol Washton Long, Matthew Baigell and Milly Heyd. Waltham, MA: Brandeis University Press, 2010. 77–89.
Halberstam, Judith. "Technologies of Monstrosity: Bram Stoker's 'Dracula.'" *Victorian Studies* 36.3 (1993): 333–352.
Harding, James M. *The Ghosts of the Avant-Garde(s): Exorcising Experimental Theater and Performance*. Ann Arbor: University of Michigan Press, 2013.

Heyd, Milly. "Man Ray/Emmanuel Radnitsky: Who Is Behind The Enigma of Isidore Ducasse." *Complex Identities: Jewish Consciousness and Modern Art*. Ed. Matthew Baigell and Milly Heyd. New Brunswick, NJ: Rutgers University Press, 2001. 115–141.

Heyd, Milly. "Tristan Tzara/Shmuel Rosenstock: The Hidden/Overt Jewish Agenda." *Jewish Dimensions in Modern Visual Culture: Antisemitism, Assimilation, Affirmation*. Ed. Rose-Carol Washton Long, Matthew Baigell and Milly Heyd. Waltham, MA: Brandeis University Press, 2010. 193–219.

Hyman, Paula. *The Jews of Modern France*. Berkeley: University of California Press, 1998.

Josephson, Matthew. *Life Among the Surrealists: A Memoir*. New York: Holt, Rinehart and Winston, 1962.

Kleeblatt, Norman L. "The Body of Alfred Dreyfus: A Site for France's Displaced Anxieties of Masculinity, Homosexuality and Power." *Diaspora and Visual Culture: Representing Africans and Jews*. Ed. Nicholas Mirzoeff. London and New York: Routledge, 2000. 76–91.

Krauss, Rosalind E. *Bachelors*. Cambridge, MA: MIT Press, 1999.

Leperlier, François. *Claude Cahun: L'Écart et la métamorphose*. Paris: Jean-Michel Place, 1992.

Leperlier, François. *Claude Cahun: L'Exotisme intérieur*. Paris: Fayard, 2006.

Levi, Neil. *Modernist Form and the Myth of Jewification*. New York: Fordham University Press, 2014.

Lindemann, Albert S. *The Jew Accused: Three Anti-Semitic Affairs (Dreyfus, Beilis, Frank) 1894–1915*. Cambridge: Cambridge University Press, 1991.

Lipton, Sara. *Dark Mirror: The Medieval Origins of Anti-Jewish Iconography*. New York: Metropolitan Books, 2014.

Pellegrini, Ann. "Whiteface Performances: 'Race,' Gender, and Jewish Bodies." *Jews and Other Differences*. Ed. Jonathan Boyarin and Daniel Boyarin. Minneapolis: Minnesota University Press, 1997. 108–149.

Perloff, Marjorie. "The Great War and the European Avant-Garde." *The Cambridge Companion to the Literature of the First World War*. Ed. Vincent Sherry. Cambridge: Cambridge University Press, 2005. 141–165.

Polizzotti, Mark. *Revolution of the Mind: The Life of André Breton*. London: Da Capo Press, 1997.

Raffles, Hugh. "Jews, Lice, and History." *Public Culture* 19.3 (2007): 521–566.

Rice, Shelley (ed.). *Inverted Odysseys: Claude Cahun, Maya Deren, Cindy Sherman*. Cambridge, MA: MIT Press, 1999.

Samuels, Maurice. *Inventing the Israelite: Jewish Fiction in Nineteenth-Century France*. Stanford: Stanford University Press, 2009.

Schechter, Ronald. *Obstinate Hebrews: Representations of Jews in France 1715–1815*. Berkeley: University of California Press, 2003.

Sell, Mike. *The Avant-Garde: Race, Religion, War*. London and New York: Seagull Books, 2012.

Seshagiri, Urmila. *Race and the Modernist Imagination*. Ithaca: Cornell University Press, 2010.

Shaw, Jennifer. *Reading Claude Cahun's Disavowals*. London: Ashgate, 2013.

Short, Robert. "Dada and Surrealism." *Modernism: A Guide to European Literature 1890–1930*. Ed. Malcolm Bradbury and James McFarlane. London: Penguin Books, 1978. 292–308.

Silverman, Lisa. "Reconsidering the Margins." *Journal of Modern Jewish Studies* 8.1 (2009): 103–120.

Silverman, Lisa. *Becoming Austrians: Jews and Culture between the World Wars*. Oxford: Oxford University Press, 2012.

Silverman, Max. *Deconstructing the Nation: Immigration, Racism, and Citizenship in Modern France*. London: Routledge, 1992.

Spitzer, Leo. "A Name Given, a Name Taken: Camouflaging, Resistance, and Diasporic Social Identity." *Comparative Studies of South Asia, Africa and the Middle East* 30.1 (2010): 21–31.
Thynne, Lizzie. "Indirect Action: Politics and the Subversion of Identity in Claude Cahun and Marcel Moore's Resistance to the Occupation of Jersey." *Papers of Surrealism* 8 (2010): 1–24.
Winock, Michel. *Nationalism, Anti-Semitism, and Fascism in France*. Trans. Jane Todd. Stanford: Stanford University Press, 2000.
Winter, Amy. *Wolfgang Paalen: Artist and Theorist of the Avant-Garde*. Westport, CN: Praeger, 2002.

Alana Sobelman
Arnold Schoenberg's Jewish Veil: The Workings of Anti-Semitic Rhetoric in *Die glückliche Hand*, Op. 18 (1913)

1

It has been widely acknowledged that the Viennese Jewish composer Arnold Schoenberg, particularly in his dramatic avant-garde works of the first two decades of the twentieth century, demonstrated his knowledge of Freudian psychoanalysis.[1] Indeed, it was during this time that Schoenberg, Bryan Simms accurately notes, "experimented with composition in a stream of consciousness and relied almost entirely on artistic instinct" (2000, 5). Nevertheless, unlike the case of Sigmund Freud's psychoanalytic works of the same time period, few studies illuminate what is particularly "Jewish" about Schoenberg's early dramatic compositions, and, more specifically, how these "Jewish" elements may be understood within the larger context of the time and place in which both Schoenberg and Freud were starting out their careers.[2] While several scholars have noted the strictly autobiographical elements at play in Schoenberg's early

---

[1] Schoenberg's dramatic works of this period include *Erwartung*, Op. 17 (1908), *Pierrot lunaire*, Op. 21 (1912, Schoenberg did not write the text for this drama but rather used German translations of a collection of French poems of the same name by Albert Giraud), and *Die Glückliche Hand* (1913). He also composed several other highly progressive orchestral works in the same time period (1908–1914) and contributed his essay, "The Relationship to the Text," as well as a facsimile of "Herzgewächse, Op. 20" (1915) to *Der Blaue Reiter Almanach* (1912). In 1911, his paintings were displayed at the first Der Blaue Reiter art exhibit in Munich. Schoenberg's involvement with Wassily Kandinsky's close-knit Der Blaue Reiter circle helps to confirm his role as an avant-garde composer. As for Schoenberg's interest in psychoanalysis, there exist several studies on the topic, both related and unrelated to Schoenberg's and Freud's relationships to Judaism. For interesting discussions on the subject, see Bryan Simms (1997); Lewis Wickes (1989); Elizabeth Keathley (2010); and Alfred Cramer (1997).

[2] Schoenberg's collaboration with the Jewish writer Gustav Hochstetter on *Brettl-Lieder* (1901), which was comprised of eight "Jewish cabaret" songs, and his entrance into the Berlin cabaret scene, beginning with his position as conductor at the literary cabaret, Überbrettl, are certainly to be regarded as "Jewish" moves in the milieu of early twentieth-century music in Germany and Austria (Bohlman 2008, 183). He did not, however, write the texts accompanying the musical scores he composed at this time. In these Jewish cabaret songs, Philip Bohlman states, "we encounter Arnold Schoenberg not as the nestor of musical modernism but as the cabaret musician" (2008, 183). A study of "Jewish" musical elements of these works, and in particular the potential

DOI 10.1515/9783110454956-010

dramatic works, like *Erwartung* (Expectation, 1908) and *Die glückliche Hand*, Op. 18 (The Fateful Hand, 1913), few studies have addressed the potential influence of popular discourse about European Jews on Schoenberg's compositions of this time period. The most common interpretation of *Die glückliche Hand*, for instance, is an autobiographical one, and suggests that Schoenberg's drama reflects events in his life, most prominently a tumultuous affair between his wife and painter Richard Gerstl. Simms asserts that the work was "no doubt triggered by the temporary breakup of Schoenberg's marriage during the summer of 1908" (2000, 100) and that the work's theme of repeated failure in love "takes its origins in the composer's marital crisis [...]" (2000, 103). This article, while acknowledging the personal references the work may generate for some critics, focuses more explicitly on Schoenberg's engagement with influential figures of the time, namely Richard Wagner and Otto Weininger. Joseph Auner rightly notes of analyses of *Die glückliche Hand*: "While the plot of romantic betrayal [...] has obvious resonances with the Gerstl affair, it is better seen not as any sort of literal representation but rather as a reworking of autobiographical material filtered through contemporary attitudes toward the relationship of the sexes expressed in the writings of August Strindberg, Otto Weininger, Kokoschka, and others" (Auner 2003, 82). In line with Auner's promotion of a non-literal interpretation of *Die glückliche Hand*, and in order to shed new light on other elements which may have found their way into Schoenberg's drama during this time period, this article argues that *Die glückliche Hand* can be read in a particular dialogue with late nineteenth- and early twentieth-century anti-Semitic claims of "Jewish disease" and "Jewish effeminacy" put forth by Richard Wagner in *Judaism in Music* (1850) and Otto Weininger in *Sex and Character* (1903). What emerges from this study is the suggestion that Schoenberg's "drama with music" features a Wagnerian-Weiningerian Jewish protagonist who is ultimately defeated by his own "diseased" and "effeminate" body, indicating that Schoenberg may have adopted, and also challenged, anti-Semitic discourse in his work. Sander Gilman's interpretation of Freud's "racially Jewish" reading of Daniel Schreber's *Memoirs of a Nervous Patient* (2000 [1903]) will help to push forward my argument that Freud and Schoenberg may be linked according to their veiled responses to racialist discourse – Freud via his case study of Schreber and Schoenberg via his dramatic *Die glückliche Hand*. The starting point of this study is a discussion of the interwoven experiences of Freud and Schoenberg in early twentieth-century Vienna, followed by a look at the anti-Semitic rhetoric employed by Wagner and

---

relationship between these elements and Freud's work, while not relevant in this article, deserves consideration.

Weininger, and Freud's complex encounters with this rhetoric, particularly illustrated in his case study of Schreber. Gilman's in-depth studies of Jewish racialism at the fin-de-siècle and his examination of Freud's "defensive" study of Schreber's *Memoirs* help to illuminate comparable complexities of Schoenberg's relation to the same anti-Semitic rhetoric Gilman extracts from Schreber. Altogether this study endeavors to engage with Schoenberg as a similarly "defensive" Jewish figure, opening the possibility for interpreting several of his works around this time as engaging with the dominant discourse about the European Jewish mind and body.

2

The first point of contact between Schoenberg and Freud is, I believe, to be found in what is known of their relationships to their own senses of Jewishness. Both men, Yosef Hayim Yerushalmi claims, "lived their lives driven by an idea and a cause that required both sacrifice and ruthlessness in the face of what Freud, borrowing from Ibsen, called the 'compact majority'" (1992, 3). Yerushalmi explains that both men were "always acutely sensitive to anti-Semitism, suffered from it, reacted to it with aggressive pride, and ended up in exile because of it [...]" (1992, 3). Both men were also, prior to the rise of Nazism, "repeatedly accused [...] of invading the sacred spiritual precincts of the *Volk* with an alien and arid 'Jewish' intellectualism, Freud thereby debasing the Aryan soul, Schoenberg corrupting German music" (1992, 4). And despite Schoenberg's conversion to Protestantism in 1898, Yerushalmi nonetheless asserts that "both felt almost mystically Jewish at their innermost core, and each came to a passionate affirmation of this essential Jewish identity" (1992, 4).[3] Yerushalmi draws further connections between Schoenberg and Freud based on their contributions to modernity:

---

[3] Schoenberg's conversion to Protestantism in 1898 is a highly curious fact, but one which will not be elaborated in depth here. Several German and Austrian Jews converted around this time for a reason that is perhaps best explained by Sander Gilman in *The Case of Sigmund Freud* (1993), wherein he asserts that a shift came about at the turn of the nineteenth century which saw a major change in the perception of the European Jew, from having a religious or national core to a racial one. While many Jews indeed converted despite this shift, Gilman claims that essentially "the Jewishness of the body and the psyche is indelible" (1993, 69) and thus Jews, once they were given a "racial label," could "not convert out of their race" (1993, 71). Schoenberg's conversion at this particular time would indicate that he made this decision on the very cusp of this shift in perception of Jews; his "reconversion" thus also came somewhat late, in the early 1930s, after he had left Germany for a safer Paris, and before he would immigrate to the United States.

> Both are among the great modern innovators; Schoenberg's revolution in music was as Copernican as was Freud's in psychology. Both were Viennese Jews (Freud arrived at age four), sons of immigrant fathers from the East, both grew up in Leopoldstadt, the crowded Jewish district of Vienna. Both loved and detested the city, admired Karl Kraus [...] and both avidly read his magazine *Die Fackel*, where, occasionally, Kraus savagely lampooned psychoanalysis but never attacked Freud. While we have no evidence that Freud was aware of Schoenberg, Schoenberg was certainly aware of Freud. (1992, 3)

Whether the two met personally is still unknown, but, as Alexander Carpenter notes, "there is a strong probability, given the social and professional overlap of their circles, that these two men would have known each other" (2010, 150). Nevertheless, the chance of their acquaintanceship is secondary here, as they are perhaps even more interestingly linked via their parallel approaches to the prevailing anti-Semitic discourse in Europe around the turn of the nineteenth century.

An interesting "Jewish" point of convergence between Freud and Schoenberg – and one which relates to their work – is, I believe, best described by Yerushalmi in *Freud's Moses: Judaism Terminable and Interminable* (1991). Borrowing the term from Philip Rieff, Yerushalmi defines the "psychological Jew":

> The psychological Jew was born before Freud. If, for all secular Jews, Judaism has become 'Jewishness' of one kind or another, the Jewishness of the psychological Jew seems, at least to the outsider, devoid of all but the most vestigial content; it has become almost pure subjectivity. Content is replaced by character. Alienated from classical Jewish texts, Psychological Jews tend to insist on inalienable Jewish traits. Intellectuality and independence of mind, the highest ethical and moral concerns, concern for social justice, tenacity in the face of persecution – these are among the qualities they will claim, if called upon, as quintessentially Jewish. (1991, 10)

Yerushalmi further states that psychological Jews "have evinced no special need to define themselves as Jews or to embrace any particular form of visible Jewish commitment, but who have felt themselves to be somehow irreducibly Jewish nonetheless" (10). Indeed, at various points in their lives, Schoenberg and Freud defined themselves according to a seemingly intangible Jewish essence. In his 1934 preface to the Hebrew translation of *Totem and Taboo* (1913), Freud writes:

> No reader of [the Hebrew translation] of this book will find it easy to put himself in the emotional position of an author who is ignorant of the language of holy writ, who is completely estranged from the religion of his fathers – as well as from every other religion – and who cannot take a share in nationalist ideals, but who has yet never repudiated his people, who feels that he is in his essential nature a Jew and who has no desire to alter that nature. If the

---

For highly varied considerations of Schoenberg's relationship to Judaism and his conversion see Móricz (2008), White (1985), and Neher (1990 [1979], 13–14).

question were put to him: 'Since you have abandoned all of these common characteristics of your countrymen, what is left of you that is Jewish?' he would reply: 'A very great deal, and probably its very essence.' (1953 [1934], xv)

The notion of Jewish "essence" also comes up in Schoenberg's writings, including his essays and letters. In a 1923 letter to Wassily Kandinsky in which he rejects an invitation to join the new Bauhaus (which "had its share of anti-Semites" [Ringer 2000, 119]) as well as the staff of the Weimar Hochschule, he wrote: "I have at last learned the lesson that has been forced upon me during this year, and I shall not ever forget it. It is that I am not a German, not a European, indeed perhaps scarcely a human being [...] but I am a Jew" (1958 [1923], 88). In 1946 Schoenberg wrote to the editor of the *Jewish Year Book*, responding to a request for information to be used in an entry on his life and work: "Jews look at me rather from a racial standpoint than from an artistic. They accordingly give me a lower rating than they give to their Aryan idols" (1958 [1946], 238). The issue of racialist perceptions of Schoenberg, particularly by Jews, comes to the surface with this sentence, but it also brings to light the universality of claims of racial Jewishness, including the prominent role that Jews themselves played in unwittingly promoting these claims.

Freud made some comparable remarks in his personal correspondences. In 1886, while working under Jean-Martin Charcot in Paris, he wrote to his fiancée Martha Bernays that he saw himself strictly as a "Jew," and one "adhering neither to Germany nor Austria" (1975 [1886], 203). And strikingly close to Schoenberg's sentiments in this letter to Kandinsky is Freud's statement in a 1926 interview with George Sylvester Viereck for Viereck's *Glimpses of the Great*: "My language is German [...] My culture, my attainments are German. I considered myself a German intellectually, until I noticed the growth of anti-Semitic prejudice in Germany and German Austria. Since that time, I prefer to call myself a Jew" (1930 [1926], 119). And still more connections can be found between the two Jewish innovators, including the psychoanalytic elements at play in Schoenberg's work of the early twentieth century.

Schoenberg's *Erwartung* (1908) and *Die glückliche Hand* are often critically studied together within a psychoanalytic framework. Indeed, several scholars discuss these two works as "companion pieces."[4] They were composed between 1908 and 1913, during what Alexander Carpenter calls Schoenberg's "intense 'psychoanalytic' period" (2010, 145). At this time, Carpenter claims, Schoenberg "was preoccupied with his own psychic unrest and was exploring a compositional aesthetic predicated on the expression of the unconscious" (2010, 145). The two works

---

4 See Payette (2008) and Simms (2000).

are "psychoanalytic" also because "they articulate Schoenberg's preoccupation with his own neurosis – a kind of hysteria manifest in repressed memory – and reflect a compositional approach that echoes Freud's contemporary writings on the nature of the unconscious" (145). Schoenberg's preoccupation with "psychic unrest" and neurosis may be an accurate depiction of his compositional process during these five years, but as the following analysis shows, it was not necessarily unrest and neurosis which were his focus; he also, and not independently of his interest in psychoanalysis, seemed preoccupied with his Jewishness.

3

It has often been pointed out that both Schoenberg and Freud were familiar with the writings of Richard Wagner and Otto Weininger. Indeed, neither Schoenberg nor Freud were exempt from what Eric Santner refers to as the "fin-de-siècle obsession with Jewish effeminacy," which was largely centered on Otto Weininger's "hugely influential treatise, *Sex and Character*" (Santner 1996, 109). Gilman acknowledges that *Sex and Character* "became an immediate best-seller" which "established [Weininger] as a serious contributor to the discourse about the relationship between race and gender at the beginning of the century" (1991, 133). Its "unprecedented influence on the scientific discourse about Jews and women at the turn of the century" meant that it was not outwardly rejected – in fact in many cases it was openly embraced by Vienna's intellectual and artistic circles – despite the rashness and gratuitousness of its claims (1991, 133). Gilman believes that its favorable recognition was in-part due to the fact that Weininger used language in *Sex and Character* which was "within the rhetoric of contemporary science" (Gilman 1991, 134), and thus he addressed a highly educated readership, including the likes of Schoenberg, Freud, and their contemporaries. But because Weininger's language in *Sex and Character* also "reflects the general view of anti-Semitic racial science about the special nature of the Jew" (Gilman 1991, 137), leading up to and immediately following the turn of the nineteenth century, its impact on figures like Freud and Schoenberg is not immediately easy to decipher.

As several scholars have pointed out, the wave of interest in Weininger in artistic and academic circles in Vienna in the first decade of the twentieth century indicates that Schoenberg must have not only known of *Sex and Character*, but also read it. Weininger's name comes up in several letters written by Alban Berg and Anton von Webern to Schoenberg between 1909 and 1912.[5] Alan

---

[5] For a discussion of Webern's and Berg's engagement with Weininger and their discussion of Weininger in letters to Schoenberg, see Brown (2014, 133–134).

Lessem suggests an influence of Weininger's theories related to female sexuality and difference on Schoenberg's compositions from around the same time period: "The text of *Erwartung*," he writes of Schoenberg's 1908 "psychoanalytic" work – a monodrama featuring a female "hysteric" who suffers hallucinations and delusions related to the death of her lover – "reflects perhaps no more than a modish preoccupation with sexual pathology, one encouraged in Viennese circles by the publication, in 1903, of a somewhat scandalous study by the young Otto Weininger" (1979, 68). Lessem summarizes the link between Weininger and Schoenberg: "Weininger's thesis in [*Sex and Character*] is that the character of a woman is determined entirely by impulses, recollections and anticipations that have to do with her sexual life. A woman is always on the brink of an identity crisis as she lacks male objectivity and the sense of a psychic continuum" (1979, 68, fn. 49). As Julie Brown notes, however, Schoenberg's view of Weininger is ultimately "difficult to pin down" (2011, 134). But what is perhaps most surprising about all of these references to Schoenberg's possible engagements with Weininger's "scandalous" text is that they do not mention Weininger's second to last chapter of the work, unabashedly entitled "Judaism." A certain reading of this chapter suggests, I believe, a far more intriguing influence of Weininger on Schoenberg, in particular Weininger's claims that Jews share the same fundamental (and negative) characteristics as women.[6]

Unlike in the case of critical studies of Schoenberg, Freud's encounters with Weininger's deterministic theories are frequently discussed in scholarship about the early development of psychoanalysis.[7] Freud read an early draft of *Sex and Character*, which, according to Gilman, turned out to be "fundamental in shaping at least some of [Freud's] attitudes toward the nature of the body [...]" (1991, 133). In fact, Gilman writes, Freud's newly developed science directly responded to the themes presented by Weininger, including the Jew as "the hysteric," the

---

[6] Distinct from any study of Schoenberg's representation of women in *Erwartung* is Jennifer Shaw's 2000 study of the theme of androgyny in the work. Her analysis elucidates Schoenberg's knowledge of Weininger's *Sex and Character*, as well as his familiarity with the writings of Wilhelm Fliess and Sigmund Freud. Nevertheless, Shaw does not focus on the relationship between femininity and Judaism (or androgyny and Judaism for that matter), a connection that directs this article's statements about Schoenberg's relationship to Weininger.

[7] See Sander Gilman (1990, 1991, 1993); Peter Gay (1988). Samuel Slipp discusses Freud's indirect influence on Weininger's text via his engagement with Wilhelm Fliess. The latter apparently came up with several ideas – particularly those pertaining to bisexuality – eventually presented in *Sex and Character*. Slipp states that Freud disclosed these ideas to his patient, Hermann Swoboda, who then relayed them to Weininger. The web of information, Slipp asserts, eventually led to the momentous falling out between Freud and Fliess (Slipp 2000, 50). See Gay (1988) for a detailed account of the Freud-Fliess-Wagner connection.

"feminized Other," and the Jew as "different, as diseased" (1991, 76). These elements together form the image of "the hysteria with which the Jewish scientist was confronted" in Freud's time (1991, 76). Yet, Gilman also acknowledges that Weininger's *Sex and Character*, with its overtly stated anti-Semitic ideas, not only had an impact on discourse about women, but also "had an unprecedented influence on the scientific discourse about Jews" at the turn of the nineteenth century (1994b, 64). And equally significant for a "racial" interpretation of Schoenberg's *Die glückliche Hand* is Richard Wagner's influence on the composer, specifically the possible impact of Wagner's *Judaism in Music* on Schoenberg's creation of his main protagonist.

Wagner's musical influence on Schoenberg is well-known, owing both to details of Schoenberg's own writings, including formal essays, lectures, and personal letters, and to critical analyses of his compositions.[8] His complex relationship to Wagner's *Judaism in Music* is clearly stated in his 1935 lecture to *Mailamm* in support of building a music department at the Hebrew University in Jerusalem[9]:

> When we young Austrian-Jewish artists grew up, our self-esteem suffered very much from the pressure of certain circumstances. It was the time when Richard Wagner's work started its victorious career, and the success of his music and poems was followed by an infiltration of his *Weltanschauung*, of his philosophy. You were no true Wagnerian if you did not believe in his philosophy [...] [Y]ou were not a true Wagnerian if you did not believe in *Deutschtum*, in Teutonism; and you could not be a true Wagnerian without being a follower of his anti-Semitic essay, *Das Judentum in der Musik*, 'Judaism in Music.' (1975, 502–503)

Here and throughout Schoenberg's lecture to *Mailamm*, Schoenberg recognizes the influence of Wagner's work on Viennese Jews (and non-Jews) of the early twentieth century, focusing specifically on the negative consequences of Wagner's major Jewish following: Jews, "deprived of their racial self-confidence, doubted a Jew's creative capacity more than the Aryans did. They were at best cautious and believed only when supported by Aryans [...]" (1975, 504).[10] Schoenberg's keen awareness of Wagner's anti-Semitic claims and the vast influence these claims had on his contemporaries makes it nearly impossible to imagine that this influ-

---

[8] See Schoenberg (1975), Brown (1994), and Danuser (1994–1995) for specific instances of Wagner's musical influence on Schoenberg.
[9] The name *Mailamm* is a Hebraized abbreviation of the "American Palestine Music Association." See Nulman (1975, 161) for more details about the origins of *Mailamm*. See Heskes (1997) for details about Schoenberg's close association with the group.
[10] David Michael Schiller makes the interesting suggestion that Schoenberg's conversion to Protestantism, as a direct consequence of his "total immersion in Wagner's music" in the late 1890s, was in order "to repair the injury to his self-esteem inflicted by Wagnerian anti-Semitism" (Schiller 2003, 77).

ence – a distinctly textual, not musical, one – did not carry over into Schoenberg's work, especially into his dramas *Erwartung* and *Die glückliche Hand*. While scholars such as Julie Brown argue that Schoenberg's writings and compositions indicate his agreement with Wagner's claims (Brown 2014, 134–136), and particularly the claims relating to the Jew's "overcoming" of Jewishness, the picture seems more complex than this, as the "racialist" reading of *Die glückliche Hand* presented here will show.

While several scholars have stressed the musical influence of Wagner specifically on Schoenberg's *Die glückliche Hand* – Bryan Simms, for example, calls the work a Wagnerian *Gesamtkunstwerk* "in which visual effects, dialogue, and music cooperate as equals" (2000, 103),[11] – few scholars have discussed the impact of *Judaism in Music* on the drama. The major element of Wagner's anti-Semitic treatise discussed in this article is the claim that the Jew invariably speaks in a foreign tongue, which is then reflected in his music:

> The hissing, shrill-sounding buzzing and grunting mannerisms of Jewish speech fall at once upon our ear as something strange and disagreeable in kind. These mannerisms also take the form of an application of the words entirely inappropriate to our national speech; of an arbitrary prolongation of them; and of a phrase-construction producing the total effect of a confused babble [...]. (1910 [1850], 13)

The Jew's speech is repellant because of its "purely aural aspect" (1973 [1850], 28): "The shrill, sibilant buzzing of his voice falls strangely and unpleasantly on our ears. His misuse of words whose exact shade of meaning escapes him, and his mistakenly placed phrases combine to turn his utterance into an unbearably muddled nonsense" (1973 [1850], 28). The closest connection between Schoenberg's *Die glückliche Hand* and Wagner's *Judaism in Music* is, I believe, to be found in Schoenberg's peculiarly speech*less* protagonist. The following close reading of the drama suggests that, like Freud, whose reading of Schreber's *Memoirs* "provides insight into Freud's defense mechanisms" (Gilman 1993, 146), certain characteristics of Schoenberg's racially Jewish protagonist in *Die glückliche Hand* offer a similar representation of the composer's methods.

---

[11] For a clear elaboration of the term *Gesamtkunstwerk*, which first appears in Wagner's 1849 writings, "Art and Revolution" and "The Artwork of the Future," see Juliet Koss (2010).

4

Schoenberg's works of 1900 to 1910 were harshly reviewed and in some cases the reviews utilized highly anti-Semitic rhetoric. Critics often focused on the compositions' "destructive" sounds. For example, the *Berliner Börsen-Courier* reported during Vienna's 1906–1907 performance season that Schoenberg's First String Quartet "is so full of restless, antithetical thematic processing that the four instruments carry on with each other in an unpleasant battle – in the first half, utter cacophony, and in the second half, a weak wallowing of sick nerves" (quoted in Painter 2001, 217). Much of this criticism, according to Karen Painter, reflected anti-Semitic tropes "made popular in Wagner's *Das Judentum in der Musik*" (2001, 217). Most striking in this review is the resemblance it has to popular depictions of the diseased, hysterical Jew, himself no more than a "weak wallowing of sick nerves." Schoenberg's *Die glückliche Hand*, which he composed in the wake of criticism such as this, may very well reflect his response to the reviews of his prior works which so much resembled the anti-Semitic writings of Wagner and Weininger in both rhetoric and rigidity.

The title of Schoenberg's "drama with music" is not easily translatable. According to Lessem, the title of the work is "a play on words which loses its full meaning in any literal translation such as 'The Lucky Hand' or even [...] 'The Hand of Fate'" (1979, 96–97). Bryan Simms translates the work as "The Magic Hand." According to Joseph Auner, the title "has proven to be very difficult to translate, because the word *glückliche* has many possible meanings, such as lucky, happy, fortunate, or fateful, all of which Schoenberg is playing upon [...]" (2003, 87). As I will elaborate, the most appropriate translation of the work for the present discussion is "The Fateful Hand."

Die glückliche Hand features three main characters: a baritone protagonist, named "Man," the "Woman" and the "Gentleman." The "Gentleman" never appears alone on stage, but only with the Woman on his arm. The Woman appears without the Gentleman, but she, too, is never alone on stage. There also exists on stage, dominantly in the first and final scenes, a chorus of twelve – six women and six men.

Lessem accurately describes the basic structure of the work: "Schoenberg's 'plot' is minimal, since the action, presented through an intricate and carefully detailed interaction of costume, abstract stage imagery, lighting and music, takes place entirely within the mind of the anonymous Man, though simultaneously projected into symbolic stage figures: a quasi-Greek chorus, a Woman and a Gentleman" (1979, 97). Of central importance for the present discussion is Schoenberg's depiction of the psychic state of his character, which, it can be assumed from the lines sung by the chorus in the work's opening scene, is one of fantasy. Despite being Schoenberg's protagonist, the Man's singing lines are minimal. As I will elaborate, the Man's lack of speech is suggestive of Schoenberg's timid approach to Wagnerian claims of "ugliness" and "repulsion" in the voice of the Jew on stage.

Important to note, perhaps, is that *none* of the three central characters in the first performance of *Die glückliche Hand*, which took place at the Vienna Volksoper in 1924 – bass-baritone opera singer Alfred Jerger (a renowned Strauss singer), the Woman, played by Hedy Pfundmayr, and the Gentleman, played by Josef Hustiger (Mesa 2007, 113) – were of Jewish origin. Schoenberg's conductor for *Die glückliche Hand*, however, Fritz Stiedry, was in fact Jewish (Saleski 1949, 165). The significance of these details lies in the possibility that Schoenberg may have intentionally kept his cast free of Jewish performers. Seeing them as "interpreters" of his compositions, he indeed may have avoided "fulfil[ling] the anti-Semites' expectation of 'mere Jewish mimicry,'" (Bohlman 2008, x), thus attempting to circumvent racialist criticism altogether.

5

The conditions of "Jewish disease" and "Jewish femininity" are revealed in Schoenberg's drama in two forms: first, via the text sung by the chorus in the opening and closing scenes; and second, through the stage movements and costume details of the protagonist himself. The text of the drama opens with Schoenberg's direction: "The stage is almost completely dark. In the front lies the Man, face down. On his back crouches a cat-like, fantastic animal (hyena with enormous, bat-like wings) that seems to have sunk its teeth into his neck" (2007 [1926], 82). The body of the Man is the focus of the drama from the very start. He is decrepit, perhaps already dead, and a hideous, unidentifiable animal gnaws at his neck. Alone on stage, suffering, under attack, it is quite possible at this early point to suppose that, as Gilman writes of Daniel Schreber, the Man "senses himself being transmuted from a 'beautiful,' masculine Aryan to an 'ugly,' feminized Jew" (1995, 147).

After the chorus's opening lines, after the "fantastic animal" is found sinking his teeth into the feeble protagonist, the chorus disappears, while "long, black, shadows fall slowly across the Man" (2007 [1926], 83). "Suddenly," Schoenberg's directions state, "behind the scene, loud, commonly gay music is heard, a joyous uproar of instruments. The shrill, mocking laughter of a crowd of people mingles with the final chord of the back-stage music" (2007 [1926], 83). At that moment, the curtains rise and the Man stands upright. His appearance is highly suggestive of a Weiningerian-Wagnerian image of the ailing Jew:

> He wears a dirty yellow-brown jacket of very coarse, thick material. The left leg of his black trousers comes down only to the knee; from there on it is in tatters. His shirt is half open, showing his chest. On his stockingless feet are badly torn shoes; one is so torn that his naked foot shows through, disclosing a large, open wound where it has been cut by a nail. His face and chest are in part bloody, part covered with scars. His hair is shorn close. (2007 [1926], 83)

The Man as a distinctly Semitic figure is clearly identifiable in Schoenberg's stage directions. He is the wounded, disheveled Jew, an example of what Carl Heinrich Stratz, in his pamphlet on Jewish anthropology in fin-de-siècle Vienna – "a pamphlet owned and read by Sigmund Freud" (Gilman 1994a, 15) – stated were the basic characteristics of the Jew: "defined by a long nose and numerous physical frailties such as a hunched back, knock knees, flat feet, etc." (cited in Gilman, 1994a, 15). His "wound," I suggest, may be indicative of two characteristics of the racial Jew: first, as a depiction of the eternal "wound" of all Jews – the circumcised penis – which, according to anti-Semitic discourse, was bodily proof of the Jew's incompleteness and ineptitude. As Gilman writes: "The Jewish male is not quite a 'whole' male, he is different and his difference is what marks the entire category of the Jew [...] Circumcision became the key to marking the Jewish body as different within the parameters of 'healthy' or 'diseased' [...]" (1991, 155). And second, the deformed "Jewish foot" of the fin-de-siècle Jew, which, Gilman writes, "marked him [...] as congenitally unable, and therefore, unworthy of being completely integrated into the social fabric of the modern state" (1991, 40). Finally, the Man's dirty appearance and torn clothes point to the image of the Jews as a disheveled and filthy vagrant: "In contemporary culture, the Jew stank of foetor judaicus. The smell, like the smell of the sewers of the nineteenth century, which epitomized the source of decay for nineteenth-century public health, was the smell of shit" (1995, 155). The Man's body remains in focus for the entirety of the drama. Considering the above assertions, it is thus possible to assume that Schoenberg deliberately presented a racially Jewish character, perhaps in part owing to Wagner's claim that "[o]ne never sees a Jew on the stage [...]"(Wagner 1973 [1850] 26). While Wagner asserts that "[w]e can conceive of no character, historical or modern, hero or lover, being played by a Jew, without instinctively feeling the absurdity of such an idea. [...]" (1973 [1850] 26–27), Schoenberg was free to depict the unaesthetic Jew precisely because his actor was not the "real thing," but rather a composite of racial characteristics.

The Man's limited number of lines, however, separates him from the image of the ostracized Jewish performer. Schoenberg's protagonist's almost silent role is reiterated in Schoenberg's proposed plan to turn *Die glückliche Hand* into a motion picture. In 1913 he presented this plan to Emil Hertzka, including in it his wish for the role of the Man: "For the film the part of the Man can be played by somebody who does not need to sing. The actor chosen should therefore be an outstandingly good one" (1964 [1913], 45). His plans were of course for a silent film – the only films appearing in the time period – a fact that may have encouraged, rather than deterred Schoenberg, as he lay out his requirements for the role.

Based on this observation, it can be suggested that Schoenberg, like Freud in his interpretation of Schreber, "aims at 'discretion'" (Gilman 1993, 143) in the former's creation of *Die glückliche Hand*. Whereas Freud's reading of Schreber "avoided any reference to the anti-Semitic rhetoric" in Schreber's *Memoirs*, so Schoenberg avoided this same rhetoric by enlisting a non-Jewish actor to "play" the fantastical role of a Semitic Jew. He thus "censored" his own readings of Wagner and Weininger, as Freud did of Schreber. From this perspective, Schoenberg's protagonist can also be seen as imbued with fears of effeminacy, and thus of Jewishness.

Perhaps the most significant turning point in Schoenberg's short work in relation to the Man's body comes when the Woman offers her goblet to the Man at the start of the second scene. Schoenberg's stage directions follow:

> The woman holds a goblet in her right hand and, stretching forth her right arm [...] offers it to the Man. Violet light falls from above upon the goblet. Rapturous pause. Suddenly the Man finds the goblet in his hand, although neither has stirred from their place and the man has never looked at her. (The Man must never look at her; he always gazes ahead; she always remains behind him.) The Man holds the goblet in his right hand, stretching out his arm. (2007 [1926], 84)

The Man has not only taken, but has taken *in* the Woman's liquid. The invisible transfer of the goblet indicates a meshing of the Man and Woman. Like Daniel Schreber of Gilman's study, the Man is perhaps "afraid he was turning into an effeminate Jew, a true composite of Weininger's images of the Jew and the woman" (1995, 142). Schoenberg's Man, however, succumbs: "He contemplates the goblet with rapture. Suddenly he becomes deeply serious, almost dejected; reflects a moment; then his face brightens again and with a joyous resolution he puts the goblet to his lips and drains it slowly" (2007 [1926], 84). The Woman quickly moves to the other side of the stage and the Man moves to the center, transformed: "He stands deep in thought, moved, entranced" (2007 [1926], 84), and says, facing only the audience: "How beautiful you are! I am so glad when you are near me. I live again" (2007 [1926], 85). By taking in the liquid originating from the Woman, he becomes the Weiningerian Jew. Here there is a distinct similarity to Schreber's memoirs, in which Schreber claims that Professor Flechsig, his supervising physician during his stay in an asylum in Leipzig, "miraculously produced in place of my healthy natural stomach a very inferior so-called 'Jew's stomach'" (1955 [1903], 144). The Man does not suffer at first from this transformation, as he can now "live again"; indeed, he seems overcome with a sense of newness. But he is soon to understand the essentialist nature of his Jewish body. The Woman is taken away by the soft hand of a third character on stage, the Gentleman, but this does not stir the Man, for he is certain that she is now part of him. Schoenberg directs the scene: "The Man does not realize that she has gone. To him, she is there at his hand, which he gazes at uninterruptedly. After a while he rises by a colossal effort, stretching his arms high in the air, and remains standing giant-like on tip-toe" (2007 [1926], 85). The Man then exclaims: "Now I possess you forever!" (2007 [1926], 86), for he believes his transformation is complete. By imbibing the Woman's drink, he has become effeminate, and according to anti-Semitic discourse, he has come into his full Jewish being. Weininger's claims – that "Judaism is saturated with femininity" and that "the Jew is more saturated with femininity than the Aryan, to such an extent that the most manly Jew is more feminine than the least manly Aryan" (1909 [1903], 187) – are given life by the Man's actions in this scene.

A counter-narrative to the above arises in the third scene of the drama, during which the Man faces his ultimate demise "at the foot" of the Woman. After a chase through a landscape full of artisans who are working "in something between a machine shop and a goldsmith's workshop," the Man appears standing below the Woman in a ravine-like structure. With urgency the Woman pushes a large stone "with her foot" (2007 [1926], 86), and it falls down upon the Man. Immediately following the act of the large stone falling upon the Man, Schoenberg's directions read: "the loud music and mocking laughter of the first scene are heard again" (2007 [1926], 86). According to a racialist Jewish reading, the Man's death thus comes as punishment for his attempt at realization of his Jewish being. Gilman writes that Schreber's memoirs are "filled with overt fear of emasculation and devirilization, expressed through the fear of becoming a Jew" (1993, 146). This idea is also suggested by the death of Schoenberg's racially Jewish protagonist. The most significant difference between the "Man" and Schreber would thus be Schoenberg's interception by way of censoring the ideas of Jewish disease and emasculation. Schoenberg "killed" his racially Jewish protagonist, indicating that he both adopted Wagnerian and Weiningerian rhetoric and simultaneously presented an elimination of it. The final lines of the Chorus are highly significant for closing the circle of Schoenberg's theme of Jewish racialism. Again the six women and six men appear and sing:

> Do you have to live again what you have so often lived? [...] Is there no peace within you? Still none? You seek to lay hold of what will only slip away from you when you grasp it. But what is in you, around you, wherever you may be, do you not feel it? Do you not hear it? Do you not understand what you hold? Do you feel only what you touch, the wounds only in your flesh, the pain only in your body? (2007 [1926], 86–87)

The possibility that the Man had neglected to understand the larger point of his bodily transformation and his Jewish wounds does not change his ultimate fate.

An alternative reading to Schoenberg's symbolic "killing" of the image of the racial Jew is that precisely because his protagonist took on characteristics of the racial Jew, he was thus fated for elimination. In light of Schoenberg's conversion, and considering Weininger's and Wagner's deterministic views of Jews as inherently wounded, effeminate, and incapable of vocalizing music, certain translations of Schoenberg's title of the drama, *Die glückliche Hand*, now appear in jest, as the Man has been delivered by a hand which is all but "lucky" or "fortunate." A more accurate translation is offered by Schoenberg himself, who stated in a 1928 lecture delivered in Breslau on the occasion of the drama's German opening that the title is directly related to the end of the second scene of the work, where his direction reads: "The Man does not realize that [the Woman] has gone" (2003, 85). Referring to this scene, he states in the lecture: "It is a certain pessimism which I was compelled to give form to at that time: Fateful Hand, which tries to grasp that which can only slip away from you, if you hold it. Fateful Hand, which does not hold what it promises!" (Auner 2003, 81). Under the English title of "Fateful Hand," the work now fully appears to present the condition of the fin-de-siècle Jew inhabiting an incurably Jewish body. A final reading of Schoenberg's drama reveals that the racial Jew of the late nineteenth and early twentieth century is at the mercy of an external fate which determines the very parameters of Jewish existence in Europe during this time period. Schoenberg's and Freud's fates, as they both have illustrated in different ways, are quite similar. Through this reading, the image of Gilman's self-censored Freud is found in the image of a self-protective Schoenberg.

As I have aimed to illustrate in this article, studies which utilize Gilman's argument that Freud's interpretation of Schreber's *Memoirs* ultimately illustrates his own battle with the racialist discourse presented by figures such as Otto Weininger are not limited to Freud's work alone, nor are they limited to strictly theoretical writings. Musical, literary, and visual works may also be included as subjects of analyses which aim to uncover a Jewish composer's (or writer's or artist's) relationship to the prevailing anti-Semitic discourse about Jews of the nineteenth and early-twentieth centuries. An example of such a study is an interpretation of Schoenberg's paintings of the avant-garde period, including *Self Portrait* (1910), which was displayed at the first *Der Blaue Reiter* exhibition in Munich. Such a study requires the use of analytic tools offered by art criticism and is well beyond the scope of the present article. Nevertheless, taking Schoenberg's paintings during this time period into account and considering the correlation between his paintings, writings, and music, these visual works would immediately appear to be intimately related to the concepts discussed in this article in regard to *Die glückliche Hand*.¹² A cross-disciplinary study of the impact of anti-Semitic writings of the late nineteenth and early twentieth centuries on such a dynamic artist as Arnold Schoenberg would surely generate some new and challenging conclusions.

Bibliography

Adams, Courtney S. "Artistic Parallels between Arnold Schoenberg's Music and Painting (1908–1912)." *College Music Symposium* 35 (1995): 5–21.

Auner, Joseph. *A Schoenberg Reader: Documents of a Life*. New Haven and London: Yale University Press, 2003.

Bohlman, Philip V. *Jewish Musical Modernism: Old and New*. Chicago and London: University of Chicago Press, 2008.

Brown, Julie. "Schoenberg's Early Wagnerisms: Atonality and the Redemption of Ahasuerus." *Cambridge Opera Journal* 6.1 (1994): 51–80.

Brown, Julie. "Understanding Schoenberg as Christ." *The Oxford Handbook of the New Cultural History of Music*. Ed. Jane F. Fulcher. New York: Oxford University Press, 2014. 117–162.

Carpenter, Alexander. "Schoenberg's Vienna, Freud's Vienna: Re-Examining the Connections between the Monodrama *Erwartung* and the Early History of Psychoanalysis." *Musical Quarterly* 93 (2010): 144–181.

Cramer, Alfred. "Music for the Future: Sounds of Psychology and Language in Works of Schoenberg, Webern, and Berg, 1909 to the First World War." PhD Dissertation. University of Pennsylvania, 1997.

Danuser, Hermann. "Musical Manifestations of the End in Wagner and in Post-Wagnerian 'Weltanschauungsmusik.'" *19th-Century Music* 18.1 (1994–1995): 64–82.

Freud, Sigmund. "Psychoanalytische Bemerkungen über einen autobiographisch beschriebenen Fall von Paranoia (Dementia Paranoides)." *Gesammelte Werke,* vol. 8. London: Imago Publishing Company, 1943 [1911]. 240–316.

Freud, Sigmund. "Preface." *Totem and Taboo. The Standard Edition of the Complete Psychological Works of Sigmund Freud,* vol. 13. Trans. James Strachey. London: Hogarth Press, 1953 [1913]. xv.

Freud, Sigmund. "Psychoanalytic Notes on an Autobiographical Account of a Case of Paranoia (Dementia Paranoides)." *The Standard Edition of the Complete Psychological Works of Sigmund Freud*, vol. 12. Trans. James Strachey. London: Hogarth Press, 1958 [1911]. 3–82.

Freud, Sigmund. *The Letters of Sigmund Freud*. Trans. Tania and James Stern. New York: Basic Books, 1975.

Gay, Peter. *Freud: A Life for Our Time*. New York and London: W.W. Norton and Co., 1988.

Gilman, Sander. *Jewish Self-Hatred: Anti-Semitism and the Hidden Language of the Jews*. Baltimore, MD: Johns Hopkins University Press, 1990.

Gilman, Sander. *The Jew's Body*. New York: Routledge, 1991.

---

12 For studies of the relationships between Schoenberg's various art mediums see Auner (2003) and Adams (1995).

Gilman, Sander. *The Case of Sigmund Freud: Medicine and Identity at the Fin-de-Siècle*. Baltimore, MD: Johns Hopkins University Press, 1994a.
Gilman, Sander. *Reading Freud's Reading*. New York: New York University Press, 1994b.
Gilman, Sander. *Freud, Race, and Gender*. Princeton, N.J.: Princeton University Press, 1995.
Heskes, Irene. "Shapers of American Jewish Music: Mailamm and the Jewish Music Forum, 1931–62."*American Music* 15.3 (1997): 305–320.
Hough, Bonny Ellen. "Schoenberg's 'Herzgewächse' and the *'Blaue Reiter' Alamnac*." *Journal of the Arnold Schoenberg Institute* 7.2 (1983): 197–221.
Kandinsky, Wassily, and Franz Marc. *The "Blaue Reiter" Almanac*. New Documentary Edition. Ed. Klaus Lankheit. New York: Viking Press, 1974.
Keathley, Elizabeth. "Revisioning Musical Modernism: Arnold Schoenberg, Marie Pappenheim, and *Erwartung*'s New Woman." PhD Dissertation. SUNY at Stony Brook, 1999.
Koss, Juliet. *Modernism After Wagner*. Minneapolis: University of Minnesota Press, 2010.
Lessem, Alan Philip. *Music and Text in the Works of Arnold Schoenberg: The Critical Years, 1908–1922*. Ann Arbor, MI: University of Michigan Research Press, 1979.
Mesa, Franklin. *Opera: An Encyclopedia of World Premieres and Significant Performances, Singers, Composers, Librettists, Arias and Conductors, 1597–2000*. Jefferson, NC: McFarland & Co., 2007.
Móricz, Klára. *Jewish Identities: Nationalism, Racism, and Utopianism in Twentieth-Century Music*. Berkeley and Los Angeles: University of California Press, 2008.
Neher, Andre. *They Made Their Souls Anew*. Trans. David Maisel. New York: SUNY Press, 1990.
Nulman, Macy. *Concise Encyclopedia of Jewish Music*. New York: McGraw-Hill, 1975.
Painter, Karen. "Contested Counterpoint: 'Jewish' Appropriation and Polyphonic Liberation." *Archiv für Musikwissenschaft* 58.3 (2001): 201–230.
Payette, Jessica. "Seismographic Screams: 'Erwartung''s Reverberations through Twentieth-Century Culture." PhD Dissertation. Stanford University, 2008.
Ringer, Alexander. *Arnold Schoenberg: The Composer as Jew*. New York: Oxford University Press, 2000.
Saleski, Gdal. *Famous Musicians of Jewish Origin*. New York: Bloch Publishing Company, 1949.
Santner, Eric L. *My Own Private Germany: Daniel Paul Schreber's Secret History of Modernity*. Princeton, NJ: Princeton University Press, 1996.
Schiller, David Michael. *Bloch, Schoenberg and Bernstein: Assimilating Jewish Music*. Oxford and New York: Oxford University Press, 2003.
Schoenberg, Arnold. *Arnold Schoenberg Letters*. Trans. Eithne Wilkins and Ernst Kaiser. London: Faber and Faber, 1964 [1958].
Schoenberg, Arnold. *Style and Idea: Selected Writings of Arnold Schoenberg*. Ed. Leonard Stein. Trans. Leo Black. London and Boston: Faber and Faber, 1975 [1950].
Schoenberg, Arnold. "Breslau Lecture on *Die glückliche Hand*." *Arnold Schoenberg, Wassily Kandinsky: Letters, Pictures, and Documents*. Ed. Jelena Hahl-Koch. Trans. John C. Crawford. London: Faber and Faber, 1984. 102–107.
Schoenberg, Arnold. *Die glückliche Hand: Drama mit Musik*. Vienna: Universal Edition, 1987.
Schoenberg, Arnold. *Die glückliche Hand: Drama with Music*. Trans. Joseph Auner. *A Schoenberg Reader: Documents of a Life*. New Haven and London: Yale University Press, 2003. 82–87.
Schreber, Daniel Paul. *Memoirs of My Nervous Illness*. Ed. and Trans. Ida Macalpine and Richard A. Hunter. New York: New York Review Books, 1955 [1903].

Simms, Bryan R. "Whose Idea Was *Erwartung*?" *Constructive Dissonance: Arnold Schoenberg and the Transformations of Twentieth-Century Culture*. Berkeley, CA: University of California Press, 1997. 100–111.

Simms, Bryan R. "The Operas *Erwartung* and *Die glückliche Hand*." *The Atonal Music of Arnold Schoenberg, 1908–1923*. New York: Oxford University Press, 2000. 89–112.

Slipp, Samuel. *The Freudian Mystique: Freud, Women, and Feminism*. London and New York: New York University Press, 1993.

Viereck, George Sylvester. *Glimpses of the Great*. New York: Macaulay Company, 1930 [1926].

Wagner, Richard. *Judaism in Music (Das Judentum in der Musik)*. Trans. Edwin Evans. London: W. Reeves, 1910 [1850].

Wagner, Richard. "Judaism in Music." *Richard Wagner: Stories and Essays*. Ed. Charles Osborne. London: Peter Owen, 1973 [1850]. 23–29.

Weininger, Otto. *Sex and Character*. London: William Heinemann and New York: G.P. Putnam's Sons, 1909 [1903].

White, Pamela A. *Schoenberg and the God-Idea: The Opera 'Moses und Aron.'* Ann Arbor: University of Michigan Press, 1985.

Wickes, Lewis. "Schoenberg's *Erwartung* and the Reception of Psychoanalysis in Musical Circles in Vienna until 1910/1911." *Studies in Music* 23 (1989): 88–106.

Yerushalmi, Yosef Hayim. *Freud's Moses: Judaism Terminable and Interminable*. New Haven and London: Yale University Press, 1991.

Yerushalmi, Yosef Hayim. "The Moses of Freud and the Moses of Schoenberg: On Words, Idolatry, and Psychoanalysis." *The Psychoanalytic Study of the Child*, vol. 47. New Haven: Yale University Press, 1992. 1–20.

Messianism, Syncretism, and Vanguard Philosophy

Małgorzata Stolarska-Fronia
Saints and Tsadikim – The Religious Syncretism of Jewish Expressionism

Jewish expressionism was a transnational cultural movement of artists who were active between 1912 and 1939 within Polish, Ukrainian, Lithuanian, and German societies. They included Ludwig Meidner and Jakob Steinhardt, members of "Die Pathetiker" group (1912); members of the Yung-yidish and Di Khalyastre groups (1919); and various artists from the Kultur-lige milieu, as well as artists whose contacts with most of the aforementioned groups were less formal (e.g., Lasar Segall, Heinrich Tischler). This informal group of artists occupied a separate cultural space within the European avant-garde, sharing its general worldview yet also expressing their own stance as modern Jewish artists. Thus, aside from the characteristic features of the expressionist movement as a whole – such as opposition to bourgeois values, a programmatic break with earlier styles of painting, a revolutionary attitude and declaration of creating new art, apocalyptic moods and messianic hopes in the face of the crisis of European culture (especially after the First World War), primitive art as a source of inspiration – Jewish expressionism involved typical Jewish motifs: a fascination with Hasidism and Kabbalah, the landscape of Eastern European Jewish towns and its mystical rendition, Jewish customs and religion, Jewish festivals, events in the Jewish life cycle, as well as a relationship with the Yiddish culture and literature of the day. Jewish artists were involved in searching for "Jewish means of expression" (Aronson and Ryback 1919, 123), and expressionism – as an opposing naturalistic representation of reality, allowing for far-reaching deformation, freedom of form and color, and forging to reveal inner, irrational and dynamic spirituality – was at this point the most appealing to young Jewish artists. The revolutionary ideas of changing values, opposing bourgeois life and assimilation, and proclaiming the rebirth of the Jewish spirit, as well as strong messianic and apocalyptic elements in the expressionist worldview, strengthened this relationship.

Note: The background research for this article was financed by the National Science Centre through a post-doctoral internship grant. Project title: *Ekspresjonizm żydowski – w poszukiwaniu przestrzeni kulturowej* (Jewish Expressionism – A Quest for Cultural Space). I would like to thank Professors Ziva Amishai-Maisels, Haim Finkelstein, Jerzy Malinowski, and Moshe Rosman for carefully reading this article and for their valuable comments and suggestions.

DOI 10.1515/9783110454956-011

This phenomenon gave rise to a specific discourse, including a debate regarding the influence of the artists' origins on both their choices of artistic language and the development of expressionism as an art movement. Central elements that dominated the discourse on Jewish expressionism in the visual arts included the connection between expressionism and religion; Jewish avant-garde engagement in the paradigm of national art; and the dilemma of choosing between style and subject matter. Discussion of the so-called "Jewish roots of expressionism" among theorists, philosophers, art critics, and the artists (both Jewish and non-Jewish) was part of this discourse.[1]

The search for authentic religious experience, a return to the original values of the Bible and Jewish mystical texts, was an important impulse behind the expressionists' output. For Jewish artists, this was a complex process, since, being familiar with and living amidst two religious cultures, Judaism and Christianity, they combined in their quest ideas and themes from both theologies. Some questions, such as the connection between Pauline teachings and Judaism, were the subjects of dissertations and articles published in the Jewish press (Kellermann 1903a, 1903b; Rappeport 1917–1918, 276–279; Strauß 1923, 1, 32–44). Themes and motifs from Christian iconography appear in expressionist art quite frequently. This coincided with a fascination with the Christian religion and with a specific manner of presenting mystical themes.

The expressionists' worldview of such artists as Ludwig Meidner and Jakob Steinhard as well as members of the Yung-yidish group (to mention only a few) was steeped in Jewish philosophy. This included Martin Buber's concept of the Jewish renaissance (Buber 1920), his philosophy of dialogue (Buber 1992), and his concept of Hasidism (Buber 1963, 1999), as well as the concepts of revelation, messianism and apocalypse that were developed, after the First World War, by Franz Rosenzweig (Rosenzweig 1998), Ernst Bloch (Bloch 1918), and Walter Benjamin (Benjamin 1971–1989), and Gershom Scholem's works on Kabbalah and Jewish mysticism (Scholem 1997). The Jewish artists were surely familiar with these works, whose excerpts were published in the contemporary Jewish press, as were related reviews and discussions.

This essay will examine the Jewish expressionists' quest for religious identity with the ultimate goal of depicting a cultural space[2] within the general expres-

---

[1] See inter alia: Goll 1917, Ryback and Aronson 1919, Weintraub 1922, Jacob 1923, *Od redakcji* (Forma, ogół, Żydzi) 1920, Chwistek 1934, Berlewi 1921. Berlewi comments that the two notions are frequently confused when it comes to Jewish art: "In my opinion, Jewish art should be expressed through a specific form, inspired by the Jewish spirit" (Berlewi 1955, n.p.).

[2] The cultural space can be defined by artistic practices (visual arts, writing, theater plays and performances) of individuals sharing the same worldview, which distinguishes them from the

sionist movement, or, more precisely, within the values represented by the second generation of expressionists.[3] It will be based on the assumption that, while the expressionists sought religious experience in order to re-sacralize art,[4] the spiritual quest of Jewish expressionists is inseparable from the search for a new, national art. Their avant-garde aesthetic experiment went hand in hand with a cultural and religious experiment. The latter constituted a search for the roots of Jewish spirituality and communality within the Hasidic movement as well as an internalization of ideas and figures from Buddhist and Christian art. I will focus on two main topics related to the Jewish expressionists' religious syncretism. The first is inspiration from Hasidic spirituality, especially the idea of ecstatic prayer, which Jewish artists identified with the creative act. Visions of religious ecstasy and the figures of tsadikim (biblical figures and spiritual masters of Hasidism), apart from conventional images of rabbis,[5] do not have a developed tradition in earlier, pre-modern traditions of Jewish art; hence depictions of these scenes often derive from patterns of Christian art, especially Baroque painting, and even art of the East. The second important issue – the very basis for constructing a religious worldview – was the messianic idea. Its reception and representation by Jewish artists is an interesting example of correspondence between, on one hand, the philosophical and literary recognition of this issue and, on the other, its portrayal in the visual arts. It is important to find a reference to the similarities and differences between an intense Christological element in the art of Jewish expressionists and expressionist art in general. In tracing this transformation I will focus primarily on artworks by members of the Yung-yidish group, and those of German-Jewish expressionism.

---

broader cultural area. Thus it exists beyond physical boundaries and territorial and national categories, and is part of an international milieu. In the case of Jewish expressionism these are artists situated in the worldview of the international avant-garde, yet expressing their particular Jewish identity expressed in the desire of identifying a modern Jewish style (see the first page of this article). Works of art created in the cultural area are identified and defined by the cultural context. (For the concept of cultural context, see Margolis 2004, 208). Therefore, my method of selection of artists and artworks largely coincides with the theory and method of cultural relativism proposed by Margolis.
3 Barron 1988.
4 Although Anderson argues that expressionists "encoded their avowedly secular project in the religious idiom" (Anderson 2011, 17), it does not preclude intentions that underlie the ultimate effect.
5 For further discussion, see Cohen 1998, 115–153.

1 In Search of an Aesthetic Paradigm – Jewish Soul and New Jewish Art

The quest for religious identity was a key element of Jewish expressionism. Clearly, intense religious pursuit and its articulation in expressionist art was a generational experience stemming from the attitudes and cultural currents typical of the early twentieth century. In 1918, the famous Neue Religiöse Kunst (New Religious Art) exhibition, which cemented the relationship between expressionism and religion, was displayed at the Kunsthalle in Mannheim. A year later, Gustav Hartlaub published *Religion und Kunst* (Religion and Art). In his view, "Der Expressionismus als Stil bildet die Grundlage alles religiösen Gefühlsausdruckes [...]" [Expressionism as a style provides the basis for expressing all religious feelings] (Hartlaub 1919, 36). Nevertheless, Hartlaub comments on "[...] idealistischen Versuchen moderner Theologen und Denker zur Erneuerung des religiösen Lebens [...]" [idealist attempts at renewing religious life by modern theologians and thinkers] (Hartlaub 1919, 107); such figures included none other than Buber, whom he labelled a *"chassidische Mystiker"* [Hasidic mystic]. Hartlaub made his observations ten years after publication of Buber's *Ekstatische Konfessionen* (Ecstatic Confessions), a synthesis of the thinker's mystical investigations. Buber confessed to an early fascination with German mysticism – the teachings of Meister Eckhart, Jakob Böhme, and Angelus Silesius – which subsequently evolved into fascination with the Kabbalah and Hasidism, culminating in publication of his tales of the Hasidim.[6] His religious thought combined with his views on art was fundamental in raising spiritual awareness among the young generation of Jews, including artists belonging to avant-garde movements.

The Jewish expressionists saw in their work a mission to reinstate proper order, to re-establish contact with lost spiritual values, with the Absolute, nature, and God, whom they understood and referred to by a variety of names, including Logos and *"shekhinah."* Often, in commenting on their art, they applied the notion of revelation – a phenomenon that in their view endowed them with cognitive powers, embodied dialogue, and allowed truth to be given a form. In their interpretation, this notion became universal, and grew into an act of cultural and artistic renewal, not only deriving from one of the most important events of Judaism, namely, the revelation at Sinai as described in the Bible, but also influenced by the

---

6 *Die Geschichten des Rabbi Nachman*. Frankfurt am Main: Rütten & Loening, 1906; *Die Legende des Baal Schem*. Frankfurt am Main: Rütten & Loening, 1908; *Der grosse Maggid und seine Nachfolge*. Frankfurt am Main: Rütten & Loening, 1922; *Tales of the Hasidim*. Foreword by Chaim Potok. New York: Schocken Books, 1991.

apocalyptic visions of John the Apostle. The concept of revelation also appeared in the context of a new Jewish national culture. Revelation, in this sense, had both a mystical and a social dimension. It was seen to naturally lead to a spiritual revolution which would produce a new quality – rebirth of Jewish culture, referred to by some explicitly as *"expressionistisches Judentum"* [expressionist Judaism] (Fuchs 1924) – and it is not without reason that this notion appears in expressionist rhetoric in connection with the idea of Jewish Renaissance introduced by Buber, as well as in German Jewish thought as represented by Rosenzweig.

Avant-garde artists felt they were creating art in a cultural void, and thus their aesthetic experimentation went hand in hand with religious experimentation. This was especially the case for artists active in the independent Polish state (e.g., members of the group *Eskpresjoniści Polscy* (Polish Expressionists, established in 1917), the Poznań group BUNT (Rebellion, established in 1918), and the Jewish Yung-yidish group (established in 1919)). For Jewish artists the First World War and its aftermath was not only a catastrophic experience; it also created the possibility to find their own cultural space within a victorious state. According to artists from the Łódź-based Yung-yidish group, the best means of achieving the latter was expressionist art. As Yankl Adler (1895–1949) stated in his manifesto:

> We, the young, have almost forsaken the relationship with the God of our Fathers; we have lost what people satisfied with themselves possess – half sin, half virtue; our trust in people was poisoned while we were still young, and in our hearts we are weighed down with the burden of a great, great longing for God and Eternity, for the power that made Creation happen, for Logos. The art of the twentieth century, Expressionist art, was born of this longing, and it is the seventh day, and the week of the commonplace is over.
> (Adler 1920, 180)

Besides the artist's own statement, Yankl Adler's art was described by contemporary critics as one that realized the paradigm of expressionist form according to Max Deri, namely, the *"symboliczno-emocjonalne odejście od natury"* [symbolic-emotional withdrawal from nature] (Zimmermann 1919, 3). Adler's manifesto proves the influence of Buberian thought. His idea of "ideal relation" had been expressed in a wish to unite with God, whereas expressionist art signified the fulfilment of this longing.[7]

Besides artistic manifestos and personal declarations by Jewish expressionists, a universal understanding of Judaism and its inclusion in the discourse on the

---

7 The formative role of religion in the creation of the new Jewish art was also noted by other contemporaries. In his article "Prolegomena to Jewish Art" published in 1919, Yehoshua Herszferder (1919, 11–12) referred to religious emotion as one element of the triad which propelled Jewish art. (The other two elements were eroticism and nature.)

significance of religious spirituality in expressionist art influenced the development of the notion and features of Jewish avant-garde art. In an article published in *Die Aktion* in 1917, Iwan Goll acknowledged the primacy of Judaism, having compared Catholicism and Judaism, and each religion's natural ability to capture "the spirit," identified as a positive and creative force. Spirituality was another key term in the discourse of expressionist art. The term "Jewish spirituality" or, more often, "Jewish soul" found its way into reviews and artistic manifestos, and exerted substantial influence on the notion of national art. A key year in the shaping of this concept was 1919, when a series of exhibitions that included Jewish expressionists was held in Poland. Among the first groups to emerge was Yung-yidish, whose members declared their desire to create avant-garde Jewish art. At the same time, branches of the Kultur-lige spread throughout Central-Eastern Europe, actively propagating their ideas, organizing lectures and exhibitions of modern Jewish artists, and aiming to introduce new forms of expression for Jewish art.[8] They maintained contacts with Jewish expressionists in Germany – including Jakob Steinhardt and Ludwig Meidner, who sought spiritual inspiration in the culture of Eastern European Jews.[9] The bond between Jewish spirituality and expressionism stemmed almost directly from the perception of Judaism as a dynamic, developing culture, full of symbolism and mysticism (the so-called *"expressionistishes Judentum"* (Fuchs 1924)). The expressionist nature of Jewish culture was counterposed against superficial secular culture, or Western culture in general, thus far associated with Impressionism. To quote Ryback and Aronson: "[...] *der Impressionismus* [ist] *der jüdischen Formenwahrnehmung fremd"* [Impressionism is alien to the Jewish perception of form], and *"sich unmittelbar auf optische Eindrücke und nicht auf Philosophie oder Symbolik gründete"* [is based on optical impressions rather than on philosophy or symbolism] (Arnonson and Ryback 2012, 131).

The desire of Jewish expressionists to distinguish their art within the overall avant-garde movement led to the designation of certain distinctive features, thereby producing a specific discourse of otherness which was a factor in mapping the cultural space of Jewish expressionism. This discourse was reinforced in the press and by art critics related and unrelated to Jewish milieu.[10] Among

---

8 The main figures of the Kultur-lige were the artists Issachar Ryback and Boris Aronson. They expressed their vision on modern Jewish art in their manifesto *Wege der jüdischen Malerei* (The Ways of Jewish Art), published in 1919 in Yiddish (Aronson and Ryback 2012, 123–141).
9 Amishai-Maisels (1982; 1995); Bertz (1995).
10 In a review of the Modern Artists exhibition in May 1921, Artur Swinarski, a member of the Poznań-based BUNT Expressionist group, with which the members of Yung-yidish were also associated, wrote of Marek Szwarc's art: *"Dusza niepokrewna ani Panieńskiemu, ani Szmajowi. Krew Szagała. Krew wschodnia, semicka; w formie w stylu odrębność – a dążność do wspólnego celu.*

the avant-garde artists, there was discussion about the primacy of form over substance; this was an attempt to distance themselves from the earlier traditions of painting, including those related to so-called ghetto art.[11]

However, even in philosophical writings, the vision of the Jewish soul (German: *Geist*) oscillated between particularism and universalism. This was a construct that united elements associated with Jewish spirituality, especially the Hasidic one, and all that it absorbed from East European culture. As I will try to show, in proclaiming the creation of a new Jewish art, Jewish artists referred to various traditions and cultures, thus indicating that their spiritual and religious worldview was the summation of the exploration of many generations. It was in fact an idiosyncratic construct, whose driving force was the emotions of a new generation that was not only seeking pathos, revelation, and ecstasy, but also identifying the role of the modern artist with the monk, prophet, priest, and finally the messiah.

2 *Hitlahavut* and the Pathos of Colors – "Purple, Through the Most Powerful Vermilion, Down to the Deepest Carmine."

The ideas of pathos, revelation, and ecstasy were known to Jewish artists primarily from Buber's writings.[12] The religious syncretism and spiritual explorations in

---

Inni są święci, prorocy, królowie jego od świętych naszych (ten bliskość przeniósł testamentowej, tu pamięć gotyku lub baroku); ekstaza ta sama, ten sam duch. Poza tym groteska, nie znana dotąd u naszych plastyków" [The soul, not akin to Panieński, nor to Szmaj [members of BUNT]. The blood of Szagał [Chagall]. Eastern, Semitic blood; distinctiveness of form and style, and yet striving for the common goal. He has other saints, prophets and kings (he conveys the Testament of immediacy, the memory of Gothic and Baroque); the same ecstasy, the same spirit. Aside from that, grotesque – thus far unknown to our own artists] (Swinarski 1920, 55).

11 By ghetto art I mean works of Jewish artists associated with realistic painting and graphic arts. They included mainly painters from Warsaw and Łódź: Maurycy Trębacz, Leopold Pilichowski, Jakub Weinles, to mention a few. They painted scenes from Jewish neighborhoods, Jewish festivals and religious customs. See Malinowski 2000, 39–63.

12 In 1904, Buber wrote his dissertation on Christian mystical philosophers Nicholas of Cusa and Böhme. The same year he started to study the Testament of Rabbi Yisra'el, known as the Ba'al Shem Tov (Scott, 2), which resulted from his former studies on Hasidism. In 1906 he published *The Tales of Rabbi Nachman* and in 1908 the first edition of *The Legend of the Ba'al-Shem*. The emphasis on relation present in the teachings of Cusanus and Böhme, as well as on the importance of the collective experience being reflected in each individual, in which the oneness of the Universe is reflected (Miller 2013), can be linked to the ideas characterising the Hasidic movement

Buber's thought established him as one of the most popular Jewish philosophers and among the major influences in shaping the worldview of Jewish artists.[13] Those who strove to strengthen and renew their contact with Jewish spirituality usually sought inspiration first from Buber's writings on Hasidism.

The Hasidic movement, recounted by Buber in the form of anecdotal legends, experienced a renaissance, especially after the First World War, when the devastating experiences of this worldwide apocalypse and the collapse of old values spurred people to embark on spiritual quests for a "new" religion. Hasidic and Kabbalistic thought also became known through the works of Gershom Scholem, as well as through the contemporary Jewish press and German translations of Yiddish works, especially the writings of Samuel Agnon and I.L. Peretz. These publications had a major impact in changing the attitudes of German Jews towards Eastern European Jews (Laor 1993, 75–93). Creating visual parallels to the emerging ideas presented in essays or short stories was part of the Jewish expressionists' (especially those from Germany) development of their worldview and identity.

Among them, Ludwig Meidner (1884–1966),[14] co-founder of "Die Pathetiker" group and who had long remained influenced by Christianity before becoming a deeply religious Jew, was the key figure in Jewish expressionism. Meidner's spiritual inspiration by Christian mysticism originated in the land of his youth: Silesia. During his studies at the *Breslau Königliche Kunstschule* (Royal School of Art) in 1903 he became interested in the writings of Angelus Silesius and Jacob Böhme, among others, whom he may have read in connection with his interest in Michael Willmann. These writings were disseminated among an informal group of Jewish artists in Berlin in which Meidner had been active since 1910; the group included most members of the Yung-yidish group from Poland. A parallel path of gaining access to these ideas was through the writings of Buber.

Raised in a secular family, though aware of his Jewish roots, Meidner experienced sudden conversions. He describes this experience on several occasions in his memoirs. In a passage composed in 1934 for a portfolio, he states:

(Scott, 9). In his 1911 *Chinesische Geister – und Liebesgeschichten*, Buber disclosed his particular interest in demonology, especially stories concerning the relations between humans and ghosts as well as the latters' adoption of a bodily form.

13 The aesthetics of representation was one of the components of his philosophy, and he was also engaged in the discussion of the notion of Jewish art. See Buber 1902, 205–210.

14 Zachary Braiterman describes Expressionism as a hybrid with a complex religious profile. He names four basic elements which he considers inherent to it: dialogue, meeting, spiritual transformation, and subjectivism coupled with a supra-subjective element, hot colours, and searing pathos. As an example of the latter element Braiterman cites the work of Ludwig Meidner (Braiterman 2007, 11–12).

Bis zum 19. Lebensjahr Atheist, – von da ab ganz einer religiöse-mystischen, aber individualistischen Erlebnisart ergeben. Vom letzten Kriegsjahr ab ganz im christlich – mystischen Denken und Erleben, 1919 bis 1923 bei der christlichen Theologie, namentlich dem Apostel Paulus. Dann trat ein Umschwung ein, nach stürmischen Jahren: Rückkehr zum Judentum, Bekanntschaft mit dem Chassidismus, Aufnahme der jüdisch – religiösen Praxis ab 1924.[15]

[Atheist until the age of 19, from then on given over to a religious-mystical though individual way of experience. From the last year of the war, fully embraced Christian-mystical thought and experience, from 1919 to 1923 [immersed] in Christian theology, namely, [the teaching of] Paul the Apostle. Then, after stormy years, came a reversal: return to Judaism, getting to know Hasidism, starting to practice Jewish religious customs since 1924.]

Earlier, Meidner had described his conversion as a revelation: "*Viele Jahre ein Gottesleugner sein; zerrüttet, zuchtlos, hämisch; böswillig, halb-verdreht; ein Kind der Zeit [...] bis eines Nachts, nie geahnt, wie ein weisser Hagelsturm, Gottes Herrlichkeit sich dir offenbart ...*" (Meidner 1918, 38) [A denier of God for many years, confused, undisciplined, gloating; malicious, half-perverse; a child of the times [...] until one night, never imagined, like a white hailstorm, the glory of God opens up before you ...].

In 1919 Meidner painted two gouaches: *Die Verzückung des Apostels Pauli / Der Laufende* (The Ecstasy of the Apostle Paul / The Running) (Fig. 1) and *Der Prophet* (The Prophet).[16] In each there appear corpulent, bearded men, their bodies, feet, and hands twisted in ecstasy. Both represent strong, hyperbolized types and reflect the artist's complex approach to religiosity. Meidner's fascination with the figure of the prophet derived from his peculiar understanding of the artist as a mediator between God and society; it was also his way of establishing dialogue with his biblical, that is, Jewish past. On the other hand, the ambiguous figure of Saint Paul in many ways reflected Meidner's own religious identity. At the particular moment when the two gouaches were created, he may have felt like a Jewish convert to Christianity who still remains firmly rooted in Judaism. This approach was not common among his Jewish contemporaries, who generally held a rather negative position towards Paul.[17] What unites the figures of Paul the Apostle and

---

15 Letter from Ludwig Meidner to Franz Landsberger, 21 February 1934. Collection of Leo Baeck Institute, Franz Landsberger Collection, AR 2318.
16 He was particularly interested in Paulinism – the teachings of Saint Paul. He read the apostolic epistles, and often invited the monk Johannes Verkade, a former Nabis who had converted to Roman Catholicism in 1902 and settled at the Benedictine abbey in Beuron, to his studio. The figure of Paul the Apostle fascinated Meidner, particularly from 1919–1924, that is, until his return to Judaism.
17 Buber belonged to Paul's critics and identified him with legalistic rabbis. See Novak 1988, 128–129.

Fig. 1: Ludwig Meidner. *Ecstasy of the Apostle Paul.* 1919 © Winfried Flammann's collection, Karlsruhe.

the Prophet in Meidner's frame of mind could be the idea of *"Hitlahabut"* (Hebrew: Hitlahavut)[18] introduced by Buber in his stories of the Ba'al Shem Tov: *"Hitlahabut ist: 'das Brennen'; die Inbrust der Ekstaze. Sie ist der Becher der Gnade und der ewige Schlüssel"* [Hitlahabut is the burning fervor of ecstasy. It is the cup of grace and the eternal key] (Buber 1908, 2). The power of fiery pathos and ecstasy was claimed by members of "Die Pathetiker" group to be the most important goal of their art.

The fact that both figures were painted by Meidner in the same year and represent a similar, mystical idea suggests more particular observations. The fineness of the boundary between the saints and tsadikim and, at the same time, the strength of the relationship between Buberian thought and Meidner's art are underscored by the correspondence between Meidner and Buber concerning the latter's project of creating drawings for the *Legend of the Ba'al Shem Tov*. By the end of 1919 Meidner offered to Buber to create illustrations for the subsequent edition of the Ba'al Shem book[19]; moreover, his further correspondence clearly indicates that Buber's philosophy had for a long time been his source of inspiration:

> *Die Welt Ihrer Bücher liegt mir in der Tat, wie ich Ihnen schon vor fünf Jahren sagte, sehr nahe und ich habe in den letzten Jahren manches Blatt gezeichnet, das eine graphische Umschreibung Ihrer Dichtungen sein könnte. Ich versuchte in letzter Zeit zu meiner eignen Freude Gebärden und Gestalten zu den Briefen des Heiligen Paulus zu zeichnen, ein Unterfangen, das Manchen sehr gewagt scheinen mag, aber es ist dennoch gut möglich (wie die Resultate beweisen).*[20]

[Indeed, the world of your books, as I told you already five years ago, is very close to me and in the recent years I have created several drawings which could be a graphic paraphrase of your poems. Recently I've been trying, for my own pleasure, to draw some gestures and figures to the epistles of Saint Paul; this endeavor might seem to be quite daring to some, but I think it is very possible nevertheless (as confirmed by the results).]

---

18 The concept of "hitlahavut" – a "flame" (Hebrew: Lahav) for God, a state of deep spiritual engagement during the prayer – occurs dozens of times in early Hasidic books in the late eighteenth and early nineteenth centuries, e.g: *Ben Porat Yosef* by Jacob Josef of Płonne (Korzec 1781), *Noam Elimelech* by Elimelech Weissblum of Leżajsk (1787), and *Kedushat Levi* by Levi Yitzchok of Berditchev (1811). I am grateful to Prof. Moshe Rosman for his expertise and comments regarding this part of my article.
19 The first edition was published in 1908: *Die Legende des Baal Schem*. Frankfurt am Main: Rütten & Loening; the second in 1916.
20 Letter from January 2 1920. Martin Buber Archive, National Library of Israel, ARC Ms. Var. 350008493.

Clearly, Meidner did not see conflict between creating illustrations for the Ba'al Shem book and his illustrations of the Apostle Paul. For him the main idea was to express religious rapture in art, and his mention of "Gebärden und Gestalten" (Gestures and Figures) could have served as universal forms applicable to both Jewish and Christian religious content. Yet, there is another, purely artistic and formal basis for this attitude. For Meidner, of all artistic traditions and styles it was the art of the Baroque that could best express and evoke religious feelings. Such art also provided an iconographic prototype for mystical prayer which did not exist in Jewish art. Therefore, for Meidner, as well as for other Jewish expressionists, Baroque art became a source of inspiration in depicting scenes expressing deep religious commitment and Hasidic spirituality, especially as applies to both the composition of images and the colors used. [21]

The Jewish expressionists drew from Baroque symbols, colors, and composition, particularly in group scenes depicting moments of ecstatic religious rapture. This is evident in Yankl Adler's *Błogosławieństwo Bal Szem Towa* (The Ba'al Shem Tov's Blessing) (Fig. 2) and *Ostatnia godzina rabiego Eleazara* (Rabbi Eliezer's Last Hour) (1918–1920) (Fig. 3).[22] As noted by earlier researchers such as Jerzy Malinowski, both images show the influence of Mannerism, as represented by the art of El Greco. The first image shows the figure of the leader of Hasidism positioned atop a cascade composition, with a man on his left and women below; his holiness is signified by rays emerging from behind his *shtreiml*, like a halo. Gestures characteristic of Mannerist painting are represented here by the symbolic gesture of priestly blessing.[23] In El Greco's painting, *Christ Blessing*, the left hand of Christ rests on a globe, whereas that of Adler's Ba'al Shem Tov opens outward and extends to the shtetl buildings below the figure – the Jewish universe representing the idea of a religious community. This image reflects the Hasidic concept of the sanctity of the tsadik, a mediator between Heaven and Earth who bears a messianic message. He is also presented as the leader of the community. The figure

---

[21] A fascination with the Baroque as a style also appears in the writings of Jewish philosophers. Apart from pursuing studies in philosophy and history, Franz Rosenzweig also attended drawing classes and lectures by Heinrich Wöllflin, who had a fundamental influence on Rozenzweig's views on art (Braiterman 2007, 44).

[22] On Meidner's influence on the art of Yankl Adler, see Malinowski (2000, 184). Adler was also familiar with art of "Die Pathetiker" group, as he was a frequent guest in the home of Jakob and Minni Steinhardt.

[23] One can draw a parallel to the blessing gesture of Christ, later called the Merciful Christ, found in Renaissance art, as in the image of *Christ Blessing Surrounded by a Donor and His Family* c. 1575–1580 by an unknown German painter from Lower Saxony; Hans Memling's painting, *Christ Blessing*, the central panel from a 1487 triptych from the Church of Santa Maria la Real, Najera, and El Greco's *Christ Blessing (The Saviour of the World)* from around 1600.

Fig. 2: Yankl Adler. *The Ba'al Shem Tov's Blessing*. 1919. Private collection.

Fig. 3: Yankl Adler. *Rabbi Eliezer's Last Hour*. 1918–1920. (painting lost). Photo – courtesy of Museum of Art in Łódź.

behind him, holding a scroll with writing on it, could be one of his disciples – the scribe Yankel or his brother-in-law Gershon of Kitev, who wrote *Igeret ha-kodesh* (The Holy Epistle) (Rosman 2010).[24] The painting thus outlines the meaning of the written account of the sanctity of the tsadik – similar to the hagiography of Christian saints. It also reveals the source of plastic imagery for the tsadik figure.

If Hasidic tales such as those published by Buber, Peretz, and Samuel Agnon – especially those which attempted to present a model of Jewish spirituality – can be regarded as Jewish hagiography, such a term can also be applied to representations of tsadikim in Jewish art. This is especially the case since contemporary Yiddish and Hebrew literature served as a primary source of knowledge and inspiration. *Rabbi Eliezer's Last Hour* is another example of this genre. This lost painting from the collection of the Museum of Art in Łódź presents the Ba'al Shem Tov's father – Rabbi Eliezer, who died when Yisra'el (later the Ba'al Shem Tov) was a child.

The painting probably refers to the scene of Eliezer transmitting his spiritual heritage to his son at the same instant the angel of death is ready to kiss his forehead. The bearded man with a prophetic look is sitting in front of a young boy, whose head is raised towards him and hand is opened upward in a gesture of acceptance. This can be also a reference to the popular legend about the last words of Eliezer to his son: "Fear nothing other than God."[25] Despite the clearly Jewish content that finds its literary parallels in different accounts concerning the life and legend of the Ba'al Shem Tov, the painting's composition reveals a Christian source; indeed, there is no doubt that direct inspiration had been drawn from El Greco's representations in *Crucifixion* with its two Maries and Saint John.

In Adler's painting there are similarly two women – the one in a red robe could be the Ba'al Shem Tov's mother, the other his future wife, with the Ba'al Shem the equivalent of Saint John – a figure associated with messianic notions and used by other members of Yung-yidish group such as Henoch Barczyński. Furthermore, the young Ba'al Shem Tov's figure itself resembles that of the saint in El Greco's *Stigmatization of Saint Francis* (1580), thereby linking the Jewish and Christian saints. Adler's painting may have resulted from his perception of a common conviction that the two shared a simple life and direct contact with nature.[26]

---

24 For further reading on the Ba'al Shem Tov see Rosman 1996.
25 This account was published in the 1906 edition of the Jewish Encyclopedia, in the Ba'al Shem Tov's biographical entry: Kaufmann Kohler and Louis Ginsburg. "BA'AL SHEM-ṬOB, ISRAEL B. ELIEZER." Jewish Encyclopedia. The unedited 1906 version online: www.jewishencyclopedia.com/articles/2252-ba-al-shem-tob-israel-b-eliezer (12 November 2015).
26 Saint Francis was a common figure linked to Hasidic ideals in Yung-yidish iconography.

It is unfortunate that we do not know what the third of Adler's painting, *Ba'al Shem Tov and the Buddha*, looked like. In a review of a 1919 winter exhibition in Łódź, Hans Zimmermann described it in enthusiastic and emotional terms: "*Von welcher Geistigkeit sind die beiden Figuren. Hier ist nichts Körper, hier ist alles Geist. Mann muß sich in die Figur des Ba'al Shem einleben, einfühlen um den 'Gefühlsinhalt' dieses Bildes ganz zu erfassen*" [Of what spirituality are the two figures. There's nothing of the body, everything here is spirit. One must settle into the figure of the Ba'al Shem, empathize, in order to capture the "emotional content"] (Zimmermann 1919, 3). Knowledge of this picture certainly would broaden consideration of the motifs from the culture of the Far East in the art of Jewish expressionists. Perhaps it would indicate that in the search for an ideal, charismatic religious attitude, their reading reached beyond the Hasidic tales and that they may also have derived their visions from Buber's *Chinesische Geister und Liebesgeschichten*.[27]

The shared feeling of ecstasy and holiness as well as the charismatic "emotional content" was, according to the expressionists, of overriding value for both the artists and the recipients of their art. The Ba'al Shem Tov, Christ, and Buddha were models of charismatic leaders of religious communities who would help attain the essence of religious spirituality. Therefore, Jewish artists visualized the essence of those personalities and their mystical teachings by creating an image of a universal model of ecstatic prayer. The Jewish artists also identified with their communal aspect in their own strivings to create a new Jewish art. Meidner and Steinhardt, co-founders of "Die Pathetiker" group, strongly identified with the character of the prophet (Bertz 1995; Amishai-Maisels 1995). For artists from Eastern Europe (Poland and Ukraine) a more direct relationship with Hasidic spirituality played a crucial role. Jankel Adler in particular keenly identified with Hasidic culture; he manifested this attachment by wearing a neo-Hasidic garment and speaking Yiddish (Malinowski 2000, 206–207).

However, for the experience of ecstatic prayer, not only was its plastic visualization important, but also the creative act itself. Longing for God can be expressed by illustrating religious scenes, but also by purely artistic means – of color, its intensity and composition. In his poem *Ikh zinge mayn tefile* (I am singing my prayer), painter and poet Jankel Adler raises a prayer to God that is full of yearning. The intensity of religious sentiment, which lifts the artist to higher levels towards the God, is expressed by colors: shades of blue, "from the cobalt to the

---

[27] Joanna Pollakówna (2012, 298) states that Adler met Buber in Germany and that there is no doubt that the philosopher had a strong impact on his iconography. See also: Malinowski (2000, 206).

deepest ultramarine"; shades of red, "purple, through the most powerful vermilion, down to the deepest carmine"; and lemon yellow and emerald green (Adler 1919). Adler could have derived his inspiration from the meaning of colors in Judaism and Christianity. Red, in Catholic theology, is the color of the apostles and martyrs and is associated with the fire of Pentecost; in Judaism it is often associated with women and feminine aspects (women in both of Adler's paintings described above wear red dresses). Blue, the color of the sky, symbolizes God and defines the boundary between the sacred and the profane. The juxtaposition of cold and warm tones expresses the tension between the profane and sacred, which was often an undertone of the Yung-yidishist art. Deep, rich, and dark colors such as dark blue and Bordeaux red had been classified by Aronson and Ryback as colors of "Jewish national painting" (Aronson and Ryback 2012, 139), and were used by Marc Chagall, whom Adler often recalled as a model.

3 Vision of Messianic Redemption and Christological Motifs

One of the main themes related to the question of the Jewish expressionists' religious syncretism and search for a true, mystical religious experience is that of Christology. Popular in Expressionist art, this theme had its own traditions within Jewish iconography. Jewish artists such as Maurycy Gottlieb, Marek Antokolsky, Samuel Hirszenberg, and Max Liebermann had been portraying Christ since the nineteenth century, and the figure had become a symbol of the ambiguous, post-emancipation identity of Jews in the modern world.[28] This was the result of an attempt, started in the eighteenth century, to include Christ in Jewish historiography, exemplified by modern Jewish thinkers such as Moses Mendelssohn, Hermann Cohen, Heinrich Graetz, and Abraham Geiger.[29] Apart from reflecting the ongoing debate on the significance of Christ for Jewish culture and history, the

---

28 The figure of Christ appears both in sculpture (Marek Antokolski's *Ecce Homo* 1873 and *The Last Breath* 1877), and painting (Maurycy Gottlieb's *Jesus Before His Judges* 1877 and *Jesus Preaching* 1878–1879; Samuel Hirszenberg's *Head of Christ* 1904; Wilhelm Wachtel's *Christ in the Pogrom District* 1920).

29 Numerous publications exist on this subject, e.g., Novak 1988, 119–138; Peter Schäfer. *The Jewish Jesus: How Judaism and Christianity Shaped Each Other*. Princeton: Princeton University Press, 2012; Zev Garber. "The Jewish Jesus: Revelation, Reflection, Reclamation." *Shofar Supplements in Jewish Studies*. West Lafayette, IN: Princeton University Press, 2011; Amishai-Maisels 1982, 84–104.

figure of Christ also appeared in the context of increasing anti-Semitism, pointing at Christianity as the source of Jewish suffering.[30]

In expressionist art, the subject of Christology is often intertwined with that of messianism. This issue is complicated by the fact that, as regards philosophy and literature, we are witnessing an increasingly prevalent view that messianic motifs, both in Christian messianism and expressionism itself, have Jewish roots (Anderson 2011, 14; Mittelmann 1993, 251–259; Milful 1983, 347–357; Tramer 1958, 33–36). This was the result of strong messianic tendencies which developed, particularly after the First World War, in both contemporary philosophy and the writings of Benjamin, Bloch, Buber, Georg Lukács, Rosenzweig, and Scholem.[31] Attempts were even made to characterize the expressionist movement as wholly intertwined with the messianic ideal, resulting in the creation of specific terminology to describe the expressionist movement, such as "messianic expressionism" (Sokel 1959) or – a term introduced recently – "expressionist messianism" (Anderson 2011, 11).[32] Messianism, rooted in Jewish thought, had great visual potential that nurtured the imagination of many Jewish avant-garde artists, both in terms of internalizing it in their art as well as shaping their own attitudes and positions as modern artists within Jewish society. By being included in art, the concept of messianism became a modern myth associated with such notions as avant-garde, novelty, modernity, and revolution.

In order to circumscribe clear boundaries of cultural space within the Messianic idea, Jewish thinkers found it relevant to list the differences between Jewish and Christian messianism. This was expressed by Gershom Scholem (Scholem

---

30 An in-depth analysis of this subject can be found in Ziva Amishai-Maisels 1982, 84–104.
31 Among the many works dealing with this issue, the most important include: Martin Kavka, *Jewish Messianism and the History of Philosophy*. Cambridge: Cambridge University Press, 2004; Wayne Cristaudo and Wendy Baker (eds.), *Messianism, Apocalypse and Redemption in 20th Century German Thought*. Adelaide: ATF, 2006; Stéphane Mosès. *The Angel of History: Rosenzweig, Benjamin, Scholem*. Stanford: Stanford University Press, 2008.
32 Anderson, the author of *German Expressionism and Messianism of a Generation*, claims that expressionists "encoded their avowedly secular project in the religious idiom" thus creating the secularised form of messianism (Anderson 2011, 16–17). By introducing the term "expressionist messianism" as opposed to "messianic expressionism" – because she considers that "expressionism as a whole demonstrates one configuration of messianism in the modern era" (Anderson 2011, 11), – she claims that in fact it led to a resacralization instead of secularization (Anderson 2011, 17). Meanwhile, in the case of Jewish expressionists, the emergence in their art of messianic and Christological motifs was both an element of defining their religious identity and an attempt to restore religious values to a generation which, due to acculturation, had lost touch with religion. The messianic new man was to be a new Jew. Therefore in their case, resacralization was the main impulse for their artistic ideas and activity, and a longing for authentic religious experience was one of their imperatives.

1971, 1–2), and his idea was developed in the pages of the Jewish press.[33] The messianic idea present in the art of Jewish avant-garde artists is characterized by lack of explicit impersonation. They do not use the repertoire of traditional Christian art, such as by showing a messiah on a donkey headed to the gates of Jerusalem. Nor do they refer as often as their predecessors – "Die Pathetiker" – to patterns of classical biblical or prophetic narration. Instead, the content of their manifests and art relates to the revolutionary element of the messianic idea. For Jewish expressionists this activist approach found its richest fulfilment in the attempt to show the messianic ritual of transfiguration revealed in turning the profane into the sacred. This is represented by the dichotomy of darkness – perceived as a post-apocalyptic emptiness where demons prowl – and light with its salvational power, and is an important component of the iconographic program of the Yung-yidish group.

The scenery for the messianic ritual of transfiguration – as in the works of Peretz[34] – is the shtetl that has declined into decadence, driven by old customs and habits and impure forces; it is a locus of mystical experience, but also the home of ordinary people and their grievances and tragedies. The shtetl night is suffused with apocalyptic imagery rooted in symbolic thought and folk beliefs. Darkness is associated with impure forces and, as the opposite of light – made on the first day of creation – with destruction. In the sacredness of the shtetl, in the dark, demons prowl and impure instincts are roused. In Icchok Brauner's (1887–1944) linocut *Dancing Devil* (Fig. 4) a naked woman (presumably Lilith) dances above the rooftops and over the head of a Jew dressed in traditional gabardine, with the outline of a town visible in the background. This graphic depiction was probably inspired by Jakob Steinhardt's linocut *Hexenverbrennung* (The Burning of the Witches), dated nine years earlier, which introduced a demonological motif into the repertoire of Jewish expressionists. The figure of naked women in Brauner's print may thus symbolize an unbounded, primordial creative power which enables the artist establish a new world order. It corresponds with Moshe Broder-

---

33 In her article entitled "The Messianic Idea," published in Martin Buber's magazine *Der Jude*, Elfriede Bergel-Groneman sought to examine Judaism's rejection of Christ as the messiah by using the dichotomy of what is abstract, and what is imagined and transferred into form (it must be emphasized that she did not refer to the doctrine of the divinity of Christ, which was often cited as a factor in the Jews' rejection of Christ). She writes that Jews did not recognize Jesus as the messiah, because his ideal was embodied, was given a form, and thus the concept of the messiah was limited. (Bergel-Gronemann, Elfriede. "Der Messiasgedanke." *Der Jude* 5, 1921–1922, 268–271.)
34 Salomon Belis-Legis. "Icchok Lejbusz Perec – Niespokojny duch żydowskiej literatury." *Opowiadania chasydzkie i ludowe*. Translation from Yiddish to Polish by Michał Friedman. Wrocław: Wydawnictwo Dolnośląskie, 1997, 21–23.

son's drama *Schwartz Shabbes* (The Black Sabbath), which introduces the idea that the coming of the Messiah will be preceded by the devil's dominion over the world.³⁵

In another of Brauner's woodcuts, *Tekiah Gedola* (Fig. 5), an ecstatically elongated figure arises. Its body is lit by a lantern on the side, beyond which a lane, with typical expressionist curves and breaks, climbs uphill. Beneath the figure's feet lies an unfolded scroll, and in the very corner of the picture tiny figures resembling Adam and Eve in their flight from paradise have been rendered; the other naked couple embracing is at the right middle. Tekiah Gedola is the third, long note of the shofar sounded at the conclusion of Yom Kippur; it symbolizes the force that infuses a person once he or she is cleansed of sin. The scroll is probably the Book of Life. People's fates are determined on the first day of the Jewish New Year. Weighing their actions, God decides whether their names should be inscribed in the Book of Life, thereby confirming that they have been righteous. In case of doubt, the decision can be postponed – the sinner then has the ten days between Rosh Hashanah and Yom Kippur to repent. This is a time of atonement and it is then that services at the synagogue are accompanied by the sound of the shofar. The shofar also appears in the Book of Revelation, announcing both victory (over oppression and evil) and the coming of the messiah.

The message of Brauner's *Tekiah Gedola* becomes even stronger, and surrounded by a double meaning, in its adding a Christological thread in deciphering the title inscribed in a tissue at the bottom of the woodcut. The title is written in Hebrew, but it seems to have been spelt incorrectly. The letter ע is omitted from the word תקיעה (tekiah), which makes the word sound like תחיה (tehiya), or resurrection³⁶. It is doubtful that this is simply a spelling mistake, and I would read it as a conscious hint of the messianic message in Brauner's work. One can see the direct link between this woodcut and Moshe Broderson's (a Yung-yidish colleague of Brauner's) poetic drama *Tchiyes-hameysim* (Resurrection of the Dead), published in 1920. Modelled on medieval mystery theater, the piece presents a syncretic vision of the rebirth of humanity through art, stimulated by positive figures from religions of the world: these figures include Shiva, Buddha, Moses, Jesus, Mahomet, and the thirty-six "Lamed Vovniks," one of whom, according to legend, is to be the Messiah.³⁷

---

35 For an extensive interpretation of Broderson's works see Rosier (1991, 61–91).
36 I am grateful to Prof. Ziva Amishai – Maisels for bringing my attention to this very important detail on Brauner's woodcut.
37 An in-depth analysis of this piece was written by Gilles Rozier (1999, 73–77).

Fig. 4: Icchok Brauner. *Dancing Devil*. Yung Yidish. 1919. Issue 2–3. 16. Illustration from the Collection of The Emanuel Ringelblum Jewish Historical Institute in Warsaw.

Fig. 5: *Tekiah Gedola*. 1919. Yung Yidish. Issue 4–6. 13. Illustration from the Collection of The Emanuel Ringelblum Jewish Historical Institute in Warsaw.

Two complementary works by Icchok Brauner – The *Dancing Devil* and *Tekiah Gedola* – reveal similar cosmic visions of a world trapped between good and evil; these visions show the transformation from apocalyptic reality into messianic future. They represent the comprehensive program of an avant-garde group of artists who have chosen the apocalyptic shtetl as the backdrop for the revival of Jewish art and culture, heralding the messianic message. Even if artists must join with the forces of evil, they are still the ones to bring back holiness. The activist aspect of their art and their attempt to go beyond traditional representations of the Jewish topos is their distinguishing feature. It should be noted that this would not have been possible without the strong connection between these artists and the Kultur-lige movement, which grasped the idea of a purifying revolution leading to a new Jewish art and culture. The *Tekiah Gedola* can be linked to the illustration, by Yoysef Tshaykov (Iosif Chaikov), for the cover of Peretz Markish's poetry collection *Shveln* (Doorways, 1919). Tshaykov, co-founder of the Kultur-lige, in his manifesto *Sculpture* explicitly manifested the syncretic, and thus special position of the Jewish artist within the world's avant-garde: "By now, a non-demonstration of his role in modern plastic arts, a Jewish artist, traversing the realms of art of the nations of the world, will create his own synthesis, using for this purpose his specific material" (Chaikov 2005, 239).

Thus, even if explicit hints were made to Christian theology in the works of Jewish expressionist artists, especially those involved in the program of creating a new Jewish culture, their works should be read in their own idiosyncratic context. This is confirmed by another picture, Yankl Adler's *Zmartwychwstanie* (The Resurrection), which corresponds to those described earlier. This work, dated 1918, is known only from a black-and-white reproduction published in the same *Yung-yidish* 4–6[38] issue as *Tekiah Gedola*. However difficult it is to judge solely from such a source, one can, at first glance, state that it is not a mere representation of the resurrected Christ. Although the composition, which is regarded as a predecessor of *Błogosławieństwo Ba'al Szem Towa* (Ba'al Shem Tov's Blessing) (1919), reveals clear inspiration from El Greco's *Resurrection*, its mystical message goes beyond religious particularities (Malinowski 2000, 184). The ascending figure in the middle has neither a crown of thorns, nor even a halo. It is presented in a geometrical, cubist background, with three figures below his feet. In fact, it is very close to the *Tekiah Gdola*, announcing the birth of a new person, although for channeling this message it uses a well-established model of Christian iconography.

---

[38] All issues of the Yung-yidish artistic journal have been digitized and are available online at: https://library.stanford.edu/blogs/digital-library-blog/2013/09/yung-yidish-digitized.

This idea could be the effect of contacts with the Poznań expressionist group BUNT, which used representations of the Crucifixion to signal the activist and revolutionary element linked to the martyrdom and resurrection of Christ. As Jerzy Malinowski notes about the Polish group, the Christological motif was just as important, symbolizing the creation of a new person in a post-apocalyptic world (Malinowski 1991, 95–119).

Although it was not explicitly expressed in the art of Polish-Jewish expressionists, one can assume that the strong thread of messianism in Polish culture, as a result of 146 years of partitions during which the Poles had strived to maintain their national identity, must have been considered by the Jewish artists as a feeling related to Jewish life in the diaspora. The year 1918, for the Germans an apocalyptic year of catastrophe, was, for Poles as well as various other ethnic and religious minorities living within the Second Polish Republic's borders, a period that signified a completely new political and social situation. The newly reborn Polish state – at least at the very beginning – seemed to be a good environment for creating new cultural spaces in which a modern Jewish spirit could find expression and independence. This kind of iconography does not occur in the iconography of the Berlin "Die Pathetiker" group. Neither Steinhardt nor Meidner dealt with these types of scenes.

The examination of the messianic aspect of Jewish expressionist art in Poland shows that Jewish artists consciously avoided direct links between the figure of Christ and the messianic message. Some stylistic forms of Christian art served only to express the messianic hopes that were associated with creating a new Jewish culture. In the new political reality after 1918, artists' convictions about the messianic mission was also common among German and Polish expressionists.

There is yet another, quite distinct issue associated with the use of the Christological motif in the art of Jewish expressionist artists, namely, the direct use of motifs such as the crucifixion or the figure of Christ or scenes of the birth of Christ. For Jewish expressionists, Christ was a complex construct, mirroring the open question of the artist's own religiosity. This notion also embodied the tension existing between accepting Jesus as a historical figure and/or the Messiah. The strongest tendency to display Christian themes among Yung-yidish artists can be seen in Marek Szwarc's *Ukrzyżowanie, Zdjęcie z krzyża, Lamentacje* (Crucifixion 1919, Descent from the Cross, The Lamentation of Christ); Szwarc, however, is an exception, as he converted to Catholicism shortly after the ephemeral group disbanded in 1921 (Malinowski 2000, 157). Furthermore, other members of the Yung-yidish group did not eschew such scenes, as evident in Icchok Brauner's *Pokłon trzech Króli* (Adoration of the Magi) or the *Madonna*. In the figure of Christ, the Jewish expressionists captured the internal tensions existing in their generation between the acceptance of Christ as one of the ancient prophets and a revolutionary, and his being perceived as a symbol of Christianity. The adaptation and manner of representing the figure of Christ in Jewish expressionist art had symbolic importance. The figure of Jesus was the basis for a cultural and religious experiment, whose effects materialized in art. This experiment was made possible by the avant-garde artists' particularly open attitude towards the figure of Christ, as was pointedly defined by Bloch:

> [...] was ist zum zweitenmal geschehen, daß jetzt plötzlich der Haß gegen Kruzifixus so spurlos und keineswegs nur opportunistisch oder aus Gleichgültigkeit gegen die religiösen Inhalte verschwinden will? Fast alle Juden des jüngeren Geschlechts gleitet der Name Jesu leicht über die Lippen. Sein vergossenes Blut brennt nicht mehr außen, aber innen; die abergläubische Scheu vor dem nazarenischen Ereignis ihrer Geistesgeschichte verschwindet, Jesus kehrt endlich zu seinem Volk zurück, und seine Name, sogar seine Symbole sind leise und allmählich, ohne Riß und ohne alles Pathos in das Herz und die Gedanken der jungen, ernsten, nachdenklichen Generation eingegangen. Sie fühlen und verstehen, daß nur sie und niemand sonst, wie sie die Geschichte Josefs und die Psalmen miterlebt haben, so auch die frühchristliche Gemeinde und die Evangelien bilden konnten.
> (Bloch 1918, 323)

> [[...] what happened for a second time that suddenly the hatred against crucifix wants to disappear without a trace, and in no way only opportunistically or out of indifference to religious topics? The name of Jesus glides over the lips of almost all the Jews of the younger generation. The blood he shed no longer burns outside but inside – the superstitious timidity of their history of ideas towards the Nazarene event is disappearing. Jesus is finally returning to his people and his name, even his symbols, have quietly and gradually, without any crack and without all the pathos, entered the hearts and thoughts of the younger, serious and pensive generation. They feel and understand that they only and nobody else – similarly to how they experienced the story of Joseph and the Psalms – can shape the early Christian congregation and the Gospels].

The image of the crucified Christ was one of the strongest symbols of the suffering, war-affected "generation 1914" (Wohl 1979), and it also concerned non-Jewish artists. Powerful, emotionally charged, and ideologically steeped scenes relating to the martyrdom of Christ appear in the art of such German expressionists as Emil Nolde, Otto Dix, and Oskar Kokoschka, as well as Polish counterparts such as Jerzy Hulewicz and Arthur Swinarski, members of the BUNT group. For members of the BUNT, the motif of physical suffering is a necessary step to cleanse the spirit and thus liberate it from the material. This concept was introduced by the Polish Romantic poet Juliusz Slowacki in his work *Genezis z ducha* (Genesis from the Spirit, 1844) (Malinowski 1991, 101). In both cases, artists identified with the figure of the suffering Christ because they were convinced that the artist, thanks to his outstanding intuition and spirituality, was able to transform the apocalyptic past into the messianic future.

Jewish artists shared this view, though undoubtedly their art is to some extent a continuation of the iconography begun by artists such as Marek Antokolski, Samuel Hirszenberg, William Wachtel, and Maurycy Gottlieb. This was a result of the existing tendency to include the figure of Christ in Jewish historiography and to situate him at the center of Christian–Jewish relations. An example of such an approach is represented by Jakob Steinhardt's two versions of *Pieta*. In these two graphics, one dated 1913, the other 1914, the Christian model for mourning the tragically crucified Jesus Christ is used to express the suffering of Jews affected by war and pogroms.[39]

The distinctive feature of the crucifixion scenes rendered by Jewish artists is the background, which resembles shtetl buildings. This indicates that, in the expressionist Jewish worldview, the center of the apocalypse is the Jewish town.[40] Thus, what in Christian iconography determines the messianic aspect of the figure of Christ – his death on the cross and subsequent resurrection – in the art of the Jewish expressionists is frozen at the universal moment in which he suffers for the sins of mankind. Therefore, it indicates that the internalization of Christological motifs by the Jewish expressionists was not based on any direct identification with Jesus as a messiah, but rather on the syncretic selection of certain features, which expressed the particular ideas and problems of their generation.

An example of an approach that oscillated between internalization and distance is the image of Christ (Fig. 6) which Steinhardt painted in 1913, the same year he created his famous *Der Prophet* (The Prophet) and other works in which biblical themes are intertwined with social issues. Emerging from deep and sharp blows of the chisel, the face of Christ, who bears a crown of thorns, stares wearily at the viewer. Seemingly suspended in a vacuum, he seems in reality to appear on the lily-blue sky, above the conventionally traced rooftops and the centrally placed cross. This representation is highly Gothic in expression, something Steinhardt's wife, Minni, draws attention to in her memories of her husband's art.[41] At the same time, this is quite an early appearance of Christ in the work of the German expressionists, and indicates Steinhardt's links to the works of Emil Nolde and Oskar Kokoschka, among others.

---

39 This theme had also been developed by Marc Chagall. In Chagall's art the suffering of the Jews before and after the Holocaust was often identified with the crucifixion. See Amishai-Maisels 1982 and 1993.
40 I have analyzed the representation of visions of the apocalyptic shtel in comparison to a common expressionist motif of metropolis in my article: "Apocalyptic City versus Apocalyptic Shtetl. The Experience of Catastrophe in the Work of the Jewish Expressionists." See Stolarska-Fronia 2015.
41 Sammlung Jakob und Mimmi Steinhardt. Erinnerungen und Lebensdokumente. DOK95/522/7–12. Jüdisches Museum Berlin.

Fig. 6: Jakob Steinhardt. *Christus*. ca. 1913. Jüdisches Museum Berlin. Photo: Jens Ziehe.

Steinhardt's Christ differs from Jewish representations of Christ that portray him in a kippah and historical costume (Samuel Hirszenberg, Wilhelm Wachtel, Maurycy Gottlieb). Contrary to these images, Steinhardt's Jesus is surrounded by Christian symbols: his crown of thorns stands out clearly from the background and the cross has an emblematic force. The position of his head *en trois-quarts* is reminiscent of how the head of the dead Christ hangs in paintings of the crucifixion. In Steinhardt's work, however, his eyes are not half-closed, nor does he lift his gaze in the final movement of a dying man. Instead, he stares directly at the viewer, his gaze reminiscent of Steinhardt's representations of *Ostjuden*. Despite the work's attributes relating to martyrdom, it is difficult to discern any strong martyrological echo in this representation, in contrast to a woodcut by Otto Lange created three years later, in which a similarly depicted face of Christ is marked by suffering, potentiated by the red of the blood streaming down his face. Here, suspended in empty space, surrounded by a violet-blue background, Christ's face suggests a connection to another type of representation in Christian iconography: the *vera icona*, "true image," the legendary face of Christ imprinted upon the veil of Saint Veronica. Steinhardt's iconic image is an attempt to confirm the idea of Jesus as a patron of, and only of, Christianity.

4 Conclusion

The fine boundary between saints and tsadikim, on one hand, and Christ and the messiah, on the other, in the art of Jewish expressionists reflects the transcultural character of their art. Yet, it shows some distinctive features of the Jewish expressionists' approach to religious subjects. They strived to resolve the assumed tension between the subject of their art and the form. They identified artistic creativity with religious engagement and perceived themselves to share the same spiritual stance as Hasidim. They did not limit themselves merely to Jewish sources but sought inspiration from the imagery of other religions and cultures. They drew most intensively, however, from Christian theology and iconography, internalizing Christological motifs into their art.

Yet, it was the fixed model of ecstatic prayer, crucifixion, and resurrection in Baroque Christian art that aided the artists from Yung-yidish and Kultur-lige to signal their generation's messianic aspirations, aimed at creating a new Jewish art. Their approach was characterized by cultural activism and a revolutionary attitude. Christian iconography depicting the lives and sufferings of Christ and the saints served as a basis of iconographical and formal experimentation, which resulted in an idiosyncratic imagery with a rich perspective and context for religious issues. Thus, for a short period of highly active creativity between 1914 and the 1920s, Jewish expressionists existed in their own cultural space.

The boundaries of this space should not be defined by either physical or political (read: national) categories. Rather, it was a particular, cultural context in which the Jewish generation of 1914 was a cluster within a larger avant-garde movement. It united artists of different national origins around the idea of creating modern Jewish art that would necessarily possess the traits assigned to revolutionary artistic movements of the time (especially expressionism and futurism), and thus also reveal the activist and innovative aspects of modern Jewish identity and culture. However ephemeral and shifting these boundaries of the Jewish expressionists' cultural space may seem, one must acknowledge, in interpreting their works of art as well as their programmatic statements, that the Jewish context of their art is as important as the fact that their art can also be read in the context of the general development of the avant-garde movements, and that the question of "Jewish roots of expressionism" remains of critical importance.

Bibliography

Adler, Yankl. "Ikh zinge mayn tfile." *Yung Yidish* 2–3 (1919): 7.
Adler, Yankl. "Ekspresjonizm (fragment z prelekcji)." *Nasz Kurier* 292 (December 5 1920). Trans. Wanda Kemp-Welch. *Between Worlds: a Sourcebook of Central European Avant-Gardes 1910–1930*. Ed. Timothy O. Benson and Éva Forgács. Cambridge, MA and London: The MIT Press. 2002. 181.
Amishai-Maisels, Ziva. "The Jewish Jesus." *Journal of Jewish Art* 9 (1982): 85–104.
Amishai-Maisels, Ziva. *Depiction and Interpretation. The Influence of the Holocaust on the Visual Arts*. Oxford: Pergamon, 1993.
Amishai-Maisels, Ziva. "Die drei Gesichter des Jakob Steinhardt." *Jakob Steinhardt. Der Prophet*. Berlin: Jüdisches Museum, 1995. 25–26.
Anderson, Lisa Marie. *German Expressionism and the Messianism of a Generation*. Amsterdam and New York: Rodopi, 2011.
Aronson, Boris, and Issachar Ber Ryback. "Wege der jüdischen Malerei (Gedanken eines Künstlers)." *Zwischen Stadt und Steppe*. Trans. and ed. Marina Dmitrieva. Berlin: Lukas Verlag, 2012. 123–141.
Bahr, Hermann. *Expressionismus*. Berlin: Delphin-Verlag, 1920.
Barron, Stephanie. *German Expressionism, 1915–1925: The Second Generation*. Los Angeles: Los Angeles County Museum of Art, 1988.
Benjamin, Walter. *Gesammelte Schriften*. Frankfurt am Main: Suhrkamp Verlag, 1972–1989.
Bergel-Gronemann, Elfriede. "Der Messiasgedanke." *Der Jude* 5 (1921–1922): 268–271.
Berlewi, Henryk. "Di zigzagn der yidisher kunst." *Almanach*. Paris 1955 (n.p.). Trans. Małgorzata Zaremba. *Polak, Żyd, Artysta. Tożsamość a awangarda*. Ed. Jarosław Suchan, Karolina Szymaniak. Muzeum Sztuki w Łodzi, 2010. 368–377.

Bertz, Inka. "Propheten und Ostjuden. Zur Verarbeitung von Zeiterfahrung im Werk Jakob Steinhardts vor und nach dem Ersten Weltkrieg." *Jakob Steinhardt. Der Prophet*. Berlin: Jüdisches Museum, 1995. 65–91.
Bloch, Ernst. *Geist der Utopie*. München and Leipzig: Duncker & Humblot, 1918.
Borsò, Vittoria, Claas Morgenroth, Karl Solibakke, and Bernd Witte (eds.). *Benjamin – Agamben: Politics, Messianism, Kabbalah*. Würzburg: Verlag Königshausen & Neumann, 2010.
Braiterman, Zachary. *The Shape of Revelation. Aesthetics and Modern Jewish Thought*. Stanford: Stanford University Press, 2007.
Buber, Martin. "Jüdische Kunst." *Ost und West* 3 (1902): 205–210.
Buber, Martin. *Die Geschichten des Rabbi Nachman*. Frankfurt am Main: Rütten & Loening, 1906.
Buber, Martin. *Die Legende des Baal Schem*. Frankfurt am Main: Rütten & Loening, 1908.
Buber, Martin. *Ekstatische Konfessionen*. Jena: Eugen Diederichs Verlag, 1909.
Buber, Martin. *Die jüdische Bewegung. Gesammelte Aufsätze und Ansprachen 1916–1920*. Berlin: Jüdischer Verlag, 1920.
Buber, Martin. *Der grosse Maggid und seine Nachfolge*. Frankfurt am Main: Rütten & Loening, 1922.
Buber, Martin. *Schriften zum Chassidismus*. München: Kösel, 1963.
Buber, Martin. *Tales of the Hasidim*. Foreword by Chaim Potok. New York: Schocken Books, 1991.
Buber, Martin. *Ja i Ty. Wybór pism filozoficznych*. Trans. Jan Doktór. Warsaw: Instytut Wydawniczy PAX, 1992.
Buber, Martin. *Gog i Magog. Kronika chasydzka*. Trans. Jan Garewicz. Warsaw: Wydawnictwo Naukowe PWN, 1999.
Chaikov, Iosif. "Rzeźba." Trans. Monika Polit. *Warszawska Awangarda Jidysz. Antologia Tekstów*. Ed. Karolina Szymania. Gdańsk: Słowo Obraz Terytoria, 2005. 233–241.
Chwistek, Leon. "Zagadnienie środowiska artystycznego." *Sztuka i życie współczesne* 1 (1934). Reprinted in: *Polak, Żyd, artysta. Tożsamość i awangarda*. Ed. Jarosław Suchan and Karolina Szymaniak. Łódź: Muzeum Sztuki w Łodzi, 2010. 388–391.
Cohen, Richard. "The Rabbi as Icon." *Jewish Icons. Art and Society in Modern Europe*. Berkeley: University of California Press, 1998. 115–153.
Cristaudo, Wayne, and Wendy Baker (eds.). *Messianism, Apocalypse and Redemption in Twentieth Century German Thought*. Adelaide: ATF, 2006.
Fuchs, Henoch. "Expressionistisches Judentum." *Jüdisch-liberale Zeitung* 4 (1924:1).
Garber, Zev. "The Jewish Jesus: Revelation, Reflection, Reclamation." *Shofar Supplements in Jewish Studies*. West Lafayette, IN: Purdue University Press, 2011.
Goll, Iwan. "Vom Geistigen." *Die Aktion* (29.12.1917): 51–52.
Hartlaub, Gustav. *Religion und Kunst*. Leipzig: Kurt Wolff Verlag, 1919.
Herszferder, Yehoshua. "Prolegomena do sztuki żydowskiej (Artykuł dyskusyjny)." *Tygodnik Nowy* I.19 (31.10.1919): 11–12.
Jacob, Heinrich Eduard. "Notitzen zur Apokalyptischen Kunstform." *Der Feuerreiter. Blätter für Dichtung, Kritik, Graphik* 2 (1923): 28.
Kavka, Martin. *Jewish Messianism and the History of Philosophy*. Cambridge: Cambridge University Press, 2004.
Kellermann, Benzion. "Paulinismus und Judentum." *Allgemeine Zeitung des Judentums* 24 (1903a): 283–285.

Kellermann, Benzion. "Paulinismus und Judentum." *Allgemeine Zeitung des Judentums* 25 (1903b): 296–299.
Kohler, Kaufmann, and Louis Ginsburg. "BA'AL SHEM-ṬOB, ISRAEL B. ELIEZER." *Jewish Encyclopedia*. The unedited 1906 version is online: www.jewishencyclopedia.com/articles/2252-ba-al-shem-tob-israel-b-eliezer (12 November 2015).
Laor, Dan. "Agnon in Germany. 1912–1924: A Chapter of a Biography." *AJS Review* XVIII. 1 (1993): 75–93.
Malinowski, Jerzy. *Sztuka i nowa wspólnota. Zrzeszenie artystów BUNT 1917–1922*. Wrocław: Wiedza o Kulturze, 1991.
Malinowski, Jerzy. *Malarstwo i rzeźba Żydów Polskich w XIX i XX wieku*. Warsaw: Wydawnictwo Naukowe PWN, 2000. 39–63, 145–226.
Margolis, Joseph. *Czym, w gruncie rzeczy, jest dzieło sztuki?* Kraków: Universitas, 2004. 57.
Meidner, Ludwig. *Im Nacken das Sternenmeer*. Berlin: Kurt Wolff Verlag, 1918.
Milful, John. "Marginalität und Messianismus: Die Situation der deutsch-jüdischen Intellektuellen als Paradigma für die Kulturkrise 1910–1920." *Expressionismus und Kulturkrise*. Ed. Bernd Hüppauf. Heidelberg: Carl Winter, 1983. 347–357.
Miller, Clyde Lee. "Cusanus Nicholaus [Nicholaus of Cusa]. *Stanford Encyclopedia of Philosophy*, 2013: http://plato.stanford.edu/entries/cusanus/ (10 November 2015).
Mittelmann, Hanni. "Expressionismus und Judentum." *Conditio Judaica: Judentum, Antisemitismus und deutschsprachige Literatur vom Ersten Weltkrieg bis 1933/38*. Munich: C.H. Beck, 1997. 251–259.
Mosès, Stéphane. *The Angel of History: Rosenzweig, Benjamin, Scholem*. Trans. Barbara Harshav. Stanford: Stanford University Press, 2008.
Novak, David. "The Quest for the Jewish Jesus." *Modern Judaism* 8.2 (May, 1988): 119–138.
"Od redakcji (Forma, ogół, Żydzi)." *Zdrój* August 1920. Published in: Ratajczak, Józef. *Krzyk i ekstaza. Antologia polskiego ekspresjonizmu*. Poznań: Wydawnictwo Poznańskie, 1987. 222–224.
Pollakówna, Joanna. „Świat ocalony (O malarstwie Janiela Adlera)." *Zapatrzenie. Myśląc o obrazach, myśląc o malarzach*. Gdańsk: Słowo/obraz terytoria, 2012: 289–306.
Rappeport, Ernst Elijahu. "Saulus." *Der Jude* 4 (1917–1918): 276–279.
Rosenzweig, Franz. *Gwiazda zbawienia*. Trans. Tadeusz Gadacz. Kraków: Wydawnictwo Znak, 1998.
Rosman, Moshe. *Founder of Hasidism: A Quest for the Historical Ba'al Shem Tov*. Berkeley, London: University of California Press, 1996.
Rosman, Moshe. "Ba'al Shem Tov." *The YIVO Encyclopedia of Jews in Eastern Europe*. New York: YIVO, 2010. www.yivoencyclopedia.org/article.aspx/Baal_Shem_Tov (11 November 2015).
Rozier, Gilles. *Mojżesz Broderson. Od Jung Idysz do Araratu*. Trans. Joanna Ritt. Łódź: Hamal Andrzej Machejek, 1999.
Schäfer, Peter. *The Jewish Jesus: How Judaism and Christianity Shaped Each Other*. Princeton: Princeton University Press, 2012.
Scholem, Gershom. "Toward an Understanding of the Messianic Idea in Judaism." *The Messianic Idea in Judaism and Other Essays*. New York: Schocken Books, 1971: 3–43.
Scholem, Gershom. *Mistycyzm żydowski i jego główne nurty*. Trans. Ireneusz Kania. Warsaw: Czytelnik, 1997.
Scott, Sarah. "Martin Buber (1878–1965)." *Internet Encyclopedia of Philosophy*. www.iep.utm.edu/buber/ (10 November 2015).
Słowacki, Juliusz. *Genezis z ducha*. Lwów: s.n., 1871.

Sokel, Walter H. *The Writer in Extremis. Expressionism in Twentieth-Century German Literature.* Stanford: Stanford University Press, 1959.

Stahl, Neta. "Uri Zvi Before the Cross: The Figure of Jesus in the Poetry of Uri Zvi Greenberg." *Religion and Literature* 40.3 (Autumn 2008): 49–80.

Stolarska-Fronia, Małgorzata. "Apocalyptic City versus Apocalyptic Shtetl. The Experience of Catastrophe in the Work of the Jewish Expressionists." *Centropa, a Journal of Central European Architecture and Related Arts* XV. 3(2015): 242–254.

Strauß, Eduard. "Paulus, der Bekehrer." *Der Jude* 1 (1923): 32–44.

Swinarski, Artur M. "Z wystaw plastyki (Wystawa Nowoczesnych Artystów w Poznaniu)." *Zdrój* XII.2 (July 1920): 55.

Tramer, Hans. "Der Expressionismus: Bemerkungen zum Anteil der Juden an einer Kunstepoche." *Bulletin des Leo Baeck Instituts* 2.5 (1958): 33–46.

Wehr, Gerhard. *Martin Buber. Biografia.* Warszawa: Wydawnictwo KR, 2007.

Weintraub, Zaw Władysław. "Moje poglądy na sztukę." *Albatros* (September 1922): 18–19. Trans. Zbigniew Targielski, Monika Polit, and Karolina Szymaniak. *Warszawska Awangarda Jidysz. Antologia Tekstów.* Ed. Karolina Szymaniak. Gdańsk: Słowo Obraz Terytoria, 2005. 227.

Wohl, Robert. *The Generation of 1914.* Cambridge, MA: Harvard University Press, 1979.

Zimmermann, H. "Die zweite Kunstaustellung des Lodzer Künstlerheims. Die Jungen." *Neue Lodzer Zeitung* 5 (15.1.1919): 3.

Tom Paulus
Between Ecstasy and Lament: Revelationism and Messianism in Epstein and Godard

The "first wave" European film theory of the 1920s includes a tendency that analytical philosopher Malcolm Turvey has labelled "revelationism" (Turvey 2008). The revelationist tradition, under whose rubric Turvey groups Frenchman Jean Epstein, Russian Dziga Vertov, Hungarian Béla Balázs and German Siegfried Kracauer, is at root an attempt to answer film theory's most basic query: what is cinema? At the time of the first filmic avant-gardes this was primarily a question about the medium's specific aesthetic qualities: what makes cinema different from the other arts, especially those, like literature, theatre, painting and music, from which it derives many of its constitutive elements? In France, resistance to the idea of a theatrically inspired cinema (captured by the derogatory label "Caligarisme," after the famous expressionist classic's fronting of elements of theatrical mise en scène) led early film critics, such as the Italian poet-critic Ricciotto Canudo, to posit cinema as more of a *Gesamtkunstwerk*, a seventh art that absolves the difference between the temporal/rhythmic basis of music or dance and the plastic/spatial basis of painting and architecture. For Jean Epstein, one of the "first wave's" most unique voices, time *was* a spatial given; his artistic practice of favoring superimposed images, rapid montage and non-linear temporality proposed to make audiences see how this was not an impossibility. Epstein atttributed to cinema a revelatory power, in that it can show an abstraction – namely, time, the fourth dimension – which cannot be perceived by the naked eye but is revealed by the "machine brain" of the film camera.[1] Like many in his intellectual milieu, Epstein's interest in the speed and ephemerality of modern experience led him to Henri Bergson's metaphysics of time, specifically the idea that reality is not monolithic but an indivisible, continuous whole, a complex process of becoming in which everything connects to everything else. Cinema reinstates the complexity of time in flux that is reduced, abstracted, "tamed" in everyday experience, and it is in this aspect rather than its trans-artistic inspiration that its medium-specificity resides (Turvey 2008, 24–25). It is only in brief moments that the spectator's bodily and affective engagement with the film aligns with the medium's full

---
[1] Turvey rejects this logic of what he labels "visual scepticism" by calling it a "category mistake," in that it starts from a logical impossibility to propose the physiological shortcomings of human vision.

potential, producing episodes of what Epstein termed "*photogénie*," which "is to film what color is to painting, volume to sculpture" (quoted in Charney 1995, 285).

Film historian Tom Gunning has characterized the epistemological aspects of Epstein's film theory as "gnostic" (Gunning 2012, 17).[2] My project here is to take a closer look at the "mystical truth" aspects of Epstein's revelationism, starting from the observation that Turvey's central figures – Epstein, Vertov, Balázs and Kracauer – were all Jewish and some, like Epstein and Kracauer, had an active interest in Jewish mysticism. Indeed, Gunning, in his preface to a recent collection of essays on Epstein, avers that new light can be shed on Epstein's thinking and film practice by acknowledging his identity as both gay and Jewish (Gunning 2012, 14). In the same volume, Christophe Wall-Romana takes up Gunning's call, linking Epstein's queerness to his repeated emphasis on the physical aspects of the aesthetic experience of "*photogénie*." Epstein's Jewishness, however, is not explicitly addressed, although Wall-Romana does find many overlapping elements between Epstein's animistic conception of a spatio-temporally reconfigured ciné-reality and Walter Benjamin's definition of "aura" in his famous *Artwork* essay (Wall-Romana 2012, 51–73).[3] Epstein, a filmmaker, critic and novelist, was born in Poland to a Polish-Jewish mother and French father; he later took a keen interest in traditions of Jewish mysticism. I argue that the visionary side to his writing derives as much from his reading of Kabbalah as from the influence of the Symbolist poetics of Mallarmé, Apollinaire and his mentor Blaise Cendrars.

In the February 1922 edition of *L'Esprit Nouveau*, the influential international review for contemporary arts, letters, science and sociology founded by Le Corbusier, Epstein published a text called "Nous kabbalistes." This piece became part of a book, *La Lyrosophie*, published the same year, which introduces Epstein's epistemological or "gnostic" project as an attempt to conflate science and sentiment into an affective logic. The book's core premise essentially rests on a pun: science depends on proof and proof is built on evidence, but evidence is itself indemonstrable because any such proof would only increase its character as being *evident*. Hence, Epstein reasons, evidence is ineffable, a feeling more than a category of the rational. This ludic attempt to break through the isolation of science from feeling has been read as Epstein's response to the intellectual fatigue he saw as arising from the dominance of rationality and instrumentalization in

---

2 In an earlier text, Gunning identifies the film camera's potential for uncovering new visual knowledge with cinema's "gnostic mission": "In Your Face: Physiognomy, Photography, and the Gnostic Mission of Early Film," in *Modernism/Modernity* 4.1 (1997): 1–29.

3 Wall-Romana establishes actual proximity between Benjamin and Epstein via the intermediary of Parisian surrealist (and translator of Proust) Léon Pierre-Quint, one of Benjamin's closest friends in the city of lights.

modernity. Kabbalah in this light becomes an alternative model for a Nietzschean poeticization of knowledge. Epstein's discussion of Kabbalah shows his Bergsonianism, in that it ignores all traditional historiography and instead commences from the emotional stimulus that mystic writing inspires in the individual reader. What the Kabbalist knows, he knows not rationally or intellectually, but directly, individually, fully: "The Kabbalist never considers the world as exterior, located outside of himself, but considers it always after he has absorbed it within himself. Everything to him is introspection. He does not differentiate between two categories of phenomena: objective and subjective. All are located for him on a unified plane of consideration, a subjective plane – that is to say, that of feeling" (Epstein 2012a, 284). A logic of feeling, a system of subjectivity, then, rationalizes apparently illogical, intuitive associations and connections. The cinema is presented as an instance of such a "lyrosophic" system, a scientific recording and revealing device that produces a logical impossibility, an extreme case of "*Je sais bien mais quand-même*": on screen there is evidence of what cannot be on the screen. Although the viewer knows that this reality does not exist, it becomes alive for him, animistically, "with all the particularitires of real life." More specifically, cinema adheres to the Kabbalist's logic of feeling:

> The cinema names things visually: as spectator I do not doubt for a second that they exist, and I link this whole drama and so much love to a few signs made of light and shadow. Never, even in the Kabbalah, was designation so thoroughly the same as creation. And, after this creation, I conserve the feeling of a second singular reality, sui generis and cinematographic. (Epstein 2012a, 285 n.)

Silent cinema's medium-specific ability to "name things visually" refers us back to the Kabbalah's origin as God's original revelation to Adam, to an Edenic state before the Fall of language and the arbitrary split between signifier and signified. In its wordless language, cinema returns us to a "savage" reality, in which things, humans and animals speak the same unmediated "mute" language of that which is evident. Cinema's project of returning to a state "before the law of words," as Epstein expresses it as late as 1950 (quoted in Witt 2013, 156), finds its roots in the cinema-related writings of visionary poet Vachel Lindsay (who shares with Epstein an interest in Egyptian hieroglyphics), specifically the poet's millennarianist conception of a universal language of the moving image. The project determined the anti-narrative bias of the *cinéma pur* movement of the twenties that most radically performed medium-specificity, and it appears throughout the revelationist discourse: in Vertov's striving towards "*absolute kinography*," an international, absolute language of cinema completely separate from that of theater and literature, and in Balázs's belief that cinema's "language without words" can undo the reign of "word culture" and teach us to become reacquainted with the nonrational emotions expressed by the face and the body (Turvey 2008, 38). The alinguistic character of cinema as a "language of physiology" heightens the animism inherent in all languages, in the sense that language brings to life objects it defines. Epstein's definition, in his text on Kabbalah, of the mystical principle as "the soul penetrating things," greatly coincides with this standard definition of animism. The most evocative statement of cinema's animism appears in Epstein's report on his expedition to Mount Etna in 1923. This text, about the filmmaker's encounter with the natural sublime, was developed into the book *Le Cinématographe vu de L'Etna* (1926). In the text, full of anthropomorphic comparison, Epstein makes the by now familiar redemptive move to read the cinema back into nature and celebrate its power to personalize. Faced with the volcano's erruption, he thinks of the cinématographe and of its first critic, Ricciotto Canudo:

> As we climbed on our mules' backs parallel to the lava flow toward the active cratrer, I thought of you, Canudo, who threw so much of your soul into things. You were the first, I think, to have sensed how cinema unites all the kingdoms of nature into a single order, posssessing the most majestic vitality. It inscribes a bit of the divine in everything. In front of me, at Nancy, a room with three hundred people moaned when they saw a grain of wheat germinate on screen. Suddenly, the true visage of life and death, of a terrifying love, appeared, provoking these religious outcries. What churches, if we only knew how to construct them, could accomodate a spectacle like this, where life itself is revealed. To discover unexpectedly, as if for the first time, everything from a divine perspective, with its symbolic profile and vaster sense of analogy, suffused with an aura of personal identity – that is the great joy of cinema. One of the greatest powers of cinema is its animism. On screen, nature is never inanimate. Objects take on airs. Trees gesticulate. Mountains, just like Etna, convey meanings. An astonishing pantheism is reborn in the world and fills it until it bursts.
> (Epstein 2012b, 288–289)

Epstein's ecstatic liturgical prose is not so ununusual for an age in which the promise of the machine and the dream of a new world were tied to the idea that, as Jacques Rancière writes, "all material and historical burdens would find themselves dissolved in a reign of luminous energy" (Rancière 2006). The question that interests me, however, is how such utopian enthusiasm – in Epstein's case, with clear echoes of Jewish messianism – can be thought back into the postmodern and what Fredric Jameson has termed its "inverse millenarianism" (Jameson 1991, 1), its discourse of endpoints, which in cinema studies is most regularly attached to the cinema of Jean-Luc Godard. I offer as a point of departure for such a query Epstein's mention, in his Kabbalah essay, of nineteenth-century Kabbalah scholar Ferdinand Christian Baur's perceiving a causal link between the resurgence of the mystical and the process of mourning after a period of turmoil. It is this connection which is of course crucial to the thinker whom Epstein most resembles, namely, Walter Benjamin. Mourning is not only the topic of Benjamin's *Habilitationsschrift*, his infamous study of the German Baroque *Trauerspiel* in which he established his theory of allegory; it is also the condition of modern man emblematically captured in Paul Klee's *Angelus Novus*, in which the philosopher perceives the angel of history as being mesmerized by the past, by an endless accumulation of wreckage from which the historicism of "progress" tries to distract. Like the revelationists and the Symbolists that inspired them, Benjamin believed that art could arrest historicism and provide a means of redemption, a mode of repair to restore the wreckage of the fall. Like Epstein, Benjamin believed that redemption, as the product of human agency, depended on both a radical deconstruction of the teleological conception of time and a restoration of the alienated relationship between words and things. It is not my purpose here to add to the already rich discussion of the messianic elements in Benjamin's philosophy, or even to explicitly connect his messianism to Epstein's utopianism. Rather, I focus on how the messianic inspiration behind Epstein's revelationism accords with Benjamin's ideas on mourning and redemption, specifically in Godard's *Hélas pour moi* (1993), the aptly titled film I discuss in more detail.

It might seem somewhat misguided to consider Godard's cinema in light of the continuing tradition of Jewish mysticism in modernist and postmodernist aesthetics, given the recent accusations of anti-Semitism levelled at the filmmaker (see Darmon 2011). These attacks, however, have been shown to be based either on unsubstantiated anecdote or on conflation of anti-Semitism with the anti-Zionist elements in Godard's vocal support for the Palestinian cause. There is also the anti-American stance of his late work, in which the death of cinema is attributed to Jewish-American mercantilization. But this should not distract us from how Jewish intellectual and theological traditions influence Godard. Indeed, his late work seems to me to start both from Gerschom Scholem's comment that there remain only two grand political options (namely, anarchy and theocracy), and from Benjamin's famous image of the dwarf in the automaton: if sixties-seventies Godard seemed to waver between Maoism, Marxism and anarchism, late Godard seems to have taken a surprising turn in the direction of theological inquiry, or "une question perdue," according to the most editorializing section in *Hélas pour moi*.

As Godard scholar David Sterritt has noted, it is in Godard's *Je vous salue Marie* (1983), his famous – and famously controversial – reworking of the Christian master narrative, that the filmmaker's interest in the spiritual and ineffable first comes to the fore and that an inquiry into aesthetics begins to overlap with one into ethics and theology (Sterritt 1999, 163). But it is only in the centerpiece of the late period, the multipart film essay *Histoire(s) du cinéma* (1988–98), that the messianic takes precedence. It is in this work also that Godard's interest in Benjamin first manifests itself, especially in the allegorical-materialist inspiration of a work consisting almost entirely of quotations that in its structural organisation closely resembles Benjamin's *Passagenwerk* (1927–40). In his masterful volume on the *Histoire(s)*, *Jean-Luc Godard: Cinema Historian*, Michael Witt elucidates that Benjamin is everywhere in Godard's work from the mid-eighties onwards, although his influence is never explicitly acknowledged (Witt 2013, 79). Benjamin's "Theses on the Philosophy of History" (1937) are cited in *Les Enfants jouent à la Russie* (1993) and in *The Old Place* (1998), a video work Godard made for MOMA. Godard's materialist montage praxis, in which the past constantly reinscribes the present, clearly derives as much from Benjamin as from the Russian Constructivists Eisenstein and Vertov. As we have seen, there are many connections between Benjamin and Epstein, who is the central figure in Godard's rediscovery of "first wave" French film theory (and rates an homage in the *Histoire(s)*). As in Benjamin, Epstein's project was to "explode the prison of real space-time" and open the continuum to another intuited world. This world, which Benjamin termed messianic *"Jetztzeit"* and Epstein dubbed *"photogénie,"* is "time filled with the actual presence of the now," in Benjamin's parlance (Benjamin 1968, 261), and "the miracle of real presence," in Epstein's (Keller 2012, 29). For Godard the crucial point of the "Theses" is the suggestion that historical materialism – the ideology of sixties-seventies Godard – misreads history and that what must be saved is not the revolutionary future but the past.

The object of redemption in Godard's film is introduced through his invocation of Martin Buber and Gershom Scholem, the figures that constitute the Jewish core in Benjamin's work. The film starts with a dorsal view of a lone figure approaching a small village. A voice-over then starts to narrate a well-known parable from Buber's *Tales of the Hasidim* (1949), a collection of stories from Hasidic oral literature that render the stories accessible to readers and scholars outside the Jewish community:

> When my father's father's father had a difficult task to accomplish [the man starts to move], he went to a certain place in the forest [pause], lit a fire [cut to a title naming the lead actors] and immersed himself in silent prayer. [Cut to a painterly but sombre shot of a lake and foliage.] And what he had to do was done. When my father's father was confronted with the same task, [cut to title "D'après une légende"] he went to the same place in the forest and said: [cut to another sombre nature shot of an empty road flanked by trees] "We no longer know how to light the fire, but we still know the prayer." [Sound of thunder on the soundtrack.] And what he had to do was done. [Cut to a title naming suppporting players] Later, [pause, cut to tableau shot in which a voice announces the theme of the story, "Rachel] he too went into the forest and said: "We no longer know how to light the fire, [cut to the reverse angle of the opening shot, with the man seemingly walking away from the village] we no longer know the mysteries of the prayer, but we still know the exact place in the forest where it occurred. And that should do." And that did do.

After a short scene that establishes the man (framed from the back, like "God" later in the story) as a book publisher who wants to buy a story from a man named Simon and a woman named Rachel, there is another shot of an empty road, and the narration resumes: "But when I was faced with the same task, I stayed at home and said: [cut to a title "Livre Premier"] 'We no longer know how to light the fire, [cut to the forest] we no longer know the prayers, we don't even know the place in the forest. But we do know how to tell the story.'" After this prologue the story proper begins. Or, that is to say, the gest starts, stops, then starts again, constantly looping back to "revealing" situations or events. When we're well into the story the publisher, who acts like a detective, starts to function as narrator, introducing himself through voice-over: "I bear the name Abraham Klimt. My parents named me Abraham Klimt." Before tackling the question of Klimt's name, let's first address his function as a buyer of stories. The tale that he wishes to buy is an "oldie but goodie" (so old it seems more legend than story): the story of Alcmene and Amphitryon, in which Jupiter adopts the guise of Amphytrion in order to possess his wife, Alcmene, a story adapted by playwrights from Plautus to Molière and – Godard's inspiration here – Jean Giroudoux. In Godard's detective version the story unfolds as follows: Klimt arrives in a small seaside town to ascertain what happened to a local couple, Simon and Rachel Donnadieu, on July 23, 1989, thereby hoping to fill the blank pages in a manuscript. He interviews witnesses who were friends of Rachel – the local curé, Monod, and his wife, the literature teacher; and their maid, Clémence – looking for "evidence" and finds that "something" happened when Simon left his wife alone one night when he travelled to Italy to buy a hotel. But about the heart of the matter – what exactly "happened" that night when Simon was away and, so it seems, someone who looked exactly like him took his place in an encounter with Rachel – he learns very little. The only local who can tell him something because she "saw something" is a young poet and "seer," Aude Amiel (related to "the author of the famous journal," Henri-Frédéric Amiel, the recluse of nineteenth-century Swiss letters). But even from Aude Klimt gets nothing substantial. By the end of Klimt's inquiry, Simon reveals that it was he, and no one else – not Rachel's lover, not "God," as is rumored and as Rachel claims – who spent that night with Rachel. We see Rachel confess to Monod, but we never hear her side of the story.

If this sounds fairly linear, although open-ended in the manner of most modernist stories, the synopsis entirely misrepresents Godard's kaleidoscopic, extremely fragmentary look at the story's central "event," a look that seems to follow Epstein's thesis that we can discover the truth only by looking through its many-sided refractions. For Epstein (via Bergson) there are no linear, chronological stories, only situations, "having neither head nor tail," open in every direction. This plurality in Godard, as in Epstein, leads to a constant shifting along the temporal axis: we begin in the fictional present, with the framing story of Klimt's investigation, then shift to the bookshop of drawing instructor and bookseller Jacques Vaché, where a plot plays out concerning a love triangle involving a woman named Angelica that only obscurely relates to the main story; from there we move to the Monod house, where Rachel arrives with Aude and her college friend Ludo, who want to learn more from their literature teacher about the "romanesque." As we later see, the Vaché and Monod episodes occur two or three days after the "event." When Klimt comes to town, much more time has passed, since in the meantime the bookseller has died and Aude's friend has been killed in the Bosnian war. "Why not start over?" Monod councils a distressed Rachel at her confession, after which the story shifts to the main temporal setting, that of the "event,"with a raincoat-clad "God" arriving at the railroad station, accompanied by his assistant, the glib Max Mercure, who likes to quote the Romantic poet and philosopher Giacomo Leopardi.

The central idea at this point seems to be a fairly conventional one, familiar from both the postmodernist detective story à la Borges or the modernist investigation plot à la *L'année dernière à Marienbad* or *Citizen Kane* (Godard has said he was thinking of a Joseph L. Mankiewicz film): as the facts pile up in a myriad of perspectives – rendered in the film by jump cuts, focus shifts and repeated or subtly altered framings – the "Truth" is lost. But Godard is also thinking like the Benjaminian historiographer, constantly questioning the truth of the present through its confrontation with the evidence of the past. Like Benjamin, Godard reasons that "nothing that has ever happened in the past is to be given as lost to history." (A quote from Benjamin's "Theses" recurs throughout the film: "There is a secret protocol between the generations of the past and that of our own. For we have been expected upon this earth.") What we are shown of the past are both the big "events" (Rachel's night with "God," her confession to Monod) and the detritus (a discussion about communism on the terrace of a café where the "[vin] rouge est fini," a discussion about art in Vaché's bookshop). And where do we place Ludo(vic), who went to Dubrovnic? Godard adds further layers through referentiality and punning: it is difficult to tell whether the names of the characters (Abraham Klimt, Max Mercure, Simon and Rachel Donnadieu – Donnadieu is the real name of Marguerite Duras, who is referenced in the film, while Monod is the maiden name of Godard's mother), the *"imperméable"* that God is wearing or the copy of the *"Nouvel Observateur"* that he carries like a means of identification, the puns on *"rouge"* and *"rougir"* (denoting both shame, lust, communism and the poppies at the side of the road) are meant to evoke allegory or farce. That Sim(e)on, Rachel and Abraham are Old Testament Hebraic names resonates in another of the film's quotes from Benjamin: "The name children are given by their parents and which corresponds to no objective knowledge is the only trace which still exists of divine language in the simple language of man."

The quote is from Benjamin's first philosophical essay, "On Language as Such and on the Language of Man" (1916). Here Benjamin opposes a referential, propositional, purely instrumental language to a fully expressible language capable of expressing both a "mental essence" and a community between man and thing (Ferber 2013). It is only in naming, which has no rational connection to the pragmatic operations of language, to objective knowledge, that a residue of divine language shines through. Benjamin's friend Gerschom Scholem similarly detected a remnant of divine language in lament, a distinct form of language that is opposite to a language conceived solely as a carrier of information, in that lament has no content other than its own expression. In the epilogue to his German translation of the Hebrew Book of Lamentations, "Über Klage und Klagelied" (1917), Scholem follows Benjamin in perceiving a fundamental tension in language between what is expressible and what is ineffable, characterizing lament as a border language between these two extremes, between revelation and silence. Indeed, for Scholem, revelation and silence are two identical points from which language originates. Lament, on the other hand, is a moment not of linguistic origin but of linguistic death (Ferber 2013). *Hélas pour moi* is a song of lament in all these senses, for it not only resumes the biblical (Book of Job), Greek epical, Shakespearian ("Woe is me!") and Romantic (Shelley, Byron) incarnations of the genre, but also preserves the lament's metaphysical dimension as (linguistic) endpoint. The only difference is that the film's subject and language is the language of cinema, of images, instead of verbal or written language. What Godard laments is the profanation and instrumentalisation of the image, its increasing alienation from its "divine" origin, i.e., the promise of early cinema or early avant-garde cinema as voiced by Epstein and the revelationists. He laments the profanation of the medium, its gross commercialization, given form in the horror and porn videos rented out by the videostore owner, Benjamin. "You sell images; you at least should know that some things are impossible to see," Klimt tells Benjamin. The cinema also was incapacitated after being confronted with its own limits, with things that escape representation, such as God, the Holocaust or the war in Yugoslavia. If cinema still seeks to unveil the naked truth, that truth has become vulgar. Klimt expresses a strange loathing of putting things crudely: "Because of the imperfection of the cinematographic medium there's always something dirty, degrading even, in exposing the naked truth," he says in voice-over. Godard then cuts to the Monods' groundkeeper reading a porn magazine. The evidence of the film (a favourite Godard metaphor) is tainted because it has become too evident. The lens is smeared, which renders the image "vague" (another favourite pun). It is in this context of the emptying of the image that we are to understand Buber's rabbinic tale, which charts an increase in distance from immanence, from "lighting the fire," which in Godard is a motif associated with artistic creation, culminating in the mediated experience of storytelling. (Godard consciously deletes the optimistic endnote of Buber's retelling: "For God made man because he loves stories.") Giraudoux's story, as myth, no longer makes sense in this day and age, which is why Klimt necessarily distances himself from the ideas of honor and shame in the story of Alcmene and Amphitryon, which are "very different from how we experience them today." To Aude's observation that the truth Klimt seeks is no longer transmissible, he replies, "Je ne vois pas." This is a statement of both moral and epistemological blindness that is nonetheless exactly the point. The "truth" that concerns Klimt, which concerns the presence of God, as Aude tells him, has "all kinds of properties or aspects, but being transmissible isn't one of them." "You'll publish a nice book," Klimt is told. "The pages are missing just where they should be," i.e., where God enters the picture. This visual scepticism is exemplified in the film's aesthetic schema: what we see or hear is mostly obfuscated, by layered sound and overlapping dialogue, compositions with blocking foregrounds, extreme long shots, low-key cinematography, framings from the back or framings that exclude the heads of characters (rendering them unrecognizable), etc.

If cinema has lost the visionary qualities it was presumed to possess in Epstein's day, should we then take Godard's lament as just another pronunciation of the death of the medium? *Hélas pour moi* certainly is a melancholy piece, in which sorrowful figures like Leopardi and Amiel figure prominently. The lament for the demise of myth and mythical or messianic time overlaps with that for the decline of classical culture (one could read the title as another pun: "*Hé(l)las pour moi*"); this lament is shared by Godard, Giraudoux and another important intellectual source for the film, the modernist author Hermann Broch, whose 1945 novel *Death of Virgil* (in which the poet's doubts in the face of his imminent death mirror the dying of Roman civilisation) is cited both here and in *Histoire(s) du cinéma*, in which it frames the tribute to Epstein. Godard's biographer Richard Brody summarizes:

> Why Jews? Why Abraham, Benjamin, and Scholem? Because their tradition had indeed been transmitted, whereas in Godard's view, the tradition of the image – of seeing the invisible – had failed to be transmitted. The cinema, as Godard understood it, had ended with its failures during World War II, and specifically, with its failures in relation to Jews and the Genocide to which they were subjected. The tradition of the image that Godard had inherited could not be transmitted, because of the insurmountable obstacles of television and material comfort, the psychic oblivion of mass culture or culturelessness, the broken thread of artistic and cultural achievement that had run from Homer to Godard himself.
> (Brody 2008, 555)

But the film is not entirely without hope. Indeed, it can be said to be messianic in its belief that redemption can still happen if the image is returned to the fire of Buber's legend,[4] to the identity of divine language as celebrated by Epstein. It does this through the very act of mourning. The transmissibility of truth that Aude puts into question by referring to Scholem is resolved in the latter's thought through the linguistic specificity of the lament, a mode of expression that both is and is not a language. The lament, observes Scholem, is a linguistic paradox: although it manifests deep feelings of sorrow in words or sounds, it communicates no content external to itself. There is no communicational exchange, no presumed interlocutor, as the lament folds back into itself. Thus, it becomes a pure act of expression that can point only to what it seeks to convey, instead of articulating that content to the full (Ferber 2013, 164). This logic of designation is quite close to Epstein's mute language of cinema that names things visually, or to the idea that the cinema's great power is to make the invisible visible *as* invisible subconscious. The metaphysical "in-between" status of lament reminds us of his lyrosophical conception of cinema as both evidence and feeling, at the same time subjective and objective. On the other hand, Scholem's conception of lament as a way to make the unsayable sayable also results from the logic of apophasis, or what Benjamin termed "negative theology." In Jewish theology, God, as the creator, is by definition separate from the physical universe and is therefore absolutely different and unknowable. The impossibility of knowing God is also related to His absolute unity, devoid of properties and therefore indescribable. (This absolute unity is the subject of the psalm that Max Mercure has "God" recite as a "sound test": "All is in One. And the Other is in One. Those are the Three Persons.") Yet to say that God defies description is already a descriptive statement. So description is still possible, but only in the negative, as description of what God is not. It is through articulating "nothing" that the lament of Godard's late films succeeds in offering an authentic aesthetic experience. This divine no-thing-ness is easy to reconcile with Godard's other philosophical influences, including Bataille's idea of "l'informe" or Sartre's idea of art becoming art precisely by negating reality (Melberg 2005). As Michael Witt has shown, Godard seems to consider cinema in Sartrean terms, as "draining the real of life before resurrecting it in the projeced image," before re-theologizing this logic of death and resurrection through a favourite eschatological quotation, from St. Paul, that "the image will come at the time of resurrection" (Witt 2013, 25). The same logic of resurrection is at work in the lament, repeating itself in an endless cycle of destruction and reconstruction, of death and resurrection.

---

4 As Michael Witt notes, in Godard's sacrificial iconography fire tends to denote the transfiguration of the real into art, a motif he borrows from André Malraux (Witt 2012, 26).

Viewed from the perspective of a postmodernist eschatology, the periodic declaration of cinema's death has become meaningless, a feedback loop comparable to the lament's language of extinction (*"Il faut recommencer la scène,"* "God" says to Rachel, unsatisfied by a first attempt at seduction). A self-declared historian, Godard is interested both in the end of cinema and in the end of history, and dubious about both. Godard's historiography is closer to Benjamin's revolutionary brand of messianism: the postmodern idea of the end of history becomes meaningless when redemption can come at any moment, instantly, when the present is transformed as the hopes, defeats and promises of past generations are reactualized in a messianic moment of *"Jetztzeit."* For Godard, redemption of the image means blasting it from its historical continuum and revealing Epstein's Bergsonian reality in flux. ("The past is not dead, it's not even past," is another favoured formula.) In the non-language of the lament, Scholem tells us, extinction is endlessly delayed by its constantly looping back to its zero point of origin (Ferber 2013, 170). For Godard, this zero point of origin is, of course, the birth of the medium and a second birth, the first filmic avant-garde. But Godard also returns to the pre-cinematic medium of painting, which in his late films is encapsulated in the (Jewish) art historian Élie Faure's writing about Rembrandt – specifically, Faure's Balázs-like observation that Rembrandt's genius lies in his proceeding inward from an exterior view of things in their everyday banality to a closer contemplation of the human face and gesture.[5] Godard's appropriation of Rembrandt, both as a visual schema and as quotation, entails an act of destruction (a "blasting") that is the essence of André Malraux's transformative historiography of art as formed out of "ancient history," the art of the past remembered, destroyed and reinvented in that of the present (Witt 2013, 86). Like Malraux in his "museum without walls," or like Benjamin's allegorist collecting and rearranging ruinous fragments, Godard creates paratactic juxtapositions – what Jacques Rancière calls Godard's "phrases" – between images that have been removed from their original context and thus reenergized. For Benjamin, such alienating of the original image or utterance is the closest art can come to revealing the fragment's vitalistic essence. As Benjamin writes, the quotation "summons the word by its name, wrenches it from its context and, in doing so, calls it back to its origins … In the word thus emancipated is mirrored the language of the angels wherein all words, shaken out of the idyllic context of meaningfulness, have become mottos in the book of creation." (Witte 1991, 127). Therein lies Godard's gnostic project.

---

5 Faure coined the term *"cinéplastique"* to account for cinema's medium-specificity at around the same time Epstein was thinking through *photogénie*.

Bibliography

Benjamin, Walter. "Theses on the Philosophy of History." Trans. Harry Zohn. *Illuminations*. Ed. Hannah Arendt. New York: Schocken Books, 1968. 253–265.
Brody, Richard. *Everything Is Cinema: The Working Life of Jean-Luc Godard*. New York: Holt, 2008.
Charney, Leo. "In a Moment: Film and the Philosophy of Modernity." *Cinema and the Invention of Modern Life*. Ed. Leo Charney and Vanessa R. Schwartz. Berkeley: University of California Press, 1995. 279–297.
Darmon, Maurice. *La question juive de Jean-Luc Godard*. Paris: Le Temps Qu'il Fait, 2011.
Epstein, Jean. "The Rule of the Kabbalah Is Such that It Espouses Passion Rather Than Opposing It." Trans. Christophe Wall-Romana. *Jean Epstein: Critical Essays and New Translations*. Ed. Sarah Keller and Jason N. Paul. Amsterdam: Amsterdam University Press, 2012a. 284–286.
Epstein, Jean. "The Cinema Seen From Etna." Trans. Stuart Liebman. *Jean Epstein: Critical Essays and New Translations*. Ed. Sarah Keller and Jason N. Paul. Amsterdam: Amsterdam University Press, 2012b. 287–292.
Ferber, Ilit. "A Language of the Border: On Scholem's Theory of Lament." *Journal of Jewish Thought & Philosophy* 21 (2013): 161–186.
Gunning, Tom. "Preface." *Jean Epstein: Critical Essays and New Translations*. Ed. Sarah Keller and Jason N. Paul. Amsterdam: Amsterdam University Press, 2012. 13–23.
Hélas pour moi. Dir. Jean-Luc Godard. Les Films Alain Sarde, 1993.
Jameson, Fredric. *Postmodernism, or the Cultural Logic of Late Capitalism*. London and New York: Verso, 1991.
Keller, Sarah. "Introduction." *Jean Epstein: Critical Essays and New Translations*. Ed. Sarah Keller and Jason N. Paul. Amsterdam: Amsterdam University Press, 2012. 23–51.
Melberg, Arne. "The Work of Art in the Age of Ontological Speculation." *Walter Benjamin and Art*. Ed. Andrew Benjamin. London and New York: Continuum, 2005. 93–108.
Rancière, Jacques. "A Thwarted Fable." *Rouge* 8 (2006). www.rouge.com.au/8/thwarted_fable.html (30 July 2016).
Sterritt, David. *The Films of Jean-Luc Godard: Seeing the Invisible*. New York: Cambridge University Press, 1999.
Turvey, Malcolm. *Doubting Vision: Film and the Revelationist Tradition*. Oxford: Oxford University Press, 2008.
Wall-Romana, Christophe. "Epstein's *Photogénie* as Corporeal Vision: Inner Sensation, Queer Embodiment, and Ethics." *Jean Epstein: Critical Essays and New Translations*. Ed. Sarah Keller and Jason N. Paul. Amsterdam: Amsterdam University Press, 2012, 51–73.
Witt, Michael. *Jean-Luc Godard: Cinema Historian*. Bloomington: Indiana University Press, 2013.
Witte, Bernd. *Walter Benjamin: An Intellectual Biography*. Trans. James Rolleston. Detroit: Wayne State University Press, 1991.

Raphael Koenig
The Mad Book: Der Nister as Unreliable Author in *From my Estate* (1929)

The production of avant-garde Soviet Yiddish writers in the year 1929 illustrates the paradoxical link between marginalization and innovation that can often be observed in Yiddish literary history (Norich 2013, 12): as the Yiddish avant-garde was threatened in its very existence, it also produced some of its most innovative works (Krutikov 2013, 224). The first signs of a comprehensive "return to order" heralded the end of radical aesthetic experimentation in the Soviet Union, leading to the official adoption of socialist realism in 1934.[1] But the "Year of the Great Turn" also corresponded to the publication of groundbreaking experimental works by Pinkhes Kahanovitsh (1884–1950), better known under his pen name "Der Nister," but also Perets Markish, Dovid Bergelson, Shmuel Godiner, and Meir Wiener (Krutikov 2013, 224–241).

The campaign orchestrated against Der Nister by the critics of the Soviet Yiddish journals *Prolit* (Proletarian Literature) in 1928–1929 is emblematic of this abrupt paradigm shift (Shneer 2004, 169–170). For them, "Nisterism" hindered the advent of a secular Yiddish proletarian culture more in line with the stipulations of the Five-Year Plan, and had to be eradicated.

Yet, Der Nister published two major collections of short stories in 1929, *Gedakht* (Imagined) and *Fun mayne giter* (From my Estate).[2] The deeply pessimistic, distressed tone of these works can be perceived as a direct answer to Der Nister's personal hardships, the changing fortunes of Yiddish culture in the Soviet Union, and the dramatic upheavals that had affected Eastern European Jews since the outbreak of the first Russian revolution in 1905. According to Khone Shmeruk, *Unter a ployt* (Under a Fence), one of the short stories in *Gedakht*, would thus constitute a "unique and original protest, powerless though it was" (Shmeruk 1965, 285; Mantovan 2014, 74). Among Der Nister's 1929 short stories, *Unter a*

---

[1] The year 1929 was declared by Stalin the "Year of the Great Turn," as he tightened his grip on power after defeating his political opponents Leon Trotsky and Nikolay Bukharin and hastened the implementation of the first Five-Year plan, promulgated in 1928 (Estraikh 2013, 50). It also marked the beginning of the end of the "romance" of Soviet Yiddish writers with communism (Estraikh 2005), as a watershed moment "between the period of relative stylistic and thematic freedom and the new era of [...] ideological dictate" (Krutikov 2013, 224).
[2] The 1929 edition of *Gedakht* is actually a republication, as it had first been published in Berlin in 1922–1923. However, this new edition features a number of more recent short stories (including *Unter a ployt*) and omits some older ones, thus constituting a literary event in its own right.

DOI 10.1515/9783110454956-013

ployt has received the most critical attention and is now part of the modern Yiddish "canon," but relatively few works of literary scholarship have been devoted to *Fun mayne giter*, the first short story of the collection that bears the same title.[3] The following article will offer an analysis of one of the most striking, yet relatively understudied aspects of *Fun mayne giter*: the highly paradoxical nature of Der Nister's literary persona as represented in the short story.

Confronted with the scalding criticism of the zealots of a new Yiddish proletarian literature, Der Nister appears to be both protesting and embracing his own marginalization by developing a radically innovative narratological conceit, which I will call "unreliable author," as opposed to the better-known "unreliable narrator."[4] Der Nister appears as the main character of *From my Estate*, depicted in turn as a madman, an amputee bereft of his writing hand, and a failed Messiah, thereby seemingly undermining his own auctorial legitimacy. This article considers successively these three figures of "de-authorization" as a radical example of experimental writing that forces us to rethink crucial narratological and historical categories.[5]

1 Writings of a Madman

In the opening paragraphs, constituting a separate narrative framework, an anonymous narrator takes a stroll in an unnamed city, happening onto fair grounds where books are sold off cheaply and even raffled off on the occasion of a state-sponsored "cheap books week." The narrator then draws a raffle ticket:

---

[3] In the following essay, *Fun mayne giter* will refer to the short story itself, and not the collection of short stories that bears the same title, unless otherwise noted. Khone Shmeruk (1965), Delphine Bechtel (1990, 261s), David Roskies (1995, 225s) and Marc Caplan (1998) all offered comprehensive analyses of *Unter a ployt*. Studies devoted to other short stories published by Der Nister in 1929 include Dara Horn's essay on the narrative structure of the *Fun mayne giter* (2013), Daniela Mantovan's thorough analysis of its symbolism and political implications (2014, 80–85), and Sabine Boehlich's book-length close reading of *Nay-Gayst* (*New Spirit*) (2008).
[4] The notion of "unreliable author" I am developing in this article addresses the specific narratological device of the depiction of the author as a character within the story, distinct from what Francis Sparshott called an "unreliable author" in his 1986 article, "The Case of the Unreliable Author," which deals with the figure of the *implied* author, i.e. the reconstruction of an auctorial persona by the reader as a necessary part of the act of reading.
[5] Der Nister's paradoxical mode of self-fashioning could be compared with the "autobiographical fictions" of other major Yiddish writers and the way they reflect exceptional historical circumstances, comprehensively analyzed in Jan Schwarz's *Imagining Lives: Autobiographical Fiction of Yiddish Writers* (2005).

Un bikher hot men in di baydlekh geplet, un ieder plet, iz geshribn geven, hot gemuzt gevinen, – hob oykh ikh ayngeshtelt un a baydl-kvitele getsoygn, un az der farkoyfer, vos farkoyft hot baydl, hot dos kvitele tseviklt, hot er mir a bikhele untergetrogn:

Der oytor – Der Nister.

Der nomen – Shrift fun a duln ; un afn shar-bletl iz oykh a gemel geven: a blas-meshugener iz in a lang meshugoim-hemd ongeton geshtanen.

(Der Nister 1929, 7)[6]

[And there was a book raffle in the booths, and every ticket, so it was written, was a winning one; I also drew a raffle ticket, and the seller who was running the booth unfolded the ticket, and handed me a little book:

The author – Der Nister.

The title: *Writings of a Madman*; and there was a picture on the front page: a pale madman was standing there, dressed in the long gown of the inmate of an insane asylum.]

The rest of the story purports to be taken from the *Shriftn fun a duln* (Writings of a Madman). These opening paragraphs constitute an unprecedented way of using a frame story to introduce a supposedly "found" manuscript or book, as it usually attributes the text of the main narrative to a different author.[7] The frame story of *From my Estate* does not deflect authorial responsibility onto a thoroughly fictional entity, but abruptly introduces the author himself, depicted as a madman.

To use the terminology of the leading theorist of "unreliable narratives," Wayne C. Booth, who distinguishes between narrator, literary persona or "implied author" (IA), and flesh-and-blood person (FBP), the narrator is the anonymous winner of the raffle, and the FBP corresponds to Pinkhes Kahanovitsh. However, there are two distinct IAs: a public literary persona (IA1) designated under the pen name Der Nister, as printed on the front page of *From my Estate*; and an avatar of this public persona within the story, whose name and imaginary photograph appear on the front page of the fictional "found" book (IA2). This frame-tale narrative involves a certain degree of playfulness. The implied reader of the story is supposed to understand the difference between the two IAs, and between them and the FBP. Der Nister's irruption in his own narrative is part of a broader tradition in Yiddish literature. The readers of *From my Estate* could be reminded of the nonchalant personal interventions of Sholem Aleichem in his own short stories (Brenner 2008, 23–97). But, by equating the words "Der Nister," "author,"

---

6 All translations are by the author unless otherwise stated.
7 For instance, in Potocki's frame-tale novel *The Manuscript Found in Saragossa*, the "found" narrative is attributed to its main character, Alfonse van Worden.

and "madman," and presenting us with a portrait of a "pale madman" in lieu of meditative photographs used as the frontispieces of works by the likes of Sholem Aleichem or Agnon (Brenner 2008, 23–24), the opening paragraphs of *From my Estate* stage frontal attacks against key symbols of authorship: the reader seems to be encouraged to question the legitimacy of the one instance that is supposed to guarantee the internal coherence and artistic validity of the narrative. No failsafe mechanism seems to remain that would preserve Der Nister (IA1) from the suspicions of insanity or incoherence that the reader might be harboring against the "mad" Der Nister (IA2).

The so-called "art of the insane" was popular among the 1920s avant-gardes, thanks to its ability to disturb, shock, and question the reader's or viewer's assumptions. As demonstrated by Hal Foster, French and German avant-garde artists from the interwar period tended to appropriate the "art of the insane" – itself often an attempt at reconstituting an idiosyncratic but internally coherent "world order"– as a means of criticizing and ironizing the prejudices and general *Weltanschauung* of their contemporaries (Foster 2001).[8]

Even in the absence of direct textual evidence documenting Der Nister's reception of their works, his stay in Berlin (1922–1924) corresponds to a moment when the works of Freud and, to a lesser extent, of Prinzhorn, were read extensively in avant-garde circles.[9] While in Berlin, Der Nister assiduously frequented the *Romanisches Café* (Romanesque Café), the central meeting point of the Berlin avant-garde, and even co-edited with fellow "Kiever" Dovid Bergelson the literary section of the first issue of the eclectic Berlin-based avant-garde Yiddish magazine *Milgroym* (Pomegranate, 1922–1924). It is fair to assume that *From my Estate* is part of this broader artistic and cultural context.

Walter Benjamin wrote about both his personal interest in the "books by the mentally ill" (which he used to seek out for his private collection) and the fact that such works had become "in vogue" among many of his contemporaries in

---

[8] Hal Foster analyzes several examples of the deep influence of the "art of the insane" on interwar avant-garde artistic creation, for instance Max Ernst's collage *Das Schlafzimmer des Meisters* (The Master's Bedroom, 1920), or Paul Klee's watercolor *Zimmerperspektive mit Einwohnern* (Room Perspective with Inhabitants, 1921). Examples abound in interwar European avant-garde literature, for instance André Breton and Paul Éluard's *L'Immaculée Conception* (The Immaculate Conception, 1930), or Kurt Schwitters' poem *An Anna Blume* (To Anna Blume, 1919).

[9] German psychiatrist Hans Prinzhorn's *Die Bildnerei der Geisteskranken* (The Artistry of the Mentally Ill, 1922), both a medical symptomatology of the artistic creations of mentally ill patients and an aesthetic evaluation of these works, was well-known in avant-garde circles, especially after the publication by Hans Prinzhorn of a short summary of his work in *G: Zeitschrift für elementare Gestaltung* (G: Journal for Elementary Form-Making, 1923–1924), one of the leading magazines of the Berlin avant-garde (MacGregor 1978).

his short essay *Bücher von Geisteskranken: Aus meiner Sammlung* (Books by the Mentally Ill: From my Collection), published in the Berlin-based *Die literarische Welt* (The Literary World) in July 1928. Benjamin expounds on the "disconcerting" nature of works written by mentally ill authors, which he attributes specifically to their ability to short-circuit established mechanisms of authorship and artistic legitimacy:

> Das Dasein von dergleichen Werken hat etwas Bestürzendes. Solange wir gewohnt sind, den Bereich der Schrift, trotz allem, als einen höheren, geborgeneren zu betrachten, ist das Auftreten des Wahnsinns, der hier mit leiseren Sohlen sich einschleicht als irgend sonst um so erschreckender. Wie ist es dahin gelangt? Wie hat er die Paßkontrolle dieses hunderttorigen Theben, der Stadt der Bücher, umgangen?
> (Benjamin, GS, 4, 619)
>
> [The mere existence of such works has something disconcerting about it. So long as we habitually regard writing as – despite everything – part of a higher, safer realm, the appearance of insanity, especially when it enters less noisily than elsewhere, is all the more terrifying. How could this happen? How did it manage to slip past the passport control of the city of books, this Thebes with a hundred doors?]
> (Benjamin 1928, 130)

Benjamin's description of the "city of books" as a fortress with strict border control unavoidably calls to mind Michel Foucault's polemical definition of the author as a functional principle according to which one "delimits, excludes, and selects." Accordingly, the specific shock value of *From my Estate* can be attributed to the general structure of the narrative itself, a complex and apparently haphazard succession of surreal and often gruesome descriptions and events that seem to defy logic and narrative conventions (Horn 2013). The shock may also be attributed to the disconcerting nature of Der Nister's self-portrayal as a "mad author," in line with the avant-garde's interest in the "art of the insane" in the 1920s.

But the relationship between Der Nister's "unreliable author" and the European avant-garde in the 1920s appears to be more complex than one of mere contemporaneity. Indeed, as Saul Zaritt explained in his essay, "'The World Awaits Your Yiddish Word': Jacob Glatstein and the Problem of World Literature" (2015), Yiddish literary works often seem to abide to a chronology of their own, one that only occasionally corresponds to the specific chronologies of major European literatures, or "Eurochronology":

> Yiddish writers were sometimes decades behind their fellow European and American practitioners in participating in these –isms [such as romanticism, symbolism, high modernism, naturalism, and expressionism]; other times they enacted artistic innovations that were very similar to their contemporaries, though such simultaneity was predominantly unacknowledged or simply unknown; and finally, when placed in comparison with later definitions of

modernism and postmodernism, these Yiddish writers could now be considered "ahead of their time." Yiddish literature, and Jewish literatures more broadly, may then prove useful in thinking beyond the constrictions of Eurochronology and in undoing traditional periodizations and geographies of world literature.
(Zaritt 2015, 179)

Der Nister's "unreliable narrator" appears to exemplify the chronological disconnection theorized by Zaritt.[10] While being unquestionably "of its time," even though Der Nister's work has never been mentioned to date in the context of the 1920s reception of the "art of the insane," it is also in dialogue with earlier trends of Yiddish and Russian literature. The title, general structure of the story, and the fact that the "pale madman in a white shirt" might be an allusion to Elya Repin's 1882 painting of Poprishchin (Mantovan 2014, 81) indicate that the work should be placed in the context of the Yiddish reception of Gogol's *Zapiski sumasshedshevo* (Diary of a Madman, 1835), alongside works of an earlier generation of Yiddish writers that were directly inspired by Gogol's *Diary of a Madman* and constitute a link between Gogol and Der Nister, for instance Mendele's 1873 and 1889 editions of *Di klyatshe* (The Nag), attributed to "Isrolik the Madman," or I.L. Peretz's short story *Der meshugener batlen* (The Mad Talmudist, 1890) and his collection of short stories *Mayselekh fun dul-hoyz* (Stories from the Madhouse, 1895–1911), which rely on various mentally ill "unreliable narrators" (Frieden 1995, 259–280).[11]

On the other hand, the originality of Der Nister's "unreliable author" as a narrative device should not be underestimated, and could even be described as being "ahead of its time." Unlike the works we just mentioned, *From My Estate* does not claim to be written from the perspective of a madman, but actually *by* a madman. However daring Gogol's, Mendele's, or Peretz's experimentation with

---

10 One could also add that Der Nister's self-styling as a "high priest" of Yiddish literature analyzed by David Roskies in "The Storyteller as High Priest" (1996) both fits perfectly within Peter Bürger's famous definition of the avant-garde as aiming at implementing deep social and political changes (as opposed, according to Bürger, to Modernism's exclusive focus on stylistic features), and seems to be singularly at odds with it, by relying on a traditional religious metaphor.

11 Of course, the fact that a work is in dialogue with earlier works of literature does not automatically imply its "belatedness." In this context, an obvious counter-example would be Lu Xun's *Kuangren riji* (A Madman's Diary, 1918), which, though inspired by Lu Xun's reading of Gogol, is nonetheless considered to be a foundational text of Chinese Modernism. Nevertheless, in the case of Der Nister, other factors could be perceived as indicating his relative "belatedness," for instance the fact that he is often described as a "symbolist" writer (Bechtel 1990), a movement that, in "Eurochronological" terms, is generally considered as dating back to the 1880s and 1890s (even though it developed further in Russia until the 1910s); or even the deep interest for folk tales that permeates his short stories, which could be perceived as neo-Romantic. Der Nister even translated Andersen's tales into Yiddish from 1919 onwards (Hoge 2014, 45).

narrative techniques and their bending of the rules of storytelling, the figure of the author himself is left unscathed. For instance, in Gogol's *Diary of a Madman*, Proprishchin, the unreliable narrator, is clearly separated from Gogol, an acclaimed author whose name guarantees the overall coherence and literary value of the text. To a certain extent, this is also the case for 1920s avant-garde works by the likes of Breton, Éluard, Klee, or Ernst: the authors' close encounters with madness are generally conceived of as the result of a deliberate experiment or carefully crafted observational process that might even allow them to reach a higher level of consciousness, such as Breton's "*surréalité*."[12] Far from potentially affecting the authors' legitimacy, it seems to be largely perpetuating what Paul Bénichou described as the Romantic "Consecration of the Writer" by other means. In fact, Der Nister's frontal attack on key symbols of auctorial legitimacy, if a reaction to specific historical circumstances, could be anachronistically described as pioneering a form of "de-authorization" akin to the debates around the "death of the author" that became a hallmark of postmodern literature from the 1960s onwards.

2 The Writer Loses his Hand

Unlike the writers mentioned by Benjamin, Der Nister was always an insider of the "city of books." Before the overwhelming success of *The Family Mashber* in 1939–1940, Der Nister's position in the Yiddish literary world could be described as that of a "writer's writer," both fairly below-the-radar and connected to a small but highly influential coterie of fellow writers and critics. Der Nister was a key member of the Kiev group (or "Kievers"), an informal group that remained active under various guises and configurations from around 1903 until the late 1940s, alongside such major figures as the novelist Dovid Bergelson, the poet Leyb Kvitko, and the critic Yekhezkl Dobrushin. In 1926–1927, Der Nister and several other Kievers founded the literary group *Boy* (Construction), which controlled the leading Soviet Yiddish literary journal *Di royte velt* (Red World) (Estraikh 2014, 10–16). Thus, several scholars have pointed out that Der Nister was far from being completely isolated in 1928–1929, when the critics of *Prolit* and *Der shtern* orchestrated a vio-

---

[12] For instance, in André Breton's *Nadja* (1928), published only a year before *From my Estate*, Breton remains a careful (if sympathetic) and lucid observer of Nadja's delirious behavior and drawings. The implied author's fascination with madness never leads to a thorough or unambiguous identification.

lent campaign against him on the grounds of the purported incompatibility of his works with the new proletarian aesthetics.[13]

Nevertheless, even though the initial critical reaction to the publication of *Gedakht* and *Fun mayne giter* was "far from entirely negative" (Krutikov 2014, 226), the "proletarian" writers undoubtedly had the upper hand in the "civil war" that raged in the Soviet Yiddish literary world between 1928 and 1932.[14] The campaign against Der Nister could be analyzed in terms of rivalries between different Soviet Yiddish literary groups.[15] However, the "Nisterism" debate is also highly significant of the abrupt paradigm shift that affected Soviet Yiddish literature:

> By 1929, the charges of mysticism and Symbolism that were leveled against Der Nister came to define a new "-ism," Nisterism, which was used negatively to refer to literature that was not proletarian. These general criticisms showed that a single definition of Soviet Yiddish literature and Soviet Yiddish culture was forming, one whose criteria would be determined by literary critics, publishers, and editors in positions of power. Yiddish prose narratives about building factories and settling Birobidzhan would come to replace expressionist poems about mental and physical destruction.
> (Shneer 2004, 169–170)

Der Nister, whose idiosyncratic, fantastic writing style was partly inspired by E.T.A. Hoffmann (Shmeruk 1965, 281; Bechtel 1990, 223–226), clashed with the realism of the "proletarian" school. He did not fare well under the new regime. He was condemned by the critics of *Prolit* and *Der shtern* for his "symbolism," which was even branded as a form of idealism, i.e. the exact opposite of Marxist

---

[13] Influential Soviet Yiddish critics such as Shakhno Epshteyn, Moyshe Litvakov, and Yitskhok Nusinov took up Der Nister's defense (Estraikh 2014, 14–15; Krutikov 2013, 224–225). However, this is only half of the story. As Delphine Bechtel has demonstrated, in a second phase of the heated polemic around the work of Der Nister, which continued until 1932, Epshteyn, Litvakov and Nusinov were in turn heavily criticized for supporting him (Bechtel 1997, 46–50). Litvakov, after writing two articles of self-criticism, even ended up turning against Nusinov, whom he accused of "methodological error and right-wing opportunism" for supporting Der Nister, which did not prevent the "Minsker" Avrom Abtshuk from violently attacking Litvakov for the same reasons a couple of months later (Bechtel 1997, 47–49). Significantly, Abtshuk's 1932 article was published in *Red World*, the journal of the Kievers that had originally supported Der Nister, thus marking the triumph of the "proletarian" writers.

[14] One could even date the beginning of this "civil war" in 1925, when the first articles attacking the Berlin edition of *Imagined* were published in *Der shtern*.

[15] Dovid Hofshteyn and the other writers of *Prolit* against the *Boy* group and *Red World*, both journals being based in Kharkov; or the "Minskers" Ber Orshanski and Yashe Bronshtyen and their journal *Der shtern* against the "Kievers" of *Boy*. One could also point out that a number of "Kievers," including Perets Markish and Leyb Kvitko, were also violently attacked by the same critics (Estraikh 2014, 14).

materialism (Bechtel 1997, 47).[16] The accusation of "mysticism" was maybe even graver. A disciple of Peretz' neo-Hasidism, Der Nister was one of the most overtly religiously inspired artists of the Soviet Yiddish avant-garde; in particular, the writings of Nachman of Breslov had a profound impact on his work (Caplan 2014, 90–110).[17] The "Great Turn" of 1928–1929 was marked by a general crackdown on independent artistic expression, but also by a violent anti-religious campaign. The eradication of all forms of religious practice (including Christian Orthodoxy, Islam, Judaism, and Buddhism) was seen as a prerequisite for the success of the Five-Year Plan. The most eloquent illustration of this notion can be found in Dziga Vertov's film *Entuziazm: Simfoniya Donbassa* (Enthusiasm: Symphony of the Donbass), a paean to the Five-Year Plan shot in 1929–1930. Its opening sequence depicts the "clearing of social space" from the twin "opiates" of religion and alcohol.

The marginalization of Der Nister that resulted from the proletarian writers' campaign against "Nisterism" was thus motivated by a range of aesthetic and ideological concerns; but it also had a concrete, devastating impact on Der Nister's ability to create and publish his works. The year 1929 represented a watershed moment in the work of Der Nister, who stopped publishing "symbolist" short stories altogether (Bechtel 1997, 39).[18] According to Daniela Mantovan, "it was almost certain that neither volume [i.e. *Gedakht* and *Fun mayne giter*] would have passed censorship" only half a year later.[19] Unable to publish another work of fiction for five years (Krutikov 2013, 224), Der Nister survived mostly by doing "hackwork": translations, documentary narratives about the "socialist reconstruction of urban centers," and, from 1934 onwards, children's tales in verse (Estraikh 2014, 17–18). Accordingly, metaphors of "de-authorization" in *From my Estate* can be read as half-veiled allusions to the fact that Der Nister's activity as a writer was then directly under threat.

---

16 For a comprehensive study of *From my Estate*'s writing style and intricate narrative structure, see Dara Horn's essay *Der Nister's Symbolist Stories* (2013).
17 For an in-depth analysis of the way in which Der Nister conceived of his role as that of a "high priest" invested with an aesthetic, social, and religious mission, see David Roskies' chapter on Der Nister, entitled "The Storyteller as High Priest," in his book *A Bridge of Longing: The Lost Art of Yiddish Storytelling* (1996).
18 However, several critics have pointed out that the "realist" novel, *The Family Mashber*, displays strong echoes of Der Nister's earlier symbolist period, thus representing a form of compromise at least superficially meeting the criteria of socialist realism (Krutikov 2014, 134).
19 As the campaign against "Nisterism," first triggered by the publication of *Gedakht*, was already in full swing when Der Nister published *Fun mayne giter*, one could surmise that the "estate" in question could hint at an artistic last will, Der Nister's "last act as a symbolist writer" (Mantovan 2014, 78).

In the opening paragraphs of the *Shriftn fun a duln* (Writings of a Madman, the story within a story of *From my Estate*), Der Nister, in a nightmarish rewriting of the scenario of *Goldilocks*, encounters a family of ten bears. As the ravenous bears demand food, Der Nister is forced to feed them the only edible item he has: his own body. Der Nister goes around the table, at the rate of one finger per bear. But the penultimate bear greedily chops off the remaining two fingers. The last bear, robbed of his fair share of fingers, is about to devour Der Nister's heart when the latter, in a desperate attempt to delay his execution, distracts him by telling him a story. The rest of the short story consists of a succession of stories told by Der Nister to the bears, thus abruptly shifting the intertextual point of reference from *Goldilocks* to the *Arabian Nights*, with Der Nister in the role of an unlikely Scheherazade.

The passage is highly ambivalent about the chances of success of this survival strategy. As Der Nister adopts the position of a traditional storyteller, he has already lost the essential tool of his trade: the hand with which he writes. The significance of this amputation is highlighted by the graphic, horrifyingly slow-paced nature of the passage. The biting off of each finger by each individual bear is narrated in great detail, complete with spouting blood and gory stumps, punctuated by the bears' grunts of satiety and Der Nister's cries of pain. Following the depiction of Der Nister as an inmate in an insane asylum, the loss of the writer's hands constitutes a second, even more visceral metaphor for "de-authorization," with clear (and probably deliberate) Freudian undertones, as the scene constitutes a textbook case of castration anxiety, linking the angst of artistic impotence with the loss of the writer's main creative appendage, the hand that holds the pen. Textual evidence both within the work of Der Nister and among the critical reactions from contemporary Soviet Yiddish critics seems to support this interpretation. As early as 1908, in a postcard addressed to Shmuel Niger, Der Nister expressed his feelings of self-doubt, isolation, and disempowerment in strong terms, linking together the failing of the writer's hand and organic decay:

> *Vi kon men gor nemen a pen in hant, az du veyst az foyln vet dos, dos mit dir ineynem ... Ikh bin azoy mat, az di pen falt mir fun hant.*[20]
>
> [How can you pick up a pen, when you know that what you write will rot, rot together with you. I am so discouraged that the pen falls from my hand.]

This postcard, possibly inspired by Hofmannsthal's *Brief des Lord Chandos* (Letter of Lord Chandos, 1902), expresses Der Nister's frustration with the difficulties en-

---

[20] Zhitomir, December 3, 1908; Postcard 8, Niger Archive, as quoted in Bechtel, 1990, 7.

countered by Yiddish writers in Russia, in the context of tight government control on Yiddish publishing and general conservative backlash in the aftermath of the violent repression of the revolution of 1905. It is significant that this image would resurface in the work of Der Nister twenty years later, in the equally dramatic context of the "Great Turn."

Immediately after the publication of *From my Estate*, a parody of the short story, entitled *Parodyes, epigramen, sharzn. Fun mayne shmates (loyt dem Nister): A mayse mit a vants, mit a floy, mit a gets Bim-Bom un mit dem Nister aleyn* (Parodies, Epigrams, Jokes. From my Rags (à la Der Nister): A Story with a Louse, a Flea, the Idol Bim-Bom, and Der Nister Himself), was published in the October 1929 edition of *Prolit*, penned by the Soviet Yiddish satirist Kofsi:

> *Zayt visn, khosheve bern, az ikh farmog gornit oyser tsen kalie finger, vos konen afile rekht keyn hentl-pen in der hant nit haltn [...], un oyb ir broygezet nit, iz nat aykh mayne tsen finger [...] un nemt un grizhet. Un ale tsen bern hobn zikh mit amol af Nistern a loz geton un genumen grizhen zayne finger un gegrizhet geshmak, un bay Nistern hobn zikh fun di hent ritshkes blut gegosn, un di greste tsvey bern hobn zikh fort nit ongezetet, hobn zey Nistern far di elnboygns a khap geton, un nokh hekher, un ingantsn opgegrizhet im di hent.*
> (Kofsi 1929, 120–121)
>
> [But, right honorable bears, do you know that I don't own anything apart from *ten damaged fingers that can't even hold a pen properly*? Go ahead, if you would have them, here are my ten fingers, take them and gnaw on them. And the ten bears threw themselves upon Der Nister all at once, started nibbling on his fingers with gusto, and streams of blood were running from the hands of Der Nister, and the two biggest bears were not quite satiated yet, grabbed Der Nister by the elbows, and gobbled down what was left of his arms.[21]]

Apart from the polemical violence and obvious malicious intent of this pastiche (the "Idol Bim-Bom" of the title being a rather unsubtle allusion to Der Nister's "mysticism"), its most striking feature consists in its displacement of the image of the severed hand. Correctly identifying it as an allusion to Der Nister's feelings of disempowerment and loss of authorial control, Kofsi, for satirical purposes, takes at face value the loss of the author's hand as proof of Der Nister's supposed literary shortcomings. This illustrates the fact that the staging of Der Nister's authorial persona within the short story's narrative did impact the image of the author as both IA1 and FPB. It is part of what Naomi Rebecca Brenner described as the "reverse expansion of literature into real life" in Yiddish literature (Brenner 2008, 9).[22] But, if Der Nister already faced a barrage of criticism from

---

[21] As quoted in Bechtel 1997, 57. Emphasis mine.
[22] As Brenner mentions in the introduction of her dissertation *Authorial Fictions: Literary and Public Personas in Modern Hebrew and Yiddish Literature*, the distinction between IA and FBP

Prolit, why would he have adopted such an apparently counter-productive and self-defeating strategy, "protesting" his marginalization by purposefully undermining an already precarious position?

The notion of unreliable author is incompatible with the theoretical frameworks generally used to analyze notions of authorship and "authorial masking." In the words of Booth (2005, 76), implied authors (IAs) are necessarily "better selves," a persona designed to present the author to the reader in the most advantageous fashion. [23] A possible answer to this aporia would be that Der Nister produced a narrative in which his literary persona was presented in an unflattering light as a gesture of defiance and an expression of utter hopelessness, denouncing the dynamics of marginalization and political repression that threatened to silence him. Der Nister's short stories, inspired by Talmudic and Hasidic parables, require several levels of interpretation. The "unreliable author" appears to shatter the bond of trust between the author and his readers, but regains a form of moral and artistic legitimacy in terms of both *ethos* and *pathos*, if we read this narratological conceit as an allusion to the fate of the author. The shattering of the symbolic authority of authorship, danger of mental illness, gruesome physical torture, and various indignities inflicted upon the author are all part of a kind of Passion Play, staging the sacrifice of the author and even his actual execution.[24] He is thus closely related to the other main characters of Der Nister's short stories from the period 1928–1929, for instance the scholar of *Unter a ployt* (inspired by Heinrich Mann's 1905 *Professor Unrat*), who faces a sham trial and is sentenced to being burned to death.

---

upon which Dan Miron insisted in *A Traveler Disguised* has to be taken with a grain of salt. Taking cues from Svetlana Boym's reading of Russian formalist Yuri Tynyanov, Brenner argues that in the context of Yiddish literature (as is the case for Russian literature according to Tynyanov), a literary persona should not be described primarily in terms of the "impersonalization" of the authorial function in the text (along the lines of the structuralist critique of the notion of author), but rather as a process of "reverse expansion of literature into actual life" (Boym 1991, 23; Brenner 2008, 9). That is to say that the literary persona (or IA) of certain authors is "transferred" unto the FBP, for instance Sholem Aleichem (IA) into Solomon Naumovich Rabinovich (Brenner 2008, 1).

23 The notion of implied author is an application in the field of narratology of Aristotle's *ethos*, one of the three modes of persuasion (with *logos* and *pathos*), by which a speaker elicits support from the audience by convincing it of his expert knowledge and upstanding moral character. An *ethos* can be more or less compelling or expertly crafted, but one that would imply the insanity or powerlessness of the speaker amounts to a theoretical impossibility.

24 Daniela Mantovan mentions that the bear, a recurring figure in the work of Der Nister, is a common symbol for Russia (Mantovan 2014, 82); one might also mention that one of the most violent critics of Der Nister in *Prolit* was called *Ber* Orchanski (a first name that, in Yiddish like in English, is a homophone of "bear").

Der Nister's staging of the sacrifice of the author as a particularly gory form of "de-authorization" is very different from what Booth calls the "assassination attempts" against the notion of the author later carried out by Barthes and Foucault (Booth 2005, 75). Foucault, in the opening paragraphs of *Qu'est-ce qu'un auteur ?* (What is an Author?), describes the "death of the author" as a *fait accompli* of twentieth-century literature:[25]

> *L'écriture est maintenant liée au sacrifice, au sacrifice même de la vie ; effacement volontaire qui n'a pas à être représenté dans les livres, puisqu'il est accompli dans l'existence même de l'écrivain. L'œuvre qui avait le devoir d'apporter l'immortalité a reçu maintenant le droit de tuer, d'être meurtrière de son auteur.*
> (Foucault 1977, 117)

> [Writing is now linked to sacrifice and to the sacrifice of life itself; it is a voluntary obliteration of the self that does not require representation in books because it takes place in the everyday existence of the writer. Where a work had the duty of creating immortality, it now has the right to kill, to become the murderer of its author.]

In Foucault's description, this sacrifice remains an abstract, purely metaphorical operation.[26] Der Nister's unreliable author, if it obtains similar results in terms of a radical debunking of the notion of authorship, is the result of a process that is diametrically opposed to the one described by Foucault. If in Der Nister's work the sacrifice of the author *does* require representation, it is precisely because it is not a figure of speech, a metaphor, or a theoretical conceit, but rather an allusion to the all-too-real eventuality of the author (FBP) being put to death. *From my Estate* does not perform the impersonalization of literature, but rather expresses tragically urgent historical and personal concerns.

By a turn of historical irony not untypical of Soviet history, some of the most fervent zealots of a Yiddish "proletarian literature," including Abtshuk, Dunets, and Litvakov, were executed before Der Nister, in 1937–1938. A power vacuum ensued, during which the position of Der Nister in the Soviet literary world vastly improved: after the success of the first volume of *Di mishpokhe Mashber* (The Family Mashber) in 1939–1940, he became a member of the Jewish Anti-Fascist Committee, chaired by Solomon Mikhoels (Estraikh 2014, 19–20). However, this was only a brief respite: Der Nister was arrested in 1949 as part of Stalin's ferocious repression against Yiddish artists and intellectuals after WWII, leading up to the "night

---

[25] Foucault is alluding to Blanchot's idea of the disappearance of the author, itself strongly influenced by Bataille's definition of sacrifice as expenditure.
[26] In Foucault's view, through a kind of "technique of the self," writers such as Joyce or Kafka perform their complete self-obliteration in and through their own works in the name of the "impersonalization" of modern literature.

of the murdered poets" in 1952.²⁷ He died in the gulag of Mineralnyi on June 4, 1950 (Maggs 1996).²⁸

It is therefore no wonder that scenes of sham trials and executions abound in the work of Der Nister, from the 1923 short story *Gekept* (Beheaded) to the mob stoning of *A mayse mit a lets, mit a moyz, un mit dem Nister aleyn* (A Story with a Goblin, with a Mouse, and with Der Nister Himself, 1929). But one the most striking example is to be found in *Dray Mayselekh* (Three Tales), a collection of children's tales in verse published by Der Nister in 1934. As a book destined for children and published by a specialized press, it was probably not taken to be "serious literature" and did not appear to be suspicious to Soviet censors. However, the front page of the work, decorated with an ominous woodcut of a threatening bear clutching the name of Der Nister in his paws, seems to be a covert allusion to *From my Estate*. And, the first short story of the collection, entitled *Der toyt fun a khinezer* (Death of a Chinese), should probably never actually be read as a bed time story to any child. It tells the story of a resistance fighter printing pamphlets in his basement, being discovered by an agent from the secret police, and then taken to police headquarters, and shot in the head. An equally grim woodcut shows us the revolutionary printer being taken away at gunpoint (a perfectly realistic Mauser) by the secret police (Fig. 1).

At first glance, the story is an edifying tale of communist martyrdom: the resistance fighter in question is a Chinese communist insurgent, and the government the secret police takes orders from is probably the Guomindang, i.e. nationalist right-wing forces.²⁹ But the timing of its publication in 1934, as political repression, party purges, and summary executions increased dramatically in the aftermath of the expulsion of Zinoviev and Kamenev from the Communist party in 1932 – by a writer who had been barred from publishing works of fiction for five years – makes it hard to believe that the martyred Chinese printer would not represent yet another avatar of Der Nister as a murdered author.

---

27 Thirteen prominent Soviet Jewish writers and intellectuals (including five former members of the Jewish Anti-Fascist Committee), who had been arrested in 1948–1949, were summarily executed on August 12 1952, a dramatic event commonly referred to as the "Night of the Murdered Poets."
28 Der Nister's words to the agents who came to arrest him in February 1949, though possibly apocryphal, are nonetheless revelatory: "Thank God. You came at last. I have waited for you for so long" (Estraikh 2014, 22).
29 The violent crackdown of the Guomindang against the Chinese communist story was a popular topic at the time among international left-wing writers, most notably in André Malraux' 1933 novel, *Man's Fate* (*La condition humaine*).

Fig. 1: M. Fradkin and B. Blank, Book Illustration for Der Nister's *Death of a Chinese*. Woodcut. Kiev, Kinder farlag, 1934. Courtesy of the Yiddish Book Center (Amherst, MA, USA).

3 Der Nister as Failed Messiah?

Even a story as dark and gruesome as *From my Estate* might not be entirely devoid of hope. In *What Is an Author?*, Foucault mentions Scheherazade as a symbol of an earlier state of literature before the "murder" of the author, in which works of literature were perceived as ensuring the survival of their authors and even their immortality. Paradoxically, *From my Estate* could be put in both categories, as both the account of an execution and a tale of survival. Like Scheherazade, his ability to tell a captivating story allows Der Nister to perpetually delay his execution. The dual poles of hope and despair, disappearance and survival, constantly interact in the story, as indicated by the cultural associations evoked by the meaning of Der Nister's pen name. "Nister," a Yiddish word from the Hebrew "nistar," meaning "the hidden," is probably an allusion to the fact that Der Nister avoided being drafted into the Russian army by hiding under a false name (Bechtel 1990, 12). But it also conjures up the image of the *Nisterim*, also known as *Lamed-Vovnik*, the thirty-six hidden just men of the Eastern European Jewish tradition, one of which might be the Messiah himself. *Nisterim* never reveal their identity:

> The hidden just men belong to a higher order because they are not subject to the temptation of conceit that is virtually inseparable from public life. Some of them devote special effort to presenting their fellow men with an image of themselves that is in the starkest contrast to their real nature.
> (Scholem 1971, 255)

These religious connotations make the tale of the demise of Der Nister in *From my Estate* a highly ambiguous one. By posing as a madman, an author bereft of his sanity and even of his writing hand, Der Nister might merely be hinting at his dire fate in the Soviet Union. But, he might also be implying that a form of redemption could still be possible. Is this redemption seen as a real possibility, or as yet another lost illusion? Der Nister might claim for himself the prestige of one of the *Nisterim*, as a messianic figure hiding in plain sight, and especially in the most abject, desperate states (or even in martyrdom, thus mixing Hasidic tradition and Christian imagery of the Passion). But, he might also be expressing his disbelief in the notion of messianic redemption itself. In *A Story with a Goblin, with a Mouse, and with Der Nister Himself*, also published in *From my Estate*, Der Nister makes a grand Messianic entrance, riding a donkey into an unnamed city that might well be Jerusalem, but his efforts to bring about radical changes are invariably followed by terrible consequences. The notion of failed Messiah is a leitmotif in the work of Der Nister, from Adam's scornful mention of a crown of spines in *Gekept* (Beheaded, 1923) to the prophecy predicting the grim fate of the main character in *Under a Fence*. But other works of Der Nister, especially *Nay-Gayst* (New Spirit), the last short story of *From my Estate*, an uplifting vision of the reconstruction of the Temple, strike a more optimistic note. Conversely, the Messianic undertones of the author's pen name might also indicate a deep-seated pessimism, in which the failure of the messianic *Nister* would only aggravate the demise of the author. In this version, the messianic allusions would maintain the appearance of tradition only to better promote a form of absolute nihilism, along the lines of Walter Benjamin's characterization of the work of Kafka as the "sickness of tradition" (Benjamin 1969, 143). On the other hand, the structure of *Fun mayne giter* as a collection of short stories, from the gruesome visions of powerlessness and despair of the opening short story bearing the same title to the uplifting visions of *Nay-Gayst*, might indicate a progression, ultimately preserving the possibility of a messianic resolution in the face of adversity and despair.

Conclusion

Not unlike Schrödinger's cat, Der Nister's "unreliable author" in *Fun mayne giter* seems to possess the rare ability to be in two places at once. It announces the demise of the auctorial function, but also a martyrdom of messianic proportions, which seems to leave open the question of a possible salvation. It arouses suspicion concerning the coherence and artistic validity of the narrative, but can also be read as the particularly dramatic staging of an artistic "last will." This "unreliable author" is situated firmly within the European avant-garde, embracing the interest of Der Nister's contemporaries for the "art of the insane" and its specific ability to shock or disturb its audiences, and appropriating it as a means of political and social critique in the specific context of the changing fortunes of Soviet Yiddish culture during the "Year of the Great Turn." But it also appears to be outside of the realm of the European avant-garde, either behind the times, by maintaining a dialogue with such literary forms as the folk tale or the religious parable; or ahead of its time, by staging a radical form of "de-authorization" that could be placed within the anachronistic context of the postmodern "death of the author." Some of these ambiguities probably cannot be dispelled, for instance the possibility of a messianic redemption or the nature of the reaction that Der Nister's apparent questioning of his own auctorial legitimacy was intended to elicit in his readers. Some others, especially pertaining to chronological discontinuities and narratological aporia, might indicate that one of the merits of *Fun mayne giter* is precisely to challenge or force us to redefine accepted categories, for instance by opening up the notion of "implied author," who might not automatically be a rhetorical "better self," or by providing us with an example of radical experimental writing that seems to fit the social and aesthetic definition of the avant-garde, while only partly corresponding to its "Eurochronological" extension. As Eurocentric approaches to the avant-garde are increasingly challenged, the conceptual displacements brought about by the study of such a rich narrative of political marginalization and symbolic disorientation seem to be particularly timely.

Bibliography

Bechtel, Delphine. *Der Nister's Work 1907–1929: A Study of a Yiddish Symbolist*. Berne: Peter Lang, 1990.
Bechtel, Delphine. "Entre tradition juive et modernité révolutionnaire: Le combat de Der Nister contre la critique littéraire soviétique." Der *Nister: Contes fantastiques et symboliques*. Ed. Delphine Bechtel. Paris: Cerf, 1997. 7–52.
Benjamin, Walter. "Books by the Mentally Ill: From my Collection." *Selected Writings Vol. 2, 1927–1934*. Ed. Michael W. Jennings, Howard Eiland, and Gary Smith. Cambridge, MA: The Belknap Press of Harvard University Press, 1999 [1928]. 123–130.
Benjamin, Walter. "Some Reflections on Kafka." *Illuminations*. Trans. Harry Zohn. New York: Schocken Books, 1969. 141–146.
Boehlich, Sabine. *"Nay-gayst": mystische Traditionen in einer symbolischen Erzählung des Jiddischen Autors "Der Nister" (Pinkhas Kahanovitsh)* ["Nay-gayst": Mystical Tradition in a Symbolist Short Story by the Yiddish Author "Der Nister" (Pinkhas Kahanovitsh)]. Wiesbaden: Harrassowitz, 2008.

Booth, Wayne C. "Resurrection of the Implied Author: Why Bother?" *A Companion to Narrative Theory*. Ed. James Phelan and Peter J. Rabinowitz. Malden, MA: Blackwell Publising, 2005. 75–88.

Boym, Svetlana. *Death in Quotation Marks: Cultural Myths of the Modern Poet*. Cambridge, MA: Harvard University Press, 1991.

Brenner, Naomi Rebecca. *Authorial Fictions: Literary and Public Personae in Modern Hebrew and Yiddish Literature*. Ann Arbor: UMI Dissertations Publishing, 2008.

Caplan, Marc. "Performance Anxieties: Carnival Spaces and Assemblages in Der Nister's *Under a Fence*." *Prooftexts* 18.1 (1998): 1–18.

Caplan, Marc. "Watch the Throne: Allegory, Kinship, and Trauerspiel in the Stories of Der Nister and Reb Nakhman." *Uncovering the Hidden: The Works and Life of Der Nister*. Ed. Gennady Estraikh, Kerstin Hoge, and Mikhail Krutikov. London: Legenda, 2014. 90–110.

Estraikh, Gennady. *In Harness: Yiddish Writers' Romance with Communism*. Syracuse, NY: Syracuse University Press, 2005.

Estraikh, Gennady. "The Stalinist 'Great Break' in Yiddishland." *1929: Mapping the Jewish World*. Ed. Hasia R. Diner and Gennady Estraikh. New York: New York University Press, 2013. 43–59.

Estraikh, Gennady. "Der Nister's 'Hamburg Score'." *Uncovering the Hidden: The Works and Life of Der Nister*. Ed. Gennady Estraikh, Kerstin Hoge, and Mikhail Krutikov. London: Legenda, 2014. 7–26.

Foster, Hal. "Blinded Insights: On the Modernist Reception of the Art of the Mentally Ill." *October 97* (Summer 2001): 3–30.

Foucault, Michel. "What is an Author?" *Language, Counter-Memory, Practice: Selected Essays and Interviews*. Ed. Donald F. Bouchard. Ithaca, NY: Cornell University Press, 1977.

Horn, Dara. "Der Nister's Symbolist Stories: Adventures in Yiddish Storytelling and their Consequences." *Choosing Yiddish: New Frontiers of Language and Culture*. Ed. Lara Rabinovitch, Shiri Goren, and Hannah S. Pressman. Detroit: Wayne University Press, 2013. 15–28.

Frieden, Ken. "I. L. Peretz: Monologue and Madness in the Early Stories." *Classic Yiddish Fiction: Abramovitsh, Sholem Aleichem, and Peretz*. Albany, NY: State University of New York Press, 1995. 259–280.

Hoge, Kerstin. "*Andersens Mayselekh* and Der Nister's Symbolist Agenda." *Uncovering the Hidden: The Works and Life of Der Nister*. Ed. Gennady Estraikh, Kerstin Hoge, and Mikhail Krutikov. London: Legenda, 2014. 41–54.

Kofsi. "Parodyes, epigramen, sharzn. Fun mayne shmates (loyt dem Nister): A mayse mit a vants, mit a floy, mit a gets Bim-Bom un mit dem Nister aleyn" ["Parodies, Epigrams, Jokes. From my Rags (à la Der Nister): A Story with a Louse, a Flea, the Idol Bim-Bom, and Der Nister Himself"]. *Prolit* (October 1929), Kharkov: Farlag "Proletari", Alukrainishe Asotsyatsye Proletarishe Shrayber ["Proletari" Editions, Pan-Ukrainian Association of Proletarian Writers], 118–121.

Krutikov, Mikhail. "Desire, Destiny, and Death: Fantasy and Reality in Soviet Yiddish Literature around 1929." *1929: Mapping the Jewish World*. Ed. Hasia R. Diner and Gennady Estraikh. New York: New York University Press, 2013. 224–241.

Krutikov, Mikhail. "'Turning My Soul Inside Out': Text and Context of The Family Mashber." *Uncovering the Hidden: The Works and Life of Der Nister*. Ed. Gennady Estraikh, Kerstin Hoge, and Mikhail Krutikov. London: Legenda, 2014. 111–144.

MacGregor, John. *The Discovery of the Art of the Insane*. Princeton, NJ: Princeton University Press, 1989.

Maggs, Peter B. *The Mandelstam and "Der Nister" Files: An Introduction to Stalin-Era Prison and Labor Camp Records*. Armonk, NY: M.E. Sharpe, 1996.
Mantovan, Daniela. "The 'Political' Writings of an 'Unpolitical' Yiddish Symbolist." *Uncovering the Hidden: The Works and Life of Der Nister*. Ed. Gennady Estraikh, Kerstin Hoge, and Mikhail Krutikov. London: Legenda, 2014. 73–89.
Nister, Der. *Fun mayne giter* [From my Estate]. Kharkov: Melukhe-farlag fun Ukrayne, 1929.
Nister, Der. "Der toyt fun a khinezer" ["Death of a Chinese"]. *Dray Mayselekh* [Three Tales]. Kiev: Kinder farlag, 1934.
Norich, Anita. "Writing on the Edge." *Choosing Yiddish: New Frontiers of Language and Culture*. Ed. Lara Rabinovitch, Shiri Goren, and Hannah S. Pressman. Detroit: Wayne University Press, 2013. 11–14.
Oyerbakh, Efraim, Yitskhok Kharlash, and Moyshe Shtarkman (eds.). "Der Nister." *Leksikon fun der nayer yidisher literatur* [Biographical Dictionary of Modern Yiddish Literature] Vol. 6. New York: Congress for Jewish Culture, 1965. 255–262.
Roskies, David. "The Storyteller as High Priest." *A Bridge of Longing: The Lost Art of Yiddish Storytelling*. Cambridge, MA: Harvard University Press, 1996. 191–229.
Scholem, Gershom. "The Tradition of the Thirty-Six Hidden Just Men." *The Messianic Idea in Judaism and Other Essays on Jewish Spirituality*. New York: Schocken, 1971. 253–256.
Schwarz, Jan. *Imagining Lives: Autobiographical Fiction of Yiddish Writers*. Madison, WI: University of Wisconsin Press, 2005.
Shmeruk, Khone. "Der Nister's *Under a Fence*: Tribulations of a Soviet Yiddish Symbolist." *The Field of Yiddish*. Second collection. Ed. Uriel Weinreich. The Hague: Mouton & Co., 1965. 265–286.
Shneer, David. *Yiddish and the Creation of Soviet Jewish Culture*, 1918–1930. Cambridge, UK: Cambridge University Press, 2004.
Sparshott, Francis. "The Case of the Unreliable Author." *Philosophy and Literature* 10.2 (October 1986): 147–167.
Zaritt, Saul. "'The World Awaits Your Yiddish Word': Jacob Glatstein and the Problem of World Literature." *Studies in American Jewish Literature* 34.2 (2015): 175–203.

Olivier Salazar-Ferrer
The Role of Judaism in Benjamin Fondane's Existential Philosophy

In the early decades of the twentieth century, the Romanian avant-garde included numerous leading Jewish artists, for example Benjamin Fondane (Benjamin Wechsler), Tristan Tzara (Samuel Rosenstock), Claude Sernet (Ernest Spirt), Ilarie Voronca (Eduard Marcus), Victor Brauner, Marcel Jancu, M.H. Maxy, Grégoire Michonze, Jules Perahim (Jules Blumenfeld), Paul Păun, and Max Blecher. Among them, Benjamin Fondane (1898–1944) played a privileged role in illustrating the confrontation between the *tabula rasa* of history and the fidelity to tradition, a confrontation which leads to a new understanding of Judaism.

Born in Iași, Fondane was the son of Isaac Wechsler, a minor tradesman from Hertsa (Bucovina), and Adela Schwarzfeld, the sister of three famous Jewish scholars: Elias (1855–1915), an historian, politician, and novelist forced into exile to France by the Romanian government in 1885; Wilhelm (1856–1894), an historian of the Romanian Jewish community; and Moses Schwarzfeld (1857–1943), who established several journals about the history, folklore, and literature of the Romanian Jews.

According to Oisteanu, the Schwarzfeld family was amenable to a post-Mendelssohnian assimilation of the Jewish community (Oisteanu 1999–2000, 181), and open to dialogue between the German Enlightenment and Judaism. Fondane's first name derives from his paternal grandfather, Benjamin Schwarzfeld (1820–1897), an educator and writer who in 1853 opened the first modern, Haskalah-based Jewish elementary school in Iași, against opposition from the conservative party among the Romanian Jews, and who was excommunicated (*The Jewish Encyclopaedia*, 1906, article on Benjamin Schwarzfeld).

Eric Freedman's bibliography (Freedman 2009) shows that, during his early period of literary activity, Fondane adopted many pseudonyms (including Alex Vilara, Ofir, Ha-shir, and Benjamin), but that his definitive Romanian pseudonym, "Fundoianu," was created from the name of his grandfather's estate, Fundoia, situated twelve miles Southwest of the small town of Hertsa (situated in what is now Ukraine). After his arrival in France in 1923, the poet adopted "Fondane" as his pen name. However, his final pseudonym would be "Isaac Laquedem," which he adopted during the German occupation, when he signed the poem "Journées de Juin" ("Days in June") in *L'Honneur des poètes – Europe II* (The Honour of Poets – Europe II, 1944), edited by Paul Eluard and published by the Éditions de Minuit.

The evolution of his pseudonyms was not just a consequence of the necessity of joining the underground during the Occupation; it also reflects the formation of a complex identity from a geographic territory to an indefinite migration, even if Fondane chose to settle in France, his elective "fatherland." His long poem *L'Exode. Super Flumina Babylonis* (Exodus. Super Flumina Babylonis, 1965) shows the interweaving between his French integration (he was naturalized and a soldier in the French army in 1940) and his Jewish cultural filiation. The publication in 2009 of an anthology of Fondane's texts on Judaism, *Benjamin Fondane à la recherche du Judaïsme* (Benjamin Fondane and the Quest for Judaism, 2009), edited by Monique Jutrin, provides a source of essential references to reevaluate Fondane's philosophical understanding of the mission of Judaism. The young poet's early quest of identity would move toward a conception of Judaism conceived as a permanent revolt against necessity and finiteness.

The Quest for Judaism

In this essay, I examine the conception of Judaism in Fondane's existential philosophy as a different area of study from the Jewish topics in his poetry which I have analyzed elsewhere (Salazar-Ferrer 2004, 2005, 2007). Before leaving Romania in December 1923, Fondane's works included numerous literary articles, some translations in Romanian of Yiddish poets (Bialik, Rosenfeld, Groper), and many poems in Jewish journals such as *Lumea Evreie*, *Mîntuirea*, *Hatikvah*, *Hasmonaea*, and *Bar-Kochba*. He personally knew the poets Jacob Groper (who represented for the young poet a source of spiritual inspiration) and Steuerman-Rodion; he worked for A.L. Zissu, editor of the Zionist journal *Mântuirea*, yet took a critical position on the question of Zionism, primarily in a series of articles published in *Mântuirea* in 1919. He declared that if *"Le sionisme n'est qu'une finalité politique. Le Judaïsme* [est] *une finalité vitale"* [Zionism is only a political objective, Judaism is a vital purpose] (Fondane 2009b, 43).[1]

---

[1] On one hand, this expression of "vital purpose" reflects his reading of Jules de Gaultier's *De Kant à Nietzsche* (From Kant to Nietzsche) Mercure de France, 1900, particularly the first chapter ("Vital instinct, Plato, Judaism"), in which De Gaultier declares that "Jewish people in a sense appear as the champions of the vital instinct" (54). Commenting on this book in 1919, Fondane remarked: "Jules de Gaultier found that Judaism represents the vital instinct from an historical perspective" (Fondane 2009g, 129). On the other hand, in a series of articles published the same year in *Mântuirea*, Fondane analyzes in sociological terms the anti-Semitic discourses in the Romanian press and offers reflections on the Zionist movement, adopting a critical distance and a

In 1919, Fondane's journalistic work for *Mântuirea* included eleven articles under the heading *Judaism and Hellenism* (Fondane 2009f, 196–126), in which he discussed the opposition between Hellenism and Judaism, examining the role of Jewish mysticism, Kabbalah, and Hassidism. However, we have no real statement about the specificity of Jewish thought, but rather a research work in this heterogeneous compilation of data, prompted by Martin Buber's reading in *Vom Geist der Judentum* (On Judaism, 1916). In the chapter "Jewish religiosity," Buber analyzes the concept of the realization of God through man, particularly in the *Zohar*: "Whether God is transcendent or immanent does not depend on Him, it depends on man" (Buber 1989, 86). Buber develops the idea that Jewish religiosity is based neither on doctrine nor on ethical prescription; Judaism implies a struggle between the prophet and the priest that "everyone, alone and from his own depth, must strive for divine freedom and unconditionality" (Buber 1989, 83). Even if Fondane's comments are related mostly to the first chapter, it is notable that in the chapter devoted to myth in Judaism, Buber rehabilitates the corporeity of the religious myth in a struggle, which opposes a mythical-monotheistic folk religion and the "intellectual structure of a rational-monotheistic rabbinic religion" (Buber 1989, 99). Buber's advocacy in favour of Jewish myth, quoting Isaac Luria and Baal Shem, may have had an influence on Fondane's late works, which bear witness to the rehabilitation of mythical thought in existential philosophy. In *La Conscience malheureuse* (The Unhappy Consciousness, 1936), for instance, Fondane takes up the stance of the Russian émigré philosopher Lev Shestov, who emphasized the opposition between Athens and Jerusalem, between reason and revelation, in a tragic attempt to save the individual from the oppression of rationalism and to liberate a God for whom everything is possible, beyond the laws of nature, logic, and morality.

A brief examination of Eric Freedman's bibliography of Fondane's works (Freedman 2009) demonstrates the importance of the Jewish imaginary and intertextuality in Fondane's poems between 1914 and 1923. More precisely, the stylistic form of the psalms offers a recurrent prosodic template for writing a series of poems whose narrative voice is addressing the Lord. This series, which is probably independent of Theodor Arghezi's famous Psalms (*Cuvinte potrivite*, 1927), includes "Adam's Psalm," "Abel's Psalm," "David's Psalm," "Shulamite's Psalm," and "The Leper's Psalm."

However, we cannot understand the multicultural formation of the young Fundoianu's identity without highlighting his fascination with French literature.

---

sharp skepticism in relation to Socialist Zionism, following Otto Warburg's article published in *Mântuirea* (I, 1919, n. 262 and 269, November 12 and 19).

His volume of essays, *Imagini și cărți din Franța* (Pictures and Books from France, 1921), devoted to Baudelaire, Gide, Maeterlinck, Francis James, Proust, Claudel, Mallarmé, Verhaeren, and Remy de Gourmont, is the best example of his exceptional perceptiveness. At this point, we are still far from the avant-garde literature; Fondane is keen to clarify the legacy of symbolism and the role of André Gide in reinventing a new classicism. However, it is impossible to neglect the dark and gloomy atmosphere in his family after the First World War: for example, his father, Isaac, died in 1917, a victim of the typhus in Iași, and Fondane, as a law student in Iași, had to cope with the *numerus closus* limiting the number of Jewish students at the university. Soon after, threats of another anti-Semitic campaign forced the young poet to close his experimental theatre company, *Insula*, which he had founded in Bucharest, drawing inspiration from Jacques Copeau and Gordon Craig.

Between 1915 and 1923, he wrote articles about the suicide of the Jewish poet Avram Steuerman-Rodion, on his uncle Elias Schwarzfeld, and about the Jewish cemetery of Iași, where his father is buried. Other articles, on Shalom Alechem and on Heine's Hebraic melodies, demonstrate the continuity of Fondane's reflections on Jewish culture. In 1919, in his article "Paroles à propos d'un ami" (A Few Words about a Friend), he declares about Jacob Groper:

> *C'était à l'époque où je cherchais ma voie, surpris de ne découvrir derrière moi aucun passé; de par mon tempérament, je recherchais une tradition [...] J'avais besoin d'un père, d'une tradition, d'une hérédité.*
> (Fondane 2009b, 43)

> [At this time, I was looking for my way, considering with surprise the absence of the past behind me; in keeping with my character, I was looking for a tradition. I needed a father, a tradition, and an inheritance.]

However, the same year, some of his articles – on the translation of the Bible and on *The Song of Songs* – adopt a sharp, Voltairean irony about the fictional component of the Old Testament (Fondane 2009b, 2009c). Moreover, he was not observant and was far from any religious dogmatism. In June 1920, he wrote: "*La Bible en tant que texte littéraire, éveillait ma curiosité, non ma foi*" [The Bible, as a literary text, aroused my curiosity. Not my faith.] (Fondane 2009c, 53). Moreover, his comparison between the *Odyssey* and the Bible includes ironic comments about the latter: "*Pourtant entre tous les livres de l'Antiquité, c'est la Bible qui a joué un rôle providentiel. On sait comment aux yeux des Juifs, elle passa pour un livre divin, miraculeusement révélé. On sait qu'à cette première falsification s'est ajoutée une autre, et ainsi fut vaincu l'univers*" [Among all books produced by Antiquity, the *Bible* has had a providential role. We know that for Jews considered it a divine book, miraculously revealed. After this first falsification, another one was produced. Then, the universe was defeated.] (Fondane 2009c, 53). About the Biblical Jehovah, he declares, in "The Translation of the Bible," published the same year:

> Quelle imagination de lettré dément a pu l'inventer? Hystérique de solitude, effrayé par son ombre, il est sanguinaire parce que craintif et maniaque. Individualiste à l'excès, il est aussi obsédé par une seule angoisse: on pourrait le confondre avec les autres dieux logés comme chacun le sait dans les fontaines, les arbres les pierres.
> (Fondane 2009, 53)

> [What mad imagination of a scholar could have invented this? Hysterical with loneliness, afraid of his own shadow, he is bloodthirsty because he is fearful and maniac. Excessively individualistic, he is also obsessed with one single idea: that he could be confused with the other gods who, as we all know, have found their abode in the fountains, the trees, and the stones.]

From 1919 to 1923, Fondane wrote *Privelişti* (Landscapes), a series of poems published in Romanian in 1930. The main topic of these poems is the country life of the traditional shtetl, where the powerful materiality of elements, animal life, and the cycles of the seasons predominant. However, we are far from the melancholic universe of Bacovia or Francis James. A secret irony and a latent catastrophism subvert the lyrical sensitivity and the harmonious relationship between man and nature. Between the exile and the tradition of the Yiddish community, the poet perceives nature as an invisible and terrifying force. The world of *Privelişti* is closed. The deep anxiety and a feeling of absurdity in front of the blind vitality of nature prevent all contemplation and peace. The climate of these poems is rather expressionist, and the opening poem, "Parade," is full of a violent Rimbaldian revolt shattering the immobility of the landscapes:

> Peut-être me suis-je trompé, Seigneur, te chantant la nature
> paisible et pure comme dans le paradis ancien;
> j'avais en moi la force, le changement, la soif, la haine.
> (Fondane 1996, 27)

> [So perhaps, I was wrong, oh Lord, to sing
> peaceful and pure nature as in the ancient paradise
> I had felt in me the power, the change, the thirst, the hatred.]

If the injunction is addressed to the Lord, the poem's apocalyptic tone and the call for a complete renewal are in line with the violent, avant-garde call for a *tabula rasa*. At the same time, a stylistic turn from 1925 to 1930 shows a clear adoption of avant-gardist audacity which draws in new myths, modernist visions, metaphors, and images, echoing the poetic worlds of Baudelaire, Rimbaud, and Apollinaire.

From the Avant-Garde to Existential Thought

The complexity of the question of Jewish filiation was increased by Fondane's links with the Romanian avant-garde, which encouraged a rejection of established traditions. Despite his close ties with the iconoclastic generation of young Jewish writers in Bucharest, including F. Brunea-Fox, Ion Călugăru, Claude Sernet-Cosma, Ilarie Voronca, Tzara, and Brauner, Fondane left Romania in December 1923, when the Romanian avant-garde was just starting. Ion Vinea's Activist Manifesto was published shortly thereafter, in May 1924, in *Comtimporanul*. Several specialists, such as Mircea Martin, Ion Pop (Pop 1999–2000), and Petre Raileanu, consider the Romanian poetry of Fondoianu as not actually avant-gardist, and certainly not dadaist, even if his poetical form includes several stylistic aspects of European modernism. His introduction to an anthology of French poems, "Le Grand ballet de la poésie française" (The Big Show of French Poetry, *Integral* 13–14), in June 1927 follows the main directions of Ion Vinea's avant-gardist manifesto (Pop 2006, 114–115), if we include a particular "catastrophism" which is the original trademark of Fondane's poetry.

From "Parade" to the long poems *Ulysse* (Ulysses, 1933), *Titanic* (1937), and *Le Mal des fantômes* (The Suffering of Ghosts, 1944), there is an obsession with the figure of wreckage, drowning, apocalyptic crisis (in which the narrator challenges the limits of human condition), the absence of meaning, the collapse of the author's certitudes, his solitude, and the impossibility of peace. This fluid universe will become the universe of exile and migration, open to the perpetual journey of the Jewish migrants who are "climbing up the night until the end of the world" [ne cessent d'escalader la nuit jusqu'à la fin du monde] (*Ulysse*, Fondane 2006, 31). In this poetic universe, the subjectivity explodes in a battle of forces and intensities, dealing with the Jewish memory of the narrator: "Juif, naturellement, tu étais juif, Ulysse" [Jewish, of course, you were Jewish, Ulysses] (Fondane 2006, 20) and the evocation of the whirlwind of the cities of the world.

> *Le monde s'ouvre en nous par la vue des navires*
> *qui partent – comme ils partent leur chevelure au vent*
> *qui rentrent – comme ils rentrent, vieillis et décrépits,*
> *dans le bal des lumières,*
> *dans la fête d'adieu des ports, pareils à des infirmes*
> *assis, pendant qu'on danse!*
>
> *Le monde s'ouvre en nous par des matins immenses*
> *(en ai-je vu briller aux cils de l'océan!)*
> *par des fées enfermées*
> *dans le noyau des fruits où les enfants ont peur,*

par des tapis jetés sous les pieds de la Reine
(comme elle avance calme dans le pays des palmes)
par des chansons de nègres sur le Mississipi
(ont-ils été aussi chassés du Paradis?)
et tout à coup par des pays de cheminées,
des asiles de nuit
où s'écoulent les eaux verdâtres de l'humain
en ai-je vu? et par des tripots clandestins,
des Parques de l'ennui
qui tricotent des bas de laine pour les morts.
(Fondane 2006, 22)

[The world opens up in us with the sight of ships
departing – as they put to sea with their hair blown back;
returning – as they re-enter, aged and decrepit,
the brightly lit ballroom
for the port's leaving-party, just like the lame do,
sitting out while the rest of us dance!

The world opens up in us with majestic mornings
(I've seen them shine on the ocean's eyelashes)
with fairies imprisoned
in the stones of fruit where children are afraid,
with carpets flung under the feet of a queen
(she walks on calmly through a land of palm trees),
with the songs of negroes along the Mississippi
(were they too driven from Paradise?)
and suddenly, with a land of smokestacks
and night-shelters,
where the greenish waters of humanity flow
(have I seen them?) and with black-market dive-bars,
the Fates of ennui
who knit woollen stockings for the dead.]
(translation by A. Rubens and H. King)

In fact, his poems represent a synthesis between symbolist, modernist, and expressionist elements which do not amount to a complete breakdown of grammatical language. However, having joined the ranks of the avant-garde, Fondane was keen to continue along this path after his exile to Paris in 1923. He was co-editor of *Integral* in Paris with Mathis Teusch and Voronca. He interviewed Tzara and Jean Cocteau and published articles on Aragon, Eluard, Delteil, Le Corbusier, Chagall, and Brancusi, reacting strongly against André Breton's theoretical and political positions. Refusing the suicide of dadaism and the "fraud" of surrealism, he was looking for a new "*porte de secours*" (way out).

Je traverse pieds nus la crise morale de ce siècle, je me cogne au suicide prêché par un mouvement artistique qui m'est proche, je m'efforce de conserver à l'Art une portée qu'on lui refuse de plus en plus.
(Letter from Fondane to Chestov, January 17 1927, Fondane 1982, 175)

[I am walking barefoot across the moral wasteland of this century, struggling with the suicide proclaimed by an artistic movement [dadaism] to which I feel close. I strive to preserve a meaning to Art when meaning is what Art is more and more denied.]

On one hand, literature seemed doomed to failure from the viewpoint of dada's radical negativism, as defined by Tzara in his *Seven Dada Manifestos*, being a movement which produces only nothingness, based exclusively on the Cartesian doubt (Fondane 1999b, 40). On the other hand, from 1927 to 1932, Fondane could not accept the surrealist movement based on the technique of automatic writing and the exploration of the Freudian subconscious through dreams. He developed a series of scathing criticisms against the theoretical position of surrealism, which amounted to the artificial rationalization of the irrational. Simultaneously, he dismissed the political ambiguity of André Breton's positions towards the revolutionary leitmotiv of the Communist party. The most relevant articles in this respect are "Les Surréalistes et la révolution" (The Surrealists and Revolution, *Integral* 12, April 1927) and a "Lettre au groupe surréaliste" (Letter to the Surrealist Group) (February 1, 1932), the latter concerning the so-called *Aragon Affair*, following publication of Aragon's poem "Front Rouge" (1931), in which he provocatively called upon workers to open fire on their enemies.[2]

However, even if it is impossible to reduce the singularity of Fondane's works to a schematic description of literary movements or manifestos, the stylistic influence of the avant-garde is obvious in his articles mainly from 1927 to 1930; these articles integrate the freedom of metaphors resulting from the stylistic influences of the surrealism and the avant-gardist constellation:

---

[2] During his stay in Russia, Louis Aragon had written a violent revolutionary poem, *Front rouge*, published in France in November 1931 in a communist journal, *Littérature de la révolution mondiale*. The authorities took the case quite seriously, seizing the journal in January 1932 and charging the poet for urging military disobedience and inciting murder. When the mainstream surrealist group tried to deny that Aragon's poem had any real political implications and started a petition in order to save the poet from public prosecution, Fondane refused to sign it and explained his position in an open letter (dated February 1 1932, and addressed to the surrealist group), in which he exposed the contradictions of surrealism and the ambiguities of its political positions.

Nous sommes venus pour accélérer la contradiction qui ronge le siècle. Nous sommes son cancer. Si à d'autres époques ce fut par la poésie qu'on prit conscience de la force vive d'un temps, c'est par la poésie que l'aujourd'hui est amené à considérer en face sa déraison. Ce n'est plus le phare en mer désignant le port en chocolat, le refuge en papier peint, c'est le cri S.O.S. du naufrage pur.
(Fondane 1999a, 54)

[We have come to deepen the contradiction that corrodes the century. We are its cancer. If, in the past, it was poetry which gave the measure of the vitality of an age, it is also poetry which nowadays confronts us with irrationality. This is no longer the lighthouse at sea which points out the chocolate harbor, the wallpaper refuge, but the S.O.S. signal of a pure shipwreck.]

In "Mots sauvages" (Wild Words), his introduction to *Priveliști*, and in two unpublished manuscripts, namely, the "Signification de Dada" (Meaning of Dada) (1928) and "De Dada au Surréalisme ou de l'idiotie pure au suicide" (From Dada to Surrealism or from Pure Idiocy to Suicide), he explores the deep crisis affecting the relationship between poetry and reality, a crisis which would modify his conception of cinema.

It is fascinating to explore this crisis and see how Fondane would find a new and original response in the adoption of Shestov's philosophy. Following Paul Valéry's metaphor of the shipwreck of civilization in his famous article "La crise de l'esprit" (The Crisis of the Mind), published in August 1919 in La *Nouvelle Revue Française,* Fondane quickly identified the Shestovian struggle against self-evidence with the crisis of reality denounced by the dadaist revolt. The main criteria of dada for Fondane is an unsuitability of the concepts of will and reason. The Cartesian *cogito* explodes to the benefit of an affective substrate, filled with intensities, which constitutes the only possible ground. In fact, the metaphor of the wreckage of classical humanism, discredited by the atrocities of the First World War, would become the central topic of his poetry (*Ulysses* (1933), *Titanic* (1937)), and the topic of catastrophe would constitute an invariant in *Exodus. Super Flumina Babylonis* (1965) and in *Baudelaire et l'expérience du gouffre* (Baudelaire and The Experience of the Abyss) (1947). Catastrophic thought is not only a source of poetic images and metaphors; it is a subversive topic able to invalidate rationalist concepts. In his final essays, Fondane seeks new access to reality through a direct "participation." Reversing the colonialist hierarchy between civilization and primitivism, based on Lévy-Bruhl's ethnological writings on the primitive mentality, he suggests that poetry can afford new access to lost reality (Salazar-Ferrer 2008, 164–169).

Following Shestov's writings, Fondane claimed that the discontinuity, the exceptional character, the singularity, the absurdity, or the irrationality of the event were dissolving the legacy of gnoseology from Aristotle to Husserl, according to the main line of argument in *La Conscience malheureuse* (The Unhappy Consciousness) (Fondane 2013). In particular, this book includes an essay published in 1929 in which Fondane elaborates a scathing criticism of Husserl's transcendental phenomenology: in "Edmund Husserl et l'œuf de Colomb du réel" (Edmund Husserl and the Columbus Egg of Reality, *Europe* 78 (June 15, 1929): 331–344), Fondane denies the validity of the phenomenological reduction which presupposes an identity between consciousness and reflection and the theory of self-evident truth (Fondane 2013, 128–130). This attempt to rehabilitate the irrational aspect of reality given through subjective experience aimed to reassess the possibility of religious thinking and the possibility of miracle.

In his essay on the art of Brancusi published in 1928, Fondane insists on the impossibility to reduce Brancusi's works to analytical thought; they are, rather, "*événements purs*" [pure events] and "exceptions" (Fondane 1995, 27). He also emphasizes the impossibility of situating them in the history of art, rejecting the Hegelian discourse on the spirit of the age (Fondane 1995, 29–31). This negation of History in the context of the avant-garde converges with the negation of the Hegelian concept of Reason in History ("*Die Vernunft in der Geschichte*"), that, after the traumatism of the First World War, was to re-surface in Fondane's work, within a Shestovian theoretical framework, most notably in his last writing, *Le Lundi existentiel ou le dimanche de l'histoire* (The Existential Monday and the Sunday of History) (1945).

The second convergence between the avant-garde and existential thought relates to the crisis of language. To the fore of a deep epistemological and ontological crisis of language which can be compared to Hermann Broch's reflection on the crisis of meaning in his article "Life Without any Platonic Idea" (Broch 1968, 321–325), Fondane considers cinematic language, following the example of René Clair's *Entr'acte* (1924), as a new access to the irrational. The silent cinema is overcoming the linguistic structure of representation and appears as a new access to reality, without the oppression of the cultural past and the social and moral codifications limiting consciousness. In 1933, in the magazine *Cahiers Jaunes* (Yellow books), he expresses the ambition of creating "*un film absurde, sur une chose absurde, pour satisfaire à mon goût absurde de liberté*" [an absurd film about something absurd, to satisfy [his] absurd taste for freedom] (Fondane 2007, 116). The most important attempt to overcome the logical structure of language appears in his *Trois scenarii – Cine-poems* (1928) which transfer the technique of screenwriting to the writing of poetry, using discontinuity and visualization. This hybridization of forms presupposes both active reception by the reader and instantaneous consumption of the image (Salazar-Ferrer and Fotiade 2012, 256). The publication, which includes two photographs by Man Ray, refers to Georges Ribemont-

Dessaignes, Arp, and Picabia, aiming to create a new *"lyrisme objectif"* [objective lyricism] produced by a rapid succession of images and metamorphoses, inspired by the plots of silent films and burlesque cinema.

According to Ramona Fotiade, the influence of Shestov's philosophy is already present in the conception of the *Trois scenarii-Cine-poems* (Salazar-Ferrer and Fotiade 2012, 258) and in his correspondence with Antonin Artaud on the new possibilities of art. In his critical writings on cinema, Fondane argues for the need to dissociate cinema from the psychological plots of drama, so as to create a *"poème cinématographique"* [cinematic poem], as illustrated by the avant-garde films of René Clair, Man Ray, Buñuel, Germaine Dulac, and Artaud. As an ambassador of the European avant-garde films in South America (where, in 1929, he was invited to present a range of recent productions, such as Clair's *Entr'acte*, Man Ray's *The Star of the Sea*, Dulac's *The Seashell and the Clergyman*, and Bunuel's *The Andalusian Dog*), Fondane developed his own conception of "pure cinema," which should reveal a tragic, burlesque, and violent reality providing a liberation from social and cultural norms. Rejecting the abstract experiments of Hans Richter and Walter Rutman, he writes:

> Mais le véritable chemin de la recherche exige de ne pas abandonner complètement l'homme, mais de briser ses systèmes de relations, ses jugements sur l'espace, le temps, la loi, la nécessité, pour explorer à travers lui le sens de la vie, de cette vie, dont chacun des actes possède quelque chose de miraculeux et de désordonné.
> (B. Fondane, "Le poème cinématographique," Salazar-Ferrer and Fotiade 2012, 270)

[However, the true direction of research is not altogether abandoning the human representation, but breaking its systems of relationships, its conception of space, time, law, necessity, in order to explore the meaning of life, of our life, whose every act reveals something miraculous and anarchic.]

Here again, we observe a convergence between the Shestovian revolt against rationality and the new possibilities provided by the avant-garde experiments.

Toward a Shestovian Interpretation of Judaism

Inevitably, this fusion of the avant-gardist revolt and Shestovian existential thought would modify Fondane's understanding and perception of Judaism. In 1934 he published a short article, "Marc Chagall," in *Les Cahiers Juifs* (Fondane 2011, 31–38). Chagall's main topic, Fondane explains, is neither the Hebrew paradise nor the Christian paradise. Instead, it is the lost Yiddish paradise,

> [...] *à la fois très tendre et douloureux, fervent et très cocasse, un paradis de misère, d'ail et de pogroms, un paradis de brocante où l'on prie encore un Dieu très ancien, un Dieu de marché aux puces.*
> (Fondane 2011, 37)

> [tender, painful, fervent and comical, a paradise of misery, garlic, and pogroms, a paradise of antiquities where man worships a very old God, a God of the second-hand market.]

Fondane compares this paradise to the paradise of Hassidim from Poland and Hungary, and Chagall's works to Yiddish writers such as I.L. Peretz (1852–1915), Sholem Aleichem (1859–1916), and Mendele Mocher Sforim (1836–1917). However, this magic universe is not Fondane's: he declares that "*Le paradis n'est pas mon lot sur la terre*" [Paradise is not my lot on earth] (Fondane 2011, 37). This is true, for Fondane's poetical world is the world of the catastrophe wounded by the absence of God, a consequence of the tragic divorce between Athens and Jerusalem. In 1934, Fondane had fully adopted the Shestovian perspective according to which Paradise (original innocence) was lost after the fall into knowledge. The presence of God was hidden by the development of rationalism or, in other words, the rationalization of faith has killed God, reducing him to the limits of morality and to human intelligibility: "*Cette philosophie impossible et cette épreuve douloureuse, cette recherche, Chestov veut bien l'appeler Dieu*" [This impossible philosophy and this painful experience means the search of God for Shestov] (Fondane 1998, 114).

At this point, the crisis of reason claimed by the dadaist revolt is identified with the crisis of reason analyzed in existential philosophy. The adoption of Shestov's existential philosophy of tragedy, around 1927–1928, certainly includes an interpretation of Judaism insofar as Fondane's perception of the mission of Jews in culture is identified with Shestov's metaphysical anarchism. In 1928, Fondane defined his conception of Judaism, in his preface to his translation of A.L. Zissu's *Spovedania unui candelabru* (Confession of a Chandelier). According Fondane, the "mission of Jews" was to produce "*un déclassement des valeurs, une décristallisation proprement une réaction morale*" [a declassification of values, a decrystallization, more precisely, a moral reaction] (Fondane 2009e, 48). Fondane declares that Zissu describes men who are not Jewish but men only, and in these men a passion of research, and in their research the "*la dédicace obscure qu'ils portent en eux, qui les oblige à devenir des dieux*" [the obscure dedication they keep in themselves, which compels them to become gods] (Fondane 2009e, 50). It is likely that this statement reflects Shestov's reference to the first chapters of *Genesis* in *Athènes et Jerusalem*, where he criticizes the drive for knowledge symbolized by the temptation of the Biblical serpent (Chestov 2011, 174, 187).

Fondane does not wish to reduce the Jewish mission to a social, historical, political aim, limited to an historical community. The essence of Judaism, according to Fondane, transcends ethics, and this represents another key Shestovian theme:

> Il y a aussi mieux que le décalogue – ou la Loi de l'effort moyen – et c'est l'exemple des Esséniens, de Jésus, de Rabbi Siméon Bar Yochaï, de l'ascétisme des cabalistes, de la joie pure des Hassidim.
> (Fondane 2009e, 49)

> [There is a better option than the Decalogue – or the Law of the average effort – and this is the example of the Essenes, of Jesus, of Rabbi Simeon Bar Yochai [the pseudonymous author of the *Zohar*], of the asceticism of Kabbalists, of the pure joy of the Hasidim.]

In other words, the aim of Judaism cannot be reduced to a moral purpose; it is an awakening of *"recherche du vivant dans le mort, de la durée dans la stagnation, de la rupture dans l'automatisme"* [search of life in death, of duration in stagnation and of breakdown in automatism] (idem). Fondane explains this mission in terms of vital dynamism, whose action is to refuse the sedimentation of culture.

However, this universal mission is possible only because the nation and its institutions are a reality of "second order" for the Jews (Fondane 2009e, 49). Fondane has no intention to deny that this mission includes a "corrosive action" belonging to a certain "messianism" according to his enemies (idem, 48–49). Surprisingly, this corrosive action is illustrated by Charlie Chaplin, the "tragic man of our times" who highlights *"le cri des antinomies irréductibles de l'homme"* [the cry of irreducible human antinomies] (Fondane 2009e, 50). This may explain why Fondane's conception of cinema points to the metaphysical role of humour and burlesque performance. Indeed, his lost film, *Tararira* (1936), included Jewish songs and musical scores to illustrate the adventures of a bohemian quartet of artists (Salazar-Ferrer and Fotiade 2012, 285). In general, this conception is not far from Georg Simmel's concept of "tragedy of culture" (1911) or from Bergson's analysis of duration and spatial automatism. According to *La Conscience malheureuse* (The Unhappy Consciousness), the role of existential philosophy is:

> La philosophie n'est pas quelque chose comme un vérificateur des poids et mesures; mais l'acte par lequel l'existant pose sa propre existence, l'acte même du vivant, cherchant en lui et hors de lui, avec ou contre les évidences, les possibilités même du vivre.
> (Fondane 2013, 20)

> [Philosophy is not something like an instrument to verify weights and measures; it is the act of the living being, which is searching for the possibility of living both inside and outside itself, in conformity with self-evident truths or against them.]

In 1929, summarizing Shestov's philosophy for students at the University of Buenos Aires, Fondane quoted the debate between Rabbi Eliezer and the scholars of the synagogue who contested the miraculous manifestations of God himself. Fondane did so to support Rabbi Eliezer's opinion and uphold the right of the majority to establish the truth (Fondane 1998, 118). This story illustrates the opposition between the irrational divine source of truth given to the individual subject and the rationalization of truth available for a majority, an essential topic in Shestovian irrationalism. The choice of Rabbi Eliezer, who was excommunicated by the scholars of the synagogue for his disobedience, is particularly significant in illustrating Shestov's transgression of the Western speculative tradition of thought, in an attempt to overcome necessity (*Anankê*) and restore the possibility of unlimited human and divine freedom (Chestov 2011, 170).

In 1936, Fondane clarified his understanding of the concept of Judaism in the article "Léon Chestov à la recherche du Judaïsme perdu" (Lev Shestov in Search of Lost Judaism), in the *Revue Juive de Genève* (Fondane 2009d, 195–198). The opposition between a "specific Judaism" and an "essential Judaism" provides the key to understand his position: the first one is temporal, historical, geographical, and psychological; the second provides a universal "revelation" for mankind:

> J'appelle « essentiels » les traits d'une figure qui se situe hors du temps, hors de l'histoire, hors des bornes d'une structure définie : géographique, historique, nationale, et qui s'attache à exprimer, ou exprime malgré soi, la densité d'une révélation qui, bien que confiée à un seul peuple, intéresse au plus haut degré le salut de l'humanité en général.
> (Fondane 2009d, 195)

> [In my view, an "essential reality" is out of time, out of History, out of the limits of a definite structure: either geographical, historical, or national, and it should convey, even in spite of itself, the density of a revelation, which, although being given to a particular people, is aimed at the salvation of mankind in general.]

In this sense, Pascal and Kierkegaard are said to be more Jewish than Bergson, Freud, or Einstein (idem). In 1938, in a letter to Jacques Maritain, Fondane adds "Kierkegaard, Luther, and even Tertullian" to represent this essential Judaism (Fondane 1997, 38). However, he excludes from this the autonomy of morality, which had produced an "alienation" of Judaism during its historical evolution: "*une tradition rompue, brisée*" [a broken tradition], according to Fondane's correspondence with Maritain about the latter's article "Impossible Anti-Semitism," published in a Catholic periodical and later in a volume entitled *Les Juifs* (Maritain 2003, 37–38). The poet replies to Maritain: "*Mais nous sommes aussi loin de Jéhova que du Christ. Israël est fier de son éthique, mais il a oublié son Dieu*" [We are as far from Jehovah than from Christ. Israel is proud of its ethics, but forgot its God]

(Fondane 1997, 38). The same central leitmotiv is repeated in an important letter from 1940 to A.L. Zissu about the latter's novel *Samson and the New Dragon*:

> C'est la grande faute doctrinale d'Israël – plus grave que tous les péchés du corps – et qui nécessairement, passant d'une autonomie à une autre, devait aboutir à Marx – c'est-à-dire à la Loi sans Dieu.
> (Fondane 2009i, 218)

> [This is the major doctrinal fault of Israel – worse than all sins of the body – which, from one autonomy to another, should lead to Marx, that is to say, to the Law without God.]

The ethical perspective is systematically perceived as an occultation of our genuine relationship to God. The only possible relationship with God is a personal one, transcending all ethical perspectives. In existential philosophy as well as in poetry, the narrator should question God directly, through direct confrontation, according to what I have elsewhere termed the Job paradigm (Salazar-Ferrer 2008, 147).[3]

In fact, the core of the essential Judaism is identified with Shestov's philosophy of tragedy, opposing Athens and Jerusalem in a radical confrontation under the hypothesis of a fall in to the rational knowledge (the "serpent of knowledge"). According Shestov, God is beyond morality or, more exactly, cannot be submitted to the rational thought of morality. For Fondane the mission of Judaism is exclusively spiritual and has no common measure with the historical or political aims of Israel. Interestingly, Maritain declares in his article that "*Israël veut le Royaume de Dieu sur la terre*" [Israel wants the kingdom of God on Earth], using the violence of the faith ("*une foi qui fasse violence à l'ordre des choses*"), claiming a restitution of its goods without having the certitude to have this faith (Maritain 1994, 79).

> D'une telle notion de la foi, et si profondément juive, la philosophie de Chestov est un témoin incomparable. Le jour seulement où il posséderait le monde, Israël serait assuré d'avoir ou d'avoir eu la foi. Jusque-là, l'angoisse et le doute demeurera au cœur de la foi juive.
> (idem)

> [Above all, Shestov's philosophy bears witness to this conception of faith, which is authentically Jewish. Israel will be sure to have a genuine faith only on the day when it will take possession of the world. Until this moment, anxiety and doubt will live in the heart of the Jewish faith.]

---

3 The "Job paradigm" is a structure of the philosophical or poetical narrative in Fondane's works in which the narrative voice is in a situation of claim and opposition to God after an irrational and catastrophic destruction of his goods and convictions.

Thus, according to the Catholic concept of redemption, the mission of the Jewish people is limited to an earthly or historical mission ("*une œuvre d'activation terrestre*"), not a supernatural one (Maritain 1994, 81). Against Maritain, Fondane argues that the will of tangible belongs not to Job's claims (in Shestov's conception) but to (Catholic) theology, whose rationalism limits God's powers and his attributes to eternal truths. The consequence of this position is a strong anti-modernism, which deconstructs the idea of progress, showing it to be an illusion produced by the Enlightenment. As we have seen, Shestov's irrationalism includes a rejection of the ethical definition of God. Consequently, Fondane's conviction, as he explains in his article "Léon Chestov à la recherche du Judaïsme perdu," is that contemporary Judaism offers no recognition of the vital importance of Shestov's religious irrationalism, despite his being the Jewish philosopher *par excellence*.

> *Convenons-en : si le Juif, seul dans l'Antiquité, a témoigné de la présence effective de Dieu, du moins pourrait-il, dans le monde moderne, et* contre *le monde moderne, être seul à témoigner, avec la même angoisse, de l'absence de Dieu !*[3] *Seul dans le monde moderne et isolé dans le judaïsme, Léon Chestov témoigne de cette angoisse-là !*
> (Fondane 2009d, 198)

> [Let us agree that if the Jew in Antiquity was the only one to bear witness to the presence of God, at least he could be alone to bear witness – *against* the modern world and with the same anxiety – *to the absence of God*! Alone in the modern world and isolated in Judaism, Lev Shestov is a witness to this anxiety!]

Witnessing the Absence of God

The Shestovian interpretation of Pascal, Nietzsche, Dostoevsky, and Kierkegaard feeds the metaphysical struggle against Husserl and Hegel. Existential thinkers are living a singular and individual tragedy which is never reducible to a system of concepts. In this sense, the role of the Jewish people today is to bear witness to the silence of God against his derealization in the rationalism of modernity.

This existential interpretation of Judaism from the point of view of Shestov's philosophy of tragedy is paramount. Contrary to Jad Hatem's interpretation, one cannot attempt to explain the role of messianism in Fondane's poetry without referring to Shestov's works (Hatem 2004, 14). It should be noted that Monique Jutrin, one of the leading specialists of Fondane's work, has interpreted the silence of God in Fondane's poetry as an illustration of *Hester Panim*, the hidden face of God and the concept of *Tsimtsoum* (contraction), by which God removed himself from the world, creating a place for the freedom and responsibility of man.

Likewise, according Claude Vigée, "*La leçon de Fondane est celle de l'ein-soft de la Cabale. Pas de fin: et c'est l'expression qui désigne le Dieu d'Israël*" [Fondane's lesson is the same than the *Ein-sof* lesson of Kabbala. *No end*: these words refer to the God of Israel] (Vigée 1998, 31).

The influence of Isaac Luria's Kabbala is certainly evident in *Exodus. Super Flumina Babylonis* (1938–1943), particularly in the conception of the meaning of exile. According to Gershom Scholem, in Luria's conception "we are provided with a cosmic conception of exile. It relates not only to the exile of Jewish people, but also to the exile of the divine presence from the origin of universe. Everything in the world is the expression of this original and essential exile" (Scholem 1974, 95). In Fondane's *Exodus*, the exile of Jewish people in History corresponds to the exile of God. The voice of the Chorus, responding to the priest of Babylon, declares that:

> *Le dieu s'est tu, disais-tu, qui habitait notre pierre.*
> *— Il s'est tu. La statue a déserté le socle.*
> *La terre est devenue opaque, la vitre s'est embuée,*
> *la vie s'est engourdie comme le sang des serpents.*
> *L'hiver de Dieu est là.*
> (Fondane 2006, 196)

[God has fallen silent, you said, you, who inhabited our stone.
He has fallen silent. The statue has left the pedestal.
Earth has become opaque, the window is misted,
Life has become sluggish like the serpent's blood.
God's winter is upon us.]

In the Chorus's discourse, God keeps silent. Life is paralyzed. God's winter has shrouded the world. Rivers are ice-cold. Either the image of the desolate face of a statue, weed-infested and moss-covered, or the metaphor of the sleep of nature in winter illustrates the idea of the absence of God. His withdrawal corresponds to the concept of God's fast in Fondane's poem. In front of this absence, the task of humanity is to resuscitate and recreate God in order to put a stop to human exile.

In Fondane's *Exodus*, this topic likely echoes the concept of *Shevirah* (break-up) in the Kabbala, which requires a *Tikkun* (rectification). According to this conception, Israel's exile is necessary to bring back the lost sparks of creation. The historical meaning of the exile of the Jewish people is in fact metaphysical. In this sense, the rectification is also a redemption (Scholem 1974, 98). This conception cannot be separated from the conception according to which the world is the consequence of an original fall, the "crack of the vases" (*Shevirat hakelim*), which is the source of imperfection, the exile of reality, and the exile of God. "Men should repair the world, not only in an external sense, the visible world, but in its totality including the visible and invisible worlds it contains. All existing things are submitted to him and depend on him" (Scholem 1974, 95). According to Scholem, this mission defined by the Kabbalists modifies the classical concept of messianism in Judaism, which is no longer a personal event in History to become a progressive task for men. The consequences of this Kabbalist concept of redemption is not limited to Israel; it is a universal mission. Moreover, it means a reconciliation between the historical meaning of exile and its metaphysical concept.

Existential Poetics and Essential Judaism

In his first essay published in French, *Rimbaud le voyou* (Rimbaud the Hooligan) (1933), Fondane quotes the *Zohar* from Edmond Fleg's edition and Jean de Pauly's translation (Fleg 1925). More precisely, he quotes the discussion between Rabbi Isaac and Rabbi Yehouda about the power of crying, superior to the power of prayer (Fleg 1925, 210–211). The immediate act of crying, which stands at the limits of language, coincides with the pure act of the existent being, the individual subject, to modify the reality. Therefore, the poetry is only an indirect, posterior, mediate expression of this act of crying. The prayer – presupposing the linguistic form – is secondary. The distance between the original act and the object "poetry," causing the Rimbaldian failure, feeds Fondane's anti-aesthetics (Salazar-Ferrer 2004b), which denounces the paradoxical seduction of poetry. The act of poetry is analyzed in terms of the personal relationship between man and God: "*Le cri de Job, du psalmiste, le cri vrai, véritablement crié à Dieu ...*" [Job's cry, the psalmist's cry, the true cry to God] (Fondane 2010b, 76).

Such references are not exceptional in the debate of the 1930s, following Abbé Brémond's famous manifestos about "pure poetry," which provided the terms of the debate with Paul Valéry, Paul Claudel, Maritain, and Albert Béguin. From 1933 to 1938, when the *False Treatise of Aesthetics* (Faux Traité d'esthétique, 1938) was published, Fondane developed a reflection on poetry as an existential affirmative act. The negative definition of poetry includes the rejection of aesthetical pleasure and its alienation to moral, social, or political ideologies. This is why in Baudelaire's poetry the function of the catastrophe is displaced toward a reflection on the abyss, revealing an existential experience of the collapse of the autonomy of aesthetical products. Anticipating Yves Bonnefoy's paradoxical value of the images and Deleuze's reflections on the catastrophic function of diagrams in visual arts, Fondane's originality consists in the development of an "anti-aesthetics" for which the poet must break with the illusions of idealism. In this sense, he will develop a performative conception of poetry, replacing a symbolist or idealist or surrealist aesthetics, able to modify the poet and the reader in a living and effective action on reality.

In a key article, "La Conscience malheureuse" (The Unhappy Consciousness), published in 1935, Fondane highlights the opposition between the act of "substantialization" of poetry and the act of "desubstantialization" of philosophy. Poetry should save existence from the process of derealization inherent in Reason. The act of poetry, producing an affirmation of existence, belongs to the *"arbre de vie"* [tree of life] while the work of magician, philosophers, theologian, and scholars produce a negation of existence.

> *A l'effort de détermination, de localisation, de mécanisation, de fixation des forces de l'univers, entrepris par les philosophes, un mouvement inverse a lieu grâce au poète, d'indétermination, d'inconstance, de libération, de désintégration* [...] *Le poète assure à nos yeux le rôle de « télégraphe vivant » entre nous et le possible; il ruisselle de solitude; il pétille de transcendance; il entretient en nous un malaise fécond; il nous empêche de guérir humainement de nos plaies; et s'il ne sait que se lamenter, il nous faut voir là la seule attitude qui nous reste possible devant le réel. Il n'est pas l'Arbre de Vie: il est soif de l'Arbre de Vie.*
> (Fondane [1935] in Stefanescu 2010, 309)

> [Against the effort of determination, localization, mechanization, fixation of the forces of the universe undertaken by the philosophers, an inverse movement takes place, owing to the poet, which includes indeterminacy, inconstancy, liberation, disintegration [...] The poet plays the role of living telegraph between us and the possible; he is dripping with solitude; he sparkles with transcendence; he maintains us in a fertile unrest; he prevents us from being cured of our wounds. Despite the fact that he has no choice except lamentation, we should consider this attitude as the only one possible faced with reality. He is not the Tree of Life; he is the thirst for the Tree of Life.]

The Biblical opposition between the Tree of Life and the Tree of Knowledge takes place in a Shestovian framework. However, Fondane's conviction was certainly that Shestov's philosophy of tragedy agrees with the Kabbalist tradition. The reading of the *Zohar* was certainly important to strengthen the Shestovian interpretation of the Tree of Knowledge. In Fondane's citation of Edmond Fleg's edition of the *Zohar*, the Tree of Life is opposed to the Tree of Death (Fleg 1925, 252–253). The dynamic and vitalist conception of the Tree of Life in Fondane's concept of poetry is perfectly compatible with the Kabbalist conception of the redemption (which supposes a spiritual participation of the Tree of Life during the period of fall under the influence of the Tree of Knowledge). As Scholem notes, "The tree of life is exclusively holiness, it is the extension of divine life in the world, excluding any mixture with evil, without kennel or waste, neither death nor limitation" (Scholem 1974, 83). In Fondane's article, existential thought should pit one's thirst for existence against the void and the *"défaillance de l'être"* [failure of Being]. However, the "mal des fantômes" [suffering of ghosts] relates not only to his own existence, the existence of the singular subjectivity, but also to the absence of God:

> *Pour le poète, tout a lieu comme si la transcendance existait, ou comme si existait une absence béante et douloureuse de cette transcendance. [...] Que Dieu soit cru existant et parfois le poète le hait; mais le hait davantage de ne pas être.*
> (Fondane 2010b, 309)

> [For the poet, it is as if transcendence existed or as if a huge and painful absence of this transcendence existed. Sometimes the poet hates God when he believes that he really exists but he hates him more because he does not exist.]

However, we should be aware that the examples illustrating poetry provided in Fondane's article are *"le Livre de Job; poésie, l'expérience mystique de Saint Jean de la Croix; poésie, la pensée de Nietzsche, de Kierkegaard"* [The Book of Job, the Mystical Experience of Saint John of the Cross, the Thought of Nietzsche and Kierkegaard]. This absence of God in the Shestovian theoretical framework is interpreted as the result of rationalist culture, as evident in *The Unhappy Consciousness* (Fondane 2013, 41). The reality of the singular being, the *"existant,"* as well as his relationship to God, has been derealized, producing the "suffering of ghosts," which provides the title of Fondane's collected poetical works (*Le Mal des fantômes*). In Fondane's poetry, Jewish emigrants are experiencing this universal "derealization" and negation of their existence. The task of the Jewish poet is to bear witness to the tragic fracture in modernity. In this sense, the absurd is not negative. If, for Camus, the absurd is the manifestation of human limits of reason, for Shestov and Fondane it is a fulminate able to shatter the finiteness of the human condition (Salazar-Ferrer 2004, 218). Fondane's response to the crisis of humanism, metamorphosing the avant-garde's revolt, is an existential philosophy and poetry which manages to remain true to the Jewish legacy in re-interpreting its meaning.

For us, today, it is highly significant that Fondane chose to live fully his convictions that the Jewish people had a spiritual mission. After he was arrested on 7 March 1944, some of his friends managed to obtain his liberation from Drancy; however, he refused to leave without his sister Line, who had been arrested with him. This decision, in one sense, identifies his fate with the fate of the Jewish people. He was subsequently murdered, on 2 October 1944, in Birkenau. His wife, Geneviève, decided to join the Catholic order of Notre-Dame de Sion in 1949. In French culture, Fondane's poem "Préface en prose" (Preface in rose) (Fondane 2006, 151–153) – a work which opposes the tragic affirmation of a human face to its negation in a moment when the human face of the Jewish people was disfigured by anti-Semitic Nazi propaganda – is considered quite rightly as emblematic of the poetic resistance against the Shoah: *"Oui, j'ai été un homme comme tous les autres hommes, / Nourri de pain, de rêve, de désespoir"* [Yes I have been a man like other men, fed with bread, dreams, despair ...], he writes. And, yet, he is reaffirming his difference:

> *Et pourtant, non!*
> *Je n'étais pas un homme comme vous.*
> *Vous n'êtes pas nés sur les routes,*
> *Personne n'a jeté à l'égout vos petits*
> *comme des chats encore sans yeux,*
> *Vous n'avez pas erré de cité en cité*
> *traqués par les polices,*
> *Vous n'avez pas connu les désastres à l'aube,*
> *les wagons de bestiaux ...*
> (Fondane 2006, 153)

> [And yet no I wasn't
> I wasn't a human being like you others.
> You weren't born on the roads,
> No one threw your babies into sewers,
> Like cats whose eyes are still shut,
> You didn't wander from slum district to slum district
> And weren't hunted down by the police,
> You didn't experience disasters at dawn
> Freight cars for animals ...]
> (translation by John Taylor, Taylor 2014, 389)

Through his tragic fate, Fondane has experienced until the last moment the metaphysical resistance inherent to existential thought, representing at its highest intensity his conception of essential Judaism.

Bibliography

Arghezi, Tudor. *Psalmi, Testament (Spiritual Psalms Testament)*. Cluj-Napoca: Dacia Publishing House, 2001.
Broch, Hermann. *La Grandeur inconnue*. Paris: Gallimard, 1968.
Buber, Martin. *On Judaism* [1916]. Ed. Nahum Glatzer. New York: Schocken Books, 1989.
Chestov, Léon. *Athènes et Jérusalem*. Paris: le Bruit du temps, 2011.
Fondane, Benjamin. *Rencontres avec Léon Chestov*. Paris: Plasma, 1982.
Fondane, Benjamin. *Constantin Brancusi*. Fontfroide le haut: Fata Morgana, 1995.
Fondane, Benjamin. "Benjamin Fondane à Jacques Maritain" (28 February 1938). *Fondane-Maritain. Correspondance de Benjamin et Geneviève Fondane avec Jacques et Raïssa Maritain*. Paris: Paris-Méditerranée, 1997. 37–39.
Fondane, Benjamin. "Léon Chestov, un nouveau visage de Dieu" [1929]. *Europe* 827 (March 1998): 110–120.

Fondane, Benjamin. "Le grand ballet de la poésie française" [*Integral* 13–14 (June–July 1927)]. *Benjamin Fondane et l'avant-garde*. Ed. Michel Carassou and Raileanu Petre. Paris: Fondation Culturelle Roumaine / Paris-Méditerranée, 1999a. 53–57.

Fondane, Benjamin. "Louis Aragon et *Le Paysan de Paris*" [*Integral* 10 (January 1927)]. *Benjamin Fondane et l'avant-garde*. Ed. Michel Carassou and Raileanu Petre. Paris: Fondation Culturelle Roumaine / Paris-Méditerranée, 1999b. 39–43.

Fondane, Benjamin. *Images et livres de France* [1921]. Trans. Odile Serre (from Romanian). Paris: Paris-Méditerranée, 2002.

Fondane, Benjamin. *Le Mal des fantômes*. Paris: Verdier Poche, 2006.

Fondane, Benjamin. *Écrits pour le cinéma. Le Muet et le parlant*. Ed. Olivier Salazar-Ferrer, Ramona Fotiade, and Michel Carassou. Paris: Verdier Poche, 2007.

Fondane, Benjamin. *Benjamin Fondane à la recherche du judaïsme*. Ed. Monique Jutrin. Paris: Parole et silence / Lethielleux, 2009a. 153–155.

Fondane, Benjamin. "Paroles à propos d'un ami" [*Lumea Evree* (November 1 1919)]. *Benjamin Fondane à la recherche du judaïsme*. Ed. Monique Jutrin. Paris: Parole et silence / Lethielleux, 2009b. 41–43.

Fondane, Benjamin. "La Traduction de la Bible" [*Rampa* IV 801 (28 June 1920): 1–2]. *Benjamin Fondane à la recherche du judaïsme*. Ed. Monique Jutrin. Paris: Parole et silence / Lethielleux, 2009c. 153–155.

Fondane, Benjamin. "Léon Chestov à la recherche du judaïsme perdu" [*Revue Juive de Genève* IV (1936): 326–328]. *Benjamin Fondane à la recherche du judaïsme*. Ed. Monique Jutrin. Paris: Parole et silence / Lethielleux, 2009d. 195–198.

Fondane, Benjamin. Preface to A.L. Zissu, *Confession d'un Candélabre* [Paris: Picart, 1928]. *Benjamin Fondane à la recherche du judaïsme*. Ed. Monique Jutrin. Paris: Parole et silence / Lethielleux, 2009e. 48–50.

Fondane, Benjamin. "Judaïsme et hellenisme" ("Judaism and Hellenism") [*Mântuirea* 230 (8 October 1919)]. *Benjamin Fondane à la recherche du judaïsme*. Ed. Monique Jutrin. Paris: Parole et silence / Lethielleux, 2009f. 95–126.

Fondane, Benjamin. "De l'éthique au spectacle (A propos de Jules de Gaultier, du Bovarysme, du peuple élu)." *Benjamin Fondane à la recherche du judaïsme*. Ed. Monique Jutrin. Paris: Parole et silence / Lethielleux, 2009g. 126–131.

Fondane, Benjamin. "Glose sur le Cantique des Cantiques de Salomon" [*Flacara* 7 (July 1922): 423–424]. *Benjamin Fondane à la recherche du judaïsme*. Ed. Monique Jutrin. Paris: Parole et silence / Lethielleux, 2009h. 56–59.

Fondane. Benjamin. "Une lettre à A.L. Zissu à propos du roman *Samson et le Nouveau Dagon*." *Entre Jérusalem, et Athènes – Benjamin Fondane à la recherche du Judaïsme*. Ed. Monique Jutrin. Paris: Parole et silence / Lethielleux, 2009i. 217–220.

Fondane, Benjamin. *Rimbaud le voyou*. Paris: Non lieu, 2010a.

Fondane, Benjamin. "La Conscience malheureuse – Fragment." [*Cahiers du Sud*, XII, 171 (April 1935)] *Benjamin Fondane ou l'épreuve du paradoxe – Pour une herméneutique existentielle*. Ed. Dorin Stefanescu. Cluj-Napoca: Eikon, 2010b: 306–310.

Fondane, Benjamin. "Marc Chagall." [*Les Cahiers Juifs* (April–May 1934)]. *Brancusi suivi de Marc Chagall*. Paris: Marguerite Waknine, 2011 : 31–39.

Fondane, Benjamin. *La Conscience malheureuse* [1936]. Introduction and notes by Olivier Salazar-Ferrer and Nicolas Monseu. Paris: Verdier / Non Lieu, 2013.

Fondane, Benjamin. "De dada au surréalisme ou de l'idiotie pure au suicide." *La Sœur de l'Ange* 13 (2014): 21–26.

Fondane, Benjamin. *The Existential Monday* ["Le Lundi existentiel et le Dimanche de l'histoire." *L'Existence*. Paris: Gallimard, 1945]. Trans. Andrew Rubens and Bruce Baught. New York: NYRB Classics, 2016.

Freedman, Eric. *Bibliographie de l'œuvre de Benjamin Fondane*. Paris: Non Lieu / Société d'Etudes Benjamin Fondane, 2009.

Hatem, Jad. *Semer le Messie selon Fondane poète*. Bruxelles: La Part de l'œil, 2004.

Jutrin, Monique (ed.). *Entre Jérusalem, et Athènes – Benjamin Fondane à la recherche du Judaïsme*. Paris: Parole et Silence / Lethielleux, 2009.

Le Livre du Zohar. Ed. Edmond Fleg. Trans. Jean de Pauly. Paris: Rieder, 1925.

Maritain, Jacques. *"L'Impossible antisémitisme"* [*Les Juifs*. Paris: Plon, 1937]. *L'Impossible antisémitisme*. Précédé de *Jacques Maritain et les Juifs*, par Pierre Vidal-Naquet, Paris: Desclée de Brouwer, 2003: 69–102.

Oisteanu, Andrei. "Benjamin Fondane. Coordonnés judaïques." *Eurésis – Cahiers Roumains d'Etudes Littéraires* (1999–2000): 178–191.

Oszi, Carmen. "La Vision d'Eretz Israël: Benjamin Fondane et le débat sioniste." *Continuum* 4 (2005–2006): 54–56.

Pop, Ion. "Fundoianu et la critique littéraire roumaine." *Euresis – Cahiers Roumains d'Etudes Littéraires* (1999–2000): 192–203.

Salazar-Ferrer, Olivier. *Benjamin Fondane*. Paris: Oxus, 2004a.

Salazar-Ferrer, Olivier. "L'Idéal de Fondane et de Valéry: l'autonomie du signifiant poétique." *Valéry, philosophes, philosophie*. Ed. A. Mairesse. Bulletin des Études Valéryennes 96–97. Paris: Éditions L'Harmattan, 2004b.

Salazar-Ferrer, Olivier. "L'Exode de Benjamin Fondane et l'attestation existentielle." *Acta Iasseyensia Comparationis* 3 (2005): 53–68.

Salazar-Ferrer, Olivier. *Benjamin Fondane et la révolte existentielle*. Paris: Corlevour, 2008.

Salazar-Ferrer, Olivier. "Benjamin Fondane et la crise de réalité." *Titanic. Bulletin International de l'Association Benjamin Fondane* 3 (2015): 19–42.

Salazar-Ferrer, Olivier and Ramona Fotiade. "Benjamin Fondane, esthétique et cinéma." *La Part de l'œil* 23 (2012): 249–291.

Scholem, Gershom. *Le Messianisme Juif – Essai sur la spiritualité du Judaïsme*. Paris: Calmann-Lévy, 1974.

Taylor, John. "Poetry Today: Discovering Benjamin Fondane." *The Antioch Review* 70.2 (Spring 2012): 382–389.

Vigée, Claude. "Un cri devenu chant." *Europe* 827 (March 1998): 28–33.

Vinea, Ion. "Manifeste activiste destiné à la jeunesse." *La Réhabilitation du rêve – Une anthologie de l'avant-garde roumaine par Ion Pop*. By Ion Pop. Paris: Nadeau, 2006. 114–115.

Jews in the Avant-Garde: A Historical Perspective

Steven E. Aschheim
The Avant-Garde and the Jews

In a topic as broad and complex as the present assignment, to provide it with a semblance of order it makes sense to think of it as consisting of four major themes. Of course, none of these can really be neatly divided the one from the other; they will constantly cross-over into each other. But at least to get some analytical grip on this confusing and complex tangle, I propose we examine firstly the role of Jews generally within the various avant-garde movements and some of the (rather problematic) attempts to account for such participation; secondly, explicitly "Jewish" avant-garde projects; thirdly, diverse avant-garde attitudes to Jews; and finally, anti-Semitic representations of Jews because they were perceived as belonging to the destructive avant-garde.

We must first attempt to understand and define what is meant by the "avant-garde." I am not at all sure that there is such a thing as "the" avant-garde. Instead we should talk about numerous avant-gardes with different pedigrees and artistic, cultural and political platforms – the very large variety of movements, countries and personalities considered just in this volume attests to that. Moreover, we can find numerous individuals who could be considered avant-garde but who did not belong to any organized school or project. Still, some preliminary, overarching heuristic scheme is needed.

The term, avant-garde, is of medieval French military origins, referring to a small unit of especially skilled soldiers who marched ahead and plotted the army's next moves. But more pertinently, especially in our present context, in its approximate modern sense – the artist as marching forward to challenge and guide society – it was first coined by the Sephardi Jewish Saint-Simonian Olinde Rodrigues in 1825.[1] It was only in the 1890s, however, that the notion of the avant-garde – typically and flamboyantly announced in manifesto form - assumed some of the artistic, cultural and political characteristics with which we presently associate it: a programatically subversive intent, a radical break with present bourgeois styles and forms and a flaunting of its conventions, a dismissal of the liberal belief in linear progress, a rejection of both high and popular culture, an activist, usually elitist, pretension (through art but not exclusively so) to create a

---

[1] See the essay "L'artiste le savant et l'industriel" where Rodrigues calls for the artist to "serve as the people's avant-garde," claiming that the power of the arts was the quickest way to social, political and economic reform. To be sure, this differed from later approaches where (apart of course from the futurists) the attitude towards science and industrial society was, to put it minimally, ambiguous. The essay is translated in Calinescu 1987.

new kind of person in a transformed, liberated civilization.² Given their emphasis on novelty, by their very nature, they are usually of a self-inflicted short-lived life-span.

I do not intend to go much beyond this and define the avant-gardes with any greater exactitude, precisely because in their variety they contain multiple directions, contradictions and ambiguities. Avant-garde movements and individuals can be variously politically reactionary and restorative, but also forward-looking and progressive; apolitical, left, right or wildly anarchic;³ determinedly secular yet also in search of some renewed faith; ideologically pacifist or obsessed with violence and war; chaotic and parodically comic and oppressively humorless.⁴ As we shall see, the self-consciously "Jewish" avant-gardes often consisted of similar internal tensions and contradictions. Equally, the different dimensions of the relationship between Jews and the avant-garde fit no simple pattern or single rubric. The nuances and dialectics need to be worked out in different concrete cases and contexts.

Historically, what has become known as "the age of the avant-gardes" spans the period of the 1890s through the late 1930s and is the focus of this essay. Yet, especially as we are considering the relation of Jews to it, it is romanticism, especially its German variation which, I believe, stands as the first prototypical avant-garde.⁵ With its cult of the strange and exotic, its emphasis on ceaseless self-creation, the emotions and the unconscious, its disavowal of bourgeois values and

---

2 In this essay I do not make a distinction between the avant-garde and the radical modernists. Raymond Williams has attempted to do so: "It is not easy to make simple distinctions between 'modernism' and the 'avant-garde', especially as many uses of these labels are retrospective. But [...] modernism can be said to begin with [...] the alternative, radically innovating experimental artists and writers – while the avant-garde begins with groups of the fully oppositional type. The old military metaphor of the vanguard which had been used in politics and in social thought from at least the 1830s – and which had implied a position within a general human progress – was now directly applicable to these newly militant movements, even when they had renounced the received elements of progressivism. Modernism had proposed a new kind of art for a new kind of social and perceptual world. The avant-garde, aggressive from the beginning, saw itself as the breakthrough to the future: its members were not the bearers of a progress already repetitiously defined, but the militants of a creativity which would revive and liberate humanity." (Williams 1988, 3).
3 In the first issues of *La Révolution surréaliste* in 1924, Breton called for an end to family, nation, army, prisons and religion. This was very different from the elitist cultural pretensions of the Stefan George Kreis. In movements such as dada the atmosphere was reminiscent of the anarchist and expressionist Erich Mühsam's admonition: "Let us be chaotic."
4 For an excellent exposition and critique of the nature of the avant-garde see Kramer 1973, 3–19.
5 As Renato Poggioli (1968, 52) correctly states: "there is not the shadow of a doubt that the [later avant-garde] would have been historically inconceivable without the romantic precedent."

conventions, its opposition to classicism and Enlightenment, its self-conscious elitism, the tension between the revolutionary, destructive impulse and the desire for restorative positive transformation, the pressing desire to create something new – all these are shared with later avant-gardes.[6]

It is, then, in their encounter with the early German romantics that we have the first Jewish engagement with the avant-garde. This was the period when Jewish integration was in its infancy and it was precisely the romantic avant-garde's flaunting of convention, its bohemian sexual style (plus the potential economic benefits that would accrue), that paradoxically provided the opportunity for this meeting and the possibility of (what later proved to be an illusory) Jewish integration. It was in the salons of Jewish women such as Dorothea Mendelssohn, Henriette Herz and Rahel Varnhagen that the famous gatherings (as well as various erotic and marital arrangements) between them and young romantic intellectuals (such as Friedrich Schlegel, Friedrich Schleiermacher, Ludwig Tieck, Jean Paul and others) took place. Yet if this proto-avant-garde encouraged a certain kind of Jewish integration, as with so many other later movements, ambiguities and dialectical contradictions were at work. As Deborah Hertz (1988, 221) expresses it: "although romanticism may have enhanced the attraction of the Jewish women to romantic intellectuals as women, the same ideology diminished the women's attractiveness as Jews. In this way the changing ideological mood in Berlin first contributed to the popularity of the Jewish salons but later helped to destroy them." Clearly, these Jewish women enthusiastically adopted the totalizing romantic sensibility, eventually to end in serious disappointment. Rahel Varnhagen's great error, wrote Hannah Arendt, was to believe that she could make a work of art of her own life, that it was not necessary to act or choose but simply be a recipient, a "mouthpiece of experience" (Arendt 1997, 81).[7]

But let us turn now to the later period and to Jewish participation within the various avant-gardes. It goes without saying that there can be no exhaustive review here of their continent-wide variety which, amongst others, included: the

---

[6] Isaiah Berlin does not employ the term avant-garde in his description of the romantics, but he attributes perhaps even a greater radicalism to their enterprise and the parallel is striking. The romantics, he argues, attacked "the foundation of the entire Western tradition," i.e. that "knowledge is virtue" and that "knowledge" itself existed. For the romantics, "not knowledge of values, but their creation, is what men achieve. You create values, you create goals, you create ends, and in the end you create your own vision of the universe, exactly as artists create works of art[.] There is only, if not the flow, the endless self-creativity of the universe [...] a process of perpetual forward self-thrusting, self-creation[.]" (Berlin 1999, 137–139).
[7] Arendt originally wanted the book to be called "R.V. Lebensgeschichte einer deutscher Jüdin aus der Romantik."

French cubists and surrealists, the Romanian dadaists in Switzerland, the Italian futurists, the German expressionists and the Stefan George Kreis, the English vorticists, the blossoming of various experimental avant-garde movements in Russia between 1905 through 1925, as well as a plethora of modernist literary projects spanning Europe. I shall mention here just a few illustrative cases and critically examine a number of theories positing explanations of such Jewish participation.

In the first place, when it comes to the avant-garde in general, with only a few exceptions, Jews did not participate *as* Jews but as integral partners. In theory (though not always in practice), most avant-gardes possessed transnational, nondenominational aspirations rendering – perhaps in illusionary fashion – the question of Jewish origins as irrelevant. The German-Jewish Marxist and expressionist philosopher Ernst Bloch remembered, perhaps with overly rose-tinted glasses, the cultural mix of Weimar's creative artistic and intellectual adventures thus: "That Reinhardt or S. Fischer or even Bruno Walter and Otto Klemperer were Jews, that Piscator or Rowohlt or Fürtwängler or Bassermann were not – that was of no interest to absolutely no one except for shady plotters or sinister tabloids. Most people didn't even know about it. Who in the world identified Weill's music for the *Three Penny Opera* as Jewish or Brecht's text as outright German? [...] The pleasant, uncomplicated everyday living and working together – that, above all, remains worthy of remembrance" (Bloch 1965, 553).

Indeed there is a danger in this exercise either of a mind-numbing, name-dropping version of "contribution" history, a feeling bordering on chauvinist pride that modernist Jewish writers like Kafka and Proust are up there with the likes of Joyce, Eliot, Conrad, Baudelaire and so on. Yet, how important is it for us to note that the founder of radical dada, Tristan Tzara was really Samuel Rosenstock and that its co-founder was the Jewish (and later Zionist) artist Marcel Janco?[8] Do we gain greater understanding of the George Kreis if we note the large number of Jewish initiates (most famously – but not inclusively – Friedrich Gundolf, Karl Wohlfskehl, Ernst Kantorowicz)? Does it tell us anything significant about the nature of expressionism itself that so many of its participants – Kurt Hiller, Ernst Toller, Alfred Döblin, Franz Werfel, Albert Ehrenstein, Carl Einstein, Alfred Lichtenstein, Jakob van Hoddis, and the painters Ludwig Meidner and Jakob Steinhardt – were Jewish or that the subsequent heated debate concerning its political

---

[8] Dada not only had many Jewish members and associates, but most were Romanian Jews. Apart from Tzara and Janco there was Arthur Segal and Maximilian Herman. Amongst the surrealists there were the Romanian Jewish Victor Brauner and the second-generation Jules Perahim. See Dagen 2011.

nature featured only one non-Jew, Bertolt Brecht?[9] And is the obverse true? Does the relative absence of Jews in the Italian futurist movement tell us much about either that movement or the Jews?

We should tread very carefully here. Occasionally, it is true that a self-conscious Jewish element did enter the work of the general avant-garde, as with, for example, Karl Wohlfskehl or Marc Chagall or (in an earlier guise) El Lissitzky. Indeed, that inveterate expressionist activist Kurt Hiller (rather unusually) insisted that his Jewish sensibility – his "in-betweeness" which exceeded the fixity of style and form – predisposed him to adopt transgressive avant-garde positions. As he put it in *The Wisdom of Ennui*: "Are there non-Jewish intellectuals? [...] perhaps 'Jewish' and 'intellectual' [should] be considered the same? Should 'Jew' be considered not an ethnological but a characterological concept? A designation for a race which uniquely germinates between races?"[10] Jeanette Malkin has gone so far as to suggest that expressionism

> forged an acting style that portrayed bodies and characters as warped, restless, distorted, vibrating with nervous energy – mirror images [...] of the over-expressive Jew[.] Moreover, its thematic emphases on isolation, rebellion, and transformation fit not only the marginal (provincial or eastern) biographies of most of its Jewish practitioners but also their ultimate integrative agenda into a (metamorphosed) German society. It thus facilitated a dual function: the emphasis on 'becoming' allowed for the possibility of a radical and abstract breakthrough (beyond the simple categories of either 'German' or 'Jew') into a regenerated world, while at the same time permitting free indulgence (albeit in transmuted form) in the normally repressed and castigated histrionic expressiveness that constituted an ongoing part of intimate Jewish subculture.
> (Aschheim 2010, 31)[11]

There are, of course, various theories which argue that the large presence of Jews within avant-garde movements derived in part from their lack of a rooted tradition, a flexibility that rendered them more open, receptive to new, even transgressive, trends and ideas. To be sure, Jews everywhere had "a vested interest in support-

---

[9] The others were Ernst Bloch, Georg Lukács, Walter Benjamin and Theodor Adorno. None of them did so in their capacity as Jews (unless one wants to equate intellectuality with Jewishness. But, intellectuality on its own is not necessarily avant-garde.) On the debate see Bloch 1977.
[10] Hiller 1913, 52–53. Quoted in Leck 2000, 214–215. Hiller was a devotee of Georg Simmel and his notion of in-betweeness, *das Zwischige*, bears a direct affinity to Simmel's "Stranger." With his aristocratic Nietzschean anticapitalism, Leck argues, Simmel created "avant-garde sociology," an entirely new discipline, and one that particularly attracted Jewish avant-garde radicals such as Hiller, Bloch, Lukács and others. Leck in general claims that Simmel's influence on the socialist, cultural, feminist, and homosexual avant-garde was profound and until now has been neglected.
[11] See also Malkin 2010.

ing a worldview that championed diversity of opinion in politics and the arts" (Jelavich 2010, 42). In this vein, Peter Jelavich (ibid., 44) has argued that because they were "faced with continued exclusion from 'official' culture, Jews created new cultural spheres, open not only to Jewish participation but to a plurality of styles, including novel and experimental forms of art." These all contain some validity but it should be noted that the Jewish relationship to both "official" and avant-garde culture and politics was in general tied to the complex dynamics, the possibilities and limits of integration and assimilation.[12]

It is true that if ever there was an avant-garde composer, the self-consciously Jewish Arnold Schoenberg stands out as exemplary. But, there is nothing "essentially" Jewish about all of this. One could argue that Felix Mendelssohn with his revival of Bach and the composing of Church music was exceedingly conservative and integrative, and that far from seeking outlandishness and transgression the Jewish operatic composers of the nineteenth century – Meyerbeer, Offenbach and Halévy – were popular precisely because they catered to popular and commercial tastes (exactly why Wagner despised them). Their path to acceptance consisted in either official "high" or "popular" culture, both quintessential enemies of the avant-garde. And while the patrons and collectors of avant-garde art – those who understood its virtues years before a wider audience began to make sense of them – were often Jews (like the German-Jewish Daniel Henry Kahnweiler, who in Paris "did most to give Cubism a cohesive identity" and who immediately recognized and championed the genius of Picasso, Braque and Léger), it is also true that Jews were equally – and perhaps more often and prominently – the great impressarios of "low" popular culture in the form of revues, vaudeville and circuses. Or as *Bildungsbürger* (traditionally educated middle-class intellectuals), Jews gravitated to respectable "high" culture (Bell 2014; Otte 2006; Jelavich 2016). Peter Gay has put it a little more strongly than I would, but he has a point: The "charge – or boast – of presumed Jewish hunger for experiment in the arts and thirst for innovation in literature is largely myth, fostered in part by Jews themselves[.] Far fewer cultural revolutionaries and far more cultural reactionaries were Jews than historians have recognized." Moreover, there "were many more Modernists who were not Jews, many Jews who were not Modernists. And many of the Jews who were Modernists were not so because they were Jews" (Gay 1978, 21, 101). The topic almost makes it embarrassingly necessary to present a list of the host of great non-Jews who populated and enriched the various cultural, artistic and political avant-gardes of the time. I shall obviously refrain from doing so.

---

[12] I am grateful for this insight, derived from discussions with Ezra Mendelsohn.

"Jewish" Avant-Garde Projects

But what of explicitly "Jewish" avant-garde movements and individuals? Given the vast amount of material and personalities involved, I am exceedingly selective and my arguments merely illustrative rather than comprehensive. On one level, this is a less problematic area, for here we are dealing with Jews acting explicitly as self-conscious Jews. Yet, here too there are levels of complexity and distinctions to be made.

The most conspicuous and fascinating place to begin is with the Russian Jewish avant-garde during the revolutionary period stretching from 1905 through 1925. As Kenneth B. Moss has shown in his superb study of the Russian Jewish Renaissance, this was the period where, quite uniquely, multiple efforts were undertaken to forge a separate, new and radical "Jewish" secular culture (in either Hebrew or Yiddish) using modernist materials and an avant-garde sensibility. As he puts it: "a significant cohort of intellectuals, writers, artists, patrons, publicists, teachers, and activists [...] organized literary journals, avant-garde anthologies, *Gesamtkunstwerk* projects and massive collective programs of literary translation" (Moss 2009, 2). Jewish plastic art, orchestral music and theater, especially the Habimah Hebrew troupe and the Moscow Yiddish Theatre thrived, all employing experimental material and modernist techniques. There was also a Hebrew Opera company in Odessa and an avant-garde Jewish theatre in Kiev. It is during this period too that El Lissitzky and Marc Chagall actively participated in this self-conscious Jewish venture and were also leading figures in the broader Bolshevik avant-garde (Hobsbawm 2013, 226).[13] Most of these figures were revolutionaries who shared the modernist convictions of the Pan-European avant-garde, "which saw wholesale cultural and psychic reinvention as essential to the creation of a new world" (Moss 2009, 4).

What made this venture so exciting and unique was the fact that these avant-gardists by and large "vociferously rejected the idea that their new culture had to be framed by some essential Jewishness; instead, they dreamed of a Hebrew – or Yiddish language culture characterized by universality of theme and individuality of expression" (ibid.). As the Yiddishist Moyshe Litvakov put it: "We do not divide literature into a 'literature of Jewishness' and a 'literature of humanity' [...] A living people, which speaks and thinks in a living language, knows of no dividing lines in its poetry" (ibid.). This too clearly influenced emerging aspects of the

---

13 See the generally useful volume *Tradition and Revolution: The Jewish Renaissance in Russian Avant-Garde Art 1912–1928*, ed. Ruth Apter-Gabriel (Jerusalem: The Israel Museum, 1987). On Chagall in that volume, see Amishai-Maisel 1987 and Apter-Gabriel 1987.

Zionist politico-cultural idea being developed in Palestine; let us not forget that the great modernist Hebrew poets, Chaim Nachman Bialik and Sha'ul Tschernikowsky, were products of, and contributors to, this wave.

Given the individualist nature of the emancipation contract in Western and Central Europe, the idea of a full-fledged and separate Yiddish or Hebrew, yet modern European-based institution of "culture" was not a possibility. This could only take place in Eastern Europe (or in Palestine or later, Israel) where collective, corporate existence remained a living, relevant, reality. As a result, for all the similarities, this Jewish avant-garde differed in a few pointed ways from the typical mold of most European avant-gardes. In addition to their universality and individuality, its proponents were cultural nationalists in service of a secular nation in the making. Thus here – unlike much of the elitist European avant-garde – the "masses" were not at all held in contempt. Rather whole institutions were formed to both mold and serve them. Moreover, as modernist and experimental as these all were, given the mass national nature of the endeavor, nineteenth century "high" culture was not entirely rejected. Thus, unlike the Italian futurists or the German expressionists – or, for that matter the Bolshevik equivalent of Proletkult which preached an iconoclastic vision of a brand new world based entirely on the experimental strivings of the workers – the institutions of the widespread Yiddishist Kultur-Lige were committed to fusing and disseminating its modernist aestheticism with that of "high" culture to the broad Jewish public (Ibid., 72).

Much of this was socialist or progressive Zionist in nature, but not exclusively so. Thus, the great poet, Uri Zvi Grinberg, who wrote in Yiddish and Hebrew, was both radically expressionist – his Yiddish journal *Albatros* took its cue from avant-garde German periodicals such as *Die Aktion* and *Der Sturm* – but he became over the years increasingly and militantly right-wing.[14]

But what of the nature of the Jewish avant-garde in Western and Central Europe? Already prior to World War I Martin Buber had called for and eventually initiated a movement of youthful Jewish renaissance.[15] It incorporated avant-garde materials with Lilien's art nouveau creations, which are the best known example

---

[14] Much of this turn, it seems, was related to his experience of anti-Semitism. He witnessed the November pogroms of 1918, narrowly escaped being shot by Polish soldiers, which convinced him early on that Polish Jews faced "physical annihilation," and in 1924 already envisioned the destruction of all of European Jewry. After his move to Palestine he was one of the founders of the activist right-wing *Brit HaBirionim*, and after the 1967 war he was a champion of the Greater Israel cause.

[15] See Gelber 1986, 105–119.

of this.[16] The most familiar – albeit disputed[17] – case is that of Weimar Germany, where specifically Jewish projects mirrored the wider explosion of experimental culture during the years 1918–1933. Michael Brenner has documented how this operated in the various fields of literature, poetry, art, theatre and music. Else Lasker-Schüler, Richard Beer-Hofman, Moritz Heiman and Stefan Zweig, Jakob Wassermann, Lion Feuchtwanger, Alfred Döblin all composed explicitly "Jewish" works, many of which were publicly performed; artists like Jakob Steinhardt and Joseph Budko and composers like Hermann Schalit and Hugo Adler applied multiple avant-garde styles to reshape Jewish musical idioms.[18] Some of these creations were more or less avant-garde in nature. But, unlike the Russian Jewish avant-garde, where more often than not a Jewish language expressed universal themes, given the "post-assimilatory" condition of Central European Jewry, the situation was reversed: the language was (and at that stage could only be) German, and the form very often modernist. But, the content and thematics were determinedly and traditionally "Jewish". In Eastern Europe, the explicitly Jewish avant-gardes were single-mindedly interested in radically forging the break with traditional Judaism, while in the West they functioned as a tool for some kind of hoped return to it, as species of re-naturalization.[19]

I turn now to the vexed relation between Zionism, as a political movement, to the avant-garde. We all know that within political Zionism there is an inherent dialectic between continuity and rebellion, tradition and radical secular innovation and that within this framework there are multiple, often competing, ideological strands.[20] While there were indeed avant-garde tendencies in early Zionism, it is of some interest that Max Nordau, perhaps Zionism's most famous intellectual at the time, was the author of the hugely popular 1892 work *Degeneration*, which attacked modernist culture, art and philosophy (especially that of Nietzsche, per-

---

16 Eric Hobsbawm (2013, 121) writes of "a peculiar contradiction at the heart of art nouveau and the *fin-de-siècle* family of avant-gardes of which it is a part [...] it was very much the style of a certain moment in the evolution of the European middle classes. But it was not designed for them. On the contrary, it belonged to an avant-garde that was anti-bourgeois and even anti-capitalist in its origins, as was the sympathy of its practitioners. Indeed, if this avant-garde had any socio-political affinity, it was for the new, mainly socialist, labour movements that suddenly sprang up in the 1880s and early 1890s."
17 See Wassermann 2004, 69–94.
18 The list goes on and these figures can all be conveniently found in Michael Brenner 1996.
19 For an explication of the differences exemplified in the cases of Micha Yosef Berdichevsky and Martin Buber, see Aschheim 1982, 122–124.
20 See Scholem 1974, 263–296.

haps the greatest influence of all on future avant-gardism),[21] as morbid, indeed insane, *fin-de-siècle* expressions of decadence, degeneration and immorality, as defective, hysterical departures from any sense of classical form and the bourgeois work-ethic (Nordau 1968).[22]

Certainly, then, the early Zionist leadership was in no way culturally avant-garde (Herzl, we should remember, was a kind of *Bildungs*-aesthete and master of the dandy-like Viennese feuillleton).[23] In any case, Zionism must above all be seen as a nationalism and all nationalisms, indeed all established political systems (for our purposes Italian Fascism, German Nazism and Russian Bolshevism) may tolerate the avant-garde for a while, but eventually their dynamism and ceaseless anti-establishmentarianism will have to be tamed, controlled or entirely marginalized. That is why almost all nationalisms will tend towards the classical and the monumental (Mosse 1980, 229–245).[24]

For all that, there were clear avant-garde tendencies within the Zionist movement, but again, these were all obviously also designed to serve national goals. Lilien's art-noveau work depicting new and old Jews in the Holy Land would be the most striking and early example of this. And, the very name "Hechalutz" literally indicated a vanguard, the youth that goes before the camp and through its visionary activism pioneered the ideals of the movement. But perhaps the most pertinent example of radical avant-gardism of early Zionism within Central Europe and Palestine was the youth movement Hashomer Hatzair and its commune Bitania (Tzur 1980; Peled 2002). It actively aimed at creating a sexually and spiritually liberated antibourgeois youth culture – a "New Zionist Man" and a transformed civilization based upon voluntary and elitist communal forms, rejecting all "mechanical" relationships. Its insistence upon constant agitation (*t'sisa*) underlying perpetual self-creation and strident cries for erotic and intellectual freedom were informed by the cultural baggage of Nietzsche, Hans Blueher, Gustav Wyneken, Gustav Landauer and, of course, Sigmund Freud.

---

21 On Nietzsche's centrality to the avant-garde in general see Aschheim 1992, 51–84. On Nordau's relationship to Nietzsche specifically, see Aschheim 2001, 3–12.
22 Indeed, it is a good thing that because of his Jewishness the later Nazi exhibition of avant-garde Degenerate Art could not invoke Nordau as the champion of this exact line of thought.
23 For an excellent portrayal of Herzl in this context, see Elon 1986.
24 The extreme was, of course, the case of Nazism and the infamous exhibition of Degenerate Art, but a certain wonder and distaste usually prevails. Thus, at the 1948 exhibition of a group of Israeli avant-garde artists called the New Horizons, Ben Gurion was dumbfounded by Joseph Zaritzky's modernist abstract painting called *Otzma* [power/strength] and he declared it incomprehensible. The painting was moved to a far less prominent position in the show. See Wollman 2014, 10.

I shall not enter into the very vexed question as to whether or not Freud and the project of psychoanalysis itself can be considered as a kind of "Jewish" avant-garde project. In a way both its friends and enemies did, and there are convincing arguments to all sides of this question. What is certain, however, is the fact that – perhaps apart from Nietzsche – Freud's influence upon parts of the liberational avant-garde was indispensably central. The expressionist emphasis on the darkness and deeper recesses of the mind, on areas of emotive pre-consciousness and its constant reworking of Oedipal themes that are no longer symbolically thought but literally enacted – in Arnolt Bronnen's play, *Parricide*, "a mother seeks to seduce her son next to the corpse of her old husband whom her fifteen-year-old son has slain" – all this is unmistakably Freudian (Sokel 1959, 44). And surrealism is virtually unthinkable without Freud. Breton's 1924 Manifesto is a homage to Freud, his foregrounding of sexual desire, his equation of poetry and the unconscious – as against rational thought – as revelatory of a superior divine and demonic reality (Collier 1988, 33–51). Salvador Dali's famous 1931 *The Persistence of Memory* provided an iconic demonstration of the power of the dream, more alive, intense and memorable than pale reality itself. Of course, this was an absurdly simplified Freud, annexed for the use of poets and visual artists – he may or may not have approved – but it is no less central for that.

Anti-Semitism and Avant-Gardes' Relations to Jews

I now consider how the avant-garde in general related to the Jews. Here, of course, I must enter into the politics of the various avant-gardes. If nationalism, Bolshevism and Fascism ultimately rejected, indeed often even persecuted, the avant-garde, it does not necessarily follow that certain exponents of the avant-garde have not been attracted to nationalism, Fascism or anti-Semitism. The permutations, again, will be various. Thus, the relationship was closest with the futurists, who, with their cult of violence, war, peripatetic activism and masculinity, both influenced the rise of, and teamed up with, Fascism. It is true that in their many manifestos there is no mention of Jews, no anti-Semitism, no hint of racism (Flint 1971). There are also reports that upon the persecution of Italy's Jews in 1938, Marinetti published an open letter denouncing anti-Semitism in the arts,[25] but I

---

[25] See "Marinetti: Follies of Futurism" by an anonymous author in http://madamepickwick artblog.com/2012/10/marinetti-follies-of-futurism.

cannot find any corroboration of this. On the contrary – despite having a futurist journal shut down by the State in June 1939 as conservatives and anti-modernists increased in influence – he not only sided with Fascism until the end but quickly adapted to Nazi influence over Mussolini. When Hitler denounced futurism by name, Marinetti in August 1937 publicly accused the German dictator of failing to understand modern art and recognizing futurism's nationalist and Fascist credentials. Hitler's error, he insisted, was to assume that there was any connection between Jews and modern art; they had always been the merchants, not the creators, of art. Nor had Jews played any part in futurism (Ialongo 2015, 260).[26]

The politics of the expressionist movement were far more complicated and diverse than that of the futurists. Claims that it had an inherent political personality would, I think, be mistaken. Many (of the non-Jewish) expressionists remained essentially apolitical before being deemed to be "un-German" and "degenerate" – the sadness and shock amongst such eminences as Ernst Ludwig Kirchner and Max Beckmann upon being so declared reads like a tragedy.[27] Still other expressionists, probably the majority, like the great artists Otto Dix and Georg Grosz were famously on the critical Weimar left. Some scholars have recently complained that these two masters resorted to crude Jewish stereotypes (especially of their rich patrons and of wealthy upper-middle-class Jews).[28] I think that even if it contains a grain of truth, this is one of gross over-interpretation. For in their work, no one was spared; their style was unexceptionally one of exaggeration, caricature and distortion. Moreover, they constantly worked with Jews and both openly condemned anti-Semitism. As Grosz put it already in 1930: "It appears as if we are moving to medieval conditions. Everything that once existed but seemed past [...] is being revived [...] anti-Semitism, war enthusiasm and a hysterical nationalism [...] One would hardly believe it unless one lived here and saw the swastika columns [...] and common slogans about a larger Germany free of Jews."[29]

This hardly applies to another famous expressionist painter, Emil Nolde. The early adherence to Nazism of this Danish-born painter is well known and even

---

[26] It is true that Jews had played little if any role in futurism, but Marinetti was being opportunistically disingenuous; he surely knew about his countryman Amedeo Modigliani and other creative modernist Jewish artists, such as Pissaro, Soutine, Lissitzky, Chagall and Jacques Lipchitz to mention just a few.
[27] Parenthetically, Beckmann's colorfully sympathetic 1919 painting of the Frankfurt synagogue, has elicited an entire panoply of interpretations, most centrally, as an uncanny anticipation of the destruction to come. See Hamlin 2016.
[28] For this argument and a review of the recent relevant literature and copious illustrations, see Washton Long 2010, 167–192.
[29] Quoted in ibid., 183.

though his art was banned in the Third Reich – 1052 of his works were removed from German museums and 48 ridiculed at the Degenerate Art Exhibition – he still remained an avid supporter. But only very recently has his really virulent anti-Semitism come to light (his champions having done everything previously to expunge it). "Jews," he declared, "have [...] little soul and little creative talent [...] the unfortunate presence of their settlements in the abodes of the Aryan peoples and their strong involvement in the innermost seats of power have led to an unbearable situation for both sides."[30] Other expressionists such as Hans Johst and Arnolt Bronnen similarly became Nazis. Perhaps the most famous case was the poet Gottfried Benn, who probed the depths of nihilism and who believed that a post-Nietzschean Nazism, through the medium of its breeding plans, could be the regenerative solution.[31] Yet, his Nazism was short-lived and no anti-Semitism is to be found in his writings.

No immanent conclusion, then, about any essential political personality in expressionism is to be found, nor can one detect any single attitude to Jews or anti-Semitism.[32] The same applies to dadaism. Three of its leading figures allow us a perspective on the range of the relevant attitudes. On the surface, its universalism and wild abandon were entirely unrelated to things Jewish. Perhaps that is the point with Tzara, who was actually born as the Jewish Samuel Rosenstock. The centrality and salience of his Romanian Jewishness, it has been argued, lies precisely in his extraordinary efforts to hide that fact. His name change – there have been various interpretations of this: thus, as in Tristan and Isolde, as in Nietzsche's Zarathustra, or as in Tzara (problem) in Yiddish and Hebrew – the constant attempts to overcome his foreignness, his dispensing with, indeed ridiculing of, all biographical data point to both the anxiety of being Jewish and the attempts to escape it (Heyd 2010).[33] That such denial was not somehow intrinsic to dadaism is shown by Tzara's Romanian Jewish co-founder, the artist and architect Marcel Janco who –and here I am radically telescoping a complex life – defined himself as "an artist who is a Jew," and in the face of anti-Semitism became militantly Jewish,

---

30 This, and other similar quotations and Nolde's Nazi attitudes are conveniently updated in Koldehoff 2013.
31 See Benn 1977 for a sample of his approach to National Socialism.
32 For all that it is worth noting, as Ian Buruma has pointed out, that radical though they may have been, there was a traditional, strongly anti-French current amongst the expressionist painters, who in many ways were consciously latter-day German Romantics (Buruma 2015, 12–13).
33 Heyd attempts to endow Tzara's work with some kind of hidden Jewish agenda. Equally fascinating is Alfred Bodenheimer's detailed formulation in the present volume which presents Tzara's radicalism, his mocking of, and alienation from, modern civilization as a form of coded Jewish protest.

emigrated to Israel, and was among the founders of the controversial Israeli artist colony at Ein Hod. As if this diversity were not enough, consider another founder of dadaism, the German Hugo Ball who upon first seeing Tzara and Janco and two other Romanian Jewish colleagues, remarked that "an Oriental-looking deputation of four little men arrived."[34] Upon leaving dada, Ball penned a species of vitriolic anti-Semitism, integrated into a wildly radical, eclectic political theology that combined Bakunist anarchism, French romantic poetry and chiliastic revolt, in order to restore original Christian (Catholic) justice against the Prussian State, Protestantism and above all against the modern, diabolic, perverting influence of the Jews (Rabinbach 1997, 66–94; Boime 2010).

The Stefan George Kreis exhibits a similar ambivalent complexity. In the present context I will leave out the attitude of the many Jewish members of the circle to their Jewishness. This ranged from identification to indifference to denial and also changed over time. Essentially, however, membership in the circle provided what seemed – at least at the time – to be an alternative path to belonging and acceptance. Their various reactions to anti-Semitism and loyalty to the Circle's ideas through the Nazi period would also need analysis. However, due to the scope of this essay, I must concentrate here on the non-Jewish members of the circle.[35]

In the first place, it may be necessary briefly to justify seeing the circle as belonging to the avant-garde in the first place. With their highly elitist vanguard pretensions, their radical dismissal of both conventional high and popular culture (many lived a life as bohemians in Munich's Schwabing), their utter contempt for the bourgeois way of life, their emphases on the mythically heroic – it was the Jewish members Gundolf and Kantorowicz who penned adulatory portraits of Alexander, Caesar, Napoleon and Friedrich II respectively – their search for an entirely transformed heroic, spiritual, "secret" Germany must surely qualify.[36]

---

[34] Quoted in Heyd 2010, 204.

[35] For a further discussion of the role and careers of the circle's Jewish members, see Raulff 2002.

[36] To be sure its insufferably dictatorial cult of leadership around George himself, and its exclusivist sense of secrecy, rendered it different from other avant-gardes, but its experimental literary styles, its oppositional stance, its sense of election and mission, and its transformational – albeit exceedingly vague post-Christian aesthetic vision, typifies it as an avant-garde of the unclassifiable right. On this, and the call for a Führer, the distinction between Fascism, conservative revolution and the George Kreis, along the spectrum of nationalisms of the Right, see Breuer 1996. Breuer documents George's radical rejection of the contemporary world and even his preparedness for violence. For George anarchy had to prevail in order that the new arise. He told Edith Landmann that perhaps revolution would be a blessing, by reducing the population from seventy to thirty million.

Jews were, of course, a very visible, even dominant, presence in the circle,[37] indeed to the point that its crucial split was over their presence, occasioned by the vitriolic anti-Semitism of Ludwig Klages and Alfred Schuler, who wrote, among many other things, that the "critical and intellectual principle, which conceals the growing barrenness of the soul and impoverishment of the instincts and is the actual parasite and cancerous growth on life: *that* is the principle which one most correctly designates with words such as Judaism, Semitism, Jehovism and whose historical carriers are the 'Jewish people.'"[38] And another prominent member, Friedrich Wolters wrote that Jews were "like all subjugated [...] races, the urge to dissolve everything that is solid, to subvert everything that is powerful, to overtax everything that is youthful and healthy[.]"[39] Moreover, given its calls for national radical renewal through a Führer, various members and associates – for longer or shorter periods – became Nazis (Fried 2008, 152).[40]

George himself, however, did allow Jews into the circle and indeed opposed Klages and Schuler on this very issue. Moreover, the great leader of the July 1944 attempt to assassinate Hitler, Klaus von Stauffenberg, was an associate of the circle. Yet, in many ways here too the "Jewish Question" was obdurately present and George's attitude remained, to put it mildly, typically ambivalent. He once contemptuously spoke of Berlin as a "mishmash of minor clerks, Jews and whores," told E. Curtius that Jews could not experience things as elementarily "as we [Germans]," and that he would never allow there to be an over-representation of Jews. And, while he clearly opposed overtly racial politics, he encouraged authors like Kurt Hildebrandt, who did advocate it (Breuer 1996, 235–236). Moreover, on National Socialism itself and its anti-Semitic policies, George maintained a deafening silence. At a late stage he commented that "this whole Jewish thing in particular is not so important to me." When asked by Jewish friends to condemn the Nazis, George replied irritably: "The Jews should not be surprised if I side more with the Nazis" (Norton 2002, 726). Perhaps, as futurism was to Fascism, given its quasi-political, mystic, nationalist bent, the George Kreis may have been more susceptible to Nazi and anti-Semitic thematics, yet its history and membership did not necessarily incline it that way; rather it demonstrated the ways in which

---

37 Apart from Gundolf, Kantorowicz and Wolfskhel there were Berthold Vallentin, Ernst Morwitz, Walter Kempner, Rudolf Borchardt, and as an associate Edith Landmann, to name just a few. See Fried 2008.
38 Schuler's words are quoted in Norton 2002, 155.
39 Ibid., 703.
40 Fried lists these as Friedrich Wolters, Ernst Bertram, Ludwig Thormaehlen and Waldemar Graf Uxkull-Gyllenband.

avant-gardes were also more conformist, more reflective of conventional tropes than they liked to admit.

Our last avant-garde group, the literary modernists, demonstrates this even more vividly. It would be wrong of course to label all of these writers as leaning toward the Fascist or authoritarian right or as being anti-Semitic. Thus, perhaps because as Irishmen they too felt like outsiders, both James Joyce and Samuel Beckett were positively philo-Semitic (Beckett joined the French resistance and championed German Jews), while in Yeats – who given his boredom with bourgeois politics and his relish for vitality, the irrational and the heroic, briefly flirted with the Irish Fascist Blueshirts – no anti-Jewish pronunciations are to be found (indeed he enjoyed toying with the Kabbalah) (Brown 2001, 340–342; Ivry 2011).

But the many literary modernists who were attracted to a post-liberal Fascism did so because, while they indulged in radical experiments with style and form, they sought a kind of revived social order and harmony. Some did so in tandem with an obscene and paranoiac anti-Semitism. Louis Ferdinand Céline and Ezra Pound, respectively, demonstrated that great modernist writers and poets could identify with Fascism and Nazism while spewing Jewish hatred. In their case one would want to separate their anti-Semitism from their genuinely accomplished literary achievements. In the case of T.S. Eliot, however, as at least one observer, Anthony Julius, has pointed out: "Anti-Semitism did not disfigure [T.S.] Eliot's work, it animated it. It was, on occasion, both his refuge and his inspiration, and his exploitation of its literary potential was virtuose" (Julius 1995, 173). To be sure, the poetry combined virtuosity with shocking racist meanness,[41] yet here too we need to make a distinction: Eliot's anti-Semitism was of the reactionary and not Fascist kind (North 2009; Surette 2011). Though modernist in literary form, Eliot's was a snobbish, religiously inflected, conservative critique of urban atheistic civilization: freethinking and capitalist Jews were its incarnation. Still, on a personal level he befriended and worked with many Jews and clearly opposed Communism and Fascism as modern totalitarian ideologies. The culture of early twentieth century avant-garde literary modernism thus witnessed numerous variations on this theme. For instance, early on in 1931, the vorticist Wyndham Lewis supported Hitler and wrote novels populated negatively with Jews (as well as homosexuals and other minorities). Yet, he soon revoked his support for the German dictator and recognizing the reality of Nazi treatment of Jews after visiting Berlin in 1937 even penned an attack on anti-Semitism, ironically named *Are the Jews Human?* In

---

41 Eliot portrayed the Jews as slumlords: "And the jew squats on the window sill, the owner" or "Rachel née Rabinovitch/Tears at the grapes with murderous paws" or "The rats are underneath the piles / The jew is underneath the lot." These quotes are to be found in Ivry 2001.

Britain, the anti-liberal literary journals such as *The New Age* and *The New Witness* shaped their counter-cultural critiques either through direct anti-Jewish tropes or as a foil for broader attacks on liberal, democratic modernity.[42]

Fascist and Nazi or conservative and reactionary literary avant-gardists alike, then, – apart from simply inheriting traditional anti-Jewish attitudes – aimed their spears at Jews, actually and symbolically, as destructive exemplars of a squalid, materialist modernity. Of course, these avant-garde modernists could not – as external critics were wont to do – accuse the avant-garde itself of being a Jewish phenomenon. Yet, in some ways their anti-Jewish accusations mimicked their critics who uttered precisely such accusations.

Coda

It would be superfluous to dwell on external anti-Semitic representations of the avant-garde as such as a destructively Jewish, subversive phenomenon. The topic is familiar enough and has been well-trodden by others. Who has not heard of Nazi denunciations of rootless modernist art as un-German and essentially Jewish, devoid of all healthy, normal forms, its cold abstraction, its indecipherable and distorted works reflective of *völkisch* non-belonging and degeneration? But this was merely the climax of a longer history of conservative anti-avant-gardist anti-Semitism. Thus, throughout the early twentieth century in France, given the large number of Jewish artists who had immigrated to Paris from Eastern Europe (most prominently Moise Kisling, Simon Mondzain, Jacques Lipchitz, Jules Pascin, Chaim Soutine, Pinchus Krémagne and many others), they became collectively identified as the Jewish École de Paris and – lumped together with Jewish art dealers who were attacked for their financial speculation and corruption – labeled as invasive, anti-traditional and essentially "Jewish" in nature. In gladiatorial fashion, the conservative, nativist École française was pitted against the "rootless" Jewish École de Paris, claiming that the Jewish sensibility was simply unable to comprehend or even appreciate the French tradition (Golan 2010).

How then are we to sum up this potpourri? It is only in the eyes of their often paranoiac enemies that the Jews constitute a single, homogenous unity. The

---

[42] *The Witness* engaged in direct political anti-Semitism. *The New Age* "was not programmatically anti-Semitic in the same way, but tried to set itself up as a free, 'manly', unsentimental area of discussion where such views could be aired with impunity. This led to a mixing of cultural modernism with anti-Semitism in its pages, which set a precedent and context for the later political and cultural ideas of Wyndham Lewis, Ezra Pound and T.S. Eliot." Villis 2006, 147.

connections between the Jews and the avant-garde can only be located in their diversity. In the first place, it would be either an anti-Semitic or chauvinistically Jewish trope to claim that the avant-garde sensibility was essentially a "Jewish" one. Indeed, its leading figures –and many of its great ones – were not Jews: for instance Joyce, Yeats, T.S. Eliot, Stefan George, Marinetti, Otto Dix, Kandinsky, Malevich, Mayakovsky, Picasso, Braque. That of course is not to say that, in one way or another, Jews – some more or less prominent – were not to be found in many of the avant-garde projects. They were more thickly present in some than in others. Indeed, in some, such as futurism, they seem to be entirely absent and, for example, amongst the early pioneers of cubism there are no Jews. Moreover, within the general European avant-garde, when they participated, they did so in the great majority of cases not as Jews. Indeed, though the avant-garde preached a disintegrative credo, joining these movements was paradoxically a means towards a post-bourgeois integration. That they often could not escape being labeled as Jewish by the very movements they had joined indicates the ironic degree to which these putatively radical, post-conventional groupings were sometimes infected by the conformist tropes of their own times. Radicalism and wild abandon often had its limits and the often inchoate nature of many avant-garde desires and sensibilities rendered them susceptible to different and sometimes undesirable political winds. When it comes to the specifically "Jewish" avant-gardes, structural differences also applied: in the Russian and East European cases, what was "Jewish" were the languages, the instruments through which universal modernist themes were to be articulated and disseminated, while in Central Europe, German was the language in which avant-garde materials were employed but sometimes to inspire Jewish national rebirth.

Some of these projects have indeed made an impact on our culture – cubism has without doubt transformed our perceptions, our ways of seeing the world,[43] and literary modernism is secure within the canon (partly because both schools paid homage to the tradition but framed it within new vision and techniques). Still, unlike nationalism and other political movements which require continuity, coherence and consensus, by their very nature avant-garde projects are anti-continuity, coherence and consensus and as such have been short-lived. As Poggioli (1968, 220) remarks, a certain dialectic causes "every avant-garde to be able (or pretend to be able) to transcend not only the academy and tradition but also the avant-garde preceding it." In any case, the great age of the avant-gardes of the twentieth century has passed. Where they presently exist, they are bereft of

---

43 Whether or not this is apocryphal, when Picasso painted Gertrud Stein she is reported to have said: "That does not look like me," to which Picasso replied: "It will."

large transformational social visions and have been comfortably integrated into the capitalist commodity culture they originally vilified; indeed, the cult of the new has been institutionalized in such a way that we are virtually incapable of shock. Thus, today, the problem of the Jews and the avant-garde possesses far less salience and little sting. It may well be that the stereotype of the Jew as a rootless, subversive and destructive outsider – or the more positive version, as a restless, creative innovator transcending conventional prejudices – will persist, but the politics and contexts in which it is now framed have been radically transformed. The dynamics of Jewish integration, self-definition and exclusion continue, but they do so outside of the anger and excitement that animated the great age of the avant-garde.

Bibliography

(anon.). "Marinetti: Follies of Futurism." http://madamepickwickartblog.com/2012/10/marinetti-follies-of-futurism (3 March 2016).

Amishai-Maisels, Ziva. "Chagall and the Jewish Revival: Center or Periphery?" *Tradition and Revolution: The Jewish Renaissance in Russian Avant-Garde Art 1912–1928*. Ed. Ruth Apter Gabriel. Jerusalem: The Israel Museum, 1987. 71–100.

Apter-Gabriel, Ruth. "El Lissitzky's Jewish Works." *Tradition and Revolution: The Jewish Renaissance in Russian Avant-Garde Art 1912–1928*. Ed. Ruth Apter Gabriel. Jerusalem: The Israel Museum, 1987. 101–124.

Arendt, Hannah. *Rahel Varnhagen: The Life of a Jewess*. Ed. Liliane Weissberg. Baltimore: Johns Hopkins University Press, 1997.

Aschheim, Steven E. *Brothers and Strangers: The East European Jew in German and German-Jewish Consciousness, 1800–1923*. Madison: University of Wisconsin Press, 1982.

Aschheim, Steven E. *The Nietzsche Legacy in Germany, 1890–1990*. Berkeley: University of California Press, 1992.

Aschheim, Steven E. *In Times of Crisis: Essays on European Culture, Germans and Jews*. Madison: University of Wisconsin Press, 2001.

Aschheim, Steven E. "Reflections on Theatricality, Identity and the Modern Jewish Experience." *Jews and the Making of Modern Theatre*. Ed. Jeanette R. Malkin and Freddie Rokem. Iowa City: University of Iowa Press, 2010. 21–38.

Bell, Julian. "Taking a Wrench to Reality." *New York Review of Books* December 4 2014: 23–25.

Benn, Gottfried. *Gesammelte Werke I. Essays, Reden. Vorträge*. Stuttgart: Klett-Cotta, 1977.

Berlin, Isaiah. *The Roots of Romanticism*. Princeton: Princeton University Press, 1999.

Bloch, Ernst. *Literarische Aufsätze*. Frankfurt am Main: Suhrkamp, 1965.

Bloch, Ernst. *Aesthetics and Politics*. London: NLB, 1977.

Boime, Albert. "Dada's Dark Secret." *Jewish Dimensions in Visual Culture: Antisemitism, Assimilation, Affirmation*. Ed. Rose-Carol Washton Long, Matthew Baigel and Milly Heyd. Waltham: Brandeis University Press, 2010. 90–115.

Brenner, Michael. *The Renaissance of Jewish Culture in Weimar Germany*. New Haven: Yale University Press, 1996.
Breuer, Stefan. *Äesthetischer Fundamentalismus. Stefan George und der Deutsche Antimodernismus*. Darmstadt: Primus Verlag, 1996.
Brown, Terence. *The Life of W.B. Yeats*. Dublin: Gill & Macmillan, 2001.
Buruma, Ian. "The Bridge to a Dangerous Future." *The New York Review of Books*. March 5 2015: 12–13.
Calinescu, Matei. *The Five Faces of Modernity: Modernism, Avant-Garde, Decadence, Kitsch, Postmodernism*. Durham: Duke University Press, 1987.
Collier, Peter. "Dreams of a Revolutionary Culture – Gramsci, Trotsky and Breton." *Visions and Blueprints: Avant-garde Culture and Radical Politics in Early Twentieth-Century Europe*. Ed. Edward Timms and Peter Collier. Manchester: Manchester University Press, 1988. 33–51.
Dagen, Philippe. "From Dada to Surrealism." *The Guardian*. July 19 2011.
Elon, Amos. *Herzl*. New York: Schocken Books, 1986.
Flint, R.W. *Marinetti: Selected Writings*. New York: Farrar, Straus and Giroux, 1971.
Fried, Johannes. "George und seine Juden." *Trumah. Zeitschrift der Hochschule für Jüdische Studien* 18 (2008): 132–160.
Gay, Peter. *Freud, Jews and Other Germans: Masters and Victims in Modernist Culture*. New York: Oxford University Press, 1978.
Gelber, Mark H. "The jungjüdische Bewegung: An Unexplored Chapter in German-Jewish Literary and Cultural History." *Leo Baeck Institute Yearbook* 31 (1986): 105–119.
Golan, Romy. "The École Francaise versus the École de Paris: The Debate about the Status of Jewish Artists in Paris between the Wars." *Jewish Dimensions in Visual Culture: Antisemitism, Assimilation, Affirmation*. Ed. Rose-Carol Washton Long, Matthew Baigel and Milly Heyd. Waltham: Brandeis University Press, 2010. 77–89.
Hamlin, Amy K. "The Conditions of Interpretation: A Reception History of the Synagogue by Max Beckmann." http://nonsite.org/article/the-conditions-of-interpretation-a-reception-history-of-the-synagogue-by-max-beckmann (March 3 2016).
Hertz, Deborah. *Jewish High Society in Old Regime Berlin*. New Haven: Yale University Press, 1988.
Heyd, Milly. "Tristan Tzara/Shmuel Rosenstock: The Hidden/Overt Jewish Agenda." *Jewish Dimensions in Visual Culture: Antisemitism, Assimilation, Affirmation*. Ed. Rose-Carol Washton Long, Matthew Baigel and Milly Heyd. Waltham: Brandeis University Press, 2010. 193–219.
Hiller, Kurt. *Die Weisheit der Langweile. Eine Zeit- und Streitschrift*, Vol. 2. Leipzig: Kurt Wolff, 1913. 52–53.
Hobsbawm, Eric. *Fractured Times: Culture and Society in the Twentieth Century*. New York: The New Press, 2013.
Ialongo, Ernest. *Filippo Tommaso Marinetti: The Artist and His Politics*. Madison and Teaneck: Fairleigh Dickinson University Press, 2015.
Ivry, Benjamin. "T.S. Eliot's On-Again, Off-Again Anti-Semitism." *Forward*. September 23 2001. http://forward.com/culture/books/142722/ts-eliots-on-again-off-again-anti-semitism/ (March 3 2016).
Ivry, Benjamin. "Samuel Beckett's Letters Reveal Roots of Resistance: New Book Details How Nobel Winner Stood up for German Jews." *Forward* November 4 2011. http://forward.com/culture/144905/samuel-becketts-letters-reveal-roots-of-resistance/ (March 3 2016).

Jelavich, Peter. "How 'Jewish' was Theatre in Imperial Berlin?" *Jews and the Making of Modern Theatre*. Ed. Jeanette R. Malkin and Freddie Rokem. Iowa City: University of Iowa Press, 2010. 39–58.
Jelavich, Peter. "Popular Entertainment and Mass Media: The Central Arenas of German-Jewish Cultural Engagement." *The German-Jewish Experience: Contested Interpretations and Conflicting Perceptions*. Ed. Steven Aschheim and Vivian Liska. Berlin: De Gruyter, 2016, 103–116.
Julius, Anthony. *T.S. Eliot, Anti-Semitism and Literary Form*. New York: Cambridge University Press, 1995.
Koldehoff, Stefan. "Noldes Bekenntnis." *Die Zeit*. October 21 2013 (Online).
Kramer, Hilton. *The Age of the Avant-Garde 1956–1972*. New York: Farrar, Straus and Giroux, 1973.
Leck, Ralph M. *Georg Simmel and Avant-Garde Sociology: The Birth of Modernity 1880–1920*. New York: Humanity Books, 2000.
Malkin, Jeanette. "Transforming in Public: Jewish Actors on the German Expressionist Stage." *Jews and the Making of Modern Theatre*. Ed. Jeanette R. Malkin and Freddie Rokem. Iowa City: University of Iowa Press, 2010. 151–173.
Moss, Kenneth B. *Jewish Renaissance in the Russian Revolution*. Cambridge: Harvard University Press, 2009.
Mosse, George L. *Masses and Man: Nationalist and Fascist Perceptions of Reality*. New York: Howard Fertig, 1980.
Nordau, Max. *Degeneration*. New York: Howard Fertig, 1968.
North, Michael. *The Political Aesthetics of Yeats, Eliot and Pound*. Cambridge: Cambridge University Press, 2009.
Norton, Robert E. *Secret Germany: Stefan George and his Circle*. Ithaca: Cornell University Press, 2002.
Otte, Marline. *Jewish Identities in German Popular Entertainment 1890–1933*. Cambridge: Cambridge University Press, 2006.
Peled, Rina. *Ha'adam He-hadash Shel Hamahpekha Hazionit: Hashomer Hazair Vshorashav Haeuropayim* [The "New Man" of the Zionist Revolution: Hashomer Hatzair and its European Roots]. Tel Aviv: Am Oved, 2002.
Poggioli, Renato. *The Theory of the Avant-Garde*. Cambridge: Harvard University Press, 1968.
Rabinbach, Anson. *In the Shadow of Catastrophe: German Intellectuals between Apocalypse and Enlightenment*. Berkeley: University of California Press, 1997.
Raulff, Ulrich. *Kreis ohne Meister. Stefan Georges Nachleben*. München: C.H. Beck, 2002.
Scholem, Gershom. "Zionism – Dialectic of Continuity and Rebellion." *Unease in Zion*. Ed. Ehud Ben Ezer. New York: Quadrangle, 1974. 263–296.
Sokel, Walter. *The Writer in Extremis: Expressionism in Twentieth Century Literature*. Stanford: Stanford University Press, 1959.
Surette, Leon. *Dreams of a Totalitarian Utopia: Literary Modernism and Politics*. Montreal: McGill-Queens University Press, 2011.
Tzur, Muki (ed.). *K'hilateinu* [Our Community]. Jerusalem: Yad Ben Tsvi, 1988.
Villis, Tom. *Reaction and the Avant-Garde: The Revolt against Liberal Democracy in Early Twentieth-Century Britain*. London: Tauris, 2006.
Washton Long, Rose-Carol. "Georg Grosz, Otto Dix, and the Philistines: The German-Jewish Question in the Weimar Republic." *Jewish Dimensions in Visual Culture: Antisemitism,*

Assimilation, Affirmation. Ed. Rose-Carol Washton Long, Matthew Baigel and Milly Heyd. Waltham: Brandeis University Press, 2010. 167–192.

Wassermann, Henry. "How to Invent a Cultural Renaissance in Weimar Germany." *Katharsis* 2 (2004): 69–94.

Williams, Raymond. "The Politics of the Avant-Garde." *Visions and Blueprints: Avant-Garde Culture and Radical Politics in Early Twentieth-Century Europe*. Ed. Edward Timms and Peter Collier. Manchester: Manchester University Press, 1988. 1–15.

Wollman, Hadass. "Driven to Abstraction." *Ha'aretz*, December 26 2014: 10.

Notes on Contributors

Steven E. Aschheim is Professor Emeritus of History at the Hebrew University of Jerusalem, where he taught cultural and intellectual history starting in 1982 and held the Vigevani Chair of European Studies. He has been a visiting scholar and professor at numerous universities in the U.S., Canada, and Europe. In 2013–2014, he was a Fellow of the Straus Institute for the Advanced Study of Law & Justice at New York University School of Law. His more recent works include: *In Times of Crisis: Essays on European Culture, Germans and Jews* (2001); *Scholem, Arendt, Klemperer: Intimate Chronicles in Turbulent Times* (2001); and *Beyond the Border: The German-Jewish Legacy Abroad* (2007). He is the editor of the conference volume *Hannah Arendt in Jerusalem* (2001) and a co-editor (with Vivian Liska) of *The German-Jewish Experience Revisited* (2015). His latest book, *At the Edges of Liberalism: Junctions of European, German and Jewish History* appeared in June 2012.

Alfred Bodenheimer is Professor of the History of Jewish Religion and Literature and Head of the Center for Jewish Studies at the University of Basel. His research focuses on European Jewish Literature as well as on concepts of Jewish modernity, especially concerning the Holocaust as well as the interdependency of Israel and the diaspora. He is editor of the *Yearbook of the Society for European-Jewish Literature* (with Vivian Liska) and co-editor of the Reihe Jüdische Moderne (Böhlau, Cologne). Among his books are *Haut ab! Die Juden in der Beschneidungsdebatte* (2012) and *Ungebrochen gebrochen. Über jüdische Narrative und Traditionsbildung* (2012). He is also the author of a series of criminal novels.

Mark H. Gelber is Senior Professor of Comparative Literature and German-Jewish Studies at Ben-Gurion University, Beer Sheva and Director of the Center for German and Austrian Studies at BGU. He was elected in 2001 to membership in the German Academy for Language and Literature (Darmstadt). He has served as visiting professor at the University of Pennsylvania, University of Graz, University of Maribor, Yale University, University of Auckland, Universiteit Antwerpen, RWTH Aachen University, New York University, and Renmin University, Beijing. His major areas of research and publication include German/Austrian-Jewish Literary and Cultural History, Cultural Zionism, Literary Anti-Semitism, Stefan Zweig, and Franz Kafka.

Raphael Koenig is a Ph.D. candidate in Comparative Literature at Harvard University and a graduate of the École Normale Supérieure and the Sorbonne in Paris. His research focuses on French, German, and Yiddish avant-garde literature and visual culture, more specifically on the reception of the so-called "art of the insane" from the early 1920s to the late 1940s. He is a member of the editorial board of *In geveb: A Journal of Yiddish Studies*.

Andreas Kramer is Reader in German and Comparative Literature at Goldsmiths, University of London. His research is primarily focused on early twentieth-century literature and culture, specifically literary and visual modernism in Germany (with an emphasis on expressionism), and the European avant-garde. He is the author of monographs on Carl Einstein, on Gertrude Stein and the German literary avant-garde, and on regionalist modernism in German culture. He has edited Eugene Jolas's autobiography, *Man from Babel* (Yale UP), and co-edited several collections, including *Carl Einstein and the European Avant-Gardes* (with Nicola Creighton, 2012). He is preparing for publication a study entitled *Inventing Maps: Geographies of the European Avant-Garde*. His current research project is on sports and expressionism, and he participates in an interdisciplinary network of scholars researching sports and the European avant-garde.

Tom Paulus teaches film history and film aesthetics at the University of Antwerp. He is co-founder of the Research Group Visual Poetics. His edited collection *Slapstick Comedy* (with Rob King) has been published by Routledge in the AFI Film Readers Series. His research centers on the history of film style, a topic explored in book chapters and essays on silent film pictorialism, Ford, Ozu, Hou Hsiao-hsien and Godard. He is editor of the online journal *Photogénie*, an environment devoted to the history and theory of cinephilia.

Zoë Roth is a lecturer in French at Durham University, UK where she researches and teaches nineteenth and twentieth century comparative literature and visual culture with a particular focus on the relation between racial experience and representation, text-image relations, and comparative approaches to the Holocaust. She has been awarded fellowships and grants by the British Academy, the Leverhulme Trust, the Harry Ransom Center, and the Vienna Wiesenthal Institute for Holocaust Studies. Her current project explores how francophone Jewish avant-garde artists in the interwar period both shaped and challenged the French racial imaginary. She has published articles in *Philip Roth Studies*, *Word & Image*, and the *Journal of Modern Literature*.

Olivier Salazar-Ferrer is lecturer at the University of Glasgow. His research focuses primarily on twentieth-century French literature and the interaction between literature, philosophy and the visual arts, with particular emphasis on European avant-garde movements. He is the author of *Benjamin Fondane* (Oxus, 2004) and *Benjamin Fondane et la révolte existentielle* (De Corlevour, 2007). He is the co-editor of *Fondane, Écrits pour le cinéma* (Verdier, 2008) with Ramona Fotiade and Michel Carassou and editor of the critical edition of Fondane's *La Conscience malheureuse* (Verdier, 2013). He is also secretary of the Association Benjamin Fondane and co-editor of *Titanic*, the journal of the Benjamin Fondane Association. His latest volume was devoted to Nicolas Bouvier (*L'Usage du monde de Nicolas Bouvier*, Infolio, 2015).

Maria Silina (Ph.D.) has been working at the Moscow Research Institute for Theory and History of Visual Arts of the Russian Academy of Arts since 2011. She is the author of a monograph on Soviet architectural sculpture of the 1920s and the 1930s published in Moscow in 2014. As a Banting postdoctoral fellow at the Université du Québec à Montréal (Canada) she studies a variety of topics including such fields as the history of Soviet art and early Marxist aesthetics, gender and museum studies, as well as the Stalinist heritage in Post-Soviet perspective.

Sami Sjöberg is an Academy of Finland Research Fellow at the University of Helsinki, holding a Ph.D. in Comparative Literature. His most recent publications include *The Vanguard Messiah: Lettrism between Jewish Mysticism and the Avant-Garde* (De Gruyter, 2015) and "Literaturrevolution in Continental Jewish Aesthetics" (arcadia, 2016). Sjöberg has translated Alfred Jarry's *Les gestes et opinions du docteur Faustroll, pataphysicien* into Finnish (2016) and published on continental avant-garde literature and its relation to Judaism, as well as contemporary European art and the poetics of the avant-garde.

Alana Sobelman is visiting lecturer at Shalem College in Jerusalem. She received her PhD from Ben-Gurion University of the Negev in Be'er Sheva, Israel. Her current research focuses on the scholar-autobiographies of Jewish scholars of the Holocaust.

Radu Stern is a Swiss art historian and curator with multiple interests. He has taught art history at Lausanne, in Dijon, Massachusetts, and Neuchâtel. He was the Deputy Director of the Applied Arts School of Vevey, Switzerland and the Director of Education at the Musée de l'Elysée, Lausanne. He regularly lectures and gives portfolio readings in universities, art schools, and photography festivals in Switzerland and abroad. His publications include *From Dada to Surrealism: Jewish Avant-Garde Artists from Romania* (JHM, 2011), *L'ubiquité de l'image* (with Christian Caujolle and Joan Fontcuberta, 2009), *Against Fashion: Clothing as Art, 1850–1930* (MIT Press, 2004), *Alexandre Rodtschenko, La femme en jeu* (1997).

Małgorzata Stolarska-Fronia (Ph.D.) is an art historian, curator, translator and academic teacher, currently implementing a post-doctoral project entitled "Jewish Expressionism – a Quest for Cultural Space." She is associate professor at the Nicolaus Copernicus University in Toruń (Poland) and was formerly the Head of the Scientific Department at the Polin – Museum of the History of Polish Jews in Warsaw. She has authored *Participation of Breslau Jews in the Artistic and Cultural Life of the City from the Emancipation until 1933* (Warsaw 2009) and several articles devoted to the issue of modern art in Jewish culture.

Laëtitia Tordjman is a Ph.D. candidate in Comparative Literature at the Université Sorbonne Nouvelle in Paris. In 2016 she was awarded the Emeric Deutsch doctoral scholarship from the Fondation pour la Mémoire de la Shoah. Her research focuses on collective representations in Yiddish and Afro-American literature in the second half of the nineteenth century and in the interwar period. Her articles cover a variety of topics such as diasporic avant-gardes, collective fictional reconfigurations in Mendele Moykher Sforim's *Di Klyatshe* (The Nag) and Oser Warszawski's *Shmuglers* (Smugglers), and literary testimonies in Yiddish during the Second World War.

www.ingramcontent.com/pod-product-compliance
Lightning Source LLC
Chambersburg PA
CBHW031724230426
43669CB00007B/234